CW00566090

Passionate Attitudes

Matthew Sturgis

Passionate Attitudes

The English Decadence of the 1890s

MACMILLAN

First published 1995 by Macmillan London

an imprint of Macmillan General Books Ltd
Cavaye Place London SW10 9PG
and Basingstoke

Associated companies throughout the world

ISBN 0 333 57238 6

1 3 5 7 9 8 6 4 2

A CIP catalogue record for this book is available from the British Library

Typeset by CentraCet Limited, Cambridge
Printed and bound in Great Britain by
Mackays of Chatham plc, Chatham, Kent

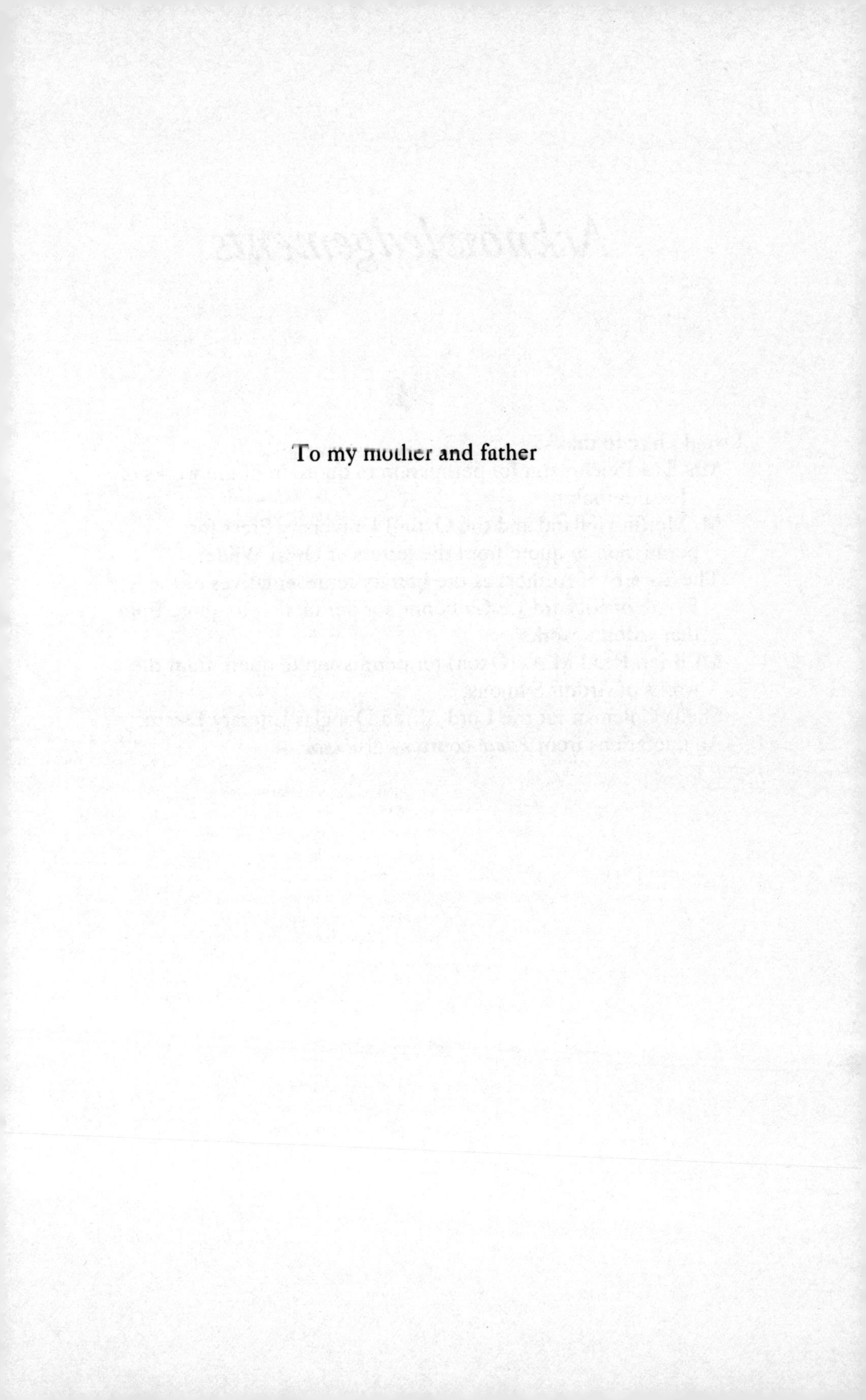

To my mother and father

Acknowledgements

I would like to thank:

Mrs Eva Reichmann for permission to quote from the works of Max Beerbohm;

Mr Merlin Holland and the Oxford University Press for permission to quote from the letters of Oscar Wilde;

The Society of Authors as the literary representatives of the Estate of Richard Le Gallienne for permission to quote from that writer's works;

Mr Brian Read M.A. (Oxon) for permission to quote from the works of Arthur Symons;

Sheila Coleman for the Lord Alfred Douglas Literary Estate;

All quotations from *Punch* courtesy of *Punch*

'Not to discriminate every moment some passionate attitude in those about us, and in the very brilliancy of their gifts some tragic dividing forces on their ways, is, on this short day of frost and sun, to sleep before evening.'

from Walter Pater's 'Conclusion' to *The Renaissance*

Contents

List of Illustrations

1. 'Some Persons of "the Nineties"' by Max Beerbohm (Courtesy of Mrs Eva Reichmann and the Ashmolean Museum, Oxford)
2. Théophile Gautier (Mansell Collection)
3. Charles Baudelaire (Mansell Collection)
4. Stéphane Mallarmé (Mansell Collection)
5. Paul Verlaine (Mansell Collection)
6. Algernon Swinburne by Simeon Solomon (Fitzwilliam Museum, Cambridge)
7. George Moore by Manet (Mansell Collection)
8. Walter Pater (Mansell Collection)
9. James McNeill Whistler by Harry Furniss (National Portrait Gallery, London)
10. Arthur Symons (Princeton University Library)
11. John Gray (Courtesy of the Reverend Bede Bailey, St Dominic's Priory, Edinburgh)
12. Ernest Dowson by Charles Conder (National Portrait Gallery, London)
13. Ricketts and Shannon by William Rothenstein (Fitzwilliam Museum, Cambridge)
14. Richard Le Gallienne (from *The Quest of the Golden Boy* by R. Whittington-Egan and Geoffrey Smerdon)
15. W. B. Yeats by J. B. Yeats (City Art Gallery, Birmingham)
16. Oscar Wilde and Lord Alfred Douglas (Mansell Collection)
17. Max Beerbohm and William Rothenstein (Mrs Ensor Holiday)
18. Robbie Ross and Reggie Turner (Estate of Giles Robertson)
19. Aubrey Beardsley by Frederick Evans (National Portrait Gallery, London)

Introduction

IN England the 1890s have developed a peculiarly powerful aura. The decade has established itself as something separate and distinct, and any one of several lurid epithets is habitually applied to characterize this ten-year span. The nineties are variously 'gay', 'yellow', 'mauve', 'naughty' or 'decadent'. The adjectives may change but the tenor remains constant; there is a suggestion of debauchery, of weariness, of sex – of everything, indeed, counter to the robust traditions of Victorianism. The period's two most memorable figures have been fixed in the popular imagination as Oscar Wilde and Aubrey Beardsley, the one a martyr to his own sexuality, the other a victim of his own fragile constitution.

This picture of the 1890s has great attractions and great stamina. It has, however, provoked much irritation amongst professional scholars and critics, as well as amongst people who lived through the nineties untouched by its mauve-yellow colouring. The period, these revisionists point out, was marked less by a feeling of decadence than by a sense of vitality and innovation, by an enthusiasm for the 'new' and an excitement in the 'modern'.

The best work of the period, they remark with ample justification, was produced not by the handful of decadents but by writers and artists working in rather different directions. The 1890s saw the mature masterpieces of James and Hardy, the early triumphs of Kipling, Shaw, Bennett, Wells and Conrad. It was, moreover, the first great age of both feminism and socialism.

Besides these serious reservations they also deplore the glib decade-ism that conceives of history as neatly divided up into ten-year parcels, each with a snappy adjective attached. This whole popular view of the period they denounce as the 'nineties myth' – and, as often as not, they blame W. B. Yeats for creating it.

In his splendidly self-dramatizing *Autobiographies* (1926) Yeats looked back on the period of his youthful development and drew it in bold colours. He took Ernest Dowson, Lionel Johnson, Arthur Symons, Count Stenbock, Wilde and Beardsley – his erstwhile confrères – and labelled them the 'tragic generation'. He cast these young men of the nineties as dejected seekers after antithesis who all went mad or died in the attempt – leaving Yeats alone free to go on to better things.

Certainly death did play a leading part in establishing the character and distinctness of the 'decadent nineties'. The demise of Beardsley, of Wilde, of Dowson, Johnson, Conder, Crackanthorpe and Stenbock, all within the decade or its immediate aftermath, strengthened the notion that the nineties were a closed and significant period, and it fixed for ever those protagonists within it. The end of the century, and the death of Queen Victoria soon after, seemed merely to confirm the picture.

In 1900, as Yeats put it, 'everybody got down off his stilts; henceforth nobody drank absinthe with his black coffee; nobody went mad; nobody committed suicide; nobody joined the Catholic Church; or if they did I have forgotten'.

The revisionists have been swift to question Yeats' memory, and to break down his rigid divisions of time. They have taken the nineties and dissolved them into a larger period which they have called the 'Age of Transition'. This age stretches from the 1870s up to the First World War, and it marks the vexed interlude between the fixed schools of Victorianism and Modernism.

Despite this remodelling of the critical landscape, the mauve-yellow-decadent-mythical nineties refuse to disappear. They continue to command attention and to repay study. For, although Yeats certainly did much to paint the decade in striking hues, he was working upon an existing schema. The origins of the nineties myth lie within the period itself.

People in the nineties were very aware of the distinctness and significance of the decade: it marked the end of the century. Side by side with the enthusiasm for the 'new' was a consciousness of the 'end'. Few ages are without their Jeremiahs and few centuries close without some prophesies of doom. The nineteenth century was certainly no exception.

In England, moreover, this sense of anxiety at the century's close was given a peculiarly French edge by the use of the term *fin de siècle*. The phrase was applied (with the same indiscriminate enthusiasm enjoyed by the adjectives 'new' and 'modern') to every striking innovation in contemporary life. And, for the insular English, France represented all that was naughty, dangerous and corrupt. It was the country of absinthe and the can-can, of Emile Zola and Paul Verlaine; it was the home of flaneurs, Bohemians and decadents.

That the English chose a French appellation for the century's end was both prompted by and conducive to ideas of decadence. Although no commentator, either at the time or subsequently, has denied the existence of this strain of thought within the period, there has been a marked tendency to narrow the scope of its influence. The suggestion that contemporary concern with the subject ever amounted to anything as definite as a 'decadent movement' has been persistently denied. The sole blame – or credit – for nineties decadence has been ascribed, rather, to a series of disparate individuals.

For some, Wilde was 'the High Priest of the Decadents'; for others, it was Beardsley who best distilled the 'essence of the decadent *fin de siècle*'. Vincent O'Sullivan (a minor figure of the age) considered that Arthur Symons 'though he was perhaps the only decadent in London . . . has managed to pass into history as the leader of a definite movement called Decadent'. While Edgar Jepson (another peripheral nineties man) scarcely allowed that the term had crossed the channel: 'When we talked of the decadent poets,' he claimed, 'we were speaking of a French school of poets of whom Verlaine was the chief.'

Rupert Croft-Cooke in his swaggering gossip-filled account of the period remarked that the 'Decadence of the nineties was not so much a literary movement as a publishing stunt . . . promoted by John Lane and Richard Le Gallienne, his friend and advisor'. Later on he suggests that it was 'something recognizable in *Punch* and popular humour but nowhere else'.

Wilde, Beardsley, Symons, Verlaine, John Lane and Richard le Gallienne, *Punch*: with so many different claimants to sole responsibility being put forward it is reasonable to wonder whether they could not all be gathered together to provide a broad base for the decadent movement of the period.

It is true that within this aggregate two very different impulses were at work – the internal and the external. There were those who espoused decadence themselves and those who remarked on it in others (with commercial excitement or moral indignation as the case might be). These two currents, however, although contrasting, are complimentary; each might be expected to stimulate the other.

The aim of this book is to chart the courses and connections of these several contemporary currents, to assess the extent to which the myth and fact of the decadent nineties was fashioned by the men and women of the period.

Part I

'Poisonous Honey'

Chapter One

IN OCTOBER 1889 Arthur Symons and Havelock Ellis, two earnest young Englishmen, set off from London for Paris. It was the year of the Exposition Universel, held to celebrate the centenary of the French Revolution. Paris, the most exciting city in Europe, was in her festive finery; the flags were flying and autumn had turned the leaves to orange. The two visitors installed themselves for a week at a modest hotel in the Rue de Choiseul off the Boulevard des Italiens and, with all the zeal of youth, set off to 'do' the Exhibition. Amongst the vast palaces and ornate pavilions on the Champs de Mars they marvelled at the newest of modern inventions, at the miracles of science and art. It was the year when Edison introduced to Europe his 'telephone' and the bottled songs of his 'phonograph'; it was the year of Edward Burne-Jones' *King Cophetua and the Beggar Girl*; it was the year in which they lit everything with electric light.

Symons and Ellis wandered, wide-eyed, through the exotic splendours of the Colonial Section, past the meticulous reconstruction of Angkor Wat; and in the fanciful setting of a Cairo street, the scent of camel dung in their nostrils, they witnessed the excitements of the Danse du Ventre. They were enchanted by the sensuous impassivity of a troupe of Javanese dancers. They ate steaks, they drank vermouth, they smoked cigarettes. They splashed out on two voluminous white-and-gold burnouses, thinking excitedly what fine dressing-gowns they might make. They looked up and saw the Eiffel Tower. All seemed novel, exciting and strange.

Nor did they neglect the city's more permanent cultural calling-ports. They made the dutiful round of the Louvre, Nôtre Dame and the City Morgue. They attended the theatre, they braved a *café chantant*. They completed, in short, the standard itinerary of the educated Englishman in Paris.

They did, however, make one extra-curricular call, unlisted in the crowded pages of the Baedeker. They visited a small fishing-tackle-cum-bookshop down on the Quai Saint Michel. This was the establishment of M. Léon Vanier. It was full of arresting curiosities. There was a photograph of the poet Paul Verlaine on the wall, and another of the *cruel conteur* Villiers de l'Isle Adam. There were hand-printed magazines with provocative titles and books by Stephen Mallarmé, Gustave Kahn and Jean Lorrain, all unavailable, unheard of even, in England.

They duly scrutinized the photographs and browsed amongst the slender paper-covered books. They admired too the shop's cat. It was, Symons noted with approval, 'most meditative, mysterious, truculent and altogether decadent'. As such it was the perfect genius of the place, for M. Vanier's establishment was the very hub of French literary 'decadence'. That indeed was why Ellis and Symons had made their excursion to the Quai Saint Michel. They were interested in this newest movement of French culture. They already understood that its prevailing tenor was feline, mysterious, meditative and truculent, but they wanted to know more.

Perhaps, in their eagerness for knowledge, they picked up a little *Glossaire* of contemporary literary terms that Vanier had published the year before, and turned to the entry for '*décadence*'. They would have read that the word, although used by Gautier, Flaubert and the Goncourts 'in the sense of literary refinement', was first employed as a specific label by the critic Maurice Barrès, in 1884, to describe Verlaine, Mallarmé and their followers.

Although the exact details of this brief entry are open to dispute, it does provide a neat framework for understanding the origins of the French *décadent* school. For while the 'school' belonged to the mid-1880s, to Verlaine and Mallarmé and their disciples, it marked the culmination of a subversive trend in French literature and culture that stretched back towards the beginning of the century. Between the 1830s and the 1870s Gautier, Flaubert and the Goncourts, to describe and justify their own attempts at a complex, heterodox style of French, had indeed all used the analogy of late Latin – the Latin of the Decadence.

The notion of Imperial Rome's decline and fall was, of course, a commonplace of historiography well before the beginning of the nineteenth century. In France the course and causes of this *chute* had been mapped out most thoroughly in Montesquieu's *Considérations sur les causes de la grandeur des Romains et de leur décadence* of 1734. While Gibbon, in his great work on the subject, placed the blame for Rome's decline upon the advent of Christianity, Montesquieu fixed on the less contentious targets of luxury and maladministration. As a symptom of this fall into enervated luxury, the example of the Latin language was felt to be useful and revealing. The elegant simplicity of language employed by the Silver Age poets had, it was argued, become corrupted towards the end of the classical period. New words, strange syntactical quirks, awkward constructions, had all confused the pure flow of Virgil's measured metres.

Throughout the nineteenth century the habits of a classical education ensured that analogies were often drawn between the contemporary scene and the history of Rome. Such comparisons were very readily made in the literary field. France, after all, boasted a long, strong and explicit classical tradition, a tradition of prescribed metres and proscribed vocabulary. The ghosts of Sophocles and Racine, plodding on alexandrine feet, still patrolled the foyer of the Comédie Française. It was these tenacious shades that Victor Hugo and his young followers hoped to exorcize in 1830 with the new romantic vigour and freedom of *Hernani*. Amongst the side-effects of Hugo's triumph, however, was the sounding of a new note in literary criticism.

If Hugo's rugged and vital verse could be said to have corrupted the traditions of French classical purity, it was but a short step to liken him to the writers of the late Roman Empire who had corrupted the clear forms of classical Latin. The critic Desiré Nisard took that step. As early as 1834 he castigated Hugo and his followers for breaking the rules of classical verse, tampering with the alexandrine and adding new words to the poetic lexicon. He noted with disapproval that the subjects of poetry were becoming buried beneath a weight of erudite details, recherché nuance, rare words, wild exaggerations and a taste for the grotesque. And he likened these sorry developments to the poetry of Rome's decadence.

The contribution of Gautier, Flaubert, the Goncourts and indeed several others was to take up Nisard's line of criticism, accept it all, but claim it as praise rather than blame. This daring espousal was not merely a hollow gesture of literary defiance. The enthusiasm of these writers for the literature of late Antiquity was genuine and erudite. They were able Latinists who knew their Apuleius at first hand. Indeed, even at school, Gautier had vexed his teachers by imitating the styles of 'corrupt' authors, rather than the sonorous cadences of Cicero.

But beyond this informed admiration there was also a deeper reason for their eager acceptance of the literary traditions of Rome's decadence. Gautier, and a few of his contemporaries, considered that nineteenth-century France was – like late Rome or Byzantium – an old and enervated civilization sinking beneath the weight of luxury into moral and physical decline. By borrowing the literary styles of decadent Rome they thought that they would be better able to reflect and express the thoughts and feelings of their own decadent age.

To most modern historians the condition of France during the nineteenth century appears positively vital. It was the great age of the country's industrialization. To many contemporary observers there seemed to be grounds for satisfaction, even complacency, in the march of material 'progress' and the spread of new-found wealth. To Gautier and his band, however, the course of the century appeared to be marked, almost from the start, by the twin evils of political cataclysm and opulent materialism. The opening years of the new era had witnessed the collapse of Napoleon's imperial (and distinctly Rome-tinted) ambitions. And in 1830, at the very start of most of their careers, the July revolution had ushered in that least poetical of rulers, the fifty-seven-year-old Louis Philippe of Orléans, the so-called Bourgeois King – a monarch who loved industry, science and money; a man who had once been reduced to seek employment as a maths teacher in Switzerland.

And even when his regime was brought down in the February revolution of 1848, the brief dawn of the Second Republic was soon obscured by Louis Napoleon's *coup d'état*. Bonaparte's nephew, having been elected President, went on to declare himself Emperor. Together, he and his Empress, Eugénie, presided over the Second Empire, a period of yet greater enrichment. The strength and confidence of France's material might was proclaimed in a series of Expositions Universels, while an unabashed delight in wealth expressed itself in a decorative style of opulent, electroplated vulgarity.

The prevailing intellectual climate of these years was inimicable not only to the finer shades of art but also to religion. Science, which was achieving so many of the triumphs of the new materialism, seemed to challenge the dogmas and 'explain' the miracles of the past. Was nothing sacred? One hard-nosed exegete claimed with bullish certitude that the celestial Cross which appeared to Constantine before the battle of Milvian Bridge, prompting him to turn the Roman Empire towards Christianity, was in fact no more than a flamingo glimpsed against the sun.

While science began by undermining the bases of religious faith, it went on to corrode man's belief in his own importance. The publication of Darwin's theories, from 1859 onwards, seemed to reduce man in stature from a unique romantic hero set above the rest of nature, to a ruthlessly fit ape set in the midst of the jungle. But even before this decisive development, advances in the study of biology had begun to suggest both the complexity and the mutability of man's position in the world. The pre-Darwinian evolutionary works of Jean-Baptiste Lamarck (1744–1829) had put forward the attractive notion that characteristics acquired by a species during life would be transmitted to the next generation as a matter of heredity.

This theory, glibly extended into the human realm through such works as Lucas' *Traité de l'hérédité naturelle*, was held up to support the notion of social decline. Successive generations of comfort and luxury, it was argued, were reducing 'modern man' to a state of neurasthenia, incapable of action, devoid of will, a prey only to his diseased and over-sensitive nerves.

The only corrective to this downward trend was likely to be barbarous. The Goncourts wrote in their Journal of 1855:

> Savagery is necessary every four or five hundred years in order to bring the world back to life. Otherwise the world would die of civilization. When bellies were full and men had lost the power of making love, hordes of barbarians six foot tall would sweep down upon them from the north. Now there are no savages it is the workers who will be doing the job in fifty years or so. And they will call it social revolution.

The barbarians were at the factory gates. But in the meantime there was nothing more to do than enjoy the descent into well-fed impotence.

The position that the Goncourts, Gautier and their confrères took up in this decadent world of their imagining was ambivalent. They were antipathetic to bourgeois materialism, yet fascinated by the new luxurious amenities it afforded, and by the prevailing grossness. They decried the decadence of society and yet they claimed that as artists they were the most extreme examples of the 'decadent' type. They had, they avowed, been brought to such a pitch by the long centuries of civilization; their nerves were so hypersensitive that they could feel, with more intensity than ever their ancestors could, all the sensations of the modern world. They acclaimed neurosis, even when it reached to madness, as the very stamp of the artist.

The same roll of years, however, that had brought them to a state of 'neurasthenia' had – they felt – also left them bored and jaded with common sensations and obvious beauties. Their palates required instead the titillation of strange spices or (as a final refinement) the knowing simplicity of the *faux naïf*.

It was the need to evoke such new super-subtle and deliberately strange sensations that encouraged these brave literary spirits to search out a new and super-subtle language, and to search for its model in the heterodox style of late Antiquity. The fullest and the most influential exposition of this idea was written by Gautier in 1868 as a tribute to his recently deceased friend and fellow-poet, Charles Baudelaire.

Baudelaire and Gautier had first met some twenty-five years before, in 1845, at the little gatherings held by their mutual friend Boissard de Boisdernier in his large apartment in the Hôtel Pimodan on the Ile Saint Louis. The Hôtel was an old building of slightly macabre aspect: there was a wholesale dyeing business on the ground floor; steam would belch infernally through the open gateway and the gutters outside ran with vivid hues. Boissard's gatherings had a similarly bizarre edge – they were hashish parties.

Hashish was readily available from the French colonies of North Africa, and the fashionable literary concern with extreme refinements of sensation had led several writers, artists and dilettanti to gather in this informal *Club des hachichins* to test out the novel effects of the drug upon their senses. Gérard de Nerval came, and Daumier. Balzac attended only once; he sniffed the hashish and then firmly handed it back. Doctor Moreau de Tours, a friend of Gautier's who had recently published a work 'On Hashish and Mental Illness', and was interested to pursue the connection between these two factors and artistic creativity, lent the meetings a quasi-scientific savour.

Gautier in 1845 was thirty-four and famous. Already he had won for himself a name as a subverter of conventions both literary and social. He had first come to the public notice as a teenage member of Hugo's celebrated gatherings of writers and artists – his *Cénacle*.

Gautier had already decided to relinquish his painter's apprenticeship for a literary career in February 1830 when a messenger arrived from Hugo at his studio with a sheaf of tickets for the first night of *Hernani*. The young Gautier, asked whether he could be relied upon to bring a party of confrères, had replied – in the approved romantic style – that he would answer for himself and his friends, 'by the skull from which Byron drank at Newstead Abbey'. He was true to his oath. On the night of 25 February, clad in an extravagant red waistcoat, his long hair spread over his shoulders, he had led his section of the crowd at the Comédie Française as they roared down the outraged shouts of the classical traditionalists and carried the day for youth and novelty. It was an occasion that coloured the rest of Gautier's life.

When, five months later, the triumphant energy of that momentous evening was drained away by the July revolution, Gautier and his young friends determined to mark their dismay at a regime and a society that seemed to them coarse, materialistic and antipathetic to art. Together they formed, in imitation of the admired Hugo, *Le Petit Cénacle* (or *Les Jeunes France* as they were dubbed by *le Figaro*). They met in a studio above a grocer's shop to wallow in self-indulgent gloom, to drink punch and to devise ingenious ways of 'shocking the burghers'. The battle lines were drawn: if society was set against the artist, then the artist would set himself against society. The gesture was a novel one. Earlier romantic poets might, in their lives, have affronted the prevailing mores and by their exaltation of inspired individuality set themselves apart from society, but they had always maintained a belief in the grand claims of humanity. They had even espoused them at a practical level. Lord Byron himself had died (albeit of dysentery) while fighting for the liberty of the Greeks. The social welfare of Gautier and the other *bousingots*, however, although charmingly playful, marked one of the first cracks in the rift between the artist and society – a rift that would draw ever wider as the century advanced.

The public – the reading, listening, looking public – was expanding with each clanking revolution of the industrial machine. But as industrial processes mass-produced coarse versions of what was once hand-made, so – it seemed to some – industrial society mass-produced a readership with coarsened tastes, lacking in those refinements that marked the aristocratic connoisseurs of the past, and wanting only amusement and relaxation at the end of exhausting labours. And there was no shortage of publishers, no lack of mechanical presses, ready to cater for such tastes.

In the face of this bourgeois philistinism the true artist – and each member of *Les Jeunes France* insisted he was that – had to make his way, derision his highest expectation, indifference his greatest fear. Popular success came to be regarded as a sure sign of mediocrity, public abuse and incomprehension the mark of real distinction.

It was a curious equation but one that developed into an orthodoxy (an orthodoxy, indeed, that maintains its power even today). It was curious because most of these defiant artists and nearly all of their small audience were drawn from the despised ranks of the bourgeoisie. How could it be otherwise? Aristocratic society was a mere vestige, the masses were still illiterate. Perhaps it was this feeling of implication that added a twist of bitterness or self-mockery to the artist's attitude as he contemplated his public.

In 1834 Gautier, together with his old school friend Gérard de Nerval and other like-minded rebels, had reaffirmed their contempt for the coarse-souled burghers by moving into the elegantly dilapidated Impasse du Doyenne, near the Louvre. To confound the bourgeois virtues of modernity, efficiency, cleanliness and sobriety, they chose to live disordered lives in a crumbling eighteenth-century palace. In unreasonably large salons decorated with their own provocative murals they discussed their theories of art, their hopes for life; they held fancy-dress balls (indeed they were almost never out of fancy dress); they cultivated a nostalgia for the seductive world of the eighteenth century, the lost age of Watteau, Pierrot and fanciful *singerie*, a world at once artistic and aristocratic. Nerval walked in the gardens of the Palais Royal leading a lobster on a pale blue ribbon.

Although some members of the Bohème du Doyenne had money, most notably the art critic Arsène Houssaye, the ambience was not so very different from the starker garret-bound Bohemia brought to life by Murger in *La Vie de Bohème* (and set, much later, to music by Puccini). The splendour of their fêtes had a tatterdemalion charm; Gautier's own rooms were tiny, and Nerval camped in the middle of his vast salon in a small tent.

While the echoes of the recently passed eighteenth century provided a wistful contrast to the inimical present, Gautier was also prepared to search further afield to justify the artistic creed he and his companions were evolving. One of his first journalistic commisions, in 1833, was to produce a series of six articles for *La France littéraire* on neglected French writers. He began with a piece on François Villon.

Villon, who was to become one of the cult figures of nineteenth-century French counter-culture, was then very little known. A poet of the fifteenth century, he had distinguished himself by his direct yet ironical ballades and, almost more importantly, by his incorrigibly riotous life. He had killed a priest, been charged with theft and, following one particularly bloody affray, was even condemned to be hanged. This last sentence (although it was later commuted) provoked Villon's masterpiece, the *Ballade des pendus*, in which the poet rounded upon the world that had condemned him.

Villon's antisocial behaviour, his fascination with death and decay, his use of thieves' slang, his mastery of the old French verse forms, all commended themselves to the young Gautier, and he eagerly commended them to the readers of *La France littéraire*. Not everyone, however, shared his enthusiasm. A semi-official newspaper called *Le Constitutionel* chose to take offence. It launched an attack on Gautier for what it considered to be his approbation of Villon's immoral life. The argument led to the courts and, although Gautier's article was cleared, the temperature of the debate was raised. Significantly, the case was the first attempt by the new regime to censor a work on moral, as opposed to political, grounds.

Gautier, stung by the prosecution and fired by his acquittal, dashed off a highly charged polemical essay, which he attached as a preface to the novel he was then completing. This novel, *Mademoiselle de Maupin*, is in itself a delightful book, a sprightly romance of crossed loves and cross-dressing, in which the eponymous heroine, disguised as a man, fascinates both the Chevalier d'Albert (who worries that he is being seduced into 'unnatural' vice) and his erstwhile mistress, Rosette (who wonders why the handsome stranger keeps failing to take full advantage of her). The book abounds with amusing incidents (including a country house production of *As You Like It* where the heroine confuses her sexual identity – and her admirers – still further by taking the part of Rosalind); it sparkles with playful eroticism and with wonderfully rich descriptions of dress and décor. Nevertheless, for all its charms and virtues, the story's impact was perhaps rather less than that of the preface that preceded it. The contentious foreword might be called the very manifesto of '*l'art pour l'art*'.

The theory of '*art for art's sake*' was not in itself new. It can be traced back to Immanuel Kant's notion that art was disinterested and that it created a parallel, man-made nature. Kant's ideas had been eagerly accepted by Goethe, Schiller and other German writers, even before being taken up in France by the rarefied intellectual circle of Madame de Staël and Benjamin Constant. It was there that the term *l'art pour l'art* was heard of for the first time. And it was at Victor Cousin's Sorbonne lectures of 1818 that the ideas behind the term had gained a wider exposure.

Gautier was certainly not the first French writer to be inspired by such theories. They lie behind the preface of Victor Hugo's *Cromwell*, with its call for complete freedom of inspiration. But while Hugo had wanted to liberate art from the cramping rules of classical drama, Gautier was seeking to free it from the constraints of social and moral responsibility. As the bohemian artist was separate from society, he argued, so too should be his art.

'Everything useful is ugly,' he wrote in the preface, 'for it is the expression of some need, and man's needs are ignoble and disgusting like his own poor and infirm nature. The most useful place in the house is the lavatory.' Art, Gautier insisted, must be an autonomous realm, free from the prevailing dogma which insisted that everything must have its social use. He maintained that art's only goal was beauty and that any attempt to impose upon it some other aim (whether moral, political or even practical) was but to contaminate the pure stream and to create ugly – or bad – art. It was an extreme position but Gautier sustained it through the sheer energy of his writing.

He carried his attack further into the camp of the utilitarians, lambasting their confident belief in 'progress'. The human race, he claimed, was certainly not perfectible, it was not even alterable. And even in its recent achievements there was little to suggest progression. Who today could perform the Labours of Hercules? And in art, while other ages could boast of Michelangelo and Raphael, 'now one has M. Paul Delaroche'.

In place of this false 'progress' Gautier offered a cult of pleasure – the pleasure of the senses. He suggested that the French government should, like Sardanapalus, institute a prize for the man who could invent a new pleasure. Gautier himself seems to have had a prodigious appetite for the sensual aspects of life: he loved stroking angora cats; he adored music; he woke each morning dreaming of breakfast, and regularly consumed five pounds of mutton and three bottles of wine in the course of a day. But above all he was 'a man for whom the visible world exists', and it was the sense of sight that, for him, led most readily to beauty. He would, he claimed, cheerfully renounce his French citizenship to see an authentic picture by Raphael or a beautiful woman naked.

Although this claim suggests that beauty can be found in both art and nature – in the Renaissance painting and the living nude – it was, Gautier conceded, more likely to be met with in the former. In his novel the character d'Albert, too often disappointed by the imperfections of real women, resolves to confine his passion to paintings and statues of them. And Gautier himself would often recall his own sense of deflation upon first meeting an artist's model known previously from the canvas alone.

Gautier decisively shifted the balance between life and art, setting the factitious above the real and insisting that life relate to art rather than art to life. For Gautier, beauty was found in formal perfection. Having refuted the utilitarian concern over art's social responsibilities he was left to exalt the supreme importance of its form. Any subject, Gautier believed, could with enough care and craft be wrought into a beautiful work of art. 'The correction of form,' as he said, 'is virtue.' Content was all but irrelevant.

With all subjects claimed for art's amoral province, it was perhaps inevitable that the artist should be drawn to areas previously forbidden as immoral. The charms of virtue having for so long been the staple of art, it was tempting to explore the lesser-worked charms of vice. And the societies of Late Antiquity offered a splendidly vicious panorama. Gautier's hero, Chevalier d'Albert, deliberately allied himself with the presiding spirits of decadent Rome: 'Tiberius, Caligula, Nero,' he apostrophizes, 'great Romans of the Empire, oh you that are so little understood, and so hounded by the mob of rhetoriticians, I too suffer from your condition.' He craves plaintively for the lost debaucheries of Heliogabulus; though in truth his own debaucheries are not unimpressive. *Mademoiselle de Maupin* is not only a *hymne à beauté* but also a carol to sex. The frank and frolicsome bedroom scenes, the titillating lesbianism, the intoxicating sexual confusion, were all well calculated to outrage convention and to win for the book the *succès de scandale* it very properly achieved. In its claims for the autonomy of art, in its relish of sensual beauty, in its fascination with the artificial and perverted, and its association of these traits with the example of decadent Rome, the book struck a series of reverberating chords.

For Gautier, however, the most immediate consequence of his triumph was a great increase in the volume of journalistic commissions he received. Balzac had admired the novel and sought to help its young author by soliciting from him regular contributions for the *Revue de Paris*. Gautier was soon writing art and music reviews for a host of other periodicals too. In 1837 he became the regular theatre critic for *La Presse*. His output was prodigious and catholic. And although he was often contributing an article to the press almost every other day, he kept up a steady flow of lurid novellas, ballet *livrets*, beautifully wrought poems and colourfully written travel books. All of them, overtly or discreetly, advanced the claims of perfect art over imperfect nature. In his poems he developed the sculptural ideal of well-chiselled and highly polished formality. His most famous collection was aptly titled *Emaux et camées* (*Enamels and Cameos*). And even in his travelogues he was wont to castigate tedious landscapes and denounce nature as 'stupid, without consciousness of itself, without thought or passion', while praising art as 'more beautiful, more true, more powerful'. They were sentiments likely to endear him to the young Charles Baudelaire.

Chapter Two

In 1845 Baudelaire was in his early twenties. Although working steadily at his poems, he had yet to publish anything of note. Relations with his beloved mother and hated stepfather had deteriorated through a series of planned disgraces – expulsion from school, riotous living, an unscheduled early return from the sea voyage that had been planned to remove him from trouble. He now found himself infected with syphilis and constrained in his prodigality by a '*conseil judicaire*' who strove to regulate his expenditure – and prevent him from running up debts. He was living in Paris in an apartment in the Hôtel Pimodan.

His reputation, such as it was, was based upon his studied eccentricity. While Gautier espoused a riotous bohemianism to distinguish himself from the respectable bourgeois crowd, the Anglomane Baudelaire marked his own sense of alienation by borrowing the pose of an English dandy. From behind this impassive mask he would launch his frequent attempts to shock. Whether he ever actually dyed his hair green or congratulated a restaurateur for producing a fillet steak that was 'as tender as the brain of a little child' is open to doubt. But such were the stories he inspired, and invented.

Gautier was certainly intrigued by the young man's unsettling presence. He noted him with care: Baudelaire's 'jet black hair was close cropped and, coming to regular points on his dazzling white forehead, it covered his head like a Saracen helmet. His eyes, the colour of Spanish tobacco, had a deep intelligent look, perhaps a little too searching. His fine delicate nose, slightly rounded, with quivering nostrils, seemed to scent some vague and far off fragrance.'

Baudelaire for his part may have admired Gautier's work but at first he was alarmed by the older poet's appearance and volubility.

With his great mane of hair, his yellow slippers, his constant cigar, his pet monkey and his proud boast that he had once struck a blow of over five hundred pounds on the *tête de Turc*, Gautier seemed altogether too ebullient.

They came, nevertheless, to realize that beneath their very different exteriors they shared many common bonds: a hatred of the bourgeoisie, a high reverence for the purity of art. They shared too an interest much discussed in French literary circles at the time: the 'transposition' of the senses and the arts.

It was thought that all the senses were subtly interrelated, that colours had their corresponding sounds and smells and textures, and that these connections could be discovered and then used by the artist in his work. While the spiritually inclined Baudelaire came to see these '*correspondances*' as a sign of the harmonious cosmos, other writers – Gautier amongst them – tended to employ the technique merely to render yet more evocative descriptions. It was Gautier who introduced the idea of using musical titles for works in other media. His '*Symphonie en blanc majeur*' appeared in the *Revue des deux mondes* at the beginning of 1849. He also enlivened his journalism with frequent transpositions. At the most obvious level he described ballet as 'music that one can see' but he also extended the practice, complaining, for instance, of Donizetti's *Lucrezia Borgia* that much of the music which should have been 'poison green' was, instead, 'fresh and pink'. The experiments of *Le Club des hachichins* seemed, moroever, to strengthen such notions. In one account of a hashish dream Gautier described how he heard colours, saw spirals of harmonious music and swam in an ocean of sonority.

By the end of the 1840s Baudelaire and Gautier were friends. Together they attended the informal recitals at the 'Divan de Peletier'; together they paid court (in their very different ways) to the captivating *demi-mondaine* Mme Sabatier. They experienced the high hopes of the 1848 Revolution and false dawn of the Second Republic. They endured the sense of betrayal that followed three years later when Louis Napoleon pronounced himself Emperor. They shared a common love for Delacroix, they developed a common enthusiasm for Wagner; in time they came even to share the same hatter.

In 1857 Baudelaire expressed his admiration by dedicating his collection of poems, *Les Fleurs du mal*, to 'the impeccable poet, the perfect magician of French literature, to my most dear and most venerated friend, Théophile Gautier'. Gautier was not a little perturbed by the honour. The book was shocking in a fashion well beyond the frisky naughtiness of *Mademoiselle de Maupin*. In 101 carefully wrought poems Baudelaire anatomized his own soul, balking at nothing that he found in its dark recesses. He had fixed his gaze with unflinching seriousness upon his own neuroses: his aching ennui, his bitter spleen, his degrading fascination with flesh, his perverse delight in the ugly and the cruel, his admiration and his envy for the wholesome, his longing – not for an impossible salvation but for sensual satiety – for escape and oblivion.

To his contemporaries such subject-matter was arrestingly new and strangely distasteful. Baudelaire, with his 'too searching eyes' and ever quivering nostrils, had charted an unknown land; Sainte-Beuve called it a 'literary Kamchatka'. And he had, moreover, dared to describe this hideous terrain in the lofty tone of high poetry, the elevated style traditionally reserved for subjects either sublime or tragic.

Yet even this high style was not left uncorrupted. Baudelaire had plundered a host of grotesque images from the musty prop-cupboard of romanticism and brought them to life. He had fixed the blank-eyed skulls and scuttling spiders as tangible symbols of his own hopeless condition. He had borrowed words from the abattoir, the morgue, the brothel, never heard before in poetry, and set them within the flow of his stately metres. The whole effect was as novel as it was arresting. Victor Hugo remarked admiringly that Baudelaire had created a '*frisson nouveau*'.

It was not, however, a *frisson* that tickled the guardians of public morality. The book provoked an immediate and fierce response. Within days of publication all copies were seized and Baudelaire charged. The courts, which had only recently failed to secure a conviction against Flaubert's *Madame Bovary*, were determined not to let another case escape them. Baudelaire tried to defend himself with Gautier's argument that art was 'unrelated to morality – unrelated but not opposed'. The judges were unimpressed. Six poems were judged obscene and ordered to be suppressed. To add to this insult Baudelaire received a further injury, a fine of three hundred francs. He was consoled only by Hugo's description of this as 'one of the rare decorations which the present regime can grant'.

For many contemporary critics it was the new and distasteful subject-matter of Baudelaire's poetry that provoked the fiercest reaction. The book belonged, they felt, to a growing body of work that dared to tackle the darker aspects of human nature and activity. The enemies of this burgeoning tradition labelled it 'realism' – a term of disparagement borrowed from the world of painting. The practitioners unwillingly accepted the brand. On its appearance *Les Fleurs du mal*, like *Madame Bovary*, was seen as a dangerous example of 'crude and indecent realism', a trend which Count Montalambert had, that very month, denounced to the Institut de France as a 'fatal influence contaminating literature, art and even philosophy'. Even though 1857 also saw the publication of a manifesto, *Le Réalisme*, by the novelist Champfleury, claiming that the new movement was specifically concerned with accurate documentation of, and sociological insight into, the everyday life of the lower classes, the word continued to be used over the next decade as an insult to be attached to any work that dealt with subjects beyond the pale of conventional taste. The fact that some writers claimed their licence to treat of such forbidden subjects on scientific and sociological grounds, and some (like Baudelaire) pleaded the rights of *l'art pour l'art*, was a discrepancy that went unremarked. Critics, shocked by the new, did not trouble to distinguish between those who scrupulously detailed ugly truths and those who lovingly delineated the subtle beauties of ugliness. Some, however, recognized the inadequacy of such a response.

When Baudelaire died in 1867, at the age of forty-six, his publishers decided to bring out a new edition of *Les Fleurs du mal*, and they asked Gautier, the book's dedicatee, to provide a biographical introduction. In this 'Notice', rather than relating the poems to any tradition of realism, Gautier focused all the contemporary notions of social and personal decadence upon Baudelaire and his *oeuvre*.

He began his disquisition with an analysis of Baudelaire's literary style, a style which he considered perfectly fitted to a period of decadence. 'The style of decadence,' Gautier claimed, was 'nothing else than art arrived at that extreme point of maturity produced by those old civilizations which are growing old with their oblique suns – a style that is ingenious, complicated, learned, full of shades of meaning and research, always pushing further the limits of language, borrowing from all the technical vocabularies, taking colours from all palettes, notes from all keyboards.'

Gautier found in this heterodox, subtilizing style an echo of the classical past: 'We may remind ourselves, in connection with it, of the language of the later Roman Empire, already mottled with the greenness of decomposition, and, as it were, gamey, and of the complicated refinements of the Byzantine school, the last form of Greek art fallen into deliquescence.' The virtue of the decadent style, Gautier suggested, was that it offered the writer a new, extended range – a range necessary to reach new areas, to touch the new tastes of a new (but infinitely weary) age. It was able 'to express in thought that which is most ineffable, and in form the vaguest and most fleeting contours; listening that it may translate them to the subtle confidences of the neuropath, to the avowals of aging and depraved passion, and to the singular hallucinations of the fixed idea verging on madness'. Such a style was, he thought, 'the inevitable and fatal idiom of peoples and civilizations where factitious life has replaced the natural life, and developed in man unknown wants . . . it expresses new ideas with new forms and words that have not yet been heard'.

It seemed, however, to be expressing not so much new 'ideas' as a new sensibility.

> In opposition to the classic style, it admits of shading, and these shadows teem and swarm with the larvae of superstitions, the haggard phantoms of insomnia, nocturnal terrors, remorse which starts and turns back at the slightest noise, monstrous dreams stayed only by impotence, obscure phantasies at which the daylight would stand amazed, and all that the soul conceals of the dark, the unformed, and the vaguely horrible, in its deepest and farthest recesses.

This equation between contemporary neuroses, monstrous subjects and the style of late Antiquity had, as already mentioned, been gaining currency in Parisian literary circles since the time of *Mademoiselle de Maupin.* It echoed through the pages of the Goncourt Journals; it underpinned Flaubert's *Salambo.* Two years before Gautier's 'Notice' appeared, the youthful Zola had written in *Mes Haines*, 'My taste, if you like, is depraved; I enjoy very spicy reading matter, decadent works in which a sort of sensitive sickliness replaces the abundant health of classical epochs. I am a child of my times.' But Gautier elucidated the point with unexampled fullness. He assembled the elements of decadence – the complex style, the neurotic sensibility, the fascination with perversion and depravity, the comparison with the later Roman Empire – and fixed them to the work of Baudelaire.

Moreover, Gautier added another element to this portrait of Baudelaire's book, or rather he highlighted one particular feature of the existing composition. He celebrated Baudelaire as the poet of the 'artificial'. Traditionally, those who decry the effects of civilization seek a refuge, or an ideal, in the example of nature. But Gautier and Baudelaire denied themselves this convenient escape. They distrusted the myth of natural virtue quite as much as they despised the myth of human progress.

The deification of nature had been a distinctive (even the dominant) feature of romanticism. From the comfort – or otherwise – of eighteenth-century Paris, Jean Jacques Rousseau had asserted that Man, a noble savage in the state of nature, was only corrupted by civilization. It was, alas, too late to do very much about the situation on a practical level, but his views did breed a recognizable romantic sensibility, which set the natural above the artificial, the primitive above the cultured, the country above the town, the simple above the ornate, the heart above the mind.

Of course anyone who has watched a spider for quarter of an hour or sat down in a nettle patch might have cause to doubt nature's claim to inherent virtue, but it had taken the Marquis de Sade to make the point in his series of porno-philosophic novels, written during the last decade of the eighteenth century. He had, moreover, gone on to make several more points. He not only questioned Rousseau's premise, he reversed the whole scale of his values: for the Marquis, 'sin' was the normal state of nature and 'good' the artificial creation of human reason. It was therefore necessary, he argued, to counter nature at every turn, to elevate the artificial above the natural, to indulge in 'unnatural vice' rather than 'natural virtue', substituting 'unnatural vice' for 'natural affection'. Only by so doing, he claimed provocatively, could Man fulfil himself. The Marquis ended his days in the lunatic asylum at Charenton in 1814, but his ideas were less easily confined.

'The shadow of the "Divine Marquis"' (in Mario Praz's phrase) stretched out over the nineteenth century. The Goncourts described Flaubert as having a mind 'haunted by de Sade'. Gautier too espoused his anti-naturalism in his own playful fashion: and at least one contemporary critic denounced *Mademoiselle de Maupin* as 'a child of the Marquis'. But Baudelaire was the most consistent and committed disciple. From his contentious assertion that he would rather hear a musical box than a nightingale, to his idiosyncratic vision of Christianity as an artificial constraint upon natural selfishness, Baudelaire always stood firmly against nature and the natural. The chain of association linking art to the artificial, the artificial to the anti-natural and the anti-natural to the perverse bound all his work together. Beauty, for him, was allied to cruelty – and depravity became the mark of art.

As Gautier observed in the 'Notice': 'That taste for the excessive, the baroque, the anti-natural, almost always contrary to classical beauty, was for [Baudelaire] a sign of the human will correcting to its liking the forms and colours furnished by matter.' This fascination with the artificial and the depraved, although here concentrated upon style, inevitably reached out to touch all aspects of Baudelaire's work. It led him to translate the works of Edgar Allan Poe. It drew him towards new and dangerous areas: the man-made metropolis was his setting, sadistic women his leading characters; the wastes of ennui and the degradations of perverted desire were his persistent themes. Gautier fixed upon this trait and allied it to those other decisive elements – the gamey savour of late Antiquity and the thrill of sensations upon a neurotic sensibility – to create a picture of Baudelaire as the poet of 'decadence'.

Two years after writing the 'Notice' Gautier, and the rest of Europe, received another pungent reminder of the fragility of empires when, in 1870, Napoleon III's plush regime crumbled before the Prussian canons at Sedan. The French, lured into war by their own pride and Bismark's cunning, were utterly defeated. The Prussians besieged Paris. Napoleon III fled across the channel to live out a hero's exile in Kent. Here were good old-fashioned barbarians shuddering the walls of the citadel. The hastily formed government at Versailles accepted humiliating terms of surrender. The citizens of Paris (Gautier amongst them) tried to institute an independent Commune but the experiment was cut short by government troops; 12,000 Parisians were shot or deported. Gautier by this time had had enough. 'This Revolution,' he announced, 'is the end of me.' He died the following year at the age of sixty-one, his last piece of writing a wistful recollection of the première of *Hernani*.

The 1868 edition of *Les Fleurs du mal*, however, lived on. It was the only version of the book available until the edition of 1916. As a result the generation coming of age during the 1870s (or that tiny fraction of the generation interested in subversive poetry) discovered their Baudelaire in Gautier's decadence-tinged portrait. And it was Gautier's 'Notice' quite as much as Baudelaire's poetry that helped to fashion the decadent school which these young men and women founded in Paris in the early 1880s.

The French have always been good at literary movements. They have a love of café intellectualism; they have the cafés in which to indulge it; they have a fondness for theories and programmes; they even sometimes have the energy to carry them out. At the beginning of the 1880s there were already several well-established cultural movements claiming hegemony. French literature was still dominated by the seventy-eight-year-old Victor Hugo. And although in his ever-fertile genius he had outgrown the narrow bounds of his early romanticism, it was in relation to that grand tradition that he continued to be regarded. The year 1880 even witnessed a jubilee production of *Hernani*. But alongside Hugo's romanticism had grown up the more careful practice of the Parnassians – the poets of the anthology *Le Parnasse contemporain*, who looked to the doctrine of *l'art pour l'art*, and took as their gospel Gautier's poem, '*L'Art*' – with its call for the diligent 'labour of the file'. As a counter to romantic energy and fire they sought their effects in complex versification, exact expression and calculated impassibility. Although Gautier had been dead for almost a decade by the beginning of the 1880s, other leading practitioners – Théodore de Banville, Leconte de Lisle, José-María de Heredia – kept the movement vital, and inspired their own imitators.

The fame of these Parnassian poets was, however, nothing compared to the more recent celebrity of Emile Zola. Prose exerted a much readier appeal than poetry over the new reading public, and Zola's novels refined and extended the tradition of 'realism' to create a new school of 'naturalism', bent – so he claimed – on examining every facet of contemporary society with scientific rigour and against a scientific model. *L'Assommoir*, his account of the tavern life of Paris, was published in 1877 and marked his first major commercial success. It established his position as a best-selling author, a position amply confirmed by *Nana* (1880) and *Germinal* (1885), and it encouraged the young writers who visited him at his house at Médan to adopt his approach.

Although rivalries and jealousies existed between these various schools, there were also points of contact. Many Parnassians admired the achievement of Hugo, and one contemporary critic drew an interesting analogy between the Parnassian poets, the naturalist novelists and the recently emerged school of Impressionist painters, suggesting that all three groups shared a common interest in the scrupulous rendition of sensation and a common distrust of discursive thought. Sensation too continued to fascinate the young writers and artists who gravitated to Paris at the beginning of the 1880s. It was, however, a fascination coloured by a new mood. Pessimism.

The generation brought up in the humiliating wake of the Franco-Prussian war and ill-fated Commune had little faith in politics, and less in the machine-driven materialism that claimed to offer a cosy salvation. The fall of the Second Empire at the hands of the Germanic 'barbarians' had not effected any revival of spirit. It had merely confirmed a belief that all action was futile, that the world was weary. It seemed to many observers that the young were entirely without spunk and without hope. A critic for the authoritative *Revue bleue* could write – by the mid-1880s – 'I have been inquiring and I have learnt, not without amazement, that the sickness of pessimism does not only apply to a few eccentrics, but that it has become a mania, and infected a remarkable number of our youth.' The works of Baudelaire found a ready audience in such a climate of personal depression and social decadence. To confirm – and endure – their *mal de jeunesse* 'a remarkable number of our youth' turned also to the philosophy of Schopenhauer and the drink of absinthe: such are the pleasures of the pessimist.

Schopenhauer, whose ideas had arrived belatedly in France during the 1870s through the popularizing works of Théodule Ribot, lent the weight of German reason to French pathological depression. His bleak belief that life was a vale of tears, controlled by the essentially malevolent Will, and that the only hope of respite was to deny the Will, escaping through renunciation of all active life or perhaps through the contemplation of an aesthetic idea, seemed to echo the vague fears and desires of his French readers. The influence of his ideas upon Wagner, moreover, gave that composer an even firmer place in the French 'decadent' pantheon. While Gautier and Baudelaire had swum in the great tide of sensual excesses poured forth when *Tannhäuser* was performed in Paris in 1861 (reproducing, as Baudelaire put it, 'the complete onomatopoeic dictionary of love'), the next generation of enthusiasts turned yet more eagerly to the Schopenhauer-influenced *Tristan und Isolde*, with its heady fusion of sex and death, and its promise that the implacable Will might be escaped through absolute abandonment to sensual passion.

Absinthe offered ersatz abandonment on the cheap. The 'green fairy' which turned white with the addition of water, mass-produced by the factories of M. Pernod, had become the favoured drink of Bohemia. It was flavoured with wormwood and the extract of this plant – even more than the high alcohol content – acted powerfully upon the nerve centres of the brain, offering the triple charm of ready oblivion, certain hangover and possible madness.

Even gloom shared produces its own camaraderie, and the young pessimists gathered eagerly together to discuss their dejected state. They met in the bars and cafés of Montmartre or at the riotous dining-societies of *Les Hirsutes* and *Les Hydropathes*. They indulged their sense of despair, they railed against society and the popularity of Zola's books, they drank their absinthe, and they enthused about Baudelaire.

Their own literary experiments found a vent in café concerts and readings, and in a host of tiny, short-lived, all but home-made periodicals. On Saturday nights the in-crowd might cram into the mock-medieval bar at Le Chat Noir to hear Maurice Rollinat recite his determinedly tortured verses to the accompaniment of the piano and his own frightful grimaces. The cognoscenti would listen to his tales of '*le meurt*, *le viol*, *le parracide*', his poems of vampires and succubi, his evocations of the most fleeting yet frightful sensations, felt with all the painful acuity of a hypersensitive nervous system; they would note the poet's pale and tortured mien, his neurotic mannerisms. Those who followed the scene closely might whisper knowledgeable gossip of Rollinat's drug habit, or tell of the pet dog which he had carefully deranged (along strict anti-naturalist lines) by beating it whenever it did anything good and rewarding it for every misdeed.

Rollinat is not admired now, and his 1882 collection, *Les Nevroses*, is an object of critical fun, but in the 1880s he was regarded as 'a second Baudelaire'. He borrowed freely from that poet (and, significantly, from Gautier's picture of him), exaggerating all the most morbid and artificial elements of his work, while in his own person he strove to present the figure of a neurotically sensitive dilettante. If he was the most extreme, he was certainly not the only example of this artistic type. Jean Lorrain, a camp figure dripping with rings, was said to keep on his desk a severed head made of wax. He aspired to nothing more than excess. The principal aim of his literary endeavour was to leave no taboo unshaken, and it was his verses which began to treat of homosexual themes with defiant frankness. He wrote not only about lesbianism – which had been coyly fashionable as a literary subject since the appearance of *Mademoiselle de Maupin* – but also of male homosexuality. His poem '*Bathylle*' about a Greek dancing boy in a Roman cabaret created a little stir when it appeared in the Chat Noir's house magazine in July 1883.

The young rebels, unsatisfied by the frigid air of the Parnassians, envious of Zola's success, relished such choice spices. The cabaret at Le Chat Noir was always crowded; the magazine was eagerly sought. More than one man sensed the dawning of a 'movement'. Léon Vanier, a small brown-skinned man of spritely energy and ambition, determined to become the publisher and promoter of the new school. Vanier had begun his retailing career selling fishing-tackle in the Rue Hautefeuille, but he had always harboured a passion for books. In 1881 he moved his shop to a site on the Quai Saint Michel and started publishing poems and stories by young writers in small editions. His shop and impress provided a more enduring platform for such work than the small stage at the back of Le Chat Noir.

In the same year that Vanier set up his shop on the Quai Saint Michel, Paul Bourget, a rather pompous young interpreter of intellectual trends, tried to give a philosophical account of the current 'decadence'. In an essay on Baudelaire which he contributed to the *Nouvelle revue* (15 November 1881), he traced the origins of the decadent literary style – first found in Baudelaire but now more widespread – to the malaise of contemporary society. 'Slowly and surely,' he wrote, 'a belief is growing in the bankruptcy of nature which promises to become the sinister faith of the twentieth century, if science or an invasion of barbarians does not save an over-reflective humanity from the fatigue of its own thought.'

The third part of his essay, '*Théorie de la décadence*', was taken up with an elaborate scientific analogy explaining the arrival of society (and literature) at this sorry state. Just as an organism degenerates if the energy of its individual cells – instead of being directed towards the functioning of the whole – becomes independent, so the 'social organism' becomes 'decadent' when 'the individual life becomes exaggerated beneath the influence of well-being and heredity'. A similar law, he continued, 'governs the development and decadence of that other organism which we call language. A style of decadence is one in which the unity of the book is decomposed to give place to the independence of the page, in which the page is decomposed to give place to the independence of the phrase, and the phrase to give place to the independence of the word.'

In July 1882, on to this increasingly self-conscious 'decadent' scene, shambled the unprepossessing figure of Paul Verlaine; bald, alcoholic, and thirty-nine, his reputation was founded more on scandal than on poetry. He had been absent from Paris for over ten years. In 1872 he had shocked the literary establishment when, as a budding poet with three well-received volumes to his credit, he had deserted his young wife and newborn child to run off with a domineering protégé, the ferociously precocious Arthur Rimbaud. Verlaine seems to have been completely in the thrall of his young companion. Together they roved across northern Europe, staying for a while in London, just behind Mornington Crescent. They sought abandonment in a life of amorality, while in their poetry they tore at the constricting bonds of French versification.

The experiment with life was not a great success, as Rimbaud ruefully records in *Un Saison en enfer*. The relationship, always unsettled, came to an ignominious end in 1873 when, during a quarrel in a Brussels hotel room, Verlaine produced a pistol and shot Rimbaud in the wrist. Despite Rimbaud's generous protestations a Belgian court condemned Verlaine to two years' imprisonment.

Verlaine, in prison and aware that he had now lost not only his wife and child but also Rimbaud, turned to God. He took first instruction and then communion from the rather amazed prison chaplain. He then transmuted the glorious experience of his conversion into the poems that would later make up *Sagesse*.

On his release from prison he continued his wanderings, taking a succession of teaching jobs, at first in England and then in France. The original force of his conversion soon dwindled; he began drinking again. In 1877, while teaching at a school in Rethel, in his native north-east, he developed a passion for one of his pupils, Lucien Létinois. Subsequently Verlaine retired from teaching and bought a farm at Juniville, where he installed himself together with Lucien and Lucien's parents. The venture, as might be guessed, was not a success. At the beginning of 1882 the farm had to be sold at a substantial loss.

It was in the wake of this financial setback that Verlaine – together with his mother and Lucien – returned to Paris and moved once more into the orbit of literary life. During the years of exile his poetry had been studiously ignored. He had been deliberately excluded from the third *Parnasse contemporain* in 1875. His two collections, *Romances sans paroles* (1874) and *Sagesse* (1881), had not been distributed from the warehouse. A few copies had been sent to the press but many editors, still shuddering at the scandal of his elopement with Rimbaud, refused to review them. The reputation he had built up with his first three collections – *Poèmes saturniens*, *Fêtes galantes* and *La Bonne chanson* – had dwindled into obscurity.

Nevertheless, where others saw a scandal to be avoided Léon Vanier saw a risk to be taken. He included four of Verlaine's poems in his periodical, *Paris moderne.* One in particular, '*Art poétique*', written some eight years before, under the influence of Rimbaud, attracted attention. Its opening and closing lines – '*De la musique avant toute chose*', and '*Et tout le reste est littérature*' – are still amongst the most quoted in French verse; its message had a decisive impact upon a generation of poets.

The poem was a call for a freer and more evocative versification. Verlaine's daring originality in this is not perhaps readily appreciated by an English reader, for French verse, despite the experiments of the romantics, had maintained a far greater measure of formality than its English counterpart. It was still dominated by the alexandrine, by the emphatic fall of the '*rhyme riche*', by a sort of rhetorical stiltedness. The efforts of the Parnassians had only served to increase the precision and rigidity of the medium, salting it with wit but leaving it cold and bright.

Verlaine turned against all this. In place of the sculptural ideal of verse, fostered by Gautier, he suggested '*la musique*', the intangible and suggestive rather than the hard-edged and descriptive. '*L'indécis*' is to be preferred to the '*précis*', '*la nuance*' set above '*la couleur*'; rhyme is to have its wings clipped, rhetoric its neck wrung. The poem itself – in '*verse impairs*' (in lines with an odd number of syllables), with its weak and internal rhymes, its tripping rhythm, its intimate rather than oratorical flavour – neatly exemplified its own programme.

The poem was written up with enthusiasm in the *Nouvelle rive gauche* by an eager young critic called Charles Morice (writing under the pseudonym Karl Mohr). Verlaine, feeling that Morice had rather overstated his position, replied to the review. The two men met and Morice, much impressed, decided to become Verlaine's champion. Morice's influence and contacts brought Verlaine further within the circle of young and provocative writers. His advocacy ensured that Verlaine's poetry began to appear in the *Nouvelle rive gauche* – or *Lutèce* as it came to be called in March 1883 – and other small periodicals.

The gathering band of admirers recognized in Verlaine a fellow disciple of Baudelaire. (Verlaine's first volume, *Poèmes saturniens*, published in 1866, had borrowed its title and not a few of its effects from *Les Fleurs du mal.*) But together with the familiar Baudelairian themes they saw and relished the novel diction of '*Art poétique*'. It seemed to them a great liberation, an escape from '*l'impeccabilité et l'impassibilité parnassiens*'. It was also a style particularly well suited to fixing the fine shades of their own ennui and exhaustion.

Verlaine's subject-matter as much as his poetic manner commended him to those neurotic young men and women reading him for the first time. His incomparable gift for evoking the subtle sadness of things – of the moonlit grove, the setting sun, the rainswept town, the passing of youth, the absence of love, the loss of hope – resonated with their spirit of pessimism.

Verlaine was quick to recognize the prevailing tenor of the young movement. Although his old-fashioned nationalism and healthy impatience with artistic theory led him to dismiss Schopenhauer and all that 'German stuff', he loved absinthe and the beauties of decay, and he allied himself deliberately to his youthful confrères. His understanding of the new movement's origins was clearly (if ironically) signposted in the edition of *Le Chat Noir* of 26 May 1883, when he published his sonnet '*Langueur*' with its emphatic declaration, 'Je suis l'Empire à la fin de la décadence.' Later that summer he expanded upon the theme, telling an interviewer:

> I like the word decadent, all shimmering with purple and gold . . . it throws out the brilliance of flames and the gleam of precious stones. It is made of carnal spirit and unhappy flesh and of all the violent splendours of the lower Empire; it conjures up the paint of courtesans, the sports of the circus, the breath of animal tamers, the bounding of wild beasts, the

> collapse amongst flames of races exhausted by the power of feeling, to the invading sound of enemy trumpets. The decadence is Sardanapalus lighting the fire in the midst of his women, it is Seneca declaiming poetry as he opens his veins, it is Petronius masking his agony with flowers.

As 'decadence' came increasingly to assert itself as the movement's watchword, so Verlaine, more and more, was seen as its figurehead.

If his poetry, with its simple and melancholic music, commended him to attention, his mode of life confirmed his position. Verlaine, far more than his young admirers, was 'made of carnal spirit and unhappy flesh'. His drinking set him against society, his homosexuality set him against nature. It was, he claimed proudly, the poet's lot and privilege to stand accurst.

He added fuel to the fire with a series of three articles in *Lutèce* towards the end of 1883. '*Les Poètes maudits*' revealed to the public – the limited public of Montmartre that is – the almost entirely unknown talents of Tristian Corbière, Rimbaud and Mallarmé: Corbière, the 'pariah' poet of the Breton fishermen; Rimbaud, the great influence upon his life, who had turned from poetry to run guns in Abyssinia; and Mallarmé, a diffident English teacher at several of the better schools in Paris, who was diligently working towards a new poetic language.

These articles – little more than mosaics of quotation grouted with biographical detail – provided the younger generation with a tradition they had not known they possessed: a trio of poets who had striven (Corbière had died in 1873, Rimbaud 'retired' in 1875) or were striving (Mallarmé was even then gathering about him a circle of like-minded intellectuals at his apartment in the Rue de Rome) towards an ideal of poetry in defiance of a hostile world. The three poets might be '*maudit*' but they, like Verlaine, rejoiced in the stigma as a mark of their calling. Verlaine, moreoever, even took the interesting step of linking his three subjects to the world of decadent Antiquity, comparing their portraits to the busts of late Roman Emperors.

By the time the articles appeared, however, Verlaine had left Paris again. Lucien had died of typhoid in April of 1883 and the distraught poet had rashly bought the Letinois family farm at Columbes from the dead boy's parents. This second attempt at pastoral life was even less successful than the first. Despite the presence of his long-suffering mother, Verlaine soon abandoned himself to drink, low company, vice and sartorial eccentricity. He tramped the country lanes in a Macfarlane plaid overcoat and broad-brimmed hat, picking up gypsies. In one drunken fit he threatened his mother with violence and, despite her protestations at the trial, was condemned to a month's imprisonment. By the spring of 1885 he had to sell the farm, at another debilitating loss, in part to pay off the five-hundred-franc fine that accompanied his gaol sentence.

That June, together as ever with his mother, he returned, now in straitened circumstances, to Paris. He discovered that while his financial position had been deteriorating his literary stock had been rising, borne upwards on the gathering tide of the new movement. Poems, stories, novels, all dressed in the robes and language of 'decadence', were (albeit in small editions) clattering from the presses. Their professed aims were to examine neglected corners of the human spirit, to dwell on new, bizarre sensations and to expose the iniquities of the age; their real desire was to shock.

They may shock us now by their mediocrity and euphuism but at the time their thumping blows struck home. Even the reviewer from *Le Chat Noir* widened his eyes at the catalogue of vice presented by Jean Lorrain's *Modernités*: 'Fellatrices, catamites, pimps, ponces, madams, club-owners, all those who traffic in lust are pictured here in all their ugliness'. As the volume of such work increased, so the characteristic themes and motifs asserted themselves: the enthusiasm for Wagner in music, for Moreau and Rops and the Pre-Raphaelites in contemporary art; for the ambiguously sexed angels of Botticelli and the mysterious smile on the face of the Mona Lisa; for the head of Antinous and the scent of flowers, for the listless truculence of cats, for all the faded glitter of Byzantium. Against the fecund, natural forces of conventional sex these authors raised an army of sterile, anti-natural erotic characters – unsexed cyphers, twice-sexed hermaphrodites, blood-lusting dominatrices, corruptible virgins, incestuous children, Bathyllic boys and Sapphic girls. In the atmosphere of unlimited literary licence some abandoned themselves to the projection of their private and peculiar fantasies, others deliberately searched out fresh vices to promote the fashion of the day – and, of course, themselves.

For all its feverish panting this sexual world was largely a realm of the imagination. It was the suppressed, rather than the indulged, desires of the decadent artists and writers that stirred up these lurid visions. Even Jean Lorrain, for all his self-advertised sinfulness, was too much of a valetudinarian to act out his homoerotic dreams. He contented himself with innuendos and with brushing his hair forward over his brow in the hope that he might be mistaken for a murderer.

One book in particular had appeared to fix the contemporary fascination with decadence and project it beyond the limited coteries of Montmartre. Useful though Bourget's essay on the '*Théorie de la décadence*' had been in focusing attention on the phenomenon, it lacked the ready accessibility of a novel that came out in May 1884. Joris Karl Huysmans' *A Rebours*, a short novel by a minor civil servant and one-time member of Zola's group at Médan, both reflected and defined the spirit of the times. It presented a vivid portrait not merely of 'decadence' but of a decadent, Comte Floréas des Esseintes. Des Esseintes, the last of an aristorcratic line, has been brought by heredity to the point of neurasthenia; his enervation, his desire for strange sensations, his inability to face the world, is pathological.

The book's very title – usually translated as 'Against the Grain' or 'Against Nature' – reveals the debt to de Sade and Baudelaire. Des Esseintes, weary of conventional debaucheries and sick of modern life, has retreated to his house outside Paris, and there, in an atmosphere of luxurious artifice, shut off from the world, he cultivates his senses. He has nothing else. The book moves in a stately procession from one sensory indulgence to the next: the symphony of liqueurs, the landscape of perfumes, the arrangement of gems, the conservatory of hideous plants.

The picture is touched with subtle and humorous satire – des Essenties disposes of his first collection of flowers (which were artificial but looked real) in favour of a second set (which are natural but look artificial). And, in a final aberration, he misreads his doctor's prescription for beef tea and takes it as an enema. Des Esseintes' experiment, moreover, ends, as inevitably it must, in failure. His nervous health deteriorates yet further under his bizarre artificial regime. His doctor orders him back to 'normal' life in Paris or else face 'insanity speedily followed by tuberculosis' and death. In an effort to lend some drama to this defeat, des Esseintes resolves to combine his return to Paris with a return to his lost faith. Despite the satirical undertone and bathetic ending, most contemporary readers took the book as a work of instruction, exciting or dangerous according to taste.

The impact of *A Rebours* was nowhere more apparent than in the passages dealing with art and literature. Huysmans provided a complete cultural guide for would-be decadents. Des Esseintes inevitably dislikes anything in painting that represents nature, preferring the visionary opulence of Gustave Moreau and Odilon Redon, or the gruesome horrors of Jan van Ruysbruck's martyrdoms. In literature his tastes are catholic but perverse. During the course of the book several visits are made to des Esseintes' library, once – and most impressively – for a brilliant overview of all late Latin literature, the literature of 'the decadence'. The corrupt and complex works of Apuleius and Petronius or St Boniface and St Aldhelm are preferred to the pure 'classics' of Virgil and Cicero.

Des Esseintes also fosters a contrary passion for various Catholic apologists. Despite such esoteric tastes he does, however, read his contemporaries too. He admires Flaubert, the Goncourts and Zola, particularly in their stranger moods; Baudelaire, and Poe, he reveres above all. Nevertheless, he also suggests that, in a time of decadence, it is often the minor writers who best – if only occasionally – distil the spirit of the times. 'In his opinion, it was in their confused efforts that you could find the most exalted flights of sensibility, the most morbid caprices of psychology, the most extravagant aberrations of language, called upon in vain to control and repress the effervescent salts of ideas and feelings.' He goes on to list some of these neglected figures who have given him such moments of pleasure. The *poète maudit* Corbière, the irredeemably bohemian Villiers de Lisle Adam, and his friend, the inventor-poet Charles Cros, who mapped out the principles of colour photography and published verse that combined jewelled splendour with creeping horror: all were fixed by Huysmans in the decadent pantheon.

Des Esseintes, ignoring the claims of Rollinat, reserves his warmest commendations for Verlaine and Mallarmé. In Verlaine he recognizes the influence of Baudelaire but praises the younger poet's individual tone, the originality of his loose-jointed versification, the expert handling of nuances, the charming naivety of *Sagesse*, and above all, that 'ability to communicate deliciously vague confidences in a whisper in the twilight'. Mallarmé he loves for his lofty scorn of society, for the Byzantine complexity of his thought and the allusive expression it finds in the strange ellipses of his hermetic language. The two poets embodied, for des Esseintes, the final decadence of French literature, a literature sick and exhausted yet determined to record its subtlest sensations of perverse pleasure and inescapable suffering. The course of the disease, he noted, had been quick. In the classical world centuries had elapsed between the variegated style of Rutilius and the gamey idiom of Sts Boniface and Aldhelm. But with French literature the 'variegated' style of the Goncourts was almost coincident with the complete liquefaction wrought by Verlaine and Mallarmé.

The achievement of *A Rebours* was to set an engrossing picture of a decadent in prose that was itself deliquescent; its effect was to give the word 'decadence' colour and to confirm Verlaine and Mallarmé as its foremost exponents. It reflected the taste of a minority and defined it for the majority. Although Huysmans put much of his own sensibility into the character of his 'hero', many of the extravagant trappings of des Esseintes' life were borrowed from Huysmans' contemporary, the minor poet and major eccentric, Robert Comte de Montesquiou-Ferzenec. The gothic chapel where de Montesquiou sermonized his tailor on taste, the parma violets he wore like a cravat in his shirt-front, the sleigh which stood in his hallway on a polar-bearskin, his habit of wearing purple to listen to Weber, his gilded tortoise, his display of silk socks, his fondness for circus performers: all these elements (carefully garnered from the gossip of those who had visited de Montesquiou's home in the Rue Franklin) found their way, more or less distorted, into Huysmans' book. They gave it the spice of a *roman à clef* for those who enjoyed such things. But the novel was much more than a portrait-sketch of a bizarre individual; it was a minutely detailed picture of decadent tastes and habits.

For most people Huysmans created, if not quite the idea, at least the pose, of 'decadence': after the publication of *A Rebours*, Robert de Montesquiou, ordering a selection of arcane volumes from an antiquarian bookseller, was appalled when the man, unaware of the Count's identity, had remarked, 'Why, Monsieur, these are books fit for des Esseintes.'

After *A Rebours* the new writers of Montmartre were very quickly branded as '*les décadents*', and Verlaine and Mallarmé were no less quickly labelled the heads of the 'decadent school'. Maurice Barrès is generally credited with having first used the adjective to define the movement, in a long essay on the influence of Baudelaire on modern literature published over two months (November/December) in 1884. The term was taken up by hostile critics and hurled as a brickbat; it was worn by the young poets as a cockade.

In May 1885 it received a fresh access of notoriety when two young journalist-poets produced a spoof volume of 'decadent' verse. The publication of *Les Déliquescences d'Adoré Floupette, poète décadent* provoked an unexpected furore. Many of the established papers reviewed the book in the mistaken belief that it was serious. And indeed its charnel-house of horrors, perversions and pessimism was certainly no more ridiculous than that of Rollinat and Lorrain. Almost from the start 'decadence' flirted with self-parody, either accidentally, through the incompetence of its practitioners, or deliberately, through a desire to escape an awful predicament by overstating its causes. The motive behind the *Déliquescences*, however, was merely mischief – allied to publicity (indeed the publisher of the slim volume was none other than Léon Vanier). The small first edition of 110 copies sold out almost immediately and a second printing of 1,500 copies was rushed through. The major publishers and the greater public were beginning to take note. There was a disapproving article in *Les Temps* on '*Les Poètes décadents*', citing Verlaine as the ringleader.

It was a propitious moment for Verlaine to return. Acclaimed in the pages of *A Rebours* and parodied in the *Déliquescences*, he arrived back in Paris to find himself being hailed as the founder and central figure of a 'movement'. His verse collection, *Jadis et naguère*, brought out by Vanier in 1884, had contained the sonnet '*Langueur*', which was now pointed to by many as the origin of the term 'decadence'. Other busy myth-makers told of how Verlaine, when approached by some young hopefuls planning to start a magazine titled *La Décade*, had replied, 'In that case you will be known as the decadents.'

Verlaine was ambivalent about his new position. He was a poet not of 'schools' but of personal vision; '*L'art*,' he would tell those who asked his advice, '*c'est d'être absolument soi-même.*' Nevertheless he bowed graciously enough in the face of his new popularity, partly because he could not avoid it and partly because it made sound financial sense. From 1886 Vanier began to publish Verlaine's verse at his own, rather than at the poet's, expense.

There was an irony in this as Verlaine's poetic gifts had very largely deserted him by this time. The great dramas of his life were over: his naïve marriage, his mad infatuation with Rimbaud, his fantastic conversion, his passion for Lucien Létinois; the intensity of his youthful vision had been spent. This decline did not, however, affect his publication programme. He produced a book almost every year. He reissued his earlier works, he used up his stock of unpublished poems, and he produced a great deal of mundane verbiage, some of it cloyingly spiritual, the rest of it flagrantly homoerotic, and all of it bereft of that musical and suggestive lightness he had advocated in '*L'Art poétique*'.

If Verlaine's ability to write poetry was declining, he lost none of his genius for 'being' a poet. He took great care to preserve his reputation as an incorrigible (though repentant) sinner. He professed his distaste for society, not by standing above it like the dandy, but by sinking below it. On his return to Paris he produced a second series of *Poètes maudits*, including himself as one of the accursed under the anagrammatic pseudonym Pauvre Lelian. With the death of his mother at the beginning of 1886 Verlaine had lost not only her stabilizing influence but also the last remnants of an income. His wife's family claimed the residue of the estate on the grounds that Verlaine had failed to provide support for his son. He sank further into squalor and ill-health. Between increasingly frequent sojourns in the public hospitals he passed his days at café tables and his nights in the arms of vast maternal prostitutes.

Nevertheless his verse and his name were much in demand. He contributed to many of the little magazines that sprang up to champion the 'decadent' cause, to *La Vogue*, *La Lutèce* and *La Décadence*. He wrote a poem on 'Parsifal' for Edouard Dujardin's *La Revue Wagnèrienne*. But above all Verlaine enjoyed – or endured – the championship of Anatole Baju's misprint-ridden publication, *Le Décadent*, which appeared, somewhat erratically, between April 1886 and April 1889.

Baju, the editor, was typical of the young men of the 'school'. He had feverish enthusiasm, unfocused ambition and no real talent. He had, like so many others, dramatized and re-created himself by adopting a pseudonym, arriving from the provinces as plain Adrien Bajut determined to make his way in the literary world of Paris. Despite an occasional job as a substitute teacher in the suburb of St Denis he devoted most of his time and almost maniacal energy to producing his tiny magazine. He wrote much of each issue himself under a variety of further pseudonyms. He set the letterpress himself and rowed with his contributors over the numerous typographical errors. In the early days of the venture he had even smuggled a small press, piece by piece, into his apartment. But the neighbours had soon complained of the noise. A fellow of such resource and tenacity was well able to bounce the half-reluctant Verlaine into his unlooked for position as the leader of the decadent school.

The young poets began – or continued – to imitate with sedulous industry what they perceived as the 'decadent' Verlainian manner: the Watteauesque settings of *Les Fêtes galantes*; the records of vague sensations mirroring yet vaguer emotions; the abandoned sense of submissive languor. Stylistically they strove for Verlaine's musicality, for his subtle interplay of assonance, alliteration and interior rhyme; they broke their sentences awkwardly and trawled the dictionary for coruscating words. Verlaine, meanwhile, sighed and allowed them to buy him another drink.

He brought an exciting sense of wickedness into their lives. Where others had only fantasized, Verlaine had acted. When Verlaine visited the young Rachilde at her fashionable home and asked if he might smoke his pipe, the author of *La Marquise de Sade* replied, with all the irresistible daring of an artistic spirit, 'Damn conventions! We're all decadents here!'

Verlaine, however, recognized clearly the limits of the 'decadent' position. It was he who is said to have whispered to Rachilde, when she was accused in the press of having invented a new sin, 'Ah, my dear child, if you had done that you would be a benefactor to mankind.' Alas, none of the decadents was able to come up with a fresh sin, and the repetition of the old transgressions – the sadism, the lesbianism, the homosexuality, the passion for artifice – rapidly began to wear itself out into mere routine. A higher ideal was needed.

The critic and dandy Barbery D'Aurevilly had already suggested that the decadent soul (as revealed by *Les Fleurs du mal*) must seek release at the foot of the Cross or the mouth of a pistol. Certainly the decadent pose was without hope; it was a creed of compensation, claiming moments of sensory pleasure as fleeting distractions from the enduring awfulness of existence.

In the face of this spiritual void some did turn to the Cross. It was des Esseintes' course at the end of *A Rebours*, and Huysmans' too. Verlaine turned to religion, fell again, and turned again, in a constant round. A few turned the pistol upon themselves. Some, like Rollinat, went mad before they could come to a decision. Many, however, took less dramatic routes out of the impasse, lapsing quietly into parody or respectability. Yet others, in the desire for some sort of spiritual value, plunged giddily into the turbid waters of spiritualism. It was in 1888 that Josephin Péladan revived the defunct medieval *Ordre kabbalistique de la rose croix*. He proclaimed himself the Sar Merodak, put on a jewelled turban and declared war against the practitioners of black magic. Although the Sar Péladan had his followers in artistic circles, the greater number of Parisian writers eventually found a focus for their transcendental urges in the literary idea of symbolism.

From the distance of a hundred years critics feel able to describe symbolism as the successor and fulfilment of decadence, as a separate – though related – school that came to a point of focus in about 1886, under the influence of Mallarmé, and went on to dominate French literature until the First World War and, indeed, beyond. It is neatly defined as an attempt to evoke, through the 'music' of language, the subtle 'correspondences' that exist between the material and spiritual worlds. Such pat descriptions and definitions would, however, have been quite unrecognizable to a Parisian of the 1880s. The term, although it had been heard in the elevated circle of Mallarmé's *mardis*, made a more dramatic appearance as a rallying call in the faction-riven world of Montmartre. As cliques formed and split, labels were needed. They could not all be 'decadents', so the cry of 'symbolism' was taken up.

The word allowed – and provided – a whole range of conflicting interpretations. In the autumn of 1886 Jean Moréas' '*Symboliste*' manifesto in the literary supplement of *Le Figaro* was rebuffed by Alfred Valette's in *Le Scapin*. René Ghil (in a magazine called, unhelpfully, *La Décadence*) claimed to be the spokesman for the new '*école symbolique*', only to be contradicted by Paul Adam in the first issue of *Le Symboliste*. Confusion reigned as the platitudes and invective flew.

Verlaine found himself embroiled. Moréas even claimed him for a founder of symbolism, as the man who had been the first to 'break the cruel bonds of verse'. His real contribution, however, was to make known the works of Rimbaud through the extensive quotations in *Les Poètes maudits*, and in a piece for *Les Hommes d'aujourd'hui*. The ideas behind the sonnet '*Voyelles*' and the startling novelty of *Illuminations* went far beyond the essentially timid innovations of '*L'Art poètique*', and offered encourgement to those, like Mallarmé, experimenting with free verse and desiring transcendence.

Mallarmé's ambitious belief that the poet could penetrate the veil of superficial reality to discover the ideal forms of an infinite and eternal realm, that nature was (in Baudelaire's phrase) but a '*forêt de symboles*' requiring only a new poetic vision and a new poetic language to reveal its secrets, was quite alien to Verlaine's temperament. Verlaine's transcendental urges were few and conventionally Christian, his 'symbolism' (for all poetry has its symbolic element) was of the human sort that finds a reflection for emotion in the world of external reality, his idea of music in verse ('*avant toute chose*') was mere euphony. Nevertheless the two poets and the two movements – decadence and symbolism – were happily confused and confounded. They were even on occasion combined into something called the 'symbolo-decadent' movement.

The press and the public, having only just taken on board the idea of a decadent school, were not anxious to give it up, especially for something so allusive and unclear as symbolism. They tended to use the terms interchangeably (although preferring the more emotive 'decadence'), to the great annoyance of all the artists concerned.

Chapter Three

IT WAS TO this scene of hectic yet vital chaos that Arthur Symons and Havelock Ellis came in the autumn of 1889. They were impressively well-prepared for the fray. In England, knowledge of – and enthusiasm for – the developments of French literature over the previous half-century, although partial, was not insignificant.

Back in 1862 the twenty-five-year-old Algernon Swinburne, travelling through France to meet his family down in the south, had stopped off in Paris. There he acquired a copy of *Les Fleurs du Mal*, which had recently been reissued in its post-trial expurgated form. Swinburne read the poems and was intoxicated (he was prone to intoxication); in the heat of the moment he wrote a review for the *Spectator*. His own masochistic tastes, awakened on the flogging block at Eton and fostered by a lubricious imagination, seemed to detect an answering echo in Baudelaire's poems. Here, he burbled, was a poet prepared 'to dwell upon sad, strange things – the perverse happiness and wayward sorrows of exceptional people . . . Not the luxuries of pleasure in their simplest first form, but the sharp and cruel enjoyments of pain, the acid relish of suffering felt and inflicted'.

Such terms, turned from praise to blame, were used four years later to condemn the hot-house sensuality of Swinburne's own *Poems and Ballads*. Even without a legal prosecution the publishers withdrew the book in alarm, and Swinburne had to place it elsewhere. The two poets swiftly became linked in the popular demonology of the times. Such a comparison now seems superficial: Swinburne's lush hymns to suffering remain, for all their technical virtuosity, the fantasies of an eccentric and private taste; while Baudelaire's cruel visions, though very personal in their way, exist within the context of a universal theme: the condition of Man in a world that offers sin but not salvation. At the time, however, the garish elements of Baudelaire's work tended to dominate any reading of him. The comparison between the two poets was readily made and readily accepted, not least by Swinburne himself, who hailed the French poet as his brother in 'Ave atque Vale'.

Swinburne also acknowledged a kinship with Gautier. He imitated his poems, he borrowed his imagery, he praised his books (*Mademoiselle de Maupin* was, he thought, 'the most perfect and exquisite book of modern times'), he adopted his ideas, he shared his interest in hermaphrodites, and he contributed no fewer than six poems to *Le Tombeau*, the memorial volume produced in 1873 to honour the dead 'magician of French literature'.

It was Swinburne who first struck the distinctly French note of artistic irresponsibility in England. Until then English writers and artists, faced with problems similar to their continental confrères – the decline of faith, the rise of industrial democracy – had been struggling towards their own artistic creed, which, for all its elevation of art, was reluctant to abandon its duties towards society. Matthew Arnold had sought to replace the (as he thought) discredited dogmas of religion with the examples of the best literature and art in an effort to preserve the traditional moral order. Ruskin, Morris and the Pre-Raphaelite Brotherhood, though they made art almost a religion, still thought to educate society to their vision. They hoped to return England to an imaginary hand-crafted medievalism, swayed by the simple socialism of the village moot and the simple faith of a vague mysticism, to make the country, in short, a fit place for Pre-Raphaelites to live in.

Swinburne, in the counterblast he issued to his critics (*Notes on Poems and Reviews*) and in the essay on William Blake that followed soon after, stepped beyond this position. Stung by the attacks upon his own poetry, he answered with the Gautieresque call of 'art for art's sake'. Taking Baudelaire as his authority, he denounced 'the heresy of instruction' as 'ruinous' to true art. Although he himself retreated in gradual stages from this extreme position – and from his extreme behaviour – ending his days (in 1909) in the sober domesticity of No. 2 The Pines, Putney, the breach was made. The influence of amoral French literature upon English practice was established.

During the 1870s England even boasted its own Parnassian school, borrowing from the example of Gautier and the precepts of Banville to polish up a glittering assortment of villanelles, ballades, rondeaus and rondels. The poetry of Austin Dobson, Andrew Lang, John Payne, Edmund Gosse, Arthur O'Shaughnessy and Theo Marzials is now largely (and sadly) forgotten, but at the time it created a new climate of awareness. The spirit of francophilia coursed with ever-quickening pulse in the arteries of English artistic – and particularly literary – life. It inspired a vogue for translations of Villon; it prompted the critical studies of Walter Beasant and George Saintsbury. And (as early as 1873) it provoked Tennyson to denounce 'Art – with poisonous honey stolen from the flowers of France'.

This toxic element of the French tradition seeped into the work of Walter Pater, a young Oxford don of sober habits and unfortunate mien. (In 1860, when Pater was twenty-one, his friends had gathered to discuss 'The External Improvement of Pater': they hit upon the idea that he should grow a moustache. He did. And perhaps it was an 'improvement', distracting attention from his close-set eyes, receding hairline and fleshy lips. But it gave him a lugubrious, military air which he was never quite able to dispel.)

Pater as a young man had felt the sting of contemporary religious scepticism very keenly. He had originally intended to take Anglican orders after his graduation, but he lost his faith early on in the course of instruction. For a brief moment he considered taking his orders anyway but, perhaps wisely, decided against it.

Deprived of religious certainty he came to believe himself adrift in a shifting state of 'flux'. The modern sciences of observation, particularly biology, were revealing a new world of previously unimagined complexity. Everything, it transpired, was continuously changing, 'evanescing by infinitesimal degrees from one state to another'. While scientists were attempting to discern the rules and patterns of this movement, in some observers it established a cast of thought which distrusted all certainties and absolutes, a cast of thought which was extended into every area of human activity and experience, even into morality and aesthetics. No points were fixed; all was relative.

In the face – or rather in the midst – of the ever-shifting flux, Pater came to think that any attempt at a comprehensive philosophy of life was futile. Instead he retreated into himself, to the last line of defence, the individual consciousness. He mapped out his ideas on this score most fully in the 'Preface' and 'Conclusion' to his first book, *Studies in the History of the Renaissance* (1873). An individual's impressions and sensations of the world around him were, Pater argued, that person's only available certainty. And the aim of life became to experience as many, as varied and as fine impressions as possible, and to discriminate them with the greatest degree of sensitivity.

Such impressions could be gathered both from nature and from art, but Pater considered art to be the superior source. Nature, as Pater remarked when oppressed by the scent of the meadowsweet in Christ Church Meadow, 'runs too much to excess'. Art, however, was nature already refined once by the scrupulous perceptions of a sensitive artist; it came 'to you proposing frankly to give nothing but the highest quality to your moments as they pass'. Life was to be a succession of high-quality moments. 'Not the fruit of experience, but experience itself is the end. A counted number of pulses only is given to us of a variegated, dramatic life. How may we see in them all that is to be seen in them by the finest senses? How can we pass most swiftly from point to point, and be present always at the focus where the greater number of vital forces unite in their purest energy?' Pater's language suggests health, vigour and steeplechasing; his notion of 'the finest senses' (in this key passage, at least) is far removed from the French obsession with the hypersensitivity of over-bred diseased nerves. French models, however, did stand behind much of his theory.

Pater admired both Gautier and Baudelaire. (He always claimed that he preferred to read Poe in Baudelaire's translations.) Their example certainly bolstered his view of art's superiority to nature as a source of impressions, and his belief that such impressions could be considered aesthetically without reference to morality or usefulness. Nevertheless, such ideas also received support from other sources – from the German aesthetic tradition of Goethe, and the recent psychological works of Herbert Spencer and Alexander Bain on the nature of human perception and the disinterestedness of man's aesthetic responses.

More peculiarly French was the colouring that Pater gave to his *Studies in the History of the Renaissance.* Although he was writing of the Renaissance he noted that even that essentially vital movement marked out its own course of rise and fall. And he displayed a fascinated enthusiasm for the later stages of this cycle. As the Renaissance advanced, Pater detected within it a strain of perversity and decay. In Leonardo da Vinci's art he discerned the 'interfusion of extremes of beauty and terror', a 'refine[ment] upon the world of common forms', 'the fascination of corruption'. This was the language of Gautier's note upon Baudelaire.

Pater's famous description of the *Giaconda* marked 'lady Lisa' as the very type of decadence. He saw her as the inheritor of centuries of human experience.

> Hers is the head upon which all 'the ends of the world are come,' and the eyelids are a little weary. It is a beauty wrought out from within upon the flesh, the deposit cell by cell, of strange thoughts and fantastic reveries and exquisite passions. Set it for a moment beside one of those white Greek goddesses or beautiful women of antiquity, and how would they be troubled by this beauty, into which the soul of all its maladies has passed.

He likened her to 'the vampire' who 'has been dead many times' and lived many lives; she has experienced 'the animalism of Greece, the lust of Rome, the mysticism of the middle age . . . the sins of the Borgias'. It is no wonder she looks 'a little weary'.

This image of the Mona Lisa as 'vampire' allied her to contemporary notions of heredity and enervation. Pater called her 'the symbol of the modern idea' of humanity as 'wrought upon by, and summing up in itself, all modes of thought and life'.

In his following chapter – on the sixteenth-century French poet, Joachim du Bellay – Pater traced still further the ripening of the Renaissance. He considered that in du Bellay's work the Renaissance was 'putting forth in France an aftermath, a wonderful late growth, the products of which have to the full that subtle and delicate sweetness which belongs to a fine and comely decadence'. Even Pater's description of the literary vocabulary employed by du Bellay and the other poets of the Pleiad echoes – in a muffled way – Gautier's disquisition upon the 'style of decadence'. Pater praises the French poets for their 'quaint and remote learning', their scholarship of language, their borrowings from Greek and Latin, and their use of 'other strange words that [they] forged themselves'. And he remarks that the 'exquisite faintness' of tone achieved by such devices was well suited to an age 'a little jaded' but with a 'constant desire for a subdued and delicate excitement'.

When the book appeared in 1873 it caused a stir of alarm. The 'Conclusion', in particular, provoked denunciation. The doctrine of 'art for art's sake' had been considered dangerous enough by some, but here was the notion of amorality extended into the realm of experience: experience for experience's sake or, perhaps, life for art's sake. Pater, shy, scrupulous, donnish and constrained, seems to have been almost perversely unaware of the fire he might be kindling. He sought not to go up in a blaze of glory but merely '[t]o burn always with a hard gem-like flame'.

Others, it was feared, would be less cautious, wanting more light – or more heat – than was offered by Pater's lambent jewel. Pater was faced by the censure of the press and the disapproval of his colleagues. The Bishop of Oxford preached a sermon against him. Taking fright, Pater removed the 'Conclusion' from the 1877 edition of *The Renaissance* because, as he put it, 'it might mislead some of those young men into whose hands it might fall'.

Something of the dangerous reputation that Pater gained can be glimpsed in the pages of a satirical novel which also appeared in 1877. W. H. Mallock's *The New Republic* contained a portrait of Pater as 'Mr Rose', a fastidious don who 'always speaks in an undertone' and whose 'two topics are self-indulgence and art'. He looks upon life as 'a chamber which we decorate as we should decorate the chamber of the woman or the youth that we love'. His connection with the decadent traditions of France and Rome is obliquely suggested by the interest he takes in a volume upon the *Cultes secrets des dames romaines*. Nevertheless the picture is somewhat confused by the fact that Mallock also refers to Mr Rose as 'the Pre-Raphaelite'. And indeed in the popular imagination Pater's ideas were not always distinguished from the more socially responsible theories of the Pre-Raphaelites. They all came to be seen as underpinning the widespread fad of 'aestheticism'.

In the late 1870s and early 1880s there was a concerted effort in cultured circles to bring 'beauty' into modern life. The strategies were various and many: wearing knee breeches and collecting blue-and-white china; adopting the dado and espousing the lily (if not the sunflower). The movement was defined most famously by the satires that were launched against it, by the *Punch* cartoons of George du Maurier and by Gilbert and Sullivan's opera, *Patience*. The general tenor of this 'movement', although it placed a high value upon art and exclusivity, saw both as contributing to the practical pleasure – and even the moral health – of life. It was not decadent. It was concerned with the beauty of Beauty – even the usefulness and the goodness of Beauty – not with the beauty of ugliness.

Nevertheless the subversive Gallic current of perversion and irresponsibility, first unstoppered by Swinburne, then channelled by Pater, continued to undermine this essentially healthy construction. Indeed the two most prominent figures of the aesthetic movement had strong allegiance with France.

James McNeill Whistler, although American by birth, had – after abandoning the prospect of a military career – studied painting in Paris during the 1850s. Ironically he trained in the same atelier as several young English artists, including George du Maurier. But, while exposure to Parisian Bohemia had confirmed the English painters in their own Englishness, Whistler imbibed the spirit of the Latin Quarter with alacrity. Indeed he had been inspired to come to Paris through reading Murger's *Scènes de la vie de Bohème.*

He developed an interest in contemporary French theories and practices. He was *au fait* with the ideas of Gautier and Baudelaire, he admired the painting of Courbet. He took up with enthusiasm the new cult for Japanese art which was even then establishing itself, after the opening up of that country once again to foreign trade. And when he came to England after his student days, he brought these interests – together with his francophilia – with him. They secured him a place in the unconventional artistic circle of Swinburne and the Pre-Raphaelite painter-poet, Rossetti.

Whistler always maintained his contacts with Parisian artistic life. In the subsequent decades he followed closely the experiments of Manet and Degas and their younger 'Impressionist' admirers. The absence of narrative in the work of these artists, the absolute concentration upon form, became the central tenet also of Whistler's artistic creed. The extremity of his position was revealed in 1877 when he exhibited one of his impressionistic views of the Thames at evening, at the first Grosvenor Gallery exhibition. The very title of the work – *Nocturne* – with its transposition of the arts, proclaimed descent from Gautier.

The exhibition was reviewed by Ruskin. The most eminent critic of the day – and the great champion of art's duty towards society – found Whistler's painting incomprehensible. He denounced the artist as a 'coxcomb' who dared 'ask two hundred guineas for flinging a pot of paint in the public's face'. Even for an artist schooled in the defiance of both public and critics, this was a hard blow to take. As

Whistler's solicitor explained in the libel writ he issued, 'Mr Ruskin's opinions are accepted as gospel in matters of art and there can be no doubt that his expressed opinion . . . is calculated to do Mr Whistler great pecuniary harm.'

The resulting legal pantomime gave Whistler a platform for his self-promotion, and presented also to the public, in dramatic form, the novel French theory that a work of art derived its significance *not* from what it represented but simply from its formal, compositional values, and from the fact that it was done by an artist. Whistler's fellow-painters balked at this estimate of their art. He could find only two (Albert Moore and William Gorman Wills) willing to appear as experts in his defence. The public – as embodied in the jury – were equally uncomfortable with his theories. Although they did give a verdict in his favour they awarded him only a farthing's damages and no costs.

The case ruined Whistler's finances but did not break his convictions. Seven years later he expanded upon his position – uninterrupted by counsel – in his 'Ten O'Clock Lecture'. There, in a steady cascade of epigrammatic wit, he proclaimed the privileged position of the artist, the freedom of art from all moral responsibility and the superiority of art to nature. ('To say to the painter, that nature is to be taken as she is, is to say to the player, that he may sit on the piano.')

Although Whistler certainly derived his ideas from France, from Gautier and Gautier's followers, his own pose of dandified self-sufficiency did not allow discipleship, and he tended to present all theories as his own. A similar posture was adopted by the youthful Oscar Wilde, who borrowed freely from many sources, from Pater, from Gautier, from Ruskin and (so Whistler claimed) from Whistler, almost always without acknowledgement. Wilde, with his flowing locks and floppy ties, rapidly became the clown-prince of aestheticism. His extravagant manner provoked and fed off the satires of du Maurier and Gilbert.

The ideas Wilde expressed during the early eighties were, by and large, less extreme than Whistler's. He tempered the call of *l'art pour l'art* with a Ruskinian sense of art's relationship with society, and he saw in the cult of beauty a reason for optimism. In 1883, however, following the success of his American lecture tour, he visited Paris. He was introduced to Edmond Goncourt, to Rollinat and Jean Lorrain. He befriended Paul Bourget, the theorist of decadence. After months of lecturing to Colorado miners and Yankee spinsters upon the virtues of wallpaper and 'The English Renaissance of Art', to encounter these strange young men proclaiming the virtues of depravity was, at the very least, intriguing. He was back in Paris the following June, for his honeymoon. He also enjoyed Huysmans' recently published *A Rebours*; it was, he told an interviewer, 'one of the best books' he had ever read.

Although in the excitement of his 1883 visit Wilde did write one poem ('The Harlot's House') and began another ('The Sphinx') which betrayed the decadent influence of Rollinat, Huysmans and their Baudelairean confrères, the decisive force of this poison percolated only slowly into his *oeuvre*, and did not produce its best effects until the 1890s.

Pater, in the meantime, was continuing his steady retreat from the daring arguments of his 'Conclusion'. He strove to elucidate and refine his views in his long historical novel of 1885, *Marius the Epicurean*. In this slow-moving spiritual odyssey of a sober and ascetic Roman of the second century AD, he suggested that the careful gathering and discriminating of sensations was, in fact, not an end in itself but a path towards conventional salvation. The goal of 'hedonism' was not, Pater now stressed, mere pleasure, but the development of one's perception to such a level that one becomes a 'complex medium of reception, towards the vision – the beatific vision – if one really cared to make it such – of our actual experience in the world'. The truly perceptive person might yet be able to grasp, beneath the flux, the hidden pattern of life.

But at the same time that he was drawing discreetly away from the perils of a wanton and amoral aestheticism of life, Pater was embracing more closely and more overtly a different strand of contemporary French tradition: the style of decadence. He had, of course, already developed his own complex literary style – ornate, self-consciously refined, eclectic, heavy with dependent clauses and anxious qualifications. It is said that he composed his sentences by first writing out the bald argument upon alternate lines of his page and then filling the interstices with qualifying sub-clauses; and then repeating the process. It is believable. As is the tale that, on his death, hundreds of slips of paper were found in his study drawers, each with a disembodied phrase awaiting its place in some still unwritten sentence. Pater, for all his rather embarrassing attempts at vitality, handled English as though it were a dead language.

Nevertheless it was not until *Marius*, a tale of the later Roman Empire, that he focused attention on the similarities between his own idiom and Latin – not the Latin of Cicero and Virgil, but rather the heterogeneous idiom of late Antiquity. In Chapter VI he gave an enthusiastic exposition of Apuleius' (and indeed his own) style, listing all the usual characteristics, the 'archaisms and curious felicities', 'racy morsels of the vernacular', touches of 'artificial artlessness', an insistence upon 'form' and 'the labour of the file'. He even explicitly likened this late Roman style to the practice of the 'modern French Romanticists', by which he meant Gautier, Baudelaire and their disciples. But then, apparently on the brink of proclaiming the 'style of decadence' to English readers, Pater drew back and labelled the creation, not 'decadence', but 'euphuism'.

To his readers the word, if it meant anything, would recall the alliterative preciosity of John Lyly's *Euphues*, the Elizabethan romance from which the term was derived. And for the Victorians the richness of Elizabethan language was generally taken as a measure of its vitality, rather than its degeneracy. For Marius, the euphuistic style of Apuleius was certainly a revitalizing force, its aim to strike a pathway between the routine sterility of the pedant's prose and the looseness of the vulgar tongue, 'to reestablish the natural and direct relationship between thought and expression, between the sensation and the term, and restore to words their primitive power'. Although these aims were echoed in Gautier's 'Notice', Pater's terminology (once again) was not of diseased nerves straining to register vague sensations; it is 'natural' and 'direct' in its quest for 'primitive power'.

Pater's ambivalent and tentative position was typical. Nevertheless, despite his caution, and insistence upon the term euphiusm (or 'eclecticism' as he had it in his 1889 essay on 'Style'), *Marius the Epicurean* introduced into English the notion that late Latin might serve as a useful model for contemporary prose.

Swinburne, the English Parnassians, Pater, Whistler, Wilde, had all provided glimpses of the French experience. They had tried on ideas and poses, borrowed forms and flourishes, advertised new names and styles. But there had been no explicit exposition of 'decadence' as a literary movement, or indeed as a socio-political phenomenon; and there had been no coherent account of how the various strands of French culture were bound together.

The series of political upheavals and collapses that had shaken

France during the first three-quarters of the nineteenth century had not been mirrored across the channel. For Britain these years had seen a steady expansion of imperial power, a steady consolidation of Victorian achievement, under the twin banners of Liberalism and Positivism. Nevertheless, the long extension of this charmed period had, by the 1880s, begun to provoke its own reaction. In an imperfect world it is hard to sustain an unbounded faith in a meliorist notion of 'progress'. Despite decades of material advancement, social ills were as pressing as ever. (They were exciting anxiety even before Charles Booth published his *Labour and Life of the People* in 1889.)

Moreover, Britain's clear advantage as both an industrial and an imperial power had been cut back by her continental neighbours. Queen Victoria's long reign was already taking on an autumnal hue even before her Golden Jubilee in 1887. The century too, drawing towards a close, was beginning to suggest to some the same season, and to others more apocalyptic visions. The notion of national decline – of decadence – became, as the 1890s approached, increasingly current in British intellectual life. It was denied by many, even by most, but it was nevertheless an issue that had to be addressed, an argument that had to be countered.

At the same time the various and exciting developments in recent French culture were brought into sharper focus for English readers by a vastly entertaining book of memoirs. George Moore's *Confessions of a Young Man*, published in 1888, gave a vivid account of the author's own progress through the artistic circles of Paris in the 1870s.

Moore had arrived in Paris as an ignorant young Irishman wanting to study painting, but had soon abandoned himself to the social and cultural excitements of the French capital, and to literature. The *Confessions* is essentially a record of youthful enthusiasms, an intellectual autobiography. Théophile Gautier was the first to win him: 'I read *Mlle de Maupin* at a moment when I was weary of spiritual passion, and this great exaltation of the visible above the invisible at once conquered and led me captive.' The revelation of Gautier's work led Moore back to the eccentric and morbid productions of the 1830s and forward to a study of Baudelaire. '*Les Fleurs du mal*!' he rhapsodized, 'beautiful flowers, beautiful in sublime decay . . . I press you to my lips.' Moore followed the scent of these 'poisonous blossoms' down to his own day. Amongst 'the French poets of the modern school' it was Verlaine who appealed most strongly, slaking his thirst for 'the strange, abnormal and unhealthy in art'.

He drank deeply: 'Verlaine became my poet, and the terraces of the "Les Fêtes galantes" the chapel of my meditations, and my desire the lady who descends her castle stairs unmindful that her page, a little nigger, is lifting her train higher than is necessary, sharing thereby with her monkey a view of her thighs.' His flat in the Rue de la Tour des Dames was done up in self-consciously 'strange, abnormal and unhealthy' style, as a cross between a gothic refectory and a seraglio. The drawing room was canopied with swathes of red material, a terracotta faun laughed in the rubescent gloom, and there were Turkish couches and lamps. In another room was an altar, a Buddhist temple, a statue of Apollo and a bust of Shelley. Moore acquired a cat (both Gautier and Baudelaire had been felidomanes) and also a python.

But then, just as he was sinking into this deliciously artificial environment, he chanced to pick up a stray copy of the *Voltaire.* There, in the magazine, was an article by Emile Zola, 'Naturalism in Art'. Naturalism. The word, the idea, the theory, reverberated in Moore's breast with all the force of 'echo augury'. Zola's theories he found positively arresting. 'I rose from breakfast, ordered my coffee, and stirred the sugar, a little dizzy, like one who has received a violent blow on the head.' It was the idea of a new aestheticism – of a 'new art corresponding to modern, as ancient art corresponded to ancient life' – that captivated him: a new art based not upon the imagination but upon the scientific exploration of modern life. He promptly renounced the sub-Baudelairean volume he was working on and resolved to produce a book of naturalist verse, to be called 'Poems of Flesh and Blood'.

Although the *Confessions* is pre-eminently a book of books and ideas, it is not devoid of its own flesh and blood. Indeed it is quite crowded with people, or, rather, with characters. The most fleshy – perhaps even the most bloody – of these dramatis personae is, of course, George Moore himself. His presence is insistent. On every page he proclaims with a charming, unaffected immodesty his involvement in the excitements of the day. He climbed the stairs to Mallarmé's Tuesday 'At Homes'; he went to see the Impressionists exhibit before anyone cared for their art; he eavesdropped on Villiers de l'Isle Adam as, with his long hair falling across his eyes, he chatted up the bovine girls in Café du Rat Mort; he attended the Nouvelle Athens, that true academy of the fine arts, the café on the Place Pigalle.

It was at this café in Montmartre, over the bocks, beneath the clouds of cigarette smoke, that Moore received his further education. He heard and disputed the theories of the day – the claims of art, the value of realism, the impossibility of verse translation, the perils of 'democratic art', the latest books, the latest gossip. It was there that the elegantly square-cut Manet sketched him, there that the slender and ironical Degas placed his absinthe drinkers, there that 'about midnight Catulle Mendès might drop in with his fine paradoxes and his strained eloquence', there that the glass door would grate upon the sanded floor to admit Duranty ('an unknown Stendhal'), Paul Alexis, Pissarro, or the saintly Carboner. They were wonderful days and nights, but – alas – they could not last.

The eruption of the 'Land War' in County Mayo in 1880 put Moore's estates in jeopardy. He was obliged to return to London, to lodgings in the Strand. The contrast between the lost excitement of Paris and the dreary respectability of Victorian England was an unhappy one.

Moore's picture of Paris was touched with fantasy. He fed his later experiences of the city, gleaned during his many return trips in the 1880s, back into his picture of the 1870s. He exaggerates, he invents. And yet the whole presents an extraordinarily vivid panorama of French literary and artistic life.

It was a picture that must have inspired Symons and Ellis as they stood thumbing through the slim volumes in Léon Vanier's shop. Perhaps it was the example of Moore, thrusting himself into the fastnesses of French culture, that resolved them to return to Paris the following year for a longer and more concerted stay. They would bring letters of introduction. They would meet Verlaine. They would pay their respects to Mallarmé. They would stand Villiers de l'Isle Adam a vermouth. It was an intoxicating vision.

Part II

'Impressions & Sensations'

Chapter Four

ARTHUR SYMONS came to French literature early. Or, rather, French literature came to him. As a babe in arms he was being carried along the sea front at Guernsey when Victor Hugo, then an exile upon the island, stopped his mother to peer and cluck at him. According to family tradition the author of *Hernani* pronounced Arthur '*un joli enfant*'. It was a propitious encounter. As Symons' literary tastes developed, so did his enthusiasm for France: at fifteen he was translating Swinburne's French lyrics; two years later he had composed 'The Defence of Delilah', an unpublished work in the Parnassian manner of Leconte de Lisle; he was, at eighteen, much struck by the poetry of Gautier and considered *Madame Bovary* 'one of the most wonderful novels [he] had ever come across'; and the first important article he contributed to the national press was a critique of the Provençal poet Frédéric Mistral. Although this folksy rustic was very different in temper from the perverse and artificial Parisian poets of the fashionable decadence, Symons' precocious literary tastes were even then drawing him towards the bizarre and the metropolitan in art. In 1887, at the age of twenty-three, he discovered the *Contes cruels* of Villiers de l'Isle Adam.

Villiers' dark tales, etched with irony and flaked with death, were then almost unknown in England. Symons was intoxicated both by the flavour of the stories and the eccentricity of their author. Fired by the urge to proselytize, he persuaded Oscar Wilde, then editing *Woman's World*, to accept an article on Villiers for the magazine. He enthused to all his friends about his new discovery. He had hopes that the controversial publisher Henry Vizetelly might bring out an English translation of the work, but feared that the stories, for all their oddness, were not quite 'indecent enough'. He even wrote boldly to Rémy de Gourmont, a noted French critic, asking to borrow any of Villiers' other works that he might be able to spare. Plans for a meeting with Villiers himself came, however, to nothing. The *cruel conteur* died, aged fifty-one, worn out by poverty and drink, just two months before Symons and Havelock Ellis arrived in Paris on their first visit.

Robert Browning, one of Symons' English heroes, also died at the end of 1889, and the sense of pressing mortality perhaps gave a heightened energy to Symons' and Ellis' second Parisian expedition the following spring. Even though their interest lay not so much with 'the venerated figures' of the generation before as with the 'new men', many of these 'new' players were themselves racing dangerously through middle age with a glass of absinthe at their elbow. With Villiers gone, who might not be next?

Happily, fate stayed her hand. In the course of their three-month visit, Symons and Ellis, two young men of ambition in a strange city, were remarkably successful in meeting almost all of the 'new men', both old and young. Ellis, who was in charge of the travel arrangements, booked them both into the Hôtel Corneille, next to the Odéon and, as Symons exclaimed excitedly, '*en plein quartier Latin*'. The hotel had been recommended by Ellis' friend Professor Geddes for its modest comforts, but Symons, who sought a literary justification for nearly all his actions, was particularly taken with it because the building was mentioned by Balzac, and Baudelaire had once had rooms there.

Symons' excitement bubbles out of the letters he wrote from Paris. To one correspondent he claimed, 'I must quote a sentence of J. A. S[ymonds], written from Venice, and apply it to myself at Paris: "The place makes me exceedingly lazy, and annihilates the moral sense." He adds: "Both of which effects seem to me good, if one does not have too much of them."' Any claims to laziness, however, are promptly discredited by an exhausting chronicle of excursions and undertakings: theatre trips, café concerts, lectures, déjeuners, dinners, salons, promenades and '*flânerie* in general'; and to these Ellis, who had just brought out an anthropological study of the criminal in society, added a round of scientific visits.

The cultural world that they explored was not exclusively decadent. The letters of introduction provided by Symons' impressive circle of London friends secured an entrée into the salon of Madame Darmasteter (formerly Miss Robinson), where they glimpsed the departing back of Hippolyte Taine, the father of Positivism and the historian of English literature; they enjoyed the world of expatriate leisure at the studio of the American artist Gifford Dyer; and they called on Leconte de Lisle, the elderly doyen of the Parnassians, to whom Symons had sent a copy of his collection, *Days and Nights*. The French poet took the book down from its place, 'spoke very admiringly of the get-up of the volume, and explained as he turned over its uncut pages, that he knew nothing of English, and could not even make anything out of [the] translations of his own poems'.

Nevertheless, it was in the byways of bohemian Paris that Symons and Ellis felt the pulse of literary and artistic life most keenly. They were fortunate in their guides, Charles Morice and Rémy de Gourmont. Morice, a shambling giant with a mop of blond hair, was one of the most lucid commentators upon the contemporary scene, as well as being Verlaine's acknowledged champion. De Gourmont was a quieter figure, erudite, unsociable and afflicted by a skin condition, yet he went out of his way to assist with introductions and explanations. Steered by these able scouts, Symons and Ellis sat in Odilon Redon's studio while the artist carefully presented albums for their inspection. They lounged at the enervated Marcel Schwob's fireside discussing the first quarto of *Hamlet*, they listened to Jean Moréas reciting his symbolist verses with a practical air to some long-suffering waitress. They flogged out to the suburbs to visit the taciturn Rodin in his workshop. They met George Moore at the house of Dr Chapman, erstwhile proprietor of the *Westminster Review*. They patronized Le Chat Noir, La Cigale and Les Deux Magots. At the Moulin Rouge they were befriended by its resident spirit of perversity, Henri de Toulouse-Lautrec.

Piloted by Morice and de Gourmont, they bobbed in the waters of literary controversy. They listened as the '*symbolistes*' and '*décadents*' fired off their salvos and the café tables of the Boul' Mich' were stained with the blood-red wine of heated debate. They were present when the *Mercure de France* tried to establish itself as the mouthpiece of the new movement, and dozens of other periodicals sprang up to contest the claim. They found Montmartre a babel, with '*symbolisme*', '*décadence*' and '*impressionnisme*' being shouted as war-cries and hurled back as insults by the little bands that gathered to discuss the books they would never write.

In this shifting scene, however, there were some fixed points. Morice and de Gourmont guided their charges towards them. De Gourmont arranged a meeting with Huysmans. They found him in the tiny bibelot-crowded salon of his mistress, Mme Courrière, lying back upon a sofa, rolling a cigarette, his eyes half-closed, as he berated the democratic and materialistic pretensions of the age with 'an accent of pained surprise' and an 'amused look of contempt, so profound that it becomes almost pity for human imbecility'. Symons and Ellis were much impressed by his disdain for the world.

Mallarmé and Verlaine, their fame secured in no small measure by *A Rebours*, continued to stand above the internecine bickering of their would-be followers. Symons and Ellis met them both. They managed to secure an invitation to one of Mallarmé's celebrated *mardis*. At the door of his small fourth-floor flat in the modestly respectable Rue de Rome, the author of *L'Après midi d'un faune*, a dapper, attractive man, with exquisite manners, greeted them. The apartment was narrow and unostentatious, elegant with what Symons called 'a scrupulous Dutch comfort'. There was a rocking chair and, of course, a cat. They were obliged to sit at the oblong table in the small oblong dining room, as this was the only room that might hold a gathering. In the middle of the table was a bowl of tobacco, all the meagre hospitality that Mallarmé could provide. The host sat at the head of the table, smoking a cigarette and, in his quiet voice, sketching ideas with 'the half apologetic air of the perfect acrobat'. That night Gabriel Mourey, the translator of Swinburne, and Henri de Régnier, a slender young novelist who affected a monocle, were also present, and the talk centred upon a promising young poet, Ephraim Mikael, who had recently died.

Ellis sat at the table awed and silent before the great theorist of symbolism. Symons, on the other hand, his high-pitched voice rising with excitement, was not shy of contributing. Unseen in the next room Mme Mallarmé and the children were sitting quietly and one of Mallarmé's daughters, on hearing Symons start up again, remarked ingenuously, 'Listen to the little bird twittering.' Perhaps Symons twittered too much; they were not invited again.

Rather more approachable was the derelict but defiant Paul Verlaine. Morice had agreed to introduce them to *Pauvre Lélian* and, as an expression of gratitude before the event, Symons and Ellis clubbed together to buy their guide dinner at a favourite café on the Boulevard Saint Michel. After their steaks they all set off towards the Café François Premier, Morice's arms windmilling extravagantly as he expatiated upon the master. Symons, unable to control his own sense of mounting excitement, began to wonder whether Verlaine might actually have cloven hooves and a green tail as he did in his caricatures.

He was not much disappointed. They discovered Verlaine amidst the white and gold splendour of his regular retreat, sitting, 'like Pan', in the midst of a rowdy group of companions. He was drinking and smiling benevolently about himself. There was no sign of a diabolical tail, but even so Symons later remembered feeling a fleeting moment of disgust at the lowness of the company, at the shabbiness of Verlaine's clothing, the absent collar, the grimed white scarf, the large grey hat set on the back of his head. The moment passed, however, and Symons saw instead the essential dignity of the man and the striking duality of his nature. 'The face,' Symons thought, 'was a strange contradictory one with its spiritual forehead, its animal jaw, its shifting faun's eyes.'

Verlaine's manner, too, contradicted his appearance. He rose with unaffected courtesy as Morice introduced the two English visitors. He engaged them in conversation about England and the English poets; he showed off his knowlege of English schoolboy slang and discoursed with feeling upon the joys of Bournemouth; he commended the distinctive flavour of the English Sunday – '*triste* yet so religious'; and, prompted by Symons, he recounted with a light impersonal frankness the story of his quarrel with Rimbaud. And all the time his body, his hands, his eyes, his brows, danced with gestures, translating the meaning of his words into movement, rather (Symons thought) as his poetry translated his meaning into music. He endured politely the interruptions of the excitable Jean Moréas, who insisted on asking Symons what the longest line in English poetry might be, largely so that he could boast of having composed one himself of twenty syllables.

The occasion was pronounced a great success. It was agreed that Symons and Ellis would visit Verlaine the following evening at the Hôtel des Mines. They duly turned up only to be told that Verlaine was out. Coming away, however, they met him in the street, leaning on the arm of a shabby little man who seemed to be his aide. They greeted him and chatted for a while, realizing with gathering certainty that the poet had quite forgotten their engagement and indeed had no idea who they were. This, however, seemed not to lessen his amiability. He insisted that they come up to his apartment.

It was a single room, small, bare and untidy. He had pinned some pencil sketches of himself on the wall. There were a few books, some of his own, and a Bible which he insisted on showing to Symons with sentimental enthusiasm. He patted it, indicated the name of the translator and confided that it was an 'excellent book'. It was, Symons would later recall, the only Bible he ever saw in Paris. Having shown off his library and touched, however briefly, upon his spiritual side, Verlaine decided it was time to indulge the other part of his nature. He produced two coins from his purse and announced, in his heavily accented English, 'I have money; I will have pleasure, pleasure, pleasure!' The decrepit factotum was dispatched to buy some rum in honour of the English guests. A young painter-friend of Verlaine's dropped by and the four of them sat about in the dim candle-light drinking their grog, smoking cigarettes and talking with restless energy about art and life and Alfred Lord Tennyson.

These meetings with Verlaine, and others that followed, proved to be the most significant encounters of Symons' Parisian visit. The extraordinary directness of Verlaine's manner and the evanescent music of his verse impressed themselves upon Symons with all the force of novelty. But then the accidents of Symons' upbringing and the interests of his youth were particularly well calculated to inspire an appreciation for the French poet, the style of his verse and the mode of his life.

Symons, the only son of a depressive Wesleyan preacher and his barely more cheerful wife, was brought up in an atmosphere that combined moral rectitude with geographical instability. Movement was a pronounced feature of the Methodist ministry; preachers and their families were regularly transferred to fresh 'circuits' in order to discourage them from developing worldly attachments. Certainly the ploy seems to have prevented the infant Arthur Symons from developing any sense of his own roots.

He was born in Milford Haven in Wales in 1865, but moved on to Guernsey in 1866 and from there to Alnwick in Northumberland two years later. This regular course of deracination continued throughout his childhood and adolescence. It cannot have aided either his education or his social confidence. He was nine years old before he was able to read but, having mastered the art, he devoured books with an almost indiscriminate voracity. His early favourites included *Don Quixote*, *Lavengro* and the novels of R. D. Blackmore. He loved escapism and the pious sobriety of his home life gave him much more to escape from. It was not surprising, given his itinerant upbringing, that he should find a kinship with wandering knights and scholar gypsies. The word 'vagabond' came to hold an actual magic for him.

Books provided a release but they also suggested action. In *Lavengro* Symons admired the scholar quite as much as the gypsy; and in imitation of the book's hero he set himself to learn Italian in two weeks. He would practise his grammar during his father's services, following the lesson in an Italian Bible. Religion itself, however, very quickly ceased to hold any interest for him. Art became his passion, literature principally, but also music. He heard Chopin's 'Funeral March' and determined to learn to play it on the piano.

In the world of books he discovered his other great passion: sex. He became a fascinated explorer at second hand. He sought out the works of Rabelais and Swinburne with what he described as 'guilty delight'. He endured agonies of frustration in his attempts to secure a copy of Byron's works that included *Don Juan*. His taste was for the 'forbidden fruit which must be delicious because it is forbidden'. This unfortunate equation between 'sex', 'sin' and 'delight' was a snare that Symons stumbled into early and never fully escaped. Study irregular verbs as he might during his father's sermons, the insidious message of Methodism got through to him: all earthly delights are subject to guilt. For the time being, however, Symons was content to search out such delights in the pages of *Poems and Ballads* and outface his silent fears of guilt. The occasional nightmares that disturbed his sleep – usually involving floors 'curdling with snakes' – were horribly vivid but struck no echo upon a pre-Freudian consciousness.

At seventeen, stuck with his pious, though not unloving, parents in Yeovil, Devon, Arthur Symons confessed, 'I was passionately in love with life; but the life I lived was not the life I wanted.' The life he wanted, so he decided, was the literary life. He had, he thought, a gift for poetry. At thirteen he had written a sub-Tennysonian epic called 'A Dream of the Garden of God', which he presented to his mother. The critical response was favourable and, thus encouraged, he had begun to fill up notebooks with his outpourings. He was engagingly frank about his own motivation: 'It was not that I had anything to say, or that I felt the need of expressing myself. I wanted to write books for the sake of writing books.' Literature, he found, raised a 'barrier' between himself and his world. It also provided a link with the more exciting world beyond Yeovil. He joined the Browning Society at its inception in 1881.

When he left school the following year he asked his former English teacher, Charles Churchill Osborne, about the prospects of a literary career. Osborne was acquainted with the world of letters, having once considered writing the history of Mount Etna. He had, moreover, recently become sub-editor and music critic for the *Western Mail.* He must have given his erstwhile pupil some slight encouragement for Symons began to bombard newspapers and periodicals, both local and national, with unsolicited articles and verses. They were all returned. His first published work did not appear until the very end of the year, when the *Wesleyan-Methodist Magazine* included his essay on 'Robert Browning as a Religious Poet'. A poem upon the birth of a child to one of his father's colleagues appeared soon afterwards in another local Methodist paper.

It was, however, the Browning Society rather than the Methodist press that decisively extended Symons' range of literary connections. The Society's irrepressible founder, Frederick Furnivall, was an extraordinary generator of literary work. He had, besides the Browning venture, started up some half-dozen other societies and was also editor of numerous medieval and Renaissance texts. At the beginning of the 1880s he was engaged in producing a series of 'Shakespeare Quarto Facsimiles' and in 1884, impressed by a paper Symons had written for the Browning Society, he asked him to write the introduction for his forthcoming edition of 'Venus and Adonis'.

Untried, largely untutored and only nineteen, Symons – after a moment's hesitation – leapt at the chance. Within the year 'Arthur Symons of Yeovil' had produced a thorough and impressive piece of richly wrought prose proclaiming the pleasures of Shakespeare's poem. It was enough to secure a further commission from Furnivall for an introduction to *Titus Andronicus* and to draw Symons further into the literary current.

His own poetry was proceeding at speed, inspired not only by Browning but also by the works of Rossetti and Gautier. In a single Saturday he 'wrote three poems during a walk in the morning, 8 triolets during a walk in the evening and a Ballade when [he] came in'. His circle of literary acquaintances expanded as Osborne introduced him to such luminaries as Leith Derwent, the sensational novelist, Philip Bourke Marston, the blind poet, and – most important – Richard Garnett, the cataloguer of the British Library. Symons' own journalism also began to bring him new contacts. He started to get pieces into the *London Quarterly Review* and *Time.*

His first important article, a lengthy and enthusiastic dissertation on the Provençal folk-poet Frédéric Mistral, appeared at the very beginning of 1886 in the *National Review.* The piece was read by, amongst others, Havelock Ellis, who was impressed. Ellis, though only twenty-seven himself and still studying for his medical exams, was employed in editing the 'Mermaid' series of unexpurgated Elizabethan and Jacobean play-texts for the dauntless Henry Vizetelly. He wrote to Symons, a correspondence ensued and a commission was arranged. It was agreed that Symons would prepare a volume of five Massinger plays for Ellis.

Symons was rapidly becoming the man of letters he wished to be. A meeting on the steps of the British Museum with a bustling young Welshman called Ernest Rhys, who like so many others had been engaged by a publisher to edit a series of literary reprints, led to a contract for a selection of Leigh Hunt's essays. The year 1886 also saw Symons' debut volume, *An Introduction to the Study of Browning,* which was published at the end of that year under the auspices of the Browning Society. This little book brought together Symons' three great literary heroes in a dramatic 'moment': it was dedicated to George Meredith, in Symons' opinion 'the greatest of living novelists'; it was written about Browning, the poet he considered 'second to Shakespeare alone'; and it was written in the manner of Walter Pater, who, next to Browning and Meredith, was 'the living English writer whom I most admire'.

Such dramatic points of focus were, as Symons noted in the book, central to both the poetry of Browning and the philosophy of Pater. Browning's 'poetry of situations' sought to reveal character at a significant moment, to 'condense the long trial of years into a single moment, and so "flash the truth out by one blow"', while Pater urged his readers to fulfil their own natures by seeking out just such moments of crisis, where 'the greatest number of vital forces unite in their purest energy'.

The book gave Symons an entrée with all three of his heroes: Meredith gratefully acknowledged the dedication; Browning graciously allowed him to come to tea; and Pater wrote a generous letter of praise on receiving an advance copy. Of the three men it was Pater, the donnish bachelor, who offered the most scope for friendship. Symons initiated a correspondence and even began sending Pater poems for criticism and praise.

It was not, however, until 1888 that Symons met the author of *Studies in the History of the Renaissance*. In August of that year he saw Pater for a brief hour in London, and in December he was invited up to Oxford for the day. He had lunch in Pater's rooms at Brasenose and then made a little tour of the city, with Pater pointing out objects of interest and providing a murmured commentary. Symons found him 'the tenderest-hearted of men, and more simple and genial when one has got through the veil or mask of formal politeness and rather forbidding gravity which he ordinarily wears'.

Even these carefully chosen words from an unabashed fan cannot quite disguise Pater's personal dullness. He was small, fifty and bald, with, moreover, that rather military moustache; his conversation was uninspiring. And yet, for Symons, as for many of the artistic men of the time, he was a touchstone. In his books, if not in his person, they found a prose style to imitate and a philosophy to follow.

For Symons, *The Renaissance*, which he read in 1885, 'opened a new world to me or, rather, gave me the key or secret of the world in which I was living. It taught me . . . that life (which had seemed to me of so little moment) could be itself a work of art.' From Pater he received confirmation of what he suspected already – that it was possible to escape the tedium of a provincial Methodism by contemplating art, by gathering and discriminating impressions and, of course, sensations. In that first flush of youthful earnestness and ambition, he was not tempted by the possibilities of amoral hedonism offered in the text. He drew out only the essential egoism of Pater's creed, the desire for intensity (of feeling, and hence experience), and the admiration of refined artistry in all things and the superiority of art to life.

The impact of Pater's prose upon the young men of the 1890s was quite as great as that of his philosophy. It returned George Moore to a love of his native tongue; it prompted W. B. Yeats to include the passage on the *Mona Lisa* (from *The Renaissance*) as the opening to his *Oxford Book of Modern Verse*. It struck Symons as being 'the most beautiful . . . in our language'.

Pater regarded his own style as an agent of linguistic regeneration, and there is no doubt that his advocacy and example awakened 'the literary conscience' of Symons (and many of his contemporaries) 'to forgotten duties towards language'. The care taken over literary composition by the men of the nineties is evident in many a delicately shaded patch of purple. Pater's programme, however, as he himself admitted, could, in hands less self-restraining than his own, lapse into 'fopperies and mannerisms'. His 'scholarly' ideal could sanction exclusivity and obscurity. The carefully wrought parts might – to borrow Paul Bourget's analogy – easily come to outweigh the whole. Even in Pater's own prose this was quite often the case, as one might expect from a man who kept stray phrases in his desk. Moreover, there is no doubt that the link Pater established between his own eclecticism and the decadent styles of late Latin and modern French quickened Symons' interest in contemporary French literature. As early as 1887 Symons was admiringly likening Pater to Baudelaire on account of their common desire to 'better nature'.

From Pater's philosophy Symons seized a new vision of life; from his prose style he gathered an exacting ideal; from his personal encouragement and interest he derived the greatest pleasure. Pater's influence, moreover, was practical as well. By his own admission never a good judge of contemporary work, Pater was nevertheless sufficiently impressed by Symons' poems to urge his own publisher, George Macmillan, to bring out a book of them.

Days and Nights, a slender volume gratefully dedicated to Pater, appeared in the spring of 1889, shortly before Symons' first visit to Paris. It was a collection of distinctly Browningesque verse, rich in significant moments and dramatic monologues, and set for the most part amidst the unfortunate poor. Although there is one poem about the miserable lot of an opium smoker, he is a very literary and conventional addict, and nothing in the book is really deserving of the epithet decadent. The collection received a generous notice from its dedicatee in the *Pall Mall Gazette* and some warm paragraphs of praise in the *Buckinghamshire Advertiser*.

Although the debt to Browning was paramount, Symons was keen to display his breadth of reading by acknowledging too the trans-channel influence of Gautier, Villiers de l'Isle Adam and Murger. In the wide embrace of Symons' literary enthusiasms, contemporary France was slowly asserting its primacy. This admiration for the modern and the foreign was one of the threads that had drawn Symons into friendship with Havelock Ellis.

It was modern French literature, however, that caused – albeit indirectly – the break-up of their professional alliance. The publisher of the Mermaid series which Ellis was editing was Henry Vizetelly, who had made his name and his business by introducing – in translation – the novels of Emile Zola to England. The unflinching naturalism of these works, many chronicling in explicit terms the bestial degradation of working-class existence, had from the start provoked scandal, publicity and, of course, sales.

In 1888, however, with the publication of *The Earth*, the guardians of public morality were stirred to action. Vizetelly was charged with obscenity for bringing out this masterpiece about the life of the Provençal peasantry; and despite the protests of Edmund Gosse and Charles Bradlaugh MP he was condemned to six months in gaol. His company was bankrupted and the Mermaid series was bought up by T. Fisher Unwin. The new broom promptly swept Ellis out over the latter's decision to publish, as an appendix to his edition of *Tamburlaine*, the charges of blasphemy brought against Christopher Marlowe. The episode, in both its phases, served as a forceful reminder of literature's power to shock and the establishment's appetite for repression.

Ellis had plenty of other work to occupy him. He was busy not only with his medical studies but also with *The New Spirit*, a collection of essays tracing, as he saw it, the 'evolution of the modern spirit' in literature through the works of Diderot, Heine, Whitman, Tolstoy and Ibsen. The title was significant, for a fascination with the 'new' was one of the abiding motifs of the 1890s. But while some saw in such novelty the signs of decay, others – like Ellis – applauded it as the mark of progress. In the introduction to *The New Spirit*, Ellis presented an overview of the contemporary scene. He acclaimed the first great achievement of the nineteenth century as the 'triumph of the middle class throughout Europe', but he suggested that the impetus of this movement was now over, and indeed that the 'huge commercial structure' on which it was founded was 'in the opinion of many, slowly and fearfully toppling down'.

He admitted that the period had not been amicable to art, but that it had provoked a number of artistic responses: Carlyle had railed against the age; Browning had retreated into 'psychological gymnastics'; Arnold had stoically turned away; while Pater, and a few other 'sensitive souls', had adopted 'another solution' and sought to 'hide the heart in a nest of roses away from the world'. Ellis paid the almost conventional respects of his generation to *Marius* ('one of the most exquisite and significant books of the century') and he emphasized the 'religious sense' that lay behind Pater's search for 'refined aesthetic joy'. But he felt that Pater's philosophy was a cul-de-sac. He lamented its effects: the 'refined development of the passive sensory sides of the human organism with [its] corresponding atrophy of the motor sides'. And he stated firmly that it was 'clearly impossible to go any further on that road'.

For Ellis, any notion of decadence – either socio-political or artistic – was already receding into the past before the 1890s began. He saw the new decade as fired by a 'new energy', an energy founded upon the sciences, particularly the sciences of observation. He felt confident that rigorous 'inquiry into traceable causes or relations of things' would yield up 'truths' which could then be applied to human and social problems. He described the duty of Man as to 'search out the facts of things' and 'found life upon them'. Society, he argued, must be built on 'the sure and simple foundation of man's organism'. And its aim must be 'to attain unity' – 'unity of standard and measure and nomenclature'.

Everywhere Ellis saw encouraging symptoms of this new energy: in the new prominence and independence that women were assuming (the 'great wave of emancipation', as he called it, 'which is now sweeping across the civilized world'); the advance of 'democracy', not just as a matter of electoral emancipation, but as a trend backed by universal 'education' (which for Ellis meant improved diet, physical exercise and fresh air, as well as the intellectual rudiments), and new forms of social organization (Ellis cited with approbation the development of trades unions and county councils). He did detect that England's position as the pre-eminent player upon the world stage was coming to an end. But he saw in the advance of France, Germany, Russia and Spain the opportunity for a new internationalism: the end of war, 'the downfall of unrestricted competition and the organization of industrialism'.

In this essentially materialist picture Ellis placed 'religion' and 'art' as palliatives 'against the excitement and hurry of modern life'. But their function was largely to 'slake our thirst' at the end of the day, and restore our spirits for the real business of life. The writers, discussed in the body of the book, were not, however, simply mental-masseurs; they actually embodied and reflected – in their different ways – the 'new spirit' of earnest enquiry into the truths of life.

Nevertheless, despite this invigorating and optimistic vision of the contemporary scene – and despite a refusal to countenance the notion of decadent aestheticism as an enduring cultural force – Ellis was certainly not uninformed upon the subject of decadence. Indeed there appear to have been very few subjects on which he was uninformed. In the autumn of 1889, just before he and Symons left for their first visit to Paris, he brought out 'A Note on Paul Bourget' in the *Pioneer*. He was the first to introduce English readers (Symons amongst them) to Bourget's theory of decadence – both social and literary – as the exaggerated importance of the parts at the expense of the whole. And in 1890, on the eve of their return to the French capital, he published a small study in social anthropology, called *The Criminal*, which drew heavily on Lombroso's ideas of a pathological connection between the 'criminal' and the 'artistic' genius. Amongst the examples of artistic reprobates put forward by Ellis were Villon, Cellini, Casanova and (with a fine disregard for libel) the 'distinctly criminal' Verlaine.

These well-structured books and essays by Ellis, and the conversations they undoubtedly inspired, provided Symons with a useful framework for developing his own ideas and working out his own attitude to 'decadence' during the sojourn in Paris. Symons' enthusiasm for Pater was too great and too fresh for him readily to accept Ellis' opinion that the creed of 'aesthetic joy' was already outmoded and that it was 'impossible to go any further on that road'. The *décadents* of Paris showed Symons how he could extend Pater's creed; they gave him a 'new aesthetic' – a means of going 'further on that road'. In the cafés of the Boul' Mich' Symons encountered young men who were searching not just for 'sweet' and 'comely' sensations, but also for bitter and illicit ones. They hid their hearts not in 'a nest of roses' but in a forest of *fleurs du mal*.

To every feature of Ellis' vital and scientific new world, Paris offered an alluring opposite: to Ellis' universal laws, Paris (like Pater) proclaimed the individual experience; Ellis placed human life in the midst of Darwinian nature, Paris (like Pater) sought to remove it into the realm of art and artifice; to Ellis' heralding of 'democracy', Paris proclaimed not only Pater's notion of the artist's superiority to the herd, but also a deliciously novel code of antisocial bohemianism; Ellis' emancipated females were transformed by Paris into cruel yet alluring *femmes fatales*; instead of Ellis' well-rounded 'education', Paris offered a regime of dissipation, immobility and dream. For Symons – a young, ambitious literary provincial, with a fascination for (sinful) sex, the choice between the two visions was not difficult to make.

Of all the important figures Symons encountered during his stay – Mallarmé, Huysmans, Rodin, Redon, Toulouse-Lautrec – the one who seemed most to embody the Parisian way was Verlaine. Symons was amazed by the defiant mode of Verlaine's existence, so entirely without the trappings of respectable bourgeois life, so very unlike Browning or Pater or any of the other English writers he knew. Verlaine's verse, too, he found novel and attractive; it became the new ideal, the new model, for his own poetry. It was, he found, 'a twilight art, full of reticence, of perfumed shadows, of hushed melodies. It suggests, it gives impressions, with a subtle avoidance of any too definite or precise effect of line or colour. The words are now *recherché*, now confidently commonplace – words of the boudoir, words of the street.'

On the technical side Symons admired, and strove to imitate, the sensuous, evocative music of Verlaine's writing, its 'singing' quality, its apparent simplicity, its avoidance of over-emphatic rhymes and rhythms. He envied Verlaine's ability to register, through suggestion rather than description, the finest shades of sensation, whether a fleeting visual impression or a fugitive human emotion. Symons saw that there was an opportunity to transpose Verlaine's method into English. It would, he realized, provide him with an ideal medium for fixing all those flickering Paterian moments.

Symons' discipleship of Verlaine was impressive in its fervour, but it did remove him from some of the other avant-garde ideas percolating through Paris at the beginning of the 1890s. It gave an idiosyncratic – Verlainian – twist to his conception of 'decadent' art. Mallarmé's esoteric notions about a new musical poetic language that could somehow reveal an unseen ideal world did not – despite that visit to the Rue de Rome – touch Symons. He recognized only Verlaine's less arcane symbolism, his subtle reflection of personal emotions in the objective and visible world. And beyond even this he tended to emphasize Verlaine's vague impressionism which sought to 'fix the last fine shade and fix it fleetingly'.

Even before Symons left Paris he had begun to experiment with poems in a distinctly Verlainian manner. The rather over-defined dramatic scenes of *Days and Nights* gave way to obliquely viewed significant moments in which the drama was more suggested than described. It was a change very much for the better.

Chapter Five

ONE OF Symons' first attempts at his new manner was 'Pastel: Masks and Faces':

> The light of our cigarettes
> Went and came in the gloom:
> It was dark in the little room.
>
> Dark, and then, in the dark,
> Sudden, a flash, a glow,
> And a hand and a ring I know.
>
> And then, through the dark, a flush
> Ruddy and vague, the grace
> (A rose!) of her lyric face.

The allusive quality and conversational style are distinctly Verlainian, as indeed are many of the poem's stylistic quirks – the internal rhyming, the repetition, the enjambment in the first and last verses, the use of assonance – while the daring introduction of those 'cigarettes' gives the poem a modern, metropolitan flavour, as well as casting a 'perfumed shadow' over the already darkened scene. It is curious too that the two adjectives most often used of Verlaine's verse – lyric and vague – both make an appearance in the piece.

Nevertheless, if the poem has the virtues of vague impressionistic verse, it does also have its drawbacks. The encounter at the heart of the poem bristles with sexual *frisson* but the setting remains obscure. Some critics have taken it as a post-coital interlude with a prostitute, but the evidence of Symons' notebooks suggests that it was based upon a chance meeting with a beguiling woman in an ill-lit corner of a Paris art gallery.

Symons returned to England in June 1890, giddy with excitement. He determined to free himself from the constraints of parental control and provincial life. He moved to London, sharing a small house with Ernest Rhys in Hampstead, and picked up once more the threads of his journalistic work, contributing unsigned pieces to the *Athenaeum* and articles to the newly established *Black and White*. For a fortnight he even stepped in to run the *Academy* while the editor was away on holiday. He was bursting to communicate all his new Parisian ideas and experiences. He attempted to interest his spreading network of journalistic contacts with articles upon French subjects. Villiers might have slipped through his fingers but there had been plenty of other encounters that deserved to be recorded.

Within a month of his return Symons published an article on Odilon Redon – the first in English – in the *Art Review*. His Parisian connections had, moreover, given him access to French periodicals; the June issue of the *Mercure de France* contained his review of a new translation of De Quincey's *Confessions of an English Opium Eater*, as well as an enthusiastic notice for *Days and Nights* from Rémy de Gourmont. Already Symons could imagine himself as the broker between English and French culture. It was a heady vision.

Although journalism was a practical necessity for Symons, it was also perhaps where his true genius lay. Nevertheless, with a perversity typical of many 1890s' figures, he insisted on considering himself as a poet first and foremost. He often fretted that if he wrote too many articles the public would, on the appearance of his next collection of verse, dismiss the book as the mere diversion of a hack. Despite such fears financial need left him quite unable to turn down any journalistic commissions, and there was also a certain pleasure at seeing his own name in print.

He did, however, find some time to write his determinedly 'modern' verses. Primed by Pater's theory and Verlaine's practice, Symons set out, in a quite deliberate intellectual fashion, to garner as many impressions and sensations ('impreshuns' and 'sensashuns' he called them) as he could. He carried about with him a small black notebook in which he would jot them down, and then would work these word-sketches into poems.

He was, as he never ceased reminding anyone who would listen, 'a man for whom the visible world exists'. Eyes agog, ever ready to receive some telling sense-data, he would peer into every omnibus, every cab, each passing face, in the hope of catching there some interesting or beautiful moment or expression before it passed. His eyes ached and yet he could not stop. 'If ever there was a religion of the eyes,' he boasted, 'I have practised that religion.'

The objects of his goggling were, he determined, to be both novel and distinctive. London, sex and bohemianism were his chosen fields. Taking Verlaine as his ideal, Symons came to regard an irregular life not merely as a source of good material but as a prerequisite of being a poet. In an early review he wrote that 'for the respectable virtues poetry has but the slightest use'. It was in abandonment, irregularity, immorality even, that the poet must look for his inspiration. 'To roam in the sun and air with vagabonds, to haunt the strange corners of cities, to know all the useless and improper and amusing people who are alone very much worth knowing; to live as well as to observe life . . . it is such things as these that make for poetry.'

This was Symons' artistic creed. He did indeed spend much of his time roaming. In the first two years of the new decade he made trips to Spain, Provence, Italy, Berlin and even Moscow. He also returned regularly to Paris, as he came increasingly to prefer 'the strange corners of cities' to the 'sun and air' of the open road. He sought out 'improper and amusing', if not 'useless', people, such as Josiah Flint, the literary tramp, and Theo Marzials, an eccentric chloral-addicted poet whose homosexual inclinations required him to spend much of his time on the continent. He also corresponded with and befriended John Addington Symonds, an historian of the Italian Renaissance and another homosexual literary exile.

Symons experimented with hashish, not because he liked it, but out of intellectual curiosity. And drink, which he explained, had 'no personal appeal', 'which, indeed, brought me no pleasures, found me intensely observant of its powers, effects and variations'.

The fruits of this determined and self-conscious research were contained in his second volume of poetry, *Silhouettes*, which came out in 1892. Although there is much that is obviously direct and personal in the collection – the self-absorption of 'The Absinthe Drinker', the mystery of the 'Javanese Dancers', the *frisson* of 'Pastel' or the emotion of 'Music and Memory' – there is also a great deal that is strained and literary. If Symons derived his technique from Verlaine, he borrowed many of his props and mannerisms from others. In the attempt to give London a poetic significance, in the preening anti-naturalism of 'Maquillage', the gentle perversity of 'Morbidezza' or the wanton sensuality of 'Perfume' there is the unmistakable trace of Baudelaire. And Baudelaire also stands behind the succession of *femmes fatales* who pursue Symons through the book. Nevertheless, despite the strident note of francophilia, the overall effect is delightfully English. The fatal vision of an enigmatic 'Monna Lisa' sitting in an omnibus, pondering 'when to wear/The latest bonnet you have bought/To match the marvel of your hair', seems to look forward to Betjeman quite as much as it looks back to *Les Fleurs du mal.*

Although Symons was confident about what he was attempting, he wanted to share his vision with others. One of the aspects of Parisian life that had attracted him most was the opportunity for intellectual discussion, and on his return to England he had hoped to find – or create – a similar atmosphere of convivial debate. He was disappointed. London, he lamented (as many have lamented since), is not easily susceptible to café society. 'This lack of easy meeting and talking,' Symons thought, 'is certainly one of the reasons why there have been in England many great writers but few schools.' He was not, however, alone in his plaints. Indeed there does seem to have sprung up during the first years of the 1890s an informal camaraderie amongst the young writers and artists of the capital – they would meet regularly, easily and often to complain about the 'lack of easy meeting and talking'.

Amongst those whom Symons met and talked with regularly was George Moore, who had rooms at 8 King's Bench Walk in the Temple. In those days the Inns of Court were not quite so exclusively the preserve of barristers; many of the chambers were taken by non-legal people and, indeed, the place was noted for its literary alumni. Fielding, Goldsmith and Thackeray had all lived there, as had William Blake. Symons was enchanted by these associations, by the cloistral calm of the place, by its proximity to both the offices of Fleet Street and the excitements of the West End.

Towards the end of 1890, when Symons' house mate, Ernest Rhys, announced his impending marriage, Symons determined to move from Hampstead to the Temple. On one of his visits to Moore he asked how he might find rooms in such a charmed spot and was directed to look in the window of the barber's shop on the corner.

He found a card advertising a set of rooms in Fountain Court. He raced round to view them. The Court itself, with its tall plane trees and single-jetted fountain, seemed an oasis in the heart of London. It also had a literary distinction as the rendezvous of John Westlock and Ruth Pinch in *Martin Chuzzlewit*. The chambers were no less satisfactory: a little garret apartment of two rooms with a small balcony looking down on to the court. There were a further two rooms, connected by a passageway, which Symons also looked at. He was particularly taken with a tiny muslin-covered window in the passageway, which gave on to the landing and would allow him a concealed view of his callers.

Symons took the first apartment immediately, and the second one soon after; he lined his room with books and installed a spinet. It was, he considered, 'the realization of a dream', placing him at the heart of things. He was close to Moore, who shared his enthusiasm for French literature. The translator Alexander Texeira de Mattos and the poet John Gray were his neighbours. He could stroll to the music halls of Leicester Square. He might encounter some acquaintances in the Strand as he – or they – returned from a necessary visit to the newspaper offices of Fleet Street. He began to feel a sense of literary community.

Young – and not so young – aspirants would meet in the Reading Room of the British Museum, and would come together for a preprandial absinthe at the Cock on Shaftesbury Avenue. They would gather at the Crown in Cranbourn Street, just off Leicester Square, after an evening at the music hall. Or they might encounter each other in the Domino Room of the Café Royal at the bottom of Regent Street. Such gatherings – informal and often crowded – undoubtedly fostered a sense of fellow-feeling amongst the jostling writers, painters and chorus girls, but to the serious and ambitious Symons they lacked a sense of purpose. They were not a satisfactory forum for artistic debate. Even in his debauchery he longed for the dedicated atmosphere of *Le Club des hachichins*, and was disappointed to find only the raucous jollity of the public house.

There were other more formal groupings which did seem to offer at least the possibility of focused discussion and concerted action, but Symons, for all his bustling desire to get on, had little access to them. He was not a resident of Bedford Park, the self-consciously 'aesthetical' suburb beyond Shepherds Bush where W. B. Yeats' family lived in an atmosphere of rustic calm and elevated discourse amongst the Norman Shaw houses, well-tended gardens and amateur theatricals. He was not party to the Sunday evening meetings of the Socialist League held at William Morris' home, just down the road in Hammersmith. He had yet to secure an entrée to the large Georgian house at 20 Fitzroy Street where Arthur Mackmurdo, Selwyn Image, Herbert Horne and the other members of the Century Guild kept alive the traditions of artistic craftsmanship and laid the foundations for the Liberty style. He was not invited to W. E. Henley's bracing Sunday soirées, where the cantankerous editor of the *National Observer* (and the model for Long John Silver) presided over his coterie of clever young writers while pontificating about imperialist politics and serving up cold meats. The glamorous circle of Oscar Wilde and his elegant disciples – all sporting green carnations in their buttonholes – was beyond his reach. He did attend the Browning Society, but its meetings were necessarily limited to a discussion of Browning. And the more convivial and exclusive literary societies, 'The Sette of Odd Volumes' or the Omar Khayyam Club, where talk might have ranged more widely, were closed to him.

It should not, however, be thought that Symons was a Cinderella. Indeed the network of his literary acquaintance spread impressively wide. He attended Coventry Patmore's sixty-seventh birthday party on his return from Paris. He was friendly with 'Michael Field', the curious dyad of Katherine Bradley and Edith Cooper, an aunt and niece who lived together in Hampstead under their singular masculine name, writing high-minded, classically inspired verse. And he enjoyed the hospitality of Edmund Gosse on Sunday afternoons at Delamere Terrace. Gosse himself was a child of non-conformity carried away by a love of literature, and he felt a natural sympathy for Symons, taking care to welcome him into the illustrious tea-sipping throng. Nevertheless Gosse (like Patmore and, to some extent, 'Michael Field') was of the generation before. He was an English Parnassian in his verse, and quite set in his ways. His Sunday gatherings, though rich in impressive guests, were both too staid and too eclectic to offer the chance of any focused artistic debate. Besides, a cup of tea is not a glass of absinthe.

Symons, however, was not the only young writer to feel the want of some semi-formalized forum for discussion; indeed on his return from Paris he discovered that a first step had been taken without him. Ernest Rhys informed him about the so-called Rhymers' Club, which he had recently set up together with W. B. Yeats and another

Irish poet, called Thomas Rolleston. The aim of the club was to give poets the opportunity of meeting, of hearing each other's verse and of commenting upon it. It had proved a popular idea and the club expanded rapidly, bringing in – amongst others – the literary members of the Fitzroy Settlement, several young Oxonians recently down from the university and a fair number of London's Irish literary mafia.

The club itself was curious in that there were no officers, no rules, no subscriptions, nor even any fixed membership. It did produce two anthologies of verse (in 1891 and 1894), which established thirteen definite Rhymers, but numerous guests attended meetings. Oscar Wilde came sometimes, his protégé John Gray more often. Some 'guests', such as John Davidson, Selwyn Image and Herbert Horne, were indeed more regular than many of the anthology contributors.

The list of those who did contribute to the two *Book[s] of the Rhymers' Club* is only partly illuminating since many of the names have now been consigned to a deserved obscurity. As a group the Rhymers represented a mixture of ages, styles, interests and backgrounds. John Todhunter, at over fifty, was the father of the group, and the only one to have secured a reputation before the formation of the club. He, together with his young Bedford Park neighbour Yeats, his old friend Edwin Ellis and the Dublin-educated Rolleston and George Greene, provided a strong London-Irish connection; while Rhys and Ernest Radford, through their positions in the publishing trade, had contacts with many of the newest generation of writers and were able to bring them into the club. Along with their coeval Yeats, these younger Rhymers – all in their early twenties – made up a definite and visible bloc within the whole. Besides Symons there was Lionel Johnson, down from New College and installed in Fitzroy Street with Herbert Horne and Selwyn Image, Ernest Dowson and Victor Plarr, also just down from Oxford, and Richard Le Gallienne, a rather ludicrous Liverpudlian busily engaged in writing journalism and being 'poetical'. The early history of the club is confused but most of these characters had probably begun their assocation with the Rhymers by the time of Symons' introduction.

The weekly meetings, though sometimes held at the Fitzroy Settlement or even out at Todhunter's house in Bedford Park, increasingly took place in an upstairs room of the Cheshire Cheese off Fleet Street. After a simple dinner downstairs the poets would withdraw to a gloomy, ill-lit panelled room above and there sit in rather self-conscious Johnsonian (if not Jonsonian) splendour with their pots of beer and church warden pipes. A sense of Paterian sobriety, even dullness, prevailed. Yeats claimed that if it had not been for the spontaneity of the Irish members the whole venture would have died of silence. It was all very different from the intellectual ferment of Montmartre.

The poets read in alphabetical order, except for Dowson who was too shy and would get Lionel Johnson to recite for him. Symons would probably have had to read between Rolleston (who barked his verse out in a 'plain military style') and the long-winded but worthy Todhunter. It was a position that must have borne home to him the disparate nature of the group.

Although there is no evidence of any self-conscious programme there was, it seems, a vague sense of camaraderie. Victor Plarr was always proud of being, as he put it, 'in the movement'. And even if it was a 'movement' without any clear direction, it was constrained by certain limits. As Yeats suggested, all the poets of that generation (not just the members of the Rhymers' Club) faced the same problem: how to get beyond the great achievements of the High Victorian tradition. Tennyson, the ancient and ennobled laureate, was approaching his end (he died in 1892) and under his care the principal strain of English verse had grown increasingly allied to the public concerns of the nation. It had become rather like the Anglican Church, both a measure of, and a medium for, the country's moral health. There had of course been dissenting voices; the fleshy excesses of Swinburne and Rossetti, and the alarming personal frankness of Meredith's *Modern Love* had all shocked by their transgression of the established code. But the established code had, by and large, prevailed. Certainly at the beginning of the 1890s it was the strongest voice, the one that the Rhymers felt they must confront.

Some poets tried to avoid their predicament by ignoring it; they strove to continue the tradition, though they were always rather conscious of their lesser power. Bolder spirits struck out in new directions: Henley with his vigorous declamatory metres and Kipling with his rollicking ballads both introduced a note of brutal, heightened realism. The Rhymers were rather less boisterous.

The elder members of the club tended to seek refuge outside themselves. They sought to combine Parnassian carefulness with a social conscience, forging verses about the dignity of labour or the pleasures of bicycling. The younger members – Symons, Yeats, Johnson, Dowson, Le Gallienne and Plarr – took the opposite route. In the face of a progressive and materialist society, they all, in their different ways and to different extents, followed the Paterian path inwards. In place of 'thoughts' they strove to express feelings, emotions, sensations and impressions. They tended to set form above content, the individual consciousness above the common good.

In spite of their shared predicament there seems, however, to have been very little communal discussion. Indeed the club's one unspoken rule, according to Yeats, was that there should be no discussion of ideas or general theories of poetry. When Symons tried tentatively to draw everyone's attention to his decadent French discoveries by suggesting 'What we are interested in is impressions', he was greeted with embarrassed silence.

Their artistic position was defined only by a few broad negatives. When Ibsen's naturalist drama, *A Doll's House*, had premièred at the Royalty Theatre in June 1889, Dowson, Symons, Yeats and most of the other Rhymers saw it. Yeats would later recall that even though he did not care for the play, finding it devoid of style – too close to nature to be art – he disliked even more the glibly hostile reactions of a 'washerwoman' and a 'theatre critic' he chanced to overhear. He felt, in the end, unable to side with these philistines against the artist: 'neither I nor my generation,' he considered, 'could escape [Ibsen and naturalism] because, though we had not the same friends, we had the same enemies.' Nevertheless, in the face of this hostile philistinism, the Rhymers' defiance was decidedly cautious.

The prevailing tone of the club was against anything conventionally poetical or flamboyant. In dress most of the members looked like bank clerks, though Symons and some of the other younger men showed the occasional flourish of sartorial eccentricity. Richard Le Gallienne was the exception, wearing his hair in a great mist of curls and even affecting knee-breeches. Dowson contented himself with the small elasticated black bow-tie which he had bought in Paris for forty-five centimes and of which he was inordinately proud. Yeats sported a brown velveteen jacket, William Theodore Peters (a regular guest) had a beautiful Renaissance-style cloak, and Symons himself had 'longish hair' and wore (perhaps in imitation of Verlaine) an Inverness cape. Daring though these touches were, they struggled to assert themselves against the general background of buttoned serge and flannel, and Lionel Johnson's ascetic dandiacal conviction that one must be at all times utterly inconspicuous.

Nor did the Rhymers indulge in the sort of bourgeois-baiting pranks that had enlivened Parisian Bohemia from the time of *Les Jeunes France.* Texeira de Mattos and another young writer, Edgar Jepson, both on the very fringes of the club, liked to bemuse 'the greater public' by waving their 'right legs gracefully at one another' whenever they met in the street. Passers-by were 'astounded' but the affectation was not adopted by others, and 'Tex' and Jepson remained on the fringe.

Unsurprisingly the gatherings seem to have been half-strangled by a sense of decorum. As the irascible Scottish poet John Davidson complained impatiently, the club lacked 'blood and guts'. Symons put it more circumspectly: 'it was not quite a satisfactory kind of *cénacle*'. Nevertheless, despite the shortcomings of the club itself, Symons hoped to find allies for his 'decadent' theories amongst the individual members, particularly the younger ones. Lionel Johnson must have seemed a likely candidate.

When Richard Le Gallienne had first caught sight of Johnson at a Rhymers' Club meeting, he had assumed that the neat, diminutive figure – barely five foot two – with that oddly glowing boyish complexion, was perhaps the teenage son of one of the other poets present. In fact Johnson was twenty-three. And, despite his physical stature, it was he who, by the force of his personality and the showiness of his erudition, assumed the role of intellectual arbiter amongst the junior members of the club.

At Oxford Johnson had been a disciple of Pater's. He had, however, drawn from his teachings neither the hedonism of Wilde nor the fervent impression-hunting of Symons, but rather a belief in the importance of ritual, of self-discipline, of *ascêcis*. Although such notions were not perhaps well calculated to dispose him towards the ideas of French decadence, he nevertheless made it his business to take an interest in the literary trends of the day.

In April 1891 he even contributed an article to the Century Guild's magazine, the *Century Guild Hobby Horse*, on 'The Practice and Theory of Verse at the Present Time Obtaining in France', which concluded with a discussion of '*décadence*' and '*symbolisme*' derived, or rather copied without translation, from a French article on the subject by Antoni Lange. Lange made a distinction between decadent literature, in which a sensation or impression is contemplated and refined upon in 'an age of afterthought', and symbolism, which presupposes a double existence in all things, an 'existence in nature' and a truer 'existence in the mind'. And it is this 'true truth' that symbolist writing sought to express; not just the visual or emotional impression as the sun sets, but the impression 'upon our mind as you say those words'. Both strains shared a common concern with language; 'poetry,' Johnson noted with approval, 'becomes a matter of infinite pains and singular attention.'

Johnson was able to give a commanding overview, using as he was an informed French source. He listed as decadents Verlaine together with his 'school' (a group which included Moréas, Laforgue and Kahn) and he differentiated them from the symbolist school of Mallarmé (which comprised Ghil, Merril, Régnier, Vièle-Griffin, Verhaeren and George Khnopff). Such an article might have provided the basis for debate amongst the Rhymers, especially when it was backed by other discussions of the topic. The Rev. W. F. Barry's ranting denunications of 'French decadence' in the *Quarterly Review* (the first appeared in July 1890, the second in April 1892) were perhaps too wild to be useful. Besides, the Rev. Barry's real ire was directed towards the realists – 'the tribe' of Zola and Maupassant – and to the seekers after pornographic postcards. Of more interest in the discussion of literary 'decadence' was the spate of reviews in the quality press during 1891 of Jules Huret's *Enquête* into the current state of French literature.

Huret's book, based on a series of interviews with contemporary writers, presented a more vital and more confused picture than Lange's article did. The starting point for the book was the notion that the old schools of Parnassianism and naturalism were being challenged by the 'psychologists' (in prose fiction) and the 'symbolist-decadents' (in poetry). Huret's enquiries, however, unearthed only bickering, contradictions, personal rivalries and ever-dividing factions. Jean Moréas did announce himself as 'chief of the symbolists', but Mallarmé – although given that title by others – disclaimed all 'schools' and 'proclaimed himself a solitary'. He then, however, gave 'perhaps the best account of the aims of the symbolist school'. Verlaine, meanwhile, dismissed 'symobolism' as an incomprehensible term ('Must be German, Eh?') and said that although he had

Max Beerbohm's 'Some Persons of "the Nineties"'; front (left to right): Arthur Symons, Henry Harland, Charles Conder, Will Rothenstein, Max Beerbohm, Aubrey Beardsley. Back (left to right): Richard Le Gallienne, Walter Sickert, George Moore, John Davidson, Oscar Wilde, W.B. Yeats, and (barely visible) "Enoch Soames".

Theophile Gautier

Charles Baudelaire

Stéphane
Mallarmé

Paul Verlaine, 1891

Algernon Swinburne
by Simeon Solomon

George Moore by Manet

Walter Pater

James McNeill Whistler
by Harry Furniss

Arthur Symons, 1891

John Gray

Ernest Dowson by Charles Conder

Ricketts and Shannon
by William Rothenstein,
1897

Richard Le Gallienne

W.B. Yeats by J.B. Yeats, 1897

taken up the title 'decadent' as a 'war-cry' after it had been flung at him as an 'insult', 'at bottom it means just nothing at all'. Most of the reviews poked fun at the French obsession with 'schools', and congratulated English literature on avoiding such a snare. 'We have not found it necessary,' remarked the critic in the *Fortnightly Review*, 'to label Mr George Meredith a "psychologue", or Mr Swinburne a "decadent"'.

Most of the Rhymers would have concurred with this verdict. Certainly there does not seem to have been any concerted discussion of the topic at the Cheshire Cheese. And even Symons, to begin with, echoed the note of disparagement. The month of Johnson's piece also saw Symons' review of Verlaine's collection *Bonheur* in the *Academy*. Symons was concerned to make a distinction not between decadents and symbolists, but between Verlaine and 'the noisy little school of *décadents*, the brain-sick little school of *symbolistes*, both claiming [him] as a master'. This equation undoubtedly reflected the very real confusion of terms and aims that Symons had encountered in the cafés of Paris, but it also carried the note of caution that he felt was necessary in introducing his admired Verlaine to the English literary public. By condemning the poet's more outrageous followers he forestalled the same charges being laid against Verlaine (and, by extension – he hoped – himself).

Johnson, on the other hand, had never spent time in Paris. He could readily accept Lange's crisp definition of two distinct schools, the one ranged under Verlaine, the other under Mallarmé, each with its own well-formulated programme. He was, moreover, never afraid to speak with seeming authority. A Wykehamist, a classicist and a Catholic convert, his education inclined him to magisterial pronouncements. It is not known what Symons made of Johnson's article. The revelation of such an area of shared interest might have seemed a spur to friendship. Or perhaps Symons detected a veiled rebuke, a demonstration that you did not have to sit about for weeks in the Café François Premier sipping absinthe to understand what was going on in contemporary French literature.

Johnson himself remained curiously distant from his subject throughout the article. He conceded only, with a lofty air, that these French experiments were 'not uninteresting, I think, to some of us English Islanders'. His own interest, however, was very limited. He could lay bare the theory of 'decadence' or 'symbolism' but the poetry he wrote showed little trace of either. He despised the 'thin diet of impressions' upon which Symons was basing his poetry. He claimed to find more life in 'the strong voices of the ancients in fame' than 'among the still-born or moribund moderns'. He was a classicist at heart, with a classicist's love of order and precedent. His verse had a clear, well-crafted energy, but little originality; it seemed always to whisper, 'the old was best'.

He longed for rules and hierarchies to shackle his wayward nature, his homosexual urges and his love of whisky. He found this sense of order in several places: in Pater's prose, in the best Latin authors, in the practice of his art, in the liturgy of the Catholic Church (to which he turned in June 1891), in the dotty pretensions of the monarchist White Rose League, in the rallying call of Yeats' Catholic Renaissance, even in his purely imaginary conversations with such authority figures as Gladstone and Cardinal Newman.

There is no doubt that some superficial aspects of the decadent stance appealed to him, but in the face of these attractions he retreated. The ideal he sought was ascetic, intellectual and cloistered. And although his hopeless addiction to drink and his largely suppressed lusts frequently threatened to upset it, he managed, for the most part, to convince himself that he had achieved such a haven.

It was, however, a constant struggle. The parody upon the decadent type that he contributed to the March 1891 issue of a small magazine called the *Anti Jacobin* was perhaps a blow in the struggle, an attempt to exorcize the appeal of the pose by laughing at it and by stressing those aspects that were furthest from his own concern. He drew a picture of 'a young man' who wilfully rejects all established thoughts and theories, and searches out instead 'graceful affectation' and 'surprising paraodox'; a man who is not so much sensitive as neurotic; who seeks the finest shades of sensation, 'the exquisite appreciation of pain, exquisite thrills of anguish, exquisite adoration of suffering'; who acknowledges the power of Gautier and Botticelli but reverences that of Baudelaire and Verlaine; who loves the aesthetic splendour and mystery of the Catholic Church, yet balks from actually joining it, in order that he might preserve his double passion – 'the sentiment of repentant yearning and the sentiment of rebellious sin'.

Although Johnson conceded that the type was to be found in England, he suggested that the 'haggard eyes of the *absintheur* and the pallid faces of "neurotic" sinners' were really the portion of 'our

Parisian friends'. And, in truth, the English imitators lived rather blameless lives, only writing about the world of sin, borrowing the plumage of 'decadent' Latin, of pagan comeliness, of fashionable lesbianism, of the Italian Renaissance, and setting it in 'strange and subtle verse'.

Those who had visited Johnson in his dark, corduroy-curtained rooms in Fitzroy Street might have recalled that he kept a jug of whisky on his shelf between *Les Fleurs du mal* and the poems of Walt Whitman, and that he drank from it often. Those who knew him well might have guessed that behind his almost clerical demeanour he was a man not unfamiliar with 'rebellious sin'; they might even have pronounced the fact a 'surprising paraodox'. In all other respects, however, they would have acknowledged that he was – or took care to be – a very different creature from his 'cultured faun'. He loved 'established thoughts and theories'; he distrusted mere sensations; he took the decisive step of entering the Catholic Church, not to lend a new spice to sin but to try and gain forgiveness; he knew Latin well and preferred the classical authors to those of the decadence.

Symons would have recognized as much. And in Johnson's disdain for an imported, pseudo-Parisian cult of sin and sensation he must have felt the sting of a personal rebuke. Johnson, he quickly realized, for all his knowledge of the subject, for all his tendency to fall, was not to be an ally in the attempt to introduce decadence into England.

Other Rhymers were less immediately disdainful. Symons certainly claimed Ernest Dowson as a companion in art. And in the biographical *Causerie* that he contributed in 1896 to the August edition of the *Savoy* magazine, he forged an enduring picture of Dowson as the very type of the decadent poet. This so-called 'Dowson myth' presented a vision of a 'demoralized Keats' refined in manner yet dilapidated in appearance, 'always, perhaps a little consciously, but at least always sincerely, in search of new sensations'; a luster after oblivion through hashish and absinthe and the aesthetic appeal of Catholicism; a frequenter of cabmen's shelters and Limehouse stews and common whores; a man whose soul was wracked by an unrequited ideal passion for the young daughter of a Soho restaurateur, and whose body was under the hereditary curse of tuberculosis; a dreamer whose hopes were always met with ruin; and yet a poet – 'a fastidious amateur of grief' – whose pure lyric gifts could transfigure all these sorrows into beauty.

The portrait was undoubtedly overdrawn but it was not entirely without point or factual basis. Dowson had come down from Queen's College, Oxford, in 1888 without taking a degree, to help his consumptive father with the running of the family's ailing dry-dock business at Limehouse. This background of decline – of decadence one might say – undoubtedly coloured Dowson's otherwise gentle, even playful, nature. He did drink a great deal, though not with Johnson's air of furtiveness. Indeed he composed a great many of his poems on the table-tops at the Cock, with a glass at his elbow. He did, while at Oxford, experiment with 'bhang', though the drug induced not oblivion but vomiting. He did convert to Catholicism in 1891 but seems to have been quite sincere in his motives, even if he was disappointed by the absence of immediate divine revelation. He certainly enjoyed the camaraderie of cabmen's shelters and, when drunk, would sleep with unprepossessing prostitutes. He did also conceive an extraordinary sentimental devotion for Adelaide 'Missie' Foltinowicz, the twelve-year-old daughter of a Polish couple who ran a small eating-house on the edge of Soho; for two years he would go almost nightly to see her and perhaps to play 'Halma' after the other customers had left; she was, in an abstract sense, his muse, but the relationship seems to have been more a sentimental adoration of innocence than an incipient grand passion.

Symons' account also suggests an intimacy between himself and Dowson that should be treated with caution. Dowson's closest friends within the Rhymers' Club were his fellow-Oxonians Johnson and Victor Plarr, neither of them allies to decadence or to Symons. Dowson himself was more tolerant. He knew France and French literature well. Due to his father's consumption the family had spent much time abroad seeking the healthier climes of the French and Italian rivieras. Despite – or because of – this irregular upbringing Ernest Dowson acquired, through private tutors and diurnal practice, a good knowledge of Latin and a fluency in French. These accomplishments had taken him to Oxford in 1886, and while at the university he had established a reputation not only for verse (his first poem 'Sonnet for a Little Girl' appeared in the November 1886 issue of *London Society*) but also for francophilia. Friends would recall his densely annotated copy of *Les Fleurs du mal*, his proud boast that he had once met Maupassant, and his excited plan to write a letter of congratulation to Emile Zola after reading *La Terre*.

Dowson certainly did not need Symons to introduce him to the French decadents. Even before they met (in May 1891) Dowson's letters are flecked with references to 'the decadent poet Paul Verlaine', to Rimbaud, to Pierre Loti and others. And the first meeting between them was less than a discovery of shared enthusiasm. 'I met Arthur Symons last night,' Dowson wrote to his friend Arthur Moore, 'do you know him? He is a standing dish with the *Academy* & knows his Paris well: but on the whole I was not greatly impressed.'

For the year and a half before they met Dowson had been flirting with 'decadent' themes in his own verse, and he had started translating works by Verlaine. But his principal understanding of what constituted 'decadent' or 'symbolist' verse (he used the terms indiscriminately) seems to have been a belief in the triumph of sound over sense. In a letter to Plarr, in March 1891, he described his latest 'versicles' as 'the merest "symbolism", almost too slight for criticism! It's an attempt at mere sound verse, with scarcely the shadow of sense in it: or hardly that so much as vague Verlainesque emotion.' And he was attracted to such verse because it chimed with his existing inclinations and practice. He does not appear to have had any interest in the sort of theories about decadence and symbolism that Johnson and Symons could bandy. Indeed the only poetic theory he ever expressed any credence in was the notion that the letter 'V' was the most beautiful in the alphabet and could not be introduced often enough into verse.

He did not share Symons' conception of decadent literature as a feverish quest for bizarre sensations. Dowson was a man for whom the visible world did not exist. His poetic universe was almost entirely taken up with conventional poetical roses, bathed in either moonlight or wine dregs. The almost invariable mood of his poems, vague, regretful, wistful and despairing, was considered Verlainian, but it was really Dowsonian. It would have been achieved without the example of Verlaine, for it was Dowson's own mood, certainly in his art but often too in his life.

His poetry can be called decadent in a certain general sense. It was a musical lament for the passing beauty of the moment, the inevitable failure of the ideal, but it lacked any of the programmatic concerns of Symons' vision. It was not 'impressionistic', it was not particularly perverse. Its lack of naturalness seemed to owe everything to Dowson's ignorance of nature, rather than to a delight in artificiality. Dowson's eccentricities on this score were formidable. Once, while walking with Plarr in the country, a newt crossed the path. Dowson announced that it was a venomous lizard and, picking up a large stick, he set about the harmless creature. The newt escaped but Dowson kept hold of his stick in case they were attacked again, and urged Plarr to arm himself too against the possible menace.

The irregularity of Dowson's personal existence makes only a very fitful appearance in his poetry, although it did of course provide the essential background to his most famous piece. 'NON SUM QUALIS ERAM BONAE SUB REGNO CYNARAE' set to thrilling music the remorseful self-disgust of one who sees the terrible discrepancy between his inescapable ideal, Cynara, and the 'bought red mouth' of the night just passed. Despite the inevitable paraphernalia of roses, lilies, wine dregs and Latin tags, the poem must have been informed in part by Dowson's own awareness of the distance between Missie, his teenage fixation, and the harlots he found 'cheaper than hotels'. Although the poem gains in intensity from its relation to life, Dowson seems to have written it partly through a youthful desire to shock. When it came out in the *Century Guild Hobby Horse* for April 1891, he wrote excitedly to a friend, 'I have just seen the proofs of my Cynara poem. It looks less indecent in print, but I am still nervous.' Certainly the poem owed nothing to Symons. Indeed any influence was in the other direction. Symons borrowed the theme for his own rather less successful 'To One in Alienation'.

Dowson's easy-going nature shied away from confrontation, and would have kept him outside any dispute between Symons and Johnson. And the general esteem in which he was held allowed him to form friendships with all his contemporaries amongst the Rhymers, with Johnson and Plarr, as well as with Gray and Symons and Yeats, and the extravagant William Theodore Peters (an American actor and poet who insisted on producing Dowson's little verse-drama, *The Pierrot of the Minute*, at Chelsea Town Hall). Dowson's poetry, for all its limitations of imagery and tone, was considered by many of the Rhymers – decadents and non-decadents alike – to be the best product of the club. It was Yeats' desire to hold 'Villanelle at Sunset' in his hand that prompted the compilation of *The First Book of the Rhymers' Club*.

Symons tried to involve Dowson in his own flights of decadent fancy. He invited him along to a small hashish-cum-tea party that he had arranged for J. A. Symonds. Dowson came but was too shy to enter into the spirit of the occasion; he 'sat, a little anxiously, with, as his habit was, his chin on his breast', surrounded by a bevy of excited ballet-girls from the Empire, 'awaiting the magic'. It never arrived. But such events, even when more successful, did not, for Dowson, belong to any programme of decadent 'sensation'-seeking. Dowson – in his verse – had really only one 'sensation', that sense of langorous world-weary resignation, and he did not need to search for it. It came to him.

Indeed, after his intitial flirtation with the pose, Dowson seems subtly to have distanced himself from the claims of French decadence. In his poem 'Transition', he ends with the lines, '. . . one by one/The roses fall, the pale roses expire/Beneath the slow decadence of the sun.' The rhythm of the verse demands that 'decadence' be given a long second syllable: it returns the word to its original meaning and frees it (and hence Dowson) from its more recent associations.

John Gray did not need Symons to proclaim him as a decadent. He adopted a decadent stance more self-consciously and consistently than Dowson ever did – and (like Dowson) his interest had developed before he encountered Symons. Born into a working-class family in London's East End in 1866 and forced to take a job as a metal-turner at the Woolwich Arsenal when only thirteen, Gray had continued to study in his spare time, learning French and the piano amongst other accomplishments. After three years he had escaped from the work-bench to a clerkship in the Civil Service. And from there his determination to be a writer, his natural good manners and his remarkable good looks had carried him into the circles of literary London.

His first mentor was Charles Ricketts, the half-French artist-typographer who lived with the painter Charles Shannon in Whistler's old house in the Vale, Chelsea. But by 1889 Gray had also been taken up by Oscar Wilde, who flirtatiously borrowed his surname for the hero of the novel he was writing. Quite when they first met is unknown, but perhaps Wilde's interest had been stimulated by reading the distinctly Wildean fairy-story which, together with an essay on the Goncourt brothers, Gray contributed to the first number of *The Dial*, an exquisitely produced periodical brought out by Ricketts and Shannon. Wilde must have been flattered by Gray's imitation and impressed by his knowledge of French literature. Certainly he would have encouraged both. Gray rapidly became one of Wilde's most conspicuous acolytes, and very probably his lover.

In the summer of 1890 Gray went to Paris (arriving just after Symons had left). He too visited Vanier's bookshop, and gained an introduction to the young poets of the Latin Quarter. His *cicerone* was Félix Fénéon, a young critic with a particular enthusiasm for Rimbaud. Fénéon secured Gray a meeting with Verlaine (who was in hospital) and presented him with 'a big pile of decadent literature'. On his return to England Gray began translating, or 'adapting', poems by Baudelaire, Rimbaud, Verlaine and Mallarmé. Occasionally he would read these French-inspired pieces at the Rhymers' Club. It was after one such meeting, at Herbert Horne's rooms in February 1891, that Dowson wrote of '"Dorian" Gray [reading] some very beautiful & obscure versicles in the latest manner of French symbolism'.

Gray, however, never formally joined the Rhymers, and he did not contribute to either of their anthologies. At the beginning of the 1890s he was moving in Wilde's dandified circle which, although it had contact with the Rhymers' Club, did not care for the bohemian ambience of the Cheshire Cheese. Nevertheless Symons, though he was not present at the meeting when Gray read his 'beautiful and obscure versicles', and though he had little access to Wilde's coterie, did come to know the precocious young 'Dorian' Gray. They were near neighbours in the Temple. Gray was a fellow enthusiast for the music hall, and in February 1892 gave a provocative lecture on 'The Modern Actor' to the Playgoer's Club, suggesting that the legitimate stage, with its cranking literalness, had fallen into 'decadence', and that the real and vital art was now to be found in the suggestive performances of the music hall. In the spring of 1892 Gray and Symons even shared the same playbill, when J. T. Grein's Independent Theatre Group presented Gray's rhymed translation of Theodore Banville's *The Kiss* together with Symons' dramatization of a Frank Harris short story (and William Archer's version of Edvard Brandes' *A Visit*).

No close friendship, however, developed between them. As was so often the case, Symons' manner seems to have made an unfavourable first impression. Gray would later refer to Symons as someone who he had 'in the past so much disliked & then liked'. They belonged to different poles of the decadent spectrum; Symons the bohemian impressionist, Gray the austere dandified artificer. Rising from the slums of Bethnal Green, Gray, far more than Symons, had had to create himself. He had taken shelter behind a mask of self-sufficient elegance, and he could find little to admire in Symons' self-absorbed sensualism.

The great majority of his early poems, whether 'adaptations' from the French or his own compositions, showed in their form, their content, their techical bravura, even in their presentation, a reverence for the superiority of artifice. His first slim collection, *Silverpoints*, published by the Bodley Head at the beginning of 1893, was sumptuously designed by Ricketts in a tall slender format derived from a Persian saddle-book and bound with boards of apple-green cloth, blocked with gold fleurs-de-lis between wavy gold lines. The book is – and was – regarded as a quintessential decadent production. A student of Paul Bourget would have noticed with interest that the poems were individually dedicated to friends and fellow-artists, and that on each page the text was almost lost in the vast prairie of surrounding margin. The parts were asserting their existence against the whole; form was triumphing over content.

It was the sight of this elegant volume that prompted Ada Leverson's famous suggestion to Wilde 'that he should go a step further than these minor poets; that he should publish a book *all* margin; full of beautiful unwritten thoughts, and have this blank volume bound in some Nile-green skin powdered with gilt nenuphars and smoothed with hard ivory, decorated with gold by Ricketts (if not Shannon) and printed on Japanese paper'. And Wilde, delighted with the idea, had replied, 'It shall be dedicated to you, and the unwritten text illustrated by Aubrey Beardsley. There must be five hundred signed copies for particular friends, six for the general public, and one for America.' For Symons, Gray's book marked 'a certain hour of the day'. It was, however, an hour that passed quickly for its author.

Silverpoints, for all its air of decadence, also contained some hints of John Gray's other side. Amongst the courtly ladies putting nature to shame, the strange erotic dreams, the terrible intimacies of the masseur, the versions of Verlaine and Baudelaire, there was a smattering of nature poems and even a few verses of a religious stamp. One of the kind acts that perhaps produced the change in

Gray's feelings towards Symons was the introduction he effected with the wealthy Russian emigré Andre Raffalovich. Raffalovich, who had literary pretensions of his own, took Gray up and supported him at first in his retreat from the influence of Wilde (who was becoming increasingly infatuated with Lord Alfred Douglas) and later in his ambition to enter the priesthood. Gray had converted to Catholicism in 1889 but, as he himself admitted, had embarked almost immediately upon a course of sin, fascinated by the worldly pleasures offered to him by Wilde. Nevertheless, as Gray's friendship with Raffalovich developed through 1893, so he renewed his commitment to the Catholic faith. His poetry became rapidly, and almost exclusively, religious. He started translating the hymns of Prudentius, of St Bernard, of St John of the Cross, and 'adapting' the religious verse of Verlaine. Symons had lost another potential ally.

Despite the interest in literary decadence and the attractions of the decadent pose, despite the knowledge of Johnson and the experiments of Dowson and Gray, despite the feeble straining of Theodore Wratislaw and William Theodore Peters, Symons remained isolated in his determined zeal. His pursuit of bizarre impressions and sensations came to be regarded with hostility, contempt, amusement or indifference by the great majority of his contemporaries.

Chapter Six

AS AN EVANGELIST of literary decadence Symons seems to have been hampered by a certain defect of charisma. Everyone agreed that he wrote lucidly and well, if sometimes with rather too much Paterian affectation, but as a personality he was disappointing. His slightly lugubrious manner was not helped by a drooping moustache. Many of his contemporaries came to respect him, even to like him, but their first impressions were almost always antipathetic. Dowson, as has been seen, was not greatly impressed. Gray disliked him initially. Yeats found him unsatisfactory on first acquaintance. Jepson was irritated by his 'high voice' and 'did not take him seriously'. George Moore remarked that he had been 'cast for a parson' and that although a good fairy had bestowed upon him a gift for writing, a bad fairy had promptly flown down the chimney and denied him the benison of conversation. Max Beerbohm found him 'perfectly agreeable, but perfectly uninteresting, like one of those white flannels that nurses give children to wipe their faces on'. There is a generous pinch of Symons in the formation of Beerbohm's woefully 'dim' 1890s' poet, Enoch Soames. Even in an age that relished paradox it was unfortunate that Symons, seeking to promote an enthusiasm for the intense evocation of personal sensations, should have been so deficient in personal intensity (or intense personality) himself. He was, in Wilde's phrase, 'an egoist without an ego'. He had the desire to gather a 'decadent school' about his ideas and practice, but he lacked the necessary qualities of projection.

Yeats, who later came to appreciate Symons, was particularly dismissive of him at first. He was too full of his own theories to listen to Symons'. Although he admired the technical virtuosity of his fellow Rhymers – especially Johnson and Dowson – he distrusted their vision of literature as 'an end in itself'. On the one hand, his commitment to the cause of Irish nationalism had led him to believe that literature must rather be the expression of conviction and the garment of noble emotion. And on the other, his involvement with the occult practices of the Order of the Golden Dawn inclined him to look beyond the realm of the senses.

Symons' most active adversary within the Rhymers' Club, however, was Richard Le Gallienne. With his extravagant haze of hair and the curiously ungrammatical affectation of the French definite article in the middle of his name, Le Gallienne might have seemed a potential ally. But appearances were deceptive. Like Symons, and unlike most of the other members of the club, he had not been to university, and had no private means of support. He was a self-educated provincial, in love with the romance of literature and determined to make a career for himself with his pen. Arriving in London from Liverpool at the end of the 1880s, he had thrown himself with unbrookable energy into the professional literary life. He contributed book notices to the *Star* (under the unabashed *nom de plume* of 'Log-roller'), he wrote criticism for numerous other periodicals, he composed stories and poems of empurpled lushness, and he read for the Bodley Head.

His manner and dress were calculated to draw attention and they succeeded. The hyacinth locks, the velvet collars, the absurd knee-breeches, were determinedly 'poetic'. But they were not determinedly 'decadent'. Perhaps Le Gallienne realized that there was a literary niche to be carved as the expert lambaster of the new phenomenon; certainly he adopted the role. As Symons embraced Frenchness and bohemianism, so Le Gallienne fell upon Englishness and romance. In his desire to escape from what he called 'the deadening thralldom of materialism and outworn conventions', he adopted – or invented – a sort of sentimental aestheticism based on hazy rose-tinted memories of Shelley and Keats and Chatterton. 'Décadence' (he always gave it its accent) he insisted on seeing as an unhealthy and foreign intruder into the gracious meadows of English poesy. It should, he thought, be weeded out.

When Symons' *Silhouettes* appeared in 1892 Le Gallienne regretted that it had been dated from Paris and disingenuously suggested that the author's enthusiasm for France was really a sign of his provincialism, revealing a strained desire not to appear provincial. Le Gallienne's own book of the same year sounded a counter-note. Its very title was *English Poems*, and its poetic preface reaffirmed Le

Gallienne's position. He claimed to be appalled that 'Youngsters blush to sing an English song'.

> Thou nightingale that for six hundred years
> Sang to the world – O art thou hushed at last!
> For not of thee this new voice in our ears,
> Music of France that once was of the spheres;
> And not of thee these strange green flowers that spring
> From daisy roots and seem to bear a sting.

The twin strains of English decadence were thus singled out and condemned: the 'strange green flowers' would have been recognized by the book's limited public as the green-dyed carnations worn by Oscar Wilde and his favoured disciples; while the 'new voice', the once (but no longer) celestial music of France, was clearly a snipe at Symons' trumpeting of Verlaine. And Le Gallienne extended his attacks on decadence even beyond the preface. Amongst his *English Poems* there was a piece entitled 'The Decadent to his Soul' which charted in very blank verse the decadent's perverse delight in developing his perception of holiness merely to give a keener edge to his sins.

The collection, however, also contained the overheated eroticism of poems such as 'Naera's Hair' ('O thy body, sweet, sweet body,/ Let me drink and drink and drink'), which made full use of the licence assumed by decadent verse, and cast some doubt on the authenticity – or consistency – of Le Gallienne's anti-decadent pose.

It was, nevertheless, a pose that he maintained with increasing assurance. By the end of 1892 he was writing a long article for the *Century Guild Hobby Horse*, mapping out the whole question of 'What is decadence in literature?' He conceded that there was a definite 'decadent style' – which he characterized somewhat confusingly as 'euphuism and its antithesis slang'. But he went on to suggest that true literary decadence was more than a question of style, it was more even than a question of theme. 'It is,' he ventured, 'in the character of the treatment that we must seek it.' Decadence, he thought, was a way of looking at things out of all proportion to their social and moral implications. 'One might say decadence consists in the euphuistic expression of isolated observations.' He condemned Gautier for noting 'only the picturesque effects of a beggar's rags', Huysmans for aestheticizing about a tapster's diseased nose; Whistler for considering his mother 'merely prismatically'. These were examples of the decadent approach: overwritten (or overpainted) delineations of isolated visual impressions. 'At bottom,' Le Gallienne concluded, 'decadence is merely limited thinking, often insane thinking.'

In informed literary circles beyond the Cheshire Cheese there was some bemusement as to what the fuss was about. E. K. Chambers, reviewing *English Poems* in the *Academy*, suggested that outside the confines of the Rhymers' Club 'the note of decadence' was quite undetectable in the work of 'our younger poets'. 'Mr Robert Bridges, Mr William Watson, Mr Alfred Austin, Mrs [Margaret] Woods – they are sane and healthy and "English" enough; they have not made cayenne pepper of their souls.' Indeed, even within the club the vast majority of Rhymers were only too 'sane and healthy' and unpipperaceous. The frequency and energy of Le Gallienne's rodomontades does, however, suggest that the decadent camp – though incoherent – was not entirely without power or support.

Nevertheless, no one, even amongst the more sympathetic Rhymers, seems to have been persuaded by Symons' particular vision of a 'decadent' art forged from the impressionist record of strange sensations. The mark of his isolation can be seen in the poems he wrote on London. Inspired by his readings of Baudelaire, Symons was convinced that the metropolis – the great artificial environment of modern man – must be one of the great subjects of modern verse, 'the very test', as he put it, 'of poetry which professes to be modern'. James Thomson had presented a doleful picture of urban alienation in 'The City of Dreadful Night' (1878); his was a terrible megalopolis, grinding out 'death and life and good and ill' without 'purpose, heart or mind or will'. While Henley, in 1893, produced the more stately pageantry of his *London Volontaries*. Symons admired Henley's achievement, and he seems to have persuaded some of his fellow Rhymers that they should attempt the genre.

Yeats was not to be drawn. He disliked urban life too much; he preferred to sit in the Strand dreaming of the lake isle of Innisfree. Johnson, however, was prepared to contemplate the town, but only from his study window, or through the mystical royalist haze cast by the statue of Charles I at the top of Whitehall. (Le Gallienne commiserated with him in the *Star* when a new electrical street light – a 'monstrosity . . . like some iron upas' – was set up beside 'that sacred statue'). Dowson also retreated, turning from the 'sullen noises of the street' to get on with the serious business of daydreaming. Le Gallienne, though, was less timid. He essayed the 'urban pastoral', a tradition almost neglected since the Restoration and but recently revived by Wilde. Wilde's 'Symphony in Yellow' had happily transformed an omnibus into 'a yellow butterfly', while Le Gallienne in his 'A Ballad of London' turned the whole town into a quaintly ridiculous English country garden where the street lamps are 'iron lilies' and the hansom cabs hover like 'dragonflies'. Le Gallienne, however, could not resist an opportunity for trite moralizing and the enthusiastic floribundance of the opening verses soon gives way to stern warnings about the corruption from whence all this brightness springs, and the ultimate oblivion to which it is all heading.

Only John Davidson amongst the Rhymers took London as his theme and accepted it. His *Fleet Street Eclogues* and modern ballads, however, tell not of the glamour of the metropolis but of its hidden hardships. They are jaunty tales of penurious existence, deceptively simple and wholly unsentimental.

Symons, though he applauded Davidson's work, was interested in a different scene. He loved all that was most modern, most artificial: the evocative world of night-time London, illuminated by the glare of the new electric lights, glimpsed from a passing train or glowing dimly along the Embankment, the 'pavement glittering with fallen rain', the Thames shaking 'with wavery gleams'; it was the shimmering, abstracted vision that Whistler had first summoned up in his 'Nocturnes'. Above all he loved the tawdry world of Leicester Square with its thronging tumultous streets, its crowded bars, its cheap hotels and its music halls.

Fountain Court was barely ten minutes' walk from the pleasures of the Empire and the Alhambra, and Symons made the trip often. From March 1892 he was, as 'Silhouette', the music hall reviewer for the *Star*, and he devoted himself to the task with eagerness. He became, in Yeats' phrase, 'a scholar of the music hall, as another might be a Greek scholar or an authority on the Age of Chaucer'.

The London music halls of the 1890s were one of the glories of the capital. They had grown from their plebeian origins to achieve a degree of respectability, but without losing any of their richness and vitality. To their traditions of sentimental song and audience participation they had added the excitements of dance, of comic monologue, of acrobatic prowess, and prestidigitation. The great houses of the Empire and the Alhambra had become veritable palaces of art. The Tivoli, the Bedford, the Oxford, Gatti's-over-the-water, the Pavilion, and a score of others kept up the popular trade. George Moore considered the music hall amongst the very few good things in Victorian England: 'What delightful unanimity of soul, what community of wit; all knew each other, all enjoyed each other's presence; in a word there was life.'

A list of once great performers accompanied by glowing epithets reads dully, and the world of the 'Lion Comique', the 'Serio', and the coster song, is lost to us. Only the echo of 'Ta-ra-ra-boom-de-ay' has carried down the years. That song, nevertheless, for all its boisterous crudity, remains tinged by the most distinctive and appealing ingredient of the music-hall brew: sex. It was performed by the wasp-waisted Lottie Collins as a sort of delirious Bacchanal. She would begin her performance deceptively, alone upon the spotlit stage, drawing out a long low note and waving a handkerchief gently in time to the orchestra; then, with an explosion of energy, she would place her hands on her hips, kick her legs in the air and move into a frenetic whirling dance, her skirts and her curls swirling about her as she span faster and faster to the piling tempo of the music. It was intoxicating stuff and for Symons it was spiced still further by the piquant disparity between the innocent mien of the dancer and the carnal depravity of her dance. He drank deep.

He found in the music halls a safety valve for the pressure-cooker of repressed Victorian sexuality. It was, he considered, the one place where there was 'a perfectly frank, healthy, and delightful display of the beauty and strength of the human form'. At a time when public pudency had all but banished Terpsichore from the legitimate stage, the music halls were a haven for the ballet, and dance has always been a sexual solvent.

Symons was certainly not alone in his enthusiasm for the halls. Moore was a fan; Max Beerbohm visited them from Oxford; William Rothenstein and Walter Sickert painted them; John Gray lectured upon them; Theodore Wratislaw wrote about them; Herbert Horne, Selwyn Image and Victor Plarr made up – with Symons – 'The Secret Society of the Believers in the Ballet'; and John Davidson's first collection of poems was even called *In a Music Hall.* The reforming clergyman Stewart Headlam ran a Church and Stage Guild which aimed to bring church members and dancers together in an attempt to defend the ballet from the strident condemnation of both pulpit and press. Within the community of art and letters only a few fastidious souls stood out against the prevailing tide; Dowson considered the halls 'unutterable'.

The reasons for the cult were various. The general opprobrium in which the halls were held by respectable persons ('cloistral pedascules' as Beerbohm called them) was quite enough to commend them to many a young iconoclast. Yeats regarded the cult as a

> reaction from the super-refinement of much recent life and poetry. The cultivated man has begun a somewhat hectic search for the common pleasures of common men and for the rough accidents of life. The typical young poet of our day is an aesthete with a surfeit, searching sadly for his lost Philistinism, his heart full of an unsatisfied hunger for the commonplace. He is an Alastor tired of his woods and longing for beer and skittles.

There was some truth in this. A distaste for high culture certainly informed Davidson's music-hall pleasures and poetry. He revelled in the 'rancid and hot' scrimmage. But many of the 'typical young poets of our day' visited the halls to emphasize, rather than to evade, their cultural super-refinement. The vulgarity of the setting merely fixed their cultivated aestheticism in yet higher relief. Beerbohm facetiously claimed to enjoy dicussing the finer points of Hesiod while sitting in the stalls of the Tivoli. Symons was more engaged by the action proceeding before him, but was scarcely less lofty in his attitude. He insisted on considering the music-hall turns as art and himself as the critic best able to explicate them. Yeats' description of him as a 'scholar' of the halls echoed, as well as mocked, Symons' pretensions in this direction.

Symons' professed scholarship was, however, but one aspect of his interest in the music halls. He was drawn to them first and foremost as an amateur of sensation, and on his frequent visits he was for ever trying to refine upon 'the common pleasures of common men'. He delighted always in what was bizarre, strange and modern. The music halls represented what was newest in art, and novelty was always to be applauded. He relished, for example, the 'serpentine dancing' of the American Loie Fuller which – reclaiming the word to its original meaning – he described as 'the sensation of the moment' and recommended to all those interested in 'what is curious, fanciful and *fin de siècle* in dancing'. He sought out new and strange ways of enjoying the acts themselves. At the Empire he would sometimes sit outside the auditorium in the promenade and follow, only by the sound of the music and the exercise of the imagination, every movement of the unseen dance. On another evening, while passing outside the theatre, he caught, 'by some rare felicity of chance', a glimpse of a final tableau when two doors giving on to the auditorium were suddenly thrown open, revealing, 'over the heads of the audience, far off in a sort of blue mist, the whole stage, its brilliant crowd drawn up in the last pose, just as the curtain was beginning to go down'.

The music hall provided Symons with a toy decadent world of which he could become the toy decadent laureate. It was artificial, it was perverse, it was sexually charged, it was overflowing with 'curious and strange and beautiful sensations', it had been ignored by Shakespeare and Shelley and Alfred Lord Tennyson. It was a new Castalian fount, and Symons was determined to win the bottling concession. Though Wratislaw and Plarr might write occasional ditties upon the subject, though Herbert Horne might celebrate in verse his love for one of the chorus dancers at the Alhambra, Symons quickly outdid them all. From 1892 onwards the music hall and its dancers became his abiding theme; his third collection, *London Nights* (1895), contained not only the assertion that 'My life is like a music hall' but also a special section of six poems entitled 'Décor de Théâtre' in which he celebrated the talents of his favourite dancers.

Many of the poems of love or sex that appear in *London Nights* and its predecessor, *Silhouettes*, also owe a debt to the music hall, for the girls described were picked up there. The sexual energy on the stage was rapidly transferred to the auditorium and the promenade, much to the horror of the self-appointed custodian of public decency, Mrs Ormiston Chant. The super-refined young men of Yeats' picture, whatever their elevated attitude to the performance, were often eager to enjoy the all too common performers or the yet more common promenaders. The thrill of this sort of slumming was not apparent to all. Dowson recalled having once met Image and Horne at midnight outside the back door of the Alhambra with a gaggle of 'trivial coryphées'. He considered there to be something 'eminently grotesque in the juxtaposition'; 'Horne very erect & slim and aesthetic – & Image the most dignified man in London, a sort of cross in appearance between a secular abbé & Baudelaire, with a manner du 18me siècle waiting in a back passage' to act escort to ballet girls. Dowson's contempt was deepened further by his belief that, for all this public show, Horne and Image never actually slept with the young women.

Symons, too, very probably exaggerated his own misdemeanours on this front. His privileged position as a critic gave him ready access to both the persons and the affections of the music-hall dancers. Yet, despite his professional familiarity with the milieu, he seems to have retained a touching stage-struck wonder. Just as some people are 'vain about their smart friends and their intimacy with the great so Symons,' according to William Rothenstein, 'was elated at knowing, however distantly, any of the dancers at the Empire or the Alhambra'. He claimed to have fallen 'casually in love' with a great many of them.

He would try to persuade himself – and his friends – that they were exotic, fascinating, perverse creatures, like the acrobat Miss Urania, or the ventriloquist, with whom des Esseintes amused himself in *A Rebours*. Symons once startled Yeats by claiming to have had an affair with a snake-charmer. In truth, however, most of these coryphées were very 'trivial' indeed. Their innocence or ignorance occasionally seasoned an affair, but the dullness of their conversation almost always ensured that the liaisons were brief. Symons recalled his own first Terpsichorean conquest – a dancer at the Alhambra with the suggestive name of Violet Pigott – as pretty, sensual and stupid, before adding with regret that she was 'not perverse'. He remembered how, while waiting for her once in Chalk Farm Road, he had come across a rare copy of Balzac's *Le Livre mystique* on a bookstall and had suddenly felt a pulse of excitement that the prospect of seeing Miss Pigott had singularly failed to produce. Art, as always, was preferable to life.

Symons could only maintain his interest by indulging in a variety, or succession, of such monotonies. Although his evil reputation existed most clearly in his own lurid imagination, his poems, notebooks and letters do attest to a steady stream of 'light loves': to Emmy 'in the midst of the villainous dancing-halls,/Leaning across the table, over the beer,'; to Renée with her 'sensitive, vaguely ironical mouth'; to Nora dancing on the pavement, 'innocently spendthrift of herself'; to Violet (not Pigott) trembling 'upon the verge of some new dawn'; to the innocent young girl in the poem 'Dawn'. He picked them up, let them down, and then 'immortalized' the shoddy transaction in minor verse. The experiences he described were – to conventional readers – novel and shocking, and his treatment of them – impressionist yet explicit – was scarcely less so.

The outcry that was raised against him was not, as has been seen, confined to the reactionary press. Richard Le Gallienne's *The Religion of a Literary Man* contained a spirited attack upon the cult of 'the demi-monde and the music hall', satirizing what he saw as the current desire that 'every one may be as indecent as his heart wishes, and he who loves the gutter may lie therein without reproach'. This critique, though it did not mention Symons in person, would have touched him in every phrase. Certainly it provoked him to a reply.

Throughout the summer of 1893 he worked on an article about literary decadence for *Harper's New Monthly Magazine* which he believed would serve as a defence of his position. Regrouping the terminology of Johnson's *Hobby-Horse* article, he suggested that literary decadence could be divided into two strains, impressionism and symbolism. Both, he claimed, were concerned with '*la vrai vérité* – the very essence of truth', but impressionism dealt with 'the truth of appearance to the senses, of the visible world to the eyes that see it', while symbolism attempted to reveal 'the truth of spiritual things to the spiritual vision' – a more nebulous concept, which he left suitably undefined.

He believed that this new movement showed 'all the qualities that mark the end of great periods, the qualities we find in the Greek, the Latin decadence': that 'intense self-consciousness', the 'restless curiosity in research', the 'over-subtilizing refinement upon refinement', the 'spiritual and moral perversity'. He likened it to a 'new and beautiful and interesting disease', but a disease that found an affinity with the already corrupted body on which it settled; '[it] reflects all the moods, all the manners of a sophisticated society; its very artificiality is a way of being true to nature.'

The decadent society bred a decadent outlook, according to Symons, and the decadent outlook required the expression of a decadent style. In France, he thought, this style had first been forged in prose by the Goncourts, whose 'écriture artiste' was itself 'almost sensation', and in verse by Verlaine, who had the rare ability, through nuance and suggestion, to 'fix the last fine shade, the quintessence of things; to fix it fleetingly; to be a disembodied voice and yet the voice of a human soul'. It is noteworthy, if unsurprising, that both these examples belong more to the impressionist than the symbolist strain of decadence. It was the ability to fix 'physical' impressions that Symons admired most in the Goncourts and Verlaine. Even when discussing Mallarmé, the acknowledged master of symbolism, he chose to praise his 'irregular, unquiet, expressive' syntax for the 'new capacities' it gave 'for the exact noting of sensation'. In the summer of 1893 his grasp of the transcendental possibilities of symbolism was still weak.

His general knowledge of the movement, however, was impressively broad. To lend weight to his thesis and to show that the movement was not just an unfortunate Gallic eccentricity, he looked beyond Huysmans, Villiers et al to the rest of Europe. He found examples of decadence in the Spain of Señora Pardo-Bazan, in the Holland of the sensitivists, in the Italy of D'Annunzio, and even in England. On the home front he pressed 'the prose of Mr Walter Pater' and 'the verse of W. E. Henley' into service. He considered them as 'attempts to do with the English language something of what Goncourt and Verlaine have done with the French', Pater by 'that morbid subtlety of analysis, that morbid curiosity of form', Henley by his 'impressionism of the moment'.

The choice of Pater is understandable, even though it would have distressed that don's fastidious and retiring temper to be forced into a spotlight together with the disreputable Paul Verlaine. Henley, however, was a curious conscript. He was bluff, he was hearty, he hated self-consciousness and affectation, he was – Yeats tells us – affected by Pre-Raphaelitism as some people are affected by a cat in the room. The circle of young writers that he gathered about himself at the *National Observer* formed a sort of unofficial opposition to the young writers who gathered at the Cheshire Cheese. Some have even suggested that Symons included him as a joke. It is true that 'In Hospital' – Henley's cycle of 'rhymes and rhythms' recounting the amputation of his leg in the Edinburgh Royal Infirmary – smacks more of 'realism' and 'Rabelaisian heartiness' (as the *Athenaeum*'s reviewer put it) than of 'spiritual and moral perversity'. His position was grim, and it is described as such; there is some humour and much courage but no sense of the beauty of ugliness. Nevertheless, there is much 'morbid curiousity of form' (not least the author's own), and there is a veritable jamboree of personal sensations and impressions. It was these last details that Symons particularly noted and considered particularly to be the marks of decadence in literature. It was what he admired so much in Verlaine's verse. It was what he aimed after in his own. By linking the established and unexpected names of Pater and Henley to his own practice he hoped to give decadence a broader base.

Even before the appearance of the *Harper's* piece at the end of 1893, Symons' reputation as Verlaine's English champion was recognized. Earlier in the year the young painter William Rothenstein, who for four years had been studying in Paris and had bustled his way determinedly into the circles of artistic excellence with all the energy of a new George Moore, had the idea of organizing an English reading tour for the impoverished Verlaine. He was advised to approach Symons, and he found in him a willing cohort. Symons was able to mobilize his not inconsiderable forces to assist the project.

He agreed to put Verlaine up in his spare room at Fountain Court; he hired the hall at Barnards Inn as a venue for the lecture; he persuaded Edmund Gosse to act as chairman for the occasion; he galvanized Horne and John Lane into assisting with the arrangements; he persuaded Horne's current mistress, Muriel Broadbent, to come and make up the bed; he alerted the press, he had tickets printed (with a face value of ten shillings). He did everything within his powers to ensure that literary and artistic London attended the auspicious event.

Verlaine's visit at the end of November was certainly enjoyable, even successful, but it was not quite the Coming of Decadence that Symons perhaps hoped for. The French poet limped into Fountain Court at 2.30 am on the morning before his lecture. The crossing had been delayed by storms. He was carrying a small valise and leaning on a large stick. Symons was waiting to help his visitor upstairs. There he regaled him with neat gin and Osborne biscuits, and kept him talking excitedly until five. The next morning Verlaine realized that he had forgotten to bring any of his books to read from. Symons leant him his own copy of *Sagesse*. Gosse arrived at eleven and took them to lunch at Court's. Horne and Muriel called in for tea at Fountain Court around four. And at seven the three men went on to sup with the publisher William Heinemann in a private room at the Roma. From there they proceeded along Holborn to Barnard's Inn.

The meeting was held in what Verlaine recalled as 'an extraordinary hall, very ancient, of a sort of rustic Gothic . . . sincere, *natural*, and marvellous in its simplicity'. Arthur Waugh (the father of Evelyn), who was reporting the event for the American press, characterized the audience as 'a strange little crowd of critics and poets, artists and musicians'. Verlaine hobbled to the platform, leaning heavily on 'the arm of Mr Arthur Symons, his most active supporter in this country'. 'Michael Field', who was one (if not two) of the 'poets' in this strange little crowd, considered that Symons, next to his mentor, looked like 'a rose bush beside a blasted thorn'. Despite reading the lecture in French, in a low tone, and seated behind a large oak table, Verlaine was well received. With an engaging informality he cited his objections to the *vers libre* experiments of some of the younger French poets and urged instead the virtues of absolute sincerity and absolute conscientiousness. He concluded what he considered to have been a 'delicious hour' by reading some poems from Symons' copy of *Sagesse.* This, Waugh reported, 'caused a positive thrill to pass through the audience'.

Although it appears to have been an eminently respectable performance, such was Verlaine's reputation that some among his highly suggestible listeners were able to derive a delightful *frisson* of alarm from the event. 'Michael Field' confided approvingly to her diary that Verlaine had been 'very, *very* judicious in the choice of his poems, and there was not a trace of "vine leaves in his hair" – I was going to write, but I must rather say round his beautiful, bald skull.' But she added, with an albeit ironical note, that it had been 'such an English scene – Satan in a frock-coat, reading religious poetry and darting pitch-spark glances at a company incapable of understanding the tragedies of hell (even the devils believe and tremble), still less its bouts of free revel.'

Verlaine himself was not up to much in the way of free revelling. His foot was causing him considerable discomfort and the next morning Symons took him to see a doctor. Then, after a visit to the Bodley Head, they returned home to receive visitors; Dowson called by, as did John Lane, Alfred Dolmetsch (the musician), Hubert Crackanthorpe, Horne and the long-suffering Muriel. At seven Symons took Verlaine to dine at the Globe with Gosse and Heinemann, and then on to the Alhambra for a performance by the Chicago Ballet. As they arrived at the theatre Verlaine confided mysteriously that he dated 'all his misfortunes from a woman he met on coming out of there twenty years ago'.The evening ended amongst familiar faces in the happy crush of the Crown.

Before leaving the following morning Verlaine autographed the wall of Symons' room, just below a little crucifix that (for the sake of affectation, it must be supposed) hung there. While Symons went down to Cornwall to stay with Havelock Ellis, Verlaine took the train up to Oxford, where Rothenstein was waiting for him. He had lunch with Professor York Powell and a select group of undergraduates (including Max Beerbohm), before telling the scarcely larger group which had gathered in the back-room of Blackwell's bookshop to hear his views on poetry that 'to be an artist it is necessary to be absolutely oneself'.

After three days of good behaviour Verlaine did, at last, manage a bohemian flourish. On his return to London he proceeded to drink all the profits from the two readings in a single weekend. In desperation a further reading was hastily arranged in Manchester by a friend of York Powell's, and Verlaine was not given his share of the receipts until he was boarding the boat train for Paris.

The appearance of the *Harper's* piece, coinciding with Verlaine's visit, might have been expected to produce a wave of interest in – and understanding of – Symons' vision of literary decadence. It did not happen. Verlaine was viewed as an interesting curiosity, while the *Harper*'s article merely provided the opposition with a clearer target.

If Verlaine had shown the two sides of his nature during his brief visit, Symons too was wandering deeper into a double-life. It was at this time that he met Lydia, a nineteen-year-old chorus dancer from the Empire. She was, or so Symons claimed, the illegitimate daughter of a Spanish gipsy and an Englishwoman, and certainly the surviving photographs of her reveal a sensual Romany beauty. For Lydia's character and, indeed, the progress of their affair, we have, of course, to rely on Symons' highly dramatized record in both verse and prose.

Symons became fascinated with her over the footlights. Their eyes had met and he had noted with excitement her 'painted, enigmatical, nervous smile'; a smile, in short, that contained the very elements of the decadent equation: the beauty of artifice, the fatal mystery of the *Mona Lisa*, and the taint of neurosis. Symons waited for her after the show.

Reading between the lines of Symons' account it would appear that for all her flashing looks Lydia was rather dull, slightly prudish and motivated almost entirely by an overweening vanity. Symons indeed admitted this last charge, claiming that the only two things that really interested her were her own beauty and the amount of attention it received. He recalled once setting her down from a cab outside the theatre and, in his absorption with her, nearly giving the cabman a sovereign instead of a shilling. When he told her of it she had remarked with real feeling, 'Oh I wish you had. It would have been to my glory.'

Lydia was content to accept Symons' attentions, although with a certain passiveness. As the affair advanced she surrendered more to her sensual nature, but she would never say very much and even Symons complained of her lack of *esprit.* Nevertheless, across the blank page of her essential dullness he sketched elaborate fantasies of depravity. He dwelt fondly upon the opposition between her prudishness and her sensuality. Here was a girl who was 'virtuous in the sense which the world uses it', who had outfaced the casting-couch demands of the Empire's toad-like proprietor, who refused to look at the nude pictures Symons tried to show her unless he would first turn away; and yet – when he finally coaxed her into bed and she responded to his kisses, which before she had only ever 'accepted' – she was 'elemental, primitive', like a tigress, or one of the Bacchic women Pater tells of, or – indeed – like any other one of the stock *femmes fatales* in the decadent pantheon.

Symons was fascinated by this dichotomy; it was precisely the spark of perversity that he needed to ignite his passion. Lydia, however, seems to have been perplexed and put out by such notions. She clearly came to enjoy the sex and to demand a great deal of it, but she saw nothing 'abnormal' or 'perverse' in such appetites. 'I am not strange,' she once complained. 'I am just like other girls; I don't want to be different from other people.' Symons cheerfully ignored such outbursts of mundanity, so caught up had he become in his self-conscious mythologizing. Sometimes Lydia apeared to him as a vampire, sometimes as a Medusa, or even as a faintly corrupted saint 'such as Luini loved to paint'.

Symons of course wanted to be different from other people. It was, he felt, his duty as an artist to be so. He relished the double-life that his passion for Lydia demanded. For, despite his bohemian habits and appetities, he still had some contact with respectable circles; he even maintained a flirtatious friendship with Katherine Willard, the daughter of an American dancing-teacher (and the dedicatee of *Silhouettes*), which might – but for his other interests – have ripened into an attachment. From decorous gatherings and suppers he would slip enigmatically away in order to be at the Empire's stage door by eleven.

His poetry, perhaps under the spell of Lydia's sexuality, was becoming even more flagrantly erotic. When John Lane launched his new literary periodical, *The Yellow Book*, in April 1894, Symons' contribution, a poem about a prostitute provocatively entitled 'Stella Maris', was – along with Aubrey Beardsley's drawings and Max Beerbohm's satire upon cosmetics – singled out for special opprobrium. Even Philip Hammerton, the critic who reviewed the first issue of *The Yellow Book* for the second, regretted the inclusion of a piece that applied the title from 'one of the most beautiful hymns to the Holy Virgin' to 'a London street walker . . . a star in the dark sea of urban life'. Although Hammerton claimed that there was no necessary connection between art and morality, he did think that the line had to be drawn somewhere, and 'why should poetic art be employed to celebrate common fornication?'

The opposition to Symons' provocative themes continued to harden throughout 1894. It was as if the Victorian establishment had become alarmed at the licence it had granted and was anxious to reassert control. During October the public was entertained by the deliberations of the Licencing Committee of the London County Council upon the subject of 'soliciting' on the promenade at the Empire. Symons contributed to the debate with a letter in the *Pall Mall Gazette*, which suavely regretted that as vice cannot be suppressed it can only be regulated, and claimed that by and large 'the question of women' was handled with 'really commendable discretion' at the Empire. Such an unapologetic stance can only have focused disapproval upon him

On the appearance of *The Second Book of the Rhymers' Club* both he and Dowson (whose 'Cynara' was included in the anthology) were condemned amidst the general chorus of faint praise. The *Nation*'s reviewer was prepared to forgive Dowson but excoriated 'the sickly and jaunty sensualism of Mr Arthur Symons, who represents the low-water mark of the "Rhymers' Club".' And when Symons submitted the poems of *London Nights* to the Bodley Head at the end of the year, John Davidson's 'reader's report', despite its praise for the 'very notable' technical accomplishment (and, indeed, its cautious recommendation of an edition of three hundred copies), presented a picture of Symons' poetic world as 'an embodiment of desire . . . utterly lonely and unimpassioned – mere and shere libidinous desire'. This was quite enough to scare off John Lane, who had recently dissolved his partnership with Elkin Matthews and was reverting rapidly to his natural caution. William Heinemann rejected it as well.

It was with some desperation that Symons turned to the splendidly improbable figure of Leonard Smithers. Smithers, then in his thirties, was only just establishing his reputation. He was a large, pasty-faced solicitor from Sheffield who had befriended the famous traveller and polymath, Sir Richard Burton. During the late 1880s Smithers had assisted Burton in his translation work for the later volumes of *The Arabian Nights*, as well as various other books of oriental and classical erotica. After Burton's death in 1890, Smithers, abandoning the law (but retaining his Yorkshire brogue), had come to London and gone into partnership with a Soho printer. Together they had continued to publish Burton's translations of erotic classics, while Smithers also dealt in literary curiosities, pictures and 'absurd and ill-written pornography'. The partnership was dissolved at the beginning of 1895, but Smithers determined to continue and expand the business on his own. He had a complete lack of moral squeamishness and a ready grasp of the commercial possibilities to be derived from shocking the public. It would become his boast that he would 'publish anything that the others are afraid of'. That Symons' manuscript had been turned down by Lane and Heinemann was for him quite enough recommendation. He agreed to bring the book out in June.

Symons and Smithers, however, were not the only figures of the period steering a course deliberately close to the chill wind of Victorian disapproval. Oscar Wilde's increasingly open infatuation with Lord Alfred Douglas was already beginning to threaten scandal. Although Symons and Wilde had been acquainted since Symons' youthful offer to write a piece on Villiers de l'Isle Adam for *Woman's World*, the two men, despite their shared interest in French literature, had never been close. Wilde tediously insisted on mispronouncing Symons' name, giving it a long 'i'; and he would deliberately ignore Symons' claims as a poet, amusing his friends instead with a routine based on the conviction that, because Symons produced so much journalistic work, he must – in fact – be a front for a syndicate. 'I have written to my solicitor,' Wilde would say, 'to enquire about shares in Symons Ltd. Naturally in mass-production of that kind you can never be quite certain of the quality. But I think one might risk some shares in Symons.'

Symons for his part regarded Wilde with a half-reluctant admiration. He recognized, however, that Wilde 'was shadowed and tracked by an evil reputation which had grown, not suddenly, but like a growth of mushrooms'. This reputation, nurtured in the dark, was finally exposed to the glare of day at the beginning of 1895.

Part III

The Cult of Celebrity

Chapter Seven

'It is personalities,' wrote Oscar Wilde, 'not principles that shape an Age.' And certainly the 1890s derived much of their decadent outline from the impress of Wilde's own personality. Wilde did – and does – tower over the period. Fluent, captivating, oracular, generous and faintly absurd, he was a pervading presence. His paradoxes, his extravagances, even his works, survive to this day; at the time they were inescapable. He came to be regarded by his contemporaries as the 'High Priest of the Decadents', and he was not short of a congregation.

Nevertheless, he presented his disciples with a problem. If Symons had too little personality to lead a movement, Wilde had perhaps too much. Symons was too dim a pilot-light, Wilde too bright. Inadvertently he blinded many of his followers with his brilliance. Some fled from the great flame, some drew close and were scorched; only a few dared to steal the fire. It was these different responses to Wilde's refulgent greatness that lent to English decadence some of its happiest – and some of its dullest – effects.

To Wilde and his admirers the word 'personality' carried a particular weight; it referred to that deliberately cultivated self which stood above, and against, rude, innate 'character'. The 'first duty in life', according to Wilde, was to 'assume a pose'. He himself assumed many during the course of his own life, but he always adopted a variation upon the aesthetic ideal of the dandy-artist: entirely above animal passion, acutely sensitive to every sensation, and in everything concerned only with beauty.

The revival of dandyism – limited though it was – remains a distinctive feature of the nineties, and particularly that corner of the nineties presided over by Wilde. The elaborate demands of dress, the scrupulous frivolities of the toilet, were a considered rebuke to the Victorian creeds of utility and seriousness. At one level they introduced the cares of art into the exercise of life; at another they harkened back to the irresponsible pre-Victorian age of the Regency, when Brummell and Nash had enlivened St James's, Bath and Brighton with the cut of their coats and the height of their stocks.

Dandyism had, moreover, received the sanction of Baudelaire. In the actions of his own life and in the pages of *Le Peintre de la vie moderne* he had championed the cause of artificiality and distinction. To the implacable enemy of nature and democracy, '*le dandysme*' was nothing less than 'the last gleam of heroism in times of decadence'. It was an attempt to establish a new élite at a moment of rising uniformity. The dandy, for Baudelaire, marked out 'the aristocratic superiority of [his] mind' by the elegant distinction of his dress; he was fired by 'the burning need to create an originality for oneself within the limits of decorum', to have 'the pleasure of astonishing and the proud satisfaction of never being astonished'. Dandyism was the 'cult of oneself'.

Wilde, though he was familiar with Baudelaire's manifesto, never achieved the fierce moral vision it put forward. His own brand of dandyism tended more towards playful subversion and self-advertisement. Baudelaire's dandiacal tenet that one 'is what one appears' offered a sly commentary upon the hypocrisies of conventional middle-class Victorianism, which – behind the concern for 'keeping up appearances' – fostered so many species of greed, dishonesty and perversion; while the apparently effeminate fascination with clothes presented a counterbalance to the boyish excesses of the so-called 'new woman'. As women increasingly sought the freedom of new spheres of activity – of stenography and medicine, of bicycling and tennis, of politics and cigarette-smoking – so men (as if to re-establish some cosmic equilibrium) turned to the cares of the wardrobe and the pleasures of the florist.

Of all Baudelaire's comments upon the dandy's way the one that appealed most readily to Wilde was that concerning 'the pleasure of astonishing'. Wilde, whatever the particular line of his jacket, was always determined to shock the middle classes – a determination which was, of course, in its own way thoroughly middle-class. Certainly he knew his audience well and was able to play up to its expectations with dazzling success. In an era that had abandoned the traditions of aristocratic patronage (and with only a limited private income of his own), Wilde recognized early that the artist must court the paying public. He recognized the virtue of having an identifiable persona. And he recognized, too, the possibilities of a courtship based on extravagantly shunning the very public he sought to gain. He was an early adept at self-publicity, and he projected his image through the willing press on to the eager public with unprecedented *élan*.

By 1889 he had metamorphosed through some of his more startling poses, past the brilliant but bumptious Oxford undergraduate and beyond the long-haired 'aesthete' who had lectured upon beauty with a lily in his hand; he had shed the thick-clustering Neronian curls acquired in Paris and the Byronic collars affected in New York. At the brink of the new decade he was thirty-five, decently shorn and elegantly dressed. He was married with two young sons (Cyril four and Vyvyan three) and living in the trim suburban comfort of Tite Street, Chelsea. He had published little that displayed the distinctive mark of 'decadence', but then he had published little altogether. He had produced a volume of lush poems, a collection of charming fairy-stories, two tedious tragedies and some amusing essays. He had lectured widely upon art, beauty and domestic furnishing, and had served a two-year stint as editor of the *Woman's World*. The only arts of which he could claim a complete mastery were those of self-promotion and conversation. The sharp thrusts of his repartee, the elegant turns of his wit, the smooth flow of his anecdotes, were all clamorously reported and repeated – at first by himself, but very soon by others.

Yet already there was a rift within the body of his achievement. For although Wilde always wore the mask of the dandy-artist, it was a mask that had two distinct aspects – the poetic and the ironic. Just as there was a bifurcation between Wilde's 'personality' and his 'character', so within his self-created persona there was a further division. His work already showed the distinctive marks of this divide: his poems and plays strained after seriousness and intensity, his lectures and short stories (being closer to his conversation) sparkled with paradoxical wit. In the former mode Wilde was self-conscious in his quest for effect – and his desire to be taken seriously; in the latter he was self-aware and self-deprecating. The ideas and practice of the decadent tradition would make an appeal to both these sides of Wilde's artistic personality.

*

At the start of the new decade Wilde's great rival as a wit – and as a self-publicist – was the expatriate American artist James McNeill Whistler. Throughout the 1880s the epigrammatic banter of their point-scoring friendship-cum-emnity was frequently (and at their own insistence) published in the press. And for the convenience of those who might have missed out the first time around Whistler provided – in 1890 – a full résumé in his manual of decorous spite, *The Gentle Art of Making Enemies*. The painter had fallen out with the poet partly from habit and partly because he claimed that Wilde (who was twenty years his junior) had plagiarized his ideas upon art.

For many years Wilde had been juggling with the essentially incompatible artistic theories of Pater and Ruskin, the one tending towards artistic autonomy and perfection of form, the other stressing the social responsibilities of art and importance of content. At the time of his American lecture tour in 1882, the Ruskinian influence had been strongest. The beautification of the home was seen by Wilde as the prelude to happiness, and the acquisition of blue-and-white china as the first step towards virtue. During the course of the eighties, however, the balance – although it continued to vacillate – moved increasingly towards the Paterian pole. Under the influence of French ideas – either met with directly in Paris or received via the francophilic and proprietorial Whistler – Wilde veered more and more towards the extremes of formalism and the elevation of art above life.

At the beginning of the 1890s Wilde published two books that sounded the note of a decadent aestheticism more strongly than ever before, as well as giving fuller substance to his reputation. *Intentions* gathered his thoughts upon aesthetics, *The Picture of Dorian Gray* projected some of those thoughts into dramatic action. Both of these works, however, announced their decadent ideas from behind an ironic mask.

The four essays of *Intentions* did not pretend to offer a coherent philosophy. The book's very title suggested its tentative nature. There were loose ends and even contradictions, but behind them loomed a gathering force of belief that borrowed heavily from the traditions of France. The portrait of Thomas Wainwright in 'Pen, Pencil and Poison' cast that artist-forger-murderer as a Baudelairean dandy, disdaining the morality of the herd and enhancing his personality – and hence his art – through a life of crime. 'The Critic as Artist' was a lengthy duologue asserting the claims of subjective criticism to a place equal or even above artistic creativity: for if art was the criticism of life, 'criticism' was the criticism of art, and – as any disciple of Gautier or Mallarmé knew – art was superior to life. In such company 'The Truth of Masks' was an anomaly, a *réchauffé* of an old plea for historically accurate costume design in Shakespearian play-productions. The piece was distinguished only by the paradoxical title at its head and the unabashed disclaimer at its end.

The fourth and most interesting essay – the best of *Intentions* – was 'The Decay of Lying' (which had first appeared at the beginning of 1889 in the *Nineteenth Century*). It was Wilde's most definite statement of decadent theories. The piece was cast as a duologue between two amiable exquisites, Cyril and Vivian, and the conversational form was perfectly suited to Wilde's ironic mode. In fact it is virtually a one-man show, with Cyril offering little more than the occasional line and cigarette, while Vivian reads out lengthy extracts from an article he is writing for the 'Retrospective Review' (house journal of the Tired Hedonists). The preoccupations of this imaginary club – faded roses, the memory of Domitian and the pleasures of boredom – introduced a note of self-parody into Wilde's exposition of his new creed, leaving the readers in some doubt as to how seriously they were to take what followed.

The theme of the essay was the relationship between art and reality, and its style was founded, like Wilde's conversation, upon the interplay of paradoxes. The argument was two-pronged and although there was an apparent contradiction between the two prongs, they shared a common origin in the theories of Gautier, Baudelaire and the later *décadents*. First Wilde contended that art is entirely free from all responsibilities, not only from the moral and social duties that many Victorians considered part of art's sphere, but even from an obligation to objective reality. Nature, he suggested, was not a fit model for the artist, such was her 'lack of design . . . her extraordinary monotony, her absolutely unfinished condition'. The artist, self-conscious and deliberate, must rely on his own craft and imagination (or 'lying', as Wilde provocatively called it) to create a fresh truth.

Upon this premise Wilde erected a new aesthetic hierarchy, working downwards from 'decorative art' (which bore no relation to life), via 'imaginative art' (which at least allowed the artist to reforge the crude forms of external reality), to 'realism', which Wilde neatly dubbed the 'real decadence'. Having set art above nature and isolated it from reality, Wilde then proceeded to re-mix the opposed elements.

Again he inverted the established order and claimed that it was not art that imitated life, but the reverse. Hamlet's dictum about 'art holding up a mirror to nature' was said, Wilde suggested, only 'to convince the bystanders of his absolute insanity in all art matters'. Art provides the forms through which life can then find expression, and even nature only shows us 'effects that we have already seen through poetry, or in paintings': Rossetti created the women his painting seemed to depict; only after Turner did people start seeing sunsets; only after Whistler did they recognize fogs; and indeed the whole nineteenth century was 'largely the invention of Balzac'.

The influence of these significant forms might be for good or ill – a beautiful Greek statue set in a bridal chamber could make the bride's children beautiful, an account of Dick Turpin's exploits could prompt a boy to apple-pilfering – it need not concern the artist. His aim was merely the creation of these puissant images, 'the telling of beautiful untrue things'. Wilde's position was an advance even beyond the precepts of Gautier's famous 'Preface'. And he mixed his subversive, decadent aesthetic with a liveliness and wit that made it doubly beguiling.

The Picture of Dorian Gray, Wilde's only novel, first appeared in the July 1890 number of *Lippincott's Monthly Magazine*. It was then published in book form – with the addition of six new chapters and an epigrammatic preface – in April of the following year. Although Wilde did not follow all the strictures laid down by Vivian regarding the novelist's art (he employed a modern setting, he touched upon the 'lower orders' and he displayed at least a superficial assiduity of research), the story is not unworthy of being called 'a beautiful untrue thing'.

Wilde told the tale of the ridiculously handsome Dorian Gray, who wished that he might remain for ever youthful while his portrait (painted by the enraptured Basil Hallward) took on the marks of age and high-living, and who found his wish strangely granted. Dorian is seduced by the hedonistic philosophy spun by the brilliant but disengaged Lord Henry Wooton. He devotes his life to pleasure – no matter how depraved. He drives the poor actress Sybil Vane to suicide by spurning her when she falls in love with him and loses her artistic talent. He kills Basil Hallward when the artist discovers the secret of the corrupted portrait and remonstrates with its subject. And then, eventually, disgusted with what the picture reveals has become of his soul, he stabs the image and thereby kills himself.

The story in both its published forms provoked considerable interest and critical abuse. Some found in it a 'malodorous putrefaction', others an 'esoteric prurience'. The *St James's Gazette* wondered whether the Treasury or the Vigilance Society might consider prosecution; while the *Daily Chronicle* thought it 'a poisonous book . . . spawned from the leprous literature of the French decadents'. And indeed the book was in many respects an English setting of *A Rebours*. It has much more plot, many more characters and rather less literary worth, but it is like Huysmans' work – a tragedy of the decadent sensibility. Dorian, like des Esseintes before him, abandons himself to every sensual experience in an effort to make his life into a work of art, and – like his predecessor – is led on, not to some unlooked for epiphany, but to self-destruction.

Huysmans' book even makes a veiled but recognizable appearance in Wilde's story. Its entrance indeed is decisive in leading Dorian on to his fatal course. This touch, however, revealed one of the essential differences between the French *décadence* and its English reflection; for while des Esseintes was prompted to his curious mode of existence by a pathological condition, Dorian is driven to his by the promptings of a plausible philosophy and the example of Huysmans' book. Dorian's conversion by Lord Henry Wooton presents a telling microcosm of the English decadent experience: Lord Henry, speaking in the unmistakable accents of Wilde himself, weans the impressionable Dorian upon an extreme misreading of Pater's 'Conclusion' and then rounds off his diet with the gift of a naughty French novel.

The origins of Lord Henry's philosophy would have been clear to most readers:

> Yes, there was to be, as Lord Henry had prophesied, a new hedonism that was to recreate life, and to save it from that harsh, uncomely puritanism that is having, in our own day, its curious revival. It was to have its service of the intellect certainly; yet it was never to accept any theory or system that would involve the sacrifice of any mode of passionate experience. Its aim, indeed, was to be experience itself and not the fruits of experience, sweet or bitter as they might be. Of the asceticism that deadens the senses, of the vulgar profligacy that dulls them, it was to know nothing. But it was to teach man to concentrate himself upon the moments of a life that is in itself but a moment.

The phraseology echoed, where it did not copy, the words of Pater's famous exhortation. But Lord Henry has chosen to ignore all those cautious qualifications that Pater elucidated so carefully in *Marius the Epicurean*, by which 'fullness of life' and moral 'insight' were set above 'pleasure' as the true guides of existence. (Pater himself noted this oversight when reviewing the novel in the *Bookman.*) Lord Henry, however, takes the words of the 'conclusion' at their lowest possible value and reduces life to a safari amongst intense momentary experiences, sought and enjoyed for their aesthetic impact only. The moral perspective is obliterated to the extent that Lord Henry convinces Dorian to look even upon 'evil' as 'simply a mode through which he could realize his conception of the beautiful'.

Lord Henry backs up his own eloquence (and Wilde points to his own sources) with the gift of a yellow-bound French novel, which fascinates and corrupts the young Dorian. The book is unnamed and uncredited, and although Wilde had originally thought of calling it '*Le Secret de Raoul*' by 'Catulle Sarrazin', in the final proofs he wisely deleted this clumsy conflation of Catulle Mendès, Gabriel Sarrazin and the hero of Rachilde's *Monsieur Venus*. The invention would have been unhelpful as, from the description of the book's contents (and by Wilde's own admission), the corrupting work was clearly 'a fantastic variation' upon *A Rebours*: 'A novel without a plot and with only one character', 'a psychological study of a young Parisian' written in 'a curious jewelled style, vivid and obscure', 'a poisonous book' to which 'the heavy odour of incense seemed to cling'.

Wilde lightly confused some of the details of the real *A Rebours*; his hero has an enthusiasm for late Roman Emperors and the misdeeds of the Renaissance, as well as an abhorrence of mirrors, which find no exact equivalents in Huysmans' original. But the central strand of artificial sensation-seeking was taken directly from the French book, and Wilde – the author – as much as Dorian – the hero – confesses the debt when he says that the unnamed novel 'seemed to contain the story of his [Dorian's] life, written before he had lived it'.

Although many of Wilde's critics considered *The Picture of Dorian Gray* 'disgusting' – and W. H. Smith refused to stock it – some affected surprise that the author allowed his hero to come to such a bad end; that the story, in other words, had a moral (or contained, as Charles Whibley facetiously put it in his *National Observer* review, 'lots of morality'). Wilde gracefully lamented the presence of the said moral, considering it, from the artistic standpoint, 'the only error in the book'. He recognized, however, that no other ending was possible; that the extreme aestheticism of the decadent lifestyle was a self-destructive cul-de-sac.

In *Dorian Gray* – as in 'The Decay of Lying' – the expounder of decadent ideas is a wit who proceeds by paradox; but in the novel the detached teacher has a pupil who attempts to put the ideas into practice. Lord Henry Wooton delineates the charms of decadence but it is Dorian who tries to enjoy them. In the attempt he destroys himself. Moreover, he is not amusing in the process. One of the awkwardnesses of the novel is the way it alternates between the lucid wit of the passages in which Lord Henry advocates the new hedonism and the meretricious tedium of those which describe Dorian's fall. This dichotomy – between the ironic and the poetic – marked (as has been suggested) all Wilde's work but only in *Dorian Gray* do the two unmixable elements appear so conspicuously side by side.

For his next literary production Wilde adopted his poetic mask exclusively. Flushed with the success of his novel he went to Paris to visit the *décadents* and to write a new play. *Salome* was a deliberate attempt to compose a 'decadent' drama, or, since '*symbolisme*' was the fashionable cry in Paris in 1891, a decadent-symbolist drama. Mixing the elements of Flaubert's *Hérodias*, Maeterlinck's plays, the Bible, and the paintings of Moreau as described by Huysmans, Wilde served up a lurid picture of the Judean princess as a *femme fatale*, a heartless and predatory virgin who desires the head of John the Baptist so that she can kiss it on the mouth and gratify a lust that he – in life – forbade.

Wilde even wrote the play in French to ally himself more closely to those decadent writers who, he felt, had achieved distinction and forged a new beauty. By using a foreign tongue he also set a distance between the play and the ironic English accents of *Intentions* and Lord Henry Wooton. The diction throughout is jewelled and heavy and slow, the atmosphere oppressive with perverse eroticism.

Although both *Salomé* and *Dorian Gray* were brilliant artificial creations in which art triumphed to the exclusion of nature, this decadent imbalance was impossible to maintain beyond the page. Indeed, even on the page the relationship between art and life was often more confused than if first appeared. Wilde would come to admit that he had put 'much of himself' into his novel.

To one correspondent he explained, 'Basil Hallward is what I think I am: Lord Henry what the world thinks me: Dorian what I would like to be . . . in other ages perhaps.' The confession is revealing on several counts. Wilde's self-identification with the upright Hallward suggests that his regard for convention, even conventional morality, was much greater that his outward – Henry Wooton-ish – pose would allow; while his apparently vain desire to be like Dorian seems to hint at a wish not only for eternal youth and beauty at a time when his own looks were fading, but also for strange sins and the mysteries of a double-life. Ironically, at the time of the book's publication, he was moving deeper into just such water.

The exact course of Wilde's homosexual education is not known. From his schooldays on he happily indulged a taste for those emotional male friendships which the Victorians, brought up on Greek literature, regarded as both normal and desirable. His extravagance of dress and manner, and his peculiar swaying walk, did, however, lead some to question his sexual proclivities. Edmond de Goncourt on meeting Wilde in 1883 had considered him '*au sexe douteux*'.

Nevertheless, doubtful or not, Wilde married Constance Lloyd in 1884, and fathered two sons in the succeeding years. For a while he was a conventionally good father and considerate husband, but his enthusiasm for the domestic idyll soon began to wane. Intimations of his fascination for the homosexual milieu began to beset him. He developed an enthusiasm for talking about the great homosexuals of history – Plato, Michelangelo, James I. He eagerly discussed the acts of homosexual love, telling his friends, 'I do not think that the people who do these things derive as much pleasure as I do from talking about them.' And once he described how, while shopping with his wife at Swan and Edgar, he had noticed the male tarts loitering in Piccadilly and felt something 'clutch at his heart like ice'.

At first, however, he wavered, trying to ennoble his urges in a haze of 'hellenic' sentiment. Some have detected a tentative realignment of his sexuality in the friendship he started up towards the end of 1885 with Harry Mariller, a young Cambridge undergraduate whom he had first known as a boy in his early London days. Certainly Wilde's letters were full of equivocal ardour: he exhorted Mariller to enter that 'unknown land full of strange flowers and subtle perfumes, a land of which it is joy of all joys to dream, a land where all things are perfect'. But despite such promptings – or perhaps because of them – the connection petered out, and Mariller took up engineering.

It is generally accepted that Wilde was not introduced to homosexual practice until 1886, when he was seduced by Robbie Ross. Wilde was thirty-two at the time and Ross but seventeen. Ross, the son of the Attorney-General of Canada, had come to London with his mother and elder brothers after his father's death, and was being 'crammed' for Cambridge at the time of their meeting. He was small, amusing and compassionate, with, as Wilde recalled, 'a face like Puck'. His manner too seems to have been similarly Puckish, for – on both their admissions – it was he who took the lead in the seduction.

Their affair was probably brief, fitful and broken by Ross's departure for King's College, Cambridge, in the autumn of 1888, but their friendship was enduring. Moreover, the decisive fact of their liaison opened up a new phase of Wilde's life; it introduced the daring of action into his campaign against conventional society. The timing of his sexual realignment was characteristically dramatic and charged with significance; for, although sodomy had been a felony since the time of Henry VIII (and was punishable, theoretically, by life imprisonment), and although acts of 'public indecency' were also open to prosecution, it was only in 1885, the year before Wilde's first encounter with Ross, that the Victorian establishment's revulsion for all homosexual acts – committed in either 'public or *private*' – had finally crystallized into law. Section 11 of the Criminal Law Amendment Act ensured that henceforth prison (up to 'two years with or without hard labour') would replace – or, rather, augment – social ostracism as the approved punishment for any homosexual encounter.

Previously Wilde had mocked convention with words and poses, now he mocked it with deeds. The artist, like the criminal (and Wilde could now claim both titles), must be against society, and indeed against nature: *à rebours*. Wilde soon came to neglect his domestic and marital duties. He sought instead the company of young men. Most were some ten years his junior, and he readily assumed the roles of mentor, guru and *chef du cénacle*. For one who enjoyed the sound of his own voice and the sight of youthful beauty, it was a happy position.

Wilde seems to have been attracted by classical profiles, boyish complexions and the vague suggestion of artistic talent. The presentation of a slim volume of poetry was usually enough to secure an entrée into his circle, and there were few aspiring young poets in London who did not court or receive his attention. To some he gave merely encouragement, hospitality and advice: it was Wilde who urged Richard Gallienne to adopt the distinctive 'Le'; he invited W. B. Yeats to Christmas dinner and read him the manuscript of 'The Decay of Lying'; Symons received a fulsome note of thanks for sending a copy of *Nights and Days*.

Others, however, were marked out for more special favour. Ross returned from a brief and traumatic university career to his mother's house in Kensington and a special place in Wilde's affections. In 1889 Wilde met John Gray through his friends Shannon and Ricketts, the artist-publishers of the Vale, and began a passionate friendship if not an affair with him, the markedly handsome young man providing the surname, perhaps even the model, for the hero of Wilde's novel. At the beginning of 1890, on a trip to Oxford to visit Pater, Wilde met Lionel Johnson, then an undergraduate at New College, and captivated him through wit and flattery. Another aspiring New College poet, John Barlas, was scarcely less enamoured. The following year the first meetings of the Rhymers' Club were dominated by Wilde's ebullient presence (Victor Plarr rather resentfully recorded the 'fascination' which Wilde exerted over Dowson and the other young poets). Wilde extended his hospitality to Theodore Wratislaw, and to Graham Robertson, the dandified young painter memorably portrayed by Sargent.

In Paris, whence he had gone at the end of 1891 to enjoy the fruits of *Dorian Gray*'s success and to work on his play, *Salomé*, Wilde swept the young literary lion-cubs, Pierre Louÿs and André Gide, into his thrall. Back in England at the start of 1892 to organize the reissue of his *Poems* by the Bodley Head, he began a brief liaison with Edward Shelley, the publisher's office boy, a somewhat neurotic youth with blond hair, broad shoulders and literary aspirations.

The group that gathered round Wilde in the early 1890s was never fixed nor formalized. It was a coterie held together only by Wilde's magnetic personality. At private views, at theatrical openings, in the Café Royal, Wilde was increasingly seen surrounded by admiring youths. Not all these young men were homosexual, and even those that were did not necessarily have sexual relations with

Wilde, but the flavour of the *cénacle* was to a large extent defined by its deviancy.

Unlike the homosexual circle that centred on the London solicitor Charles Kains Jackson (and published poems about 'boy love' in his discreetly 'uranian' magazine *The Artist and Journal of Home Culture*), or the elaborately named 'Order of Chaeronaea', established by George Ives as a clandestine power-base for homosexuals, Wilde's coterie was not concerned to promote the 'cause' (as it was called). It merely sought the clear air of beauty and self-fulfilment above the oppressive fogs of Victorian 'respectability'. Wilde may have contributed to the underground serial-novel *Teleny* (which charted the homosexual liaisons of a French count), but in his own acknowledged works homosexual themes appear only obliquely. They colour the ambience of *Dorian Gray* for instance, but they remain unstated. His young friends tended to adopt a similar course in their own behaviour.

Their ways may seem affected but they had the charm of charm. When Louÿs visited London (with his mistress) in June 1892, he wrote excitedly to Gide of how Wilde and his friends 'envelop everything in poetry'. He was particularly taken with their habit of, when asked for a cigarette, lighting it first and not handing it over until after they had taken a preliminary drag. Revealingly, it is 'poetry' – rather than irony – in which they 'envelop everything'. For all Wilde's own wit, the temper of his followers was decidedly earnest; it was to their master's intense, poetic side that they were drawn.

Although many of these young men had ambition and talent, they all had considerably less than Wilde. They were also much younger than him, and lacked his confidence, his education, his famous fluency. They became little more than an audience for his talk, a sop to his vanity. Wilde himself described them as 'exquisite Aeolian harps that play in the breeze of my matchless talk'. The strains they echoed, however, were not the sprightly paradoxes of his wit but the overblown flights of his poetic fancy. The early poetry of John Gray, for instance, was little more than an agglomeration of tropes and mannerisms borrowed, either directly from Wilde himself or from those whom Wilde favoured, in a vain attempt to be new, daring and poetic.

*

Throughout the brief course of his seduction of Edward Shelley, Wilde was engaged – beyond his minor responsibilities at the Bodley Head – in overseeing, or undermining, the rehearsals of his first comedy, *Lady Windermere's Fan*, which George Alexander was putting on at the St James's Theatre. The play marked yet another phase in Wilde's work. He had assumed a fresh mask, adopted a new voice. After the decadent hues and tones of *Intentions*, *Dorian Gray* and *Salomé*, here was a piece that followed all the most conventional conventions of the London stage. The tale of Lady Windermere and her moral strictures against the 'fallen' Mrs Erlynne, who (unbeknownst to her) is her own mother, does not seek a place in the literary avant-garde.

Wilde himself never rated his comedies highly as art; he is said to have told Gide: 'mes pièces ne sont pas du tout bonnes; et je n'y tiens pas du tout . . . Mais si vous saivez comme elles amusent!' It was popular drama, however, that gave him a far wider audience (and far greater remuneration) than he had previously achieved. The dandies who appeared in his plays (in *Lady Windermere's Fan* there are two: Lord Darlington and Cecil Graham) gave him a new and public mouthpiece for his own *bons mots*, and blurred once again the boundaries of art and life.

Lady Windermere's Fan had its première on 20 February 1892 and, despite a mixed reception from the critics, the audience – as Wilde remarked in his curtain speech – liked the piece almost as much as he did himself. The opening night was further distinguished by the first public appearance of the notorious 'green carnation'. The young friends to whom Wilde sent complimentary tickets – a group that included Shelley, Ross, Louÿs (over from Paris) and Graham Robertson – were all instructed to buy a specially doctored 'green carnation' from Goodyear's in the Royal Arcade, and to wear it at the performance. Wilde wore one himself, and so did the actor Ben Webster, who played the part of Cecil Graham.

The effect of these curious blooms upon the other members of the audience must have been disquieting: the flowers were clearly an affront to nature; their shift from white to green reversed the colour-change wrought on absinthe by the addition of water; while the colour green (according to Wilde in *Intentions*) was 'always the sign of a subtle artistic temperament' and 'a laxity, if not a decadence, of morals'. The buttonholes linked the artificial world of the stage with the supposedly real world of the auditorium; they seemed to be a 'secret symbol', but of what? Wilde, when asked by Graham Robertson what the flowers meant, predictably replied, 'Nothing whatever, but that is just what nobody will guess.' He claimed merely to be teasing the audience with hints of a non-existent secret. But, of course, Wilde – and most of his entourage – did have a secret. The green carnation, which must have appeared to many as the badge of some esoteric society, was almost a challenge to the public to discover that secret.

At first the press, used to Wilde's extravagances, assumed that the flower's import was philosophical. When, two weeks after the première of his play, Wilde and 'a suite of young gentlemen' all turned up wearing 'the vivid dyed carnation' for the first performance of John Gray's adaptation of Banville's *The Kiss* (in the Independent Theatre triple bill that also included Symons), the *Star* reported that this artificial creation had now 'superseded the lily and the sunflower' as the emblem of the aesthetic cutting-edge. And although the April issue of *The Artist and Journal of Home Culture* – the magazine of homosexual subversion and interior decoration edited by Charles Kains Jackson – tellingly included full DIY instructions on how to turn a carnation green, most of its (very small) readership was already in the know.

If the advent of the green carnation confirmed the new strenuously anti-natural phase of Wilde's philosophy and life, the success of *Lady Windermere's Fan* propelled him into a fresh sphere of celebrity and wealth. Drawing-room comedy proved to be the ideal medium for marketing his unique gifts as a conversationalist. *Lady Windermere* opened up his wit to a world beyond the London dinner party, beyond even the book-buying public and the readers of the quality press. The play ran to large houses until the end of July, made a tour of the provinces, and was back in town by 31 October. The fashionable came because 'everyone' was talking about it, and their servants came to find out what it was 'everyone' was talking about. Even the Prince of Wales came. Wilde was interviewed, Wilde was quoted; Wilde's movements were reported in the press. The twin strands of his life were twisting against each other: as his private liaisons became more dangerous and more in need of concealment, so his professional successes made him more conspicuous and more confident of his own security.

It was in the spreading gloriole of fame produced by *Lady Windermere's Fan* that Wilde began his fateful affair with Lord Alfred

Douglas, a gilded youth with an alluringly arrogant profile and a stunningly modest poetic talent. They had met the year before. Douglas, the youngest son of the Marquis of Queensberry, was an Oxford friend of Lionel Johnson, although three years his junior. (They had been at Winchester together and Johnson, as he liked to recall, had, in one of those quaint customs that brighten Wykehamical life, held up Douglas' shirt-tails while he was being birched by the headmaster.) During the Oxford summer term of 1891 Johnson, who had been so excited by *The Picture of Dorian Gray* that he had written its author an elegant Latin poem of praise, lent his copy of the book to Douglas. Bosie (as his friends called him) fell upon the novel with passion. By his own fevered estimate he read it 'fourteen times running'. He wanted to meet the author, and what Bosie wanted Bosie got.

Later that summer Johnson obligingly took Bosie to call on Wilde at Tite Street, and Wilde was suitably struck by his new admirer – so pale, so beautiful, so boyish, and so titled. He asked him to dine at his club, and Douglas accepted the invitation. At this next meeting Wilde presented Bosie with a copy of the large-paper limited edition of *Dorian Gray* which had recently come out. He inscribed it with rare restraint: 'Alfred Douglas from his friend who wrote this book. July 91. Oscar.' The gift, if not the dedication, revealed Wilde's interest. He called on Douglas at Oxford during the Christmas term and sent him a 'comp' for the opening of *Lady Windermere's Fan*; nevertheless, the seeds of attraction did not blossom until the following spring.

Wilde always claimed that the intimacy sprang up in April 1892 after Douglas had written from Oxford requesting his help with a man who was blackmailing him over an indiscreet letter. Certainly they seem to have started seeing each other more regularly from that time. Wilde's biographers, however, have tended to portray their subject as an all but innocent victim drawn into the toils of the supremely selfish and irresponsible Bosie. There is no doubt that Bosie Douglas *was* spectacularly selfish and irresponsible, self-deceiving and extravagant, and, indeed, unreliable as a witness to the course of the affair. Nevertheless, his version of events, in which Wilde began making 'overtures' to him as early as their second meeting over dinner at the Albermarle Club and only made his conquest after many encounters and many months of eloquently exerted pressure, carries a certain plausibility.

In a letter to Frank Harris written in 1925 Douglas gave an all too graphic account of his seduction: he finally gave in to Wilde's advances, so he claimed, after a night on the town. They had returned to Tite Street in the early hours after 'dinner at the Savoy, a play (or music hall) and supper at the Lyric club'. Mrs Wilde, the children and the servants were away, and – after much discussion – Wilde persuaded the inebriated Bosie to stay the night in the spare room, rather than return to his mother's house in Cadogan Place. And it was there that 'he succeeded in doing what he wanted to do ever since the first moment he saw me'.

Douglas even goes into the details of what it was that Wilde had so long wanted to do to him: 'I did with him and allowed him to do just what was done among boys at Winchester and Oxford . . . Sodomy never took place between us; nor was it thought or dreamt of. Wilde treated me as an older boy treats a younger one at school, and he added what was new to me and was not (as far as I knew) known or practised among my contemporaries: he "sucked" me.'

Bosie's tone of bemused detachment seems overstated but, nonetheless, the dynamics of the event ring true. Wilde was thirty-seven and flushed with success, Douglas, twenty-one and vain. Wilde had devoted his life to the pursuit of beauty, and Douglas combined the beauty of an alabaster complexion with a taste for being adored. After his introduction to homosexual sex by the much younger Ross Wilde had quickly developed into an adept and enthusiastic seducer. Douglas did not possess Ross's 'Puck'-like openness; he was self-centred and neurotic. It is difficult not to see him as the pursued and Wilde as the pursuer.

Douglas, though, was clearly no stranger to homosexuality, and he was always far keener than Wilde on promoting the 'cause'. (His famous sonnet on 'the Love that dare not speak its name' was one of the least ambiguous rallying calls to appear in a short-lived undergraduate magazine called the *Chameleon*.) He was certainly not corrupted by Wilde. Nevertheless, his own tastes ran towards 'youth and beauty and softness', and although photographs suggest that Wilde was achieving the last of these distinctions (particularly around his middle), he could lay few claims to beauty and youth. Wilde was soon forced to accept that Douglas only consented to his attentions in order to oblige him, and the sexual side of their affair very quickly foundered. This breach, however, did nothing to break the relationship between them; indeed their intimacy continued to grow in claustrophobic intensity. Their sexual energy was merely diverted elsewhere.

Douglas' problems with blackmailers during the spring of 1892 suggest that he was already initiated in the seamy underworld of homosexual vice. Extortion was one of the time-honoured means by which male prostitutes and their pimps reaped a second return on their transactions. And it was Douglas who seems to have introduced Wilde to this new thrill.

Compared to the little circle of aspirational camp-followers in which Wilde had previously moved, this was dingy and sordid terrain. Wilde's guides, apart from Douglas, were Maurice Schwarbe (a nephew of the Attorney-General) and the touchingly pathetic Alfred Taylor, an Old Marlburian who had managed to run through the fortune he had inherited from his cocoa-manufacturing father and was, by the age of thirty-two, reduced to living in humble rented accommodation near the Houses of Parliament. Taylor was engaged as a sort of unofficial pimp to comb Piccadilly, the Leicester Square music halls and the public ice-rink at Knightsbridge, in search of suitable bits of rough for Wilde and Douglas. He would then present these finds, perhaps in his own rooms – an incense-clouded bower of cut-price exoticism, decked out with paper fans and artificial flowers, and screened by three sets of curtains from the harsh light of reality – or else over dinner in one of the private dining rooms at Kettners in Soho.

They were a dreary and unexceptional lot that he presented for approval, with little more than youth to recommend them. History (or the transcript of the Wilde trials) has preserved the memory of Sidney Mavor (known to his friends as Jenny), who went on to become a Church of England parson; of Freddy Atkins, a cheeky boy of eighteen who hoped to become a drag-artist in the music halls but, in the meantime, worked as a billiard marker; of Alfred Wood, another personable teenager, who ran a blackmailing racket; of Charlie Parker, a girlish valet; and of Parker's brother Bill; of a young actor, Harry Barford; of a clerk called Ernest Scarfe; and of Tankard, a page-boy at the Savoy.

In the depths of this sordidness Wilde strove to maintain the unimpassioned pose of the dandy. He tried to pretend that – like Dorian Gray or des Esseintes – he was merely sampling a new mode of pleasure, a new sensation, a new aesthetic thrill. But the truth was that he had succumbed to his animal nature; he had allowed passion to master pose. There was an ever-widening gap opening between exalted vision and base reality, and Wilde could only paper over it with self-delusion. He gave his boys dinner at Kettners or the Florence, wooed them with champagne and cigarette-cases, and dazzled them with what Charlie Parker called talk of 'poetry and art and the old Roman days', before taking them off, to whichever hotel he was staying at, for sex. He managed to convince himself that he was 'feasting with panthers', though in truth it was no more than 'supping with renters'.

This new period of Wilde's clandestine existence brought with it a much increased peril of exposure. The world of his *cénacle* was bound by its own idealized mores, but this other region was altogether more cynical. Previously Wilde had felt secure enough to flirt with exposure himself, but by the beginning of 1893 the initiative was in danger of slipping from him; he was facing the threat of blackmail for the first time.

The cause of his discomfort was Alfred Wood. Both Wilde and Douglas had slept with this youth, and Douglas had even taken him up to Oxford and given him a set of cast-off clothes. Wood claimed that he found some compromising letters from Wilde to Bosie carelessly left in the pocket of this suit, although it seems rather more likely that he stole them deliberately. However he came by them, Wood recognized their worth and – explaining that he needed the money to start a new life in America – demanded thirty pounds for their safe return. Wilde grandly paid the sum, or something near it.

Wood's associates, Clibburn and Allen, had, however, taken care to hold back one particularly florid letter – likening Bosie to 'Hyacinthus, whom Apollo loved so madly'. They made copies of it and sent one of them to Herbert Beerbohm Tree, the actor-manager who was then rehearsing Wilde's next play, *A Woman of No Importance.* Beerbohm Tree, a man of the world and of the theatre, was unimpressed. He passed the note on to Wilde with a word of caution, and Wilde was thus primed for Allen's approach. By his own account (given at the trial) he handled the confrontation brilliantly.

He disarmed Allen on his appearance by asserting, 'I suppose you have come about my beautiful letter to Lord Alfred Douglas. If you had not been so foolish as to send a copy of it to Mr Beerbohm Tree, I would gladly have paid you a very large sum of money for the letter, as I consider it to be a great work of art.' Allen, taken aback, suggested that a very different contruction could be put upon the document, but Wilde dismissed the insinuation with the *aperçu* that 'Art is rarely intelligible to the criminal classes'. When Allen then told him that 'a man had offered him sixty pounds' for the letter, Wilde earnestly advised him to sell, saying that he himself had never 'received so large a sum for any prose work of that length' but that he was delighted to find someone in England who considered a letter of his to be worth sixty pounds. Allen, his bluff called, changed tack and began whining about the expenses he had incurred in trying to find Wilde. Wilde generously gave him half a sovereign for his pains and sent him on his way.

About five minutes later there was a knock on the door and Allen's partner, Clibburn, appeared, proffering the disputed letter. He explained that he and Allen had decided that there was no use trying to 'rent' someone who merely laughed at them, and they were returning the letter as a mark of respect. Wilde thanked him for his trouble, scolded him on the state of the notepaper ('I think it quite unpardonable that better care was not taken of an original manuscript of mine'), and dismissed him with the other half of the sovereign.

Despite this minor triumph Wilde could not be sure that other copies of the letter were not in circulation. To cast a further veil of art between himself and reality, and to substantiate his claim that the document was in fact a 'prose poem', he asked Pierre Louÿs to turn the letter into French verse. Louÿs' poem was then published in the May issue of the undergraduate magazine that Douglas was editing.

Wilde, more daringly than ever, was turning his life into art, but the cracks in the canvas were beginning to show. The whole affair, though outfaced with panache, revealed with new force the dangers of his double-life. For the time being, however, he was content to provoke the fates. His second play, *A Woman of No Importance*, opened at the Royal Haymarket Theatre on 19 April 1893 and repeated the triumph of *Lady Windermere's Fan*, vexing the critics and delighting the audiences. Beerbohm Tree was well pleased, not only by the success of his production but also by the part he acted. 'Lord Illingworth' was another Wildean dandy, many of whose epigrams had appeared already either in Wilde's own conversation or in Lord Henry Wooton's advice to Dorian Gray (often in both). Tree even played the part much in the manner of Wilde, to the author's amused pleasure: 'Ah,' Wilde is said to have remarked, 'every day dear

Herbert becomes *de plus en plus Oscarisé*; it is a wonderful case of nature imitating art.'

Even more gratifying for Wilde than the demonstration of his theories, however, were the financial rewards of his play. The piece brought him a hundred pounds a week, and the money was desperately needed to support Bosie's expensive whims. With a regular round of lunch at the Café Royal, dinner at the Savoy and supper at Willis's, Wilde's weekly expenditure was never less than eighty pounds and often as much as a hundred and thirty. Fame, fortune, three meals a day and the company of Lord Alfred Douglas soon began to take their toll on Wilde's figure, and his manners. He could be blasé and overbearing when drink eroded his natural courtesy. And increasingly he drank to excess.

The flagrancy of Wilde's behaviour with Douglas was enraging Bosie's volatile father and distressing his formidable mother; it was upsetting hoteliers; it was even breaking up the old *cénacle*. The dissenters from Wilde's own circle of friends were alarmed as much by Wilde's lack of style as by his lack of discretion. In March John Gray wrote to Pierre Louÿs 'about the falling out with Oscar', saying only that it was 'absolute'. The following month Louys, over from Paris for the première of *A Woman of No Importance*, visited Wilde in the hotel room which he was ostensibly using for his work but was in truth sharing with Douglas and using for assignations with rent boys. He noted that there was only one bed – with two pillows – and his dismay was compounded when Wilde's wife came in – on her daily visit from Tite Street with the mail – and burst into tears. He tried to remonstrate with Wilde, to urge him to break off his 'fatal connection' with Douglas, but, on being rebuffed, he too broke with his former friend 'completely'. Lionel Johnson, an intimate of Douglas', saw the destructive relationship from the opposite perspective; he cast Wilde rather than Bosie as the corruptor, and composed a poem, entitled 'To the Destroyer of a Soul', denouncing Wilde's influence.

The heedless arrogance of Wilde's attitude which prompted these desertions from his standard also allowed him to bear them. Buoyed by an olympian self-confidence, he travelled up to Oxford during the summer term of 1893. It was May, the month before 'Finals', and Wilde spent three weeks happily distracting Bosie and his friends from their work with tales of unbelieving saints and unbelievable popes. One of the stories he told appeared in the June issue of the *Spirit Lamp*, the determinedly decadent little magazine that Douglas edited.

'The Disciple' is barely a page long and bears retelling. Wilde himself retold it many times. The story recounts how, when Narcissus died, the flowers and trees were stricken with grief and asked the river to lend them some water for their tears. The river declined, regretting that it needed all its own water to mourn for the lost Narcissus. 'I loved him,' the river explains simply. 'How could you help loving Narcissus?' reply the flowers. 'He was so beautiful.' The river sounds surprised: 'Was he beautiful?' 'Who should know that better than yourself?' reply the flowers, 'for every day, lying on your bank, he mirrored his beauty in your waters . . .' 'I loved him,' murmurs the river, 'because, when he hung over me, I saw the reflection of my own beauty in his eyes.'

The story's title was, of course, ironic, for the tale suggested that there are no disciples, only self-regarding egoists. But Wilde, seeing his own brilliance daily reflected back in the admiring eyes of Bosie's enrapt undergraduate friends, must have doubted – with complacency – the truth of his own fable. If he had looked closely, however, he might have noticed one pair of eyes – large, dark, slow-moving eyes – glazed with fluvial self-absorption.

Chapter Eight

MAX BEERBOHM had gone up to Merton College in the autumn of 1890 and in his first two years had steadily built up a reputation for his wit and for his caricatures of the dons (which were often scrawled in the margins of the essays he subsequently – if rarely – handed them). He had first glimpsed Wilde back in 1889 at a dinner arranged by his half-brother, Herbert Beerbohm Tree, who was even then courting a play from Wilde. Beerbohm, then only seventeen, had been fascinated by him and began to develop a cult for Wilde. He used to claim to his Oxford contemporaries that he had only ever read three books, Thackeray's *Four Georges*, Lear's *Book of Nonsense* and Wilde's *Intentions* or, as he often called it 'the Book'.

Beerbohm was certainly not alone amongst his Oxford contemporaries in his admiration of Wilde, but his interest seems to have been focused by a desire not merely to worship but also to learn. Almost from the outset of his undergraduate career Beerbohm had aspirations to become an artist – a writer and caricaturist – and he recognized the importance of being, before these, a 'personality'. For him, Wilde represented the model of the artist as self-dramatized, fully finished persona. And amongst Wilde's works it was those that spiced the aesthetic quest for beauty with a liberal dose of ironic wit that appealed most strongly to him.

At first Beerbohm was obliged to view his idol from a distance. He copied his actions – attending Pater's notoriously arid lectures and making fun of Pater's notoriously arid manner. And he followed Wilde's progress – writing poems in praise of him, annotating his books and revelling in the drama surrounding Sarah Bernhardt's aborted production of *Salomé* in June 1892. Already Beerbohm had learnt the stylistic lessons of *Intentions*: the lightness of touch, the high unseriousness, the ironic detachment and knowingness, and was applying them to everything and everyone – even to Wilde in his most poetic guise. When the Lord Chamberlain refused to give *Salomé* a licence, on the grounds that the portrayal of biblical characters was not allowed on stage, Beerbohm wrote excitedly to his Oxford friend (and fellow Wilde-watcher), Reggie Turner, of his own plans to draw an elaborate picture – to be called the 'Modern Salome' – depicting Lord Lathom (the Lord Chamberlain) presenting the 'head of Oscar the Poetast' to King Bull and Mrs Grundy.

Towards the end of 1892, however, Beerbohm was drawn more closely into Wilde's orbit when his half-brother secured the rights to produce *A Woman of No Importance.* The development of their relationship – or rather of Beerbohm's chaging attitude to Wilde over the next three years – is vividly preserved in the letters Beerbohm wrote to Reggie Turner.

Turner, the illegitimate son of a wealthy Jewish banker, was two years ahead of Beerbohm at Merton, but their friendship prospered early and swiftly, and indeed lasted throughout their lives. During his undergraduate days Turner was famous for his indolence, his ugliness and his humour. His performances at college 'smokers', his spontaneous mimicry, his flights of comic lunacy, led many of his contemporaries – including Somerset Maugham and Beerbohm himself – to judge him the most amusing man they had ever encountered.

Turner shared Beerbohm's enthusiasm for Wilde, and indeed Wilde's works became the currency of their friendship: Max gave Reggie a copy of *Lord Arthur Savile's Crime*; Reggie replied with *Salomé*, and, for Max's twenty-first birthday present, had a copy of *Intentions* specially bound in vellum. On receiving the handsomely got-up French edition of *Salomé* – in February 1893 – Beerbohm wrote to thank Turner in a letter that parodied Wilde's two manners: he mixed the extravagance of his poetic diction ('It has charmed my eyes from their sockets and through the voids has sent incense to my brain') with touches of his paradoxical wit ('In construction it is very like a Greek play, I think: yet in conception so modern that its publication in any century would seem premature').

To admiration and imitation Beerbohm soon added the homage of advertisement. His first published article, written at exactly this time, was a portrait – albeit a mildly satirical one – entitled 'Oscar Wilde by an American', which was published in a new periodical called the *Anglo-American Times* in March 1893. From behind the ill-fitting mask of an American in Paris catching sight of Wilde as he entered the Maison Doreé, Beerbohm gave a sprightly encomium of 'the Master', spiced with liberal pinches of irony and rather crude jests. He made the – even then – conventional claims for Wilde's powerful personality, his genius as a talker, his protean facility as critic, poet, wit, scholar, novelist, dramatist, conteur and philosopher, his position as 'an amateur of beautiful things and a *dilettante* of things delightful'. But the picture of praise is spiked with some revealing reservations about Wilde's 'disciples' who, sitting 'eternally at the feet of Gamaliel . . . have learned nothing but the taste of boot-polish'.

Beerbohm pretended to point up the difficulty of being one of Wilde's apostles. The 'harm', he suggested, 'that Mr Wilde has done within a certain radius is incalculable.' The knowing reader might perhaps have expected a veiled reference to homosexual corruption at this point, but instead Beerbohm proceeds with 'For the love of beauty for its own sake, which has absorbed his whole system and inspired everything he has written, is a very rare thing indeed. It is inborn and cannot ever be communicated. And thus the young men who have tried to reproduce not only the manner of "the Master" but his spirit also have, for the most part, failed absurdly.'

The criticism is apt enough applied to the sterile verses of John Gray ('one of the corrupt'), but it focuses on Wilde's claims as an evangelist of beauty (his poetic manner) rather than on his genius as a wit and ironist. The distortion was no doubt deliberate, diverting attention from the fact that the witty manner and ironic spirit of Beerbohm's own prose had clearly been learnt from Wilde. By attacking the established 'disciples' for their inability to claim one half of Wilde's legacy, Beerbohm was clearing a space for himself close to the 'Master's' throne and proclaiming his rights to the other half.

Beerbohm, as any debutant author might be, was much pleased with the piece, telling Turner ingenuously that it was 'brilliant'. Wilde himself, to Beerbohm's yet greater pleasure, concurred, pronouncing it 'incomparably clever'. Wilde was always exceedingly generous to Beerbohm. He recognized his talent and praised it, even when he himself was the object of its barbed wit. He rather envied Beerbohm his extraordinary detachment; and his famous remark that 'The gods have bestowed on Max the gift of perpetual old age' saluted this unimpassioned calm, as well as striking the poignant note of one who had set such store by youth and was rapidly losing it.

In the spring of 1893 Beerbohm, from behind his inscrutable mien, saw much of Wilde during rehearsals for *A Woman of No Importance*. The frequent letters to Turner at this time took on an almost formulaic structure, combining eagerly reported Wildean anecdotes, stern criticisms of Wilde's physique and manners, and little essays at Wildean wit. Beerbohm's admiration is obvious, as is his desire to set a distance between himself and his master. A report of Wilde's attack on the 'wretched little donkeys of critics' who had savaged Henry Irving's *King Lear* ('Surely,' Wilde had said, 'a gentleman has a right to fail if he chooses') was followed by the tart assertion that 'Oscar drinks far more than he ought . . . He has deteriorated very much in appearance; his cheeks being quite dark purple and fat to a fault. I think he will die of apoplexy on the first night of the play.' An anecdote about Wilde ordering a watercress sandwich in a restaurant leads into the (almost certainly wrong) declaration that 'it seems he [Wilde] speaks French with a shocking accent . . . and that when he visits the decadents he has to repeat once or twice everything he says to them'.

Beerbohm's account of the play's opening night combined criticism, praise and parody. He ended, 'The notices are better than expected; the piece is sure of a long, of a very long run, despite what the critics may say in its favour.' The detached superiority of Beerbohm's tone is still rather strained, and the paradox of the last phrase – although amusing – is too obviously in imitation of 'the Master'. Beerbohm's artistic dependence upon Wilde emerges even more clearly in his next letter to Turner, which gives an excited account of the post-theatre supper at the Albermarle, with Tree, Wilde and Alfred Douglas ('who is staying with him'). He begins with a detailed report of the (further) praise that Wilde lavished upon his little article – 'He said . . . that my style was like a silver dagger. I am becoming vainer than ever' – and passes on that evening's magisterial *bon mot* – 'a lovely thing' about Wilde telling an insolent journalist, 'I remember your name perfectly but I can't recall your face.' Beerbohm then attempts to place himself in Wilde's paradoxical universe by telling Turner of how, while walking home that night, he had seen 'a glare in the sky like some false dawn. A cabman told me it was a fire and drove me to it . . . It was quite lovely, though there was no life lost I am afraid.' It was only in a cunningly placed postscript that he recorded a Whistlerian barb about *Salome* ('Oscar has scored another brilliant exposure') to check the balance.

The introduction of Whistler was telling, for the artist (in his own mind at least) was Wilde's master. Since their falling out – and the resumé of its course in *The Gentle Art of Making Enemies* – loyalty to Whistler was akin to subversion of Wilde. It was a disrespect which Beerbohm and Turner indulged. At the beginning of 1892 Reggie had presented Max with a copy of Whistler's book, inscribed with Baudelaire's dandiacal stricture, '*doit aspirer à être sublime sans interruption, il doit vivre et dormir devant un miroir*'. The quotation from Baudelaire served to lower Wilde yet another notch on the historical scale, for if Whistler was Wilde's intellectual master, Baudelaire, in many respects, was Whistler's.

Whistler's oft-reiterated cavil was with Wilde's supposed 'plagiarism'. He could never forget that in 1885 he had helped Wilde to prepare a lecture on art for the students of the Royal Academy. Whistler ignored the fact that his own ideas were largely derived from Gautier and Baudelaire, and, that Wilde – moreover – had transformed whatever he borrowed through the prism of his iridescent wit. For Whistler, a master of subtle shades in painting but a black-and-white practitioner in matters of thought, the equation was simple: the notions were his own and Wilde had used them without acknowledgement. Nor was Whistler the only person to level such charges. That Wilde was a plagiarist became a cheap crack of late Victorian criticism.

Beerbohm, ready to learn not only from Wilde's achievements but also from his mistakes, was quick to perceive the fine line that separated plagiarism from homage. He did not want to blunder across it as Wilde too often did – particularly in his serious or 'poetic' mode. The mask of irony which Beerbohm was forging allowed him always to maintain a margin of detachment between himself and his subject, a margin which marked the boundary between what could be condemned as plagiarism and what had to be accepted as parody.

During 1893 Beerbohm was already beginning to jostle for independence from Wilde. And, as he later recalled, he received a decisive and unexpected boost to his *amour propre* towards the middle of the year:

> In the Summer Term of '93 a bolt from the blue flashed down on Oxford. It drove deep, it hurtlingly embedded itself in the soil. Dons and undergraduates stood around, rather pale, discussing nothing but it. Whence came it, this meteorite? From Paris. Its name? Will Rothenstein. Its aim? To do a series of twenty-four portraits in lithograph. These were to be published from the Bodley Head, London. The matter was urgent. Already the Warden of A, and the Master of B, and Regius Professor of C, had meekly 'sat'. Dignified and doddering old men, who had never consented to sit to any one, could not withstand this dynamic little stranger. He did not sue: he invited; he did not invite: he commanded. He was twenty-one years old. He wore spectacles that flashed more than any other pair ever seen. He was a wit. He was brimful of ideas. He knew Whistler. He knew Edmond de Goncourt. He knew everyone in Paris. He knew them all by heart. He was Paris in Oxford. It was whispered that, so soon as he had polished off his selection of dons, he was going to include a few undergraduates. It was a proud day for me when I – I – was included.

Rothenstein, the son of a Bradford cloth-merchant, was a prodigy of drive and self-confidence. By the age of twenty-one, without the benefits of artistic or social connection, he had bustled his way first to the very hub of the Parisian art world and then – on his return to London – into the offices of John Lane, and into a commission for a series of Oxford portraits. It was while he was casting around for some undergraduate celebrities to add to his gallery of worthy dons that he was introduced to Beerbohm. He was at once enchanted by a personality that matched his own in precosity and differed from it in every element of style. To Rothenstein's energy, Beerbohm opposed languor; to his bustle, manners; to his enthusiasms, the clarity of wit. Rothenstein resolved to draw him, and to promote him. Provocatively (but with much truth) he would refer to Beerbohm as the most brilliant man he had met at the university. With such an encomium from such an ally Beerbohm could pretend to himself (and his friends) that he was rising to an equality with Wilde. He had a ready opportunity to try his new stilts.

The summer term of 1893 was distinguished not only by Rothenstein's meteoric descent upon the city but also by Wilde's solar appearance there during May. Beerbohm had recently forged a friendship with Wilde's beloved Bosie, although he assured Turner that there were no grounds for jealousy, Douglas being 'for one thing, obviously mad (like all his family I believe)'. Beerbohm characterized his new friend – who was striving to gain recognition for his own literary efforts – as 'a very pretty reflection of Oscar', whereas he himself was ready to assume the mantle of equality. He told Turner of one Oxford dinner at which he, Oscar and Bosie had been present together with Viscount Encomb, the Earl of Kerry and Lord Basil Blackwood; he characterized it as 'quite a peers' dinner: at any rate as regards aristocracy of intellect as represented by me and the Divinity'.

Beerbohm and Wilde also appeared together in print; the same issue of the *Spirit Lamp* that contained 'The Disciple' also included 'H. M. Beerbohm's' essay on 'The Incomparable Beauty of Modern Dress'. The piece asserted – with a cod seriousness which perhaps masks sincerity – that the great achievement of the Victorian era had been the solving of 'the problem of costume'. At last a universally accepted mode of dress had been found. Uniformity, however, did not in Beerbohm's opinion deny individuality; small details become especially significant and revealing. He lavished special praise upon a certain 'poet' who had brought an understanding of this into literature: 'the writer of that splendid, sinister work *Dorian Gray* has given an entirely modern setting to his characters. In every scene of the story we find him dwelling upon and drawing rich dramatic effect from such things as the wing of an Inverness cape or a pair of straw-coloured gloves or, even, a pair of patent leather boots. Foppishness is woven, with exquisite effect, through the very fabric of the work.'

Wilde's own dress sense had, of course, undergone a dramatic alteration. The foppish excesses that proclaimed the 1880s 'aesthete' – the velvet breeches, the coat cut like a cello, the voluminous cape – had been replaced by an opulent exaggeration of the most conventional clothing. His collars were high, his jackets well-buttoned, his waistcoats portentous. On one level this marked a victory for Beerbohm's incomparably beautiful 'Modern Dress', but on another it revealed a break with the strict code of the dandy. For the true dandy, appearance both created and revealed personality: the buttonhole proclaimed the man. For Wilde, however, dress had become increasingly a disguise. His clothes – if they could not quite hide his corpulence – did at least suggest a false respectability.

Beerbohm was close enough to Bosie and Wilde to be aware of this deception. Back in London, after the end of term, he clearly realized the need to set not only an artistic but also a social distance between himself and Wilde. With Rothenstein to pilot him he felt confident of making his own way. It was not that he was intolerant of homosexuals. He enjoyed their company and was amused to recount their gossip, giving Turner (for example) a lively précis of the scandalous débâcle involving Bosie, Robbie Ross and the 'schoolboy Helen'. But he gracefully deflected such attentions away from himself. Turner was always more than a little in love with him and although Beerbohm was flattered by the attention and the gifts bestowed, his letters always sought to preserve a degree of distance. It was not, however, so much homosexuality that alarmed Beerbohm as sexuality itself. Indeed, the display of any appetite unsettled the studied calm of his pose.

Perhaps it was in an effort – conscious or otherwise – to oppose himself to the mad, impassioned and unhealthy relationship he had been witnessing between Wilde and Douglas that he embarked upon his own highly idiosyncratic first 'love affair'. That August on the stage of the Tivoli – the newest and smartest music hall in the Strand – Beerbohm saw for the first time a fifteen-year-old prodigy, Cissie Loftus. She was an innocent waif-like girl, dressed in an innocent waif-like frock of palest pink, who had a quite extraordinary ability to imitate the voices and mannerisms of other famous music-hall comedians. She was, as the play bills had it, a 'Mimetic Marvel'. Beerbohm was smitten.

Did he recognize a reflection of himself in this tiny, poised figure whose genius – though real and particular – relied entirely upon parodying the performances of others? There is a grain of narcissism in most loves, and Beerbohm's passion for Cissie Loftus seems to have been almost entirely self-reflecting. True, he went night after night '*au* Tivoli' to worship her; he would wait at the stage door after the show to catch a glimpse of her stepping into her rather shabby coach chaperoned by her rather shabby mother; he would even spend afternoons loitering around the leafy suburban streets of Herne Hill, where he knew she lived; but he barely spoke to her once – and, that once, he pretended to be a journalist writing an interview for the *Pall Mall Gazette*. Although she sent him – at his timid request – two photographs of herself (one inscribed to 'My scrumptious Soosey Tooscy' after a line in one of her songs), she was an absent figure.

She was even more absent than Ernest Dowson's Missie. She very quickly became little more than a mirror in which Beerbohm could pose, a stone upon which he could whet the 'silver dagger' of his prose style, and an ideal on to which he could project his fantasies. Even these fantasies tended to be dreams of absence. In the series of letters he bombarded Turner with during the late summer of 1893 he fondly imagined Cissie carried off to an early grave in childbirth, or shut away from him behind a convent wall.

Beerbohm's excursions were not confined to Herne Hill. Throughout the summer and autumn – as a fourth-year undergraduate, Beerbohm was allowed to spend the term away from Oxford – he was bustled about London by the indefatigable Rothenstein, being introduced to all the clever, useful and amusing people who could be found. Together with Rothenstein he visited the Crown and the Cock to sample (very briefly) the bohemian bustle so beloved of Symons and Dowson. They went (far more often and for longer) to the domino room of the Café Royal, where, in that 'exuberant vista of gilding and crimson velvet set amidst opposing mirrors and upholding caryatids, with fumes of tobacco ever rising to the painted and pagan ceiling, and with the hum of presumably cynical conversation broken into so sharply now and again by the clatter of dominoes shuffled on marble tables', Beerbohm felt with wonder that here, indeed, was 'life'.

One afternoon they made an excursion to Pimlico and called at a house in Cambridge Street to meet a young artist who was achieving rapid celebrity with some bizarre black-and-white book illustrations which seemed to combine the sensual flow of Burne-Jones' line with the cruel exoticism of Japanese art. Beerbohm could not fail to be struck by Aubrey Beardsley: he was as tall and angular as Beerbohm was short and compact; while Beerbohm looked like an owl, Beardsley had the startling physique of an ungainly marsh-bird. He was very pale, yet seemed to burn with a febrile energy; both were symptoms of the consumption which had already infected his frame. His nose was prominent and his hair-style almost without precedent, the 'tortoise-shell' locks combed forward in a narrow Plantagenet fringe. He had, moreover, begun to win the fame and notoriety which Beerbohm himself desired. But, then, he was three days older than his visitor.

Both Beardsley and Beerbohm were twenty and both were almost 'complete', their personalities self-fashioned and self-willed, their talents marshalled and expressive. Beerbohm admired Beardsley's affectations – the butterfly tie; the recently decorated studio, painted in orange distemper with black woodwork in homage to des Esseintes' décor; the passion for candlelight; the camp exclamations ('Really, how perfectly entrancing') – and yet he saw beneath them the reassuring bedrock of 'a stony common sense'. It was a foundation that they shared. They shared too the fascination with Wilde. Indeed, at the time of their first meeting Beardsley was busily engaged on the work which would link his name inextricably with that of 'the Master', to the subsequent annoyance of both parties.

Beardsley had first encountered Wilde two years previously in Sir Edward Burne-Jones' garden, when Beardsley was still a teenage aspirant tied to a hateful day-job at the Guardian Fire and Life Assurance office in Lombard Street. Together with his sister, Mabel, he had made the pilgrimage to Burne-Jones' house in West Kensington, under the mistaken impression that the painter held 'open studio' on Sunday afternoons. Burne-Jones, despite the fact that he had long since abandoned this practice, took pity upon the pair and showed them round. 'By the merest chance' Beardsley happened to have a small portfolio of his own drawings with him, and he needed little prompting to show them. Burne-Jones immediately recognized their worth, as well as their considerable debt to his own style. Both discoveries pleased him, and he offered some generous words of encouragement and some tea. Also taking tea in the Burne-Jones' garden were Oscar Wilde and his wife and, as Beardsley wrote to a friend, 'We came home with the Oscar Wildes – charming people.' Within two years, however, the charm and the awe would wear off.

Aubrey Beardsley had been born in Brighton in 1872, and something of that town's Regency naughtiness entered into his soul. His father was a vestigial and hapless figure, and it was left largely to his capable mother to support the family. She taught the piano and French privately, and inspired her son with a love and knowledge of both.

Despite being diagnosed a consumptive at the age of seven, Aubrey enjoyed an active existence. The benign régime of Brighton Grammar School encouraged his drawing, writing and acting, and together with his sister Mabel (one year his senior) he lived out a rich fantasy life in private theatricals and musical charades. When he left school in 1888 and took a job as a humble clerk with a firm of city surveyors, he knew that he wanted more.

That first endorsement of his talent from Burne-Jones was all the encouragement he needed. He began attending night classes at the Westminster School of Art. He visited the National Gallery to absorb the Renaissance masters. He went to Hampton Court to see the great procession by Mantegna. He made – with Mabel – a special pilgrimage to 40 Prince's Gate to see the famous 'Peacock Room' that Whistler had created there in his most gorgeous Japanese-aesthetic style. And, following Whistler's example, he studied Japanese prints himself, adding their flat colour-surfaces and curious asymmetries to his own rapidly expanding arsenal of effects.

His precocity was soon noted. Aymer Vallance, an art connoisseur and a friend-of-a-friend of the family, was the first to become excited by Beardsley's nascent talent. He effected an introduction to William Morris – who declined to become the second. Morris appears to have been displeased by what he considered the too obvious debt Beardsley's early work owed to Burne-Jones. Vallance had more luck introducing Beardsley to Robbie Ross, who, down from Cambridge, was making his way as an art critic.

At that first meeting in February 1892, Beardsley – after overcoming his initial shyness – began to amaze Ross and Vallance's other guests with the breadth and lightness of his erudition, with his detailed knowledge of Balzac's works, with his thorough familiarity with both the National Gallery and British Museum collections. Their astonishment was complete when he opened his portfolio: Ross was so struck by one picture – the 'Procession of Joan of Arc' – that he asked immediately to buy it. Beardsley demurred, explaining that it was only a pencil sketch, and offered instead to make a pen-and-ink version. Ross agreed, and promptly set about improving the value of his investment, taking Beardsley up and arranging dinners at which he could introduce his discovery to clever, amusing and useful people.

Beardsley's first significant professional commission followed soon after. But it did not arrive via Ross. It was Beardsley's custom during the office lunch hour to browse through the eighteenth-century volumes in a little antiquarian bookshop in Queen Street, off Cheapside. The co-proprietor of the shop, Frederick Evans – an odd little man with passions for music, acting and amateur photography –

became intrigued by his curious-looking customer. He discovered that Beardsley drew, asked to see his work, and promptly developed a passion for that too. He even agreed to accept Beardsley's pictures in exchange for books.

When Evans heard that his friend J. M. Dent, the publisher, was looking for an illustrator who could work in the Burne-Jones manner to decorate a new, popular edition of Malory's *Morte D'Arthur*, he urged him to come and see some examples of Beardsley's work. Dent called round at once, and was stroking his moustache approvingly over the drawings when Beardsley himself strolled in for his daily browse. Evans introduced the publisher to the illustrator with such contagious enthusiasm that the former was bold enough to suggest a commission and the latter was rash enough to accept it.

Although the project, which turned out to comprise twenty full or double-page illustrations and over five hundred mock-medieval borders, illuminated letters and assorted flourishes, became, during the eighteen months it took to complete, a wearisome chore, it gave Beardsley the money (two hundred and fifty pounds) and the confidence to climb down from his high stool. At the end of the summer of 1892 he resigned from his job at the Assurance office to dedicate himself to art.

Vallance's tireless good offices, meanwhile, brought Beardsley to the attention of a young critic called C. Lewis Hind, who was busy trying to set up a new art magazine, to be called *The Studio*. Hind was 'amazed' by the 'astonishing degree of proficiency' that Beardsley's art had attained, and was convinced that here was the 'unique thing' to give the first number of his periodical a sensational start. He in turn enthused the Anglo-American artist and critic, Joseph Pennell, with the idea of writing the piece.

In the event Hind was lured away by the Astor millions to edit the *Pall Mall Budget*, and the first number of *The Studio* (now under the editorship of Gleeson White) containing Pennell's piece – 'A New Illustrator' – did not appear until April 1893. Beardsley had given some thought to the pictures that should accompany the article. Several of the *Morte D'Arthur* designs were to be included, but he also needed a prodigy piece to arrest the public's attention on his début.

The most striking literary event of the year had been the publication in January (and in the original French) of Oscar Wilde's *Salomé*. Beardsley, like Beerbohm and, indeed, every other young avant-gardist worth his absinthe, had been intoxicated by the jewelled horrifics of the play, by its decadent admixture of eroticism and sin. He was impressed too, no doubt, by the controversy and publicity that it generated. Beardsley saw an opportunity to ally himself to both art and fame: with the naked courage of concealed ambition he chose to draw a picture in his newest 'Japanese' style, illustrating the lurid climax of the play when Salome presses the lips of John the Baptist's head against her own; and he submitted it for inclusion in *The Studio*.

Even before the magazine appeared in proof, Wilde was aware of this tribute. Very probably Ross had hastened to acquaint him with it. He generously acknowledged the homage with a copy of the Paris edition inscribed, 'For Aubrey: for the only artist who, besides myself, knows what the dance of the seven veils is, and can see that invisible dance'. Wilde's enthusiasm for his new admirer was as generous and impulsive as ever. He even suggested that they should go together to see the New Salon in Paris that spring.

Beardsley, whose habitual shyness was quickly melting under the sun of so much rapid success, informed Wilde that he would like to do the translation for the English language edition of the play, which John Lane was planning to bring out. Wilde seems not to have objected, but Lane – already aware of Beardsley's commercial potential as an illustrator – scotched the scheme and redirected the young man back to his drawing-board. He commissioned Beardsley to produce the pictures to accompany the translation: ten full-page drawings and a cover-design, all for the fee of fifty guineas. The task of turning the play into English was swiftly claimed – on the author's ill-judged recommendation – by Lord Alfred Douglas.

In May 1893 Beardsley did go to Paris for the New Salon, although he travelled in a party organized by Pennell, rather than with Wilde – who was on his visit to Oxford at the time. Perhaps it was as well: Beardsley might have struggled in Wilde's shadow, free of it he stood out. Immaculately attired in a symphony of muted greys, his grey silk tie knotted in the loose Parisian fashion, a gold-topped cane held nonchalantly in the fingers of a grey-gloved hand, a straw boater placed eccentrically on his narrow head, he was – according to Mrs Pennell at least – the cynosure of the Champs de Mars. He had both the dandy's sense of poise and his gift for affectation. He had learnt quickly from Wilde, and was quickly presented with an opportunity for displaying his knowledge.

One of the few who was not impressed by the display was Whistler, who had recently moved to Paris and was living on the Rue du Bac. When Pennell tried to introduce Beardsley one night in the Café de la Paix, that other great dandy-artist of the period affected to ignore him. The reason for the antipathy seems to have been entirely instinctual. For some obscure reason Whistler considered Beardsley to be covered in hair; he complained to Pennell that even his shoes had 'hairs growing out of them'. Pennell defended his young friend and persuaded Whistler to let him bring Beardsley round to the Rue du Bac on Sunday afternoon.

That visit, too, was not a success. Whistler was perfectly polite to Beardsley's face, but he took Pennell aside at one point to lament with mock horror at 'those hairs – hairs everywhere'. And he failed to make their rendezvous that evening. Beardsley was badly hurt by this sting from the armed butterfly. The promptness and aptness of his response, however, revealed how much he himself already knew about the gentle art of making enemies: even that night he worked up a biting caricature of Whistler (the first of many) which he then presented to the Pennells.

Wilde never crossed Beardsley so crassly, although the confusion over the translation of *Salomé* certainly vexed the artist. Nevertheless, the young draughtsman, having been spurned by one hero, began to turn away from the other. He realized quickly that while Wilde's play would provide him with a platform, he must act out his own drama upon it. Indeed, Beardsley's prosecution of the whole *Salome* commission became an act of subversion upon Wilde and his play, subtly unbalancing the traditional relationship between text and illustration to such an extent that – to some observers – it seemed to have been entirely reversed.

Beardsley's drawings – always brilliant – were by turns shocking, facetious, cruel and splendidly irrelevant. Throughout the latter half of 1893 he would bring them – almost singly – into the Vigo Street offices of the Bodley Head for the amazed but anxious inspection of John Lane. Lane had no doubt of Beardsley's genius – and saleability – but he was much alarmed by his habit of introducing lewd details unobtrusively into his compositions. Several drawings had to be withdrawn entirely because – as Beardsley rather gleefully explained – booksellers would not be able to stick them up in their windows.

One picture, 'Enter Herodias', was held back on account of the naked youth standing coyly beside the queen with a powder puff in one hand and a mask in the other. Lane insisted upon the introduction of a fig leaf, while Beardsley versified nimbly in one corner of the discarded proof sheet:

> Because one figure was undressed
> This little drawing was suppressed.
> It was unkind, but never mind,
> Perhaps it was all for the best.

Lane's stricture upon the drawing revealed the prosaic limits of his vision, for – in his anxiety to cover up the page boy's genitalia – he failed to notice the large erection distorting the robe of the other monstrous attendant, or indeed the unmistakable caricature of Wilde's features in the portrait of Herodias.

Although there were exceptions, Beardsley by and large used caricature in his drawings as an offensive weapon. It had been his first means of attack against Whistler's hauteur and he also used it upon Wilde's domineering personality. Even before he began the *Salome* job he had privately mocked Wilde's pretensions to both originality and scholarship in a picture entitled 'Oscar Wilde at Work': the corpulent playwright sits complacently at his desk surrounded by the tools of his trade – the works of Swinburne and Gautier, Flaubert's *Trois Contes* and a 'Family Bible'; there is also a French dictionary and a useful volume called 'French verbs at a glance'.

It was, however, in the illustrations for *Salome* that Beardsley made his most devastating assaults upon Wilde. 'Enter Herodias' was not the only one of his pictures to be marked by the author's distinctive visage. The frontispiece (as well as the later 'A Platonic Lament') lent Wilde's features to the Moon, the poor sad 'Moon' which passes much of the play being compared to a 'mad', 'drunken' woman 'seeking everywhere for lovers'. Was Beardsley transposing the portentous 'symbolism' of the play on to a less elevated plane of reference: Oscar the abandoned and effeminate sensualist 'seeking everywhere for [homosexual] lovers'?

Beardsley was certainly inclined to treat the subject of Wilde's sexuality playfully; his own intense curiosity about sexual matters was always touched with an almost child-like innocence. Perhaps he thought that Wilde might even enjoy the mischievous joke, which was, after all, almost as much at the incomprehending public's

The Woman in the Moon,
frontispiece for *Salomé*.

expense as it was at Wilde's own. Wilde, however, was hurt. Moreover, he did not care for Beardsley's illustrations. He recognized their technical excellence, he acknowledged their inimitable style, but, as he explained to Ricketts, they were altogether 'too Japanese' for a play which was essentially 'Byzantine'. He disapproved too of the rather strained indecency which infected some of Beardsley's drawings (even after the scrutiny of Lane), reducing them to the level of those 'naughty scribbles a precocious boy makes in the margins of his copybook'. Behind such reservations, however, was an uneasy awareness that Beardsley had stolen the show.

The critics were not slow to point it out. The *Saturday Review* thought that Beardsley's drawings could not be 'quite agreeable to Mr Wilde'. 'Illustration,' their reviewer considered, 'by means of derisive parody of Felicien Rops, embroidered on to Japanese themes, is a new form of literary torture, and no one can question that the author of *Salome* is on the rack . . . Mr Beardsley laughs at Mr Wilde.' *The Times* struck a similar, if louder, note, considering the drawings 'fantastic, grotesque, unintelligible for the most part and so far as they are intelligible, repulsive. They would seem to represent the manners of Judea as conceived by Mr Oscar Wilde portrayed in the style of the Japanese grotesque as conceived by a French *décadent*. The whole thing must be a joke, and it seems to us a very poor joke!'

Funny or not, the *Salome* illustrations greatly advanced Beardsley's fame and the notoriety of his art. In his drawings he had managed to create a new self-contained world, a world that abandoned all allegiance to nature and owed everything to art. Wilde was right to detect the dominant influence of Japanese art, but there were other forces at work too. Indeed, Beardsley's pictorial language had achieved a truly decadent heterogeneity; besides the Japonic and Pre-Raphaelite borrowings, it was now spiced with medical technicalities, pornographic slang, Renaissance appropriations, daring neologies, and touches of eighteenth-century French. The relationship between form and content was deliberately upset. Characters floated without moorings, dominated by their fabulous clothes or by the decorative devices that – without reference to sense or probability – swirled about them. Their figures were drawn out (beyond even the elongations of Burne-Jones) and smoothed down to a disconcerting androgyny. These oddly sexless bodies were then given faces that spoke of untold depravity.

Beardsley's art, despite its numerous influences, was like nothing that had gone before; it seemed, moreover, exactly to reflect those notions of cultural and social degeneration – of unhealthfulness, licence, sexual and moral confusion – that were being canvassed with increasing vigour as the 1890s progressed. His work provided the press and the public with a focus for, and illustration of, contemporary decline; it distilled, as *The Studio* remarked, 'the very essence of the decadent *fin de siècle*'.

The effect of his art was unnerving. Even the critics who admired its accomplishment could not ignore its oddness. The reviewer for *Public Opinion*, when confronted by Beardsley's 'Girl in a Bookshop' at a New English Art Club show, fretted that 'the whole has charm, but it is undoubtedly the charm of degeneration and decay. These things do not belong to the sane in body or mind, and they do not find their out and out admirers in men of robust intellect, or of a wholly healthy moral tone . . .'

Beardsley, who was so clearly not 'sane in body', began from the first to acquire a reputation also for unhealthiness of 'mind' and deficiency of 'moral tone'. Elongated and androgynous himself, he was readily confused with his own degenerate pictures. It was a confusion that the press was delighted to make, the public happy to accept. And Beardsley – relishing the attention – did nothing to disabuse them. Very rapidly he became the human embodiment of 'the decadent *fin de siècle*'. He shared the position with Wilde, but he was in many ways a more satisfactory symbol than the author of *Salomé*. Wilde had already appeared as the human embodiment of 1880s aestheticism, he wrote popular dramas, he was fat, florid and successful. Beardsley, like 'decadence', was new, diseased and curious in form – and, like the century, he was hastening towards his end.

Beardsley, moreover, was not the only person to have his life coloured by his depraved and novel work. Other lives paid his art the homage of imitation: the so-called 'Beardsley woman' acceded to the ranks of contemporary *femmes fatales* as the very type of *fin de siècle* feminity – languorous, neurotic, sexually aware and very slender.

Despite the provocation of the caricatures, Wilde affected to befriend Beardsley. Throughout the time of the *Salomé* commission (May 1893 to February 1894) he showed him much real kindness, offering him theatre tickets, praising his work, introducing him to useful contacts, taking him on the inevitable round of pleasures between Kettners, the St James's restaurant and the Café Royal. But there seems to have been an almost unprecedented thread of anxiety in the relationship, the more noticeable for being exceptional. Wilde is habitually – and quite rightly – praised for having had a wit devoid of malice, but in his recorded exchanges with, or about, Beardsley the button appears to have slipped from the foil.

To each of Beardsley's presumptions Wilde replied with a direct counter-thrust. If Beardsley's drawings made play of Wilde's coarse sensuality, so Wilde attacked Beardsley's freakish asexuality: 'Don't sit on the same chair as Aubrey,' he once queenishly declared. 'It's not compromising.' If Wilde looked like the Moon, Beardsley had 'a face like a silver hatchet and grass green hair'. The artist's cosmopolitan pose drew the retort, 'Dear Aubrey is too Parisian; he cannot forget that he has been to Dieppe – once.' His claim to a knowledge of literature and an admiration of Pope was chastened with the lordly observation that 'There are two ways of disliking poetry: one is to dislike it and the other is to like Pope.' Even Wilde's praise was tinged with acid. In one elaborately sustained analogy he likened Beardsley's work to absinthe in its strength, seductiveness and luminosity, before adding that, also like absinthe, 'it gets on one's nerves and is cruel'. And cruelty became the quality that Wilde most often associated with Beardsley and his art.

Beardsley for his part, although he occasionally sniped at Wilde behind his back (he told Frank Harris that 'At noontide Oscar will know the sun has risen'), was content to maintain the pose of friendship. He even kept a photograph of Wilde on his mantelpiece. He could learn much from 'the Master' – and did. Beardsley's remark that he had caught a chill by inadvertently leaving the tassel off his cane revealed its provenance; as did his languid assertion that, when 'Nero set Christians on fire, like large tallow candles', it was 'the only light Christians have ever been known to give'.

Nevertheless, Beardsley absorbed his lessons rapidly, and soon his affectations and staccato repartee developed a distinctive character. He wore the dandy's mask of poised indifference with a composure that even Wilde could not match. He put it on, not to conceal a secret life, but to outface an imminent mortality. He even tried to subsume his medical condition beneath his pose, declaring with unflinching wit, 'Really I believe I'm so affected, even my lungs are affected.'

His cultivated anti-naturalism achieved its zenith when he asked his friend Ada Leverson to come early to one of his Thursday afternoon 'At Homes' to help 'scent the flowers'. Mrs Leverson supposed this to be a mere verbal conceit, but arrived to discover her host spraying the gardenias and tuberose with opopanax. He handed her some frangipani and urged her to perfume the stephanotis.

Chapter Nine

PERHAPS it was on one of the highly perfumed Thursday afternoon 'At Homes' that Beerbohm paid his first call on Beardsley. Certainly their friendship developed quickly in the latter half of 1893. A collaboration was even mooted but came to nothing. They sought each other out in idleness; exquisitely dressed, they would parade around the town, indulging in conspicuous leisure – drinking at the Café Royal, attending the theatre, or passing the afternoon – as spectators – in the Regency atmosphere of Angelo's fencing school in St James's Street. They drew caricatures of each other, Beardsley lampooning Beerbohm's youthful precociousness (and hence his own) by drawing him as a naked baby in a top hat. And they encouraged each other in their escape from Wilde.

In this conspiracy of insurrection Mrs Leverson was an inadvertent ally. Although she had only met Oscar Wilde the year before, she was already a favoured friend; Wilde was a frequent guest at the large house in South Kensington where she and her husband, Ernest, lived. While Mr Leverson was a conventional product of late-Victorian wealth, with a passion for gambling and a deficient business sense, his young wife (she was thirty in 1893) was conspicuous for her wit and charm. Wilde was delighted by her. He was soon calling her 'the wittiest woman in the world'. Her wit, however, was quite irresponsible, and when, in the summer of 1893, she started contributing occasional sketches to *Punch*, she began with a lampoon of Wilde. Although, for her, such skits were a form of flattery – the tribute of wit to wit – and Wilde received them as such, Beerbohm would have recognized their subversive power. His own attitude to Wilde was becoming increasingly facetious.

Writing to Rothenstein on the appearance of the English edition of *Salome*, he referred to Wilde's drama as 'the play of which the drawings are illustrative'. He confessed to having reread it recently, adding '[I] like it immensely – there is much, I think, in it that is beautiful, much lovely writing – I almost wonder Oscar doesn't dramatize it.' The wit is sharp, the criticism just, and the combination reveals how far Beerbohm had advanced since the parodic homage of just six months before.

Beerbohm's letters to Turner continued to be filled with 'Oscar' anecdotes, but the tone was frequently and deliberately flippant, with 'poor Oscar' being viewed through the wrong end of the temporal telescope. At once moment Beerbohm describes his deportment as distinctly 'Georgian', at another Wilde is said to have been in a 'very 1880' mood.

Beerbohm and Beardsley, two incorporeal virgins of twenty-one, delighted in emphasizing the age, the fleshliness, the sexuality, the opulence, and the appetite of their thirty-something mentor. Beerbohm's caricatures were scarcely less swingeing than Beardsley's. Edward Backhouse's claim that during the summer of 1893 Beerbohm drew a cartoon depicting Wilde as a satyr copulating with Bosie seems improbable. Nevertheless, by the beginning of 1894, under Beerbohm's pencil, Wilde had swollen into an 'enormous dowager'. Earlier drawings by Beerbohm had shown him trim and well-coiffed, now he became gross and effeminate, his hair bouffant, his hands plump yet tiny, his clothes excessive, his chins innumerable.

There was of course some truth in this changing vision, but the pictures still retain an aura of revulsion. When the long-suffering Wilde ventured to remonstrate, Beerbohm wrote briskly to Turner complaining, 'Don't you think it is a fearful cheek on his part? So long as a man's head interests me, I shall continue to draw it. He is simply an unpaid model of mine and as such he should behave.'

In his writings, the 'infant' Beerbohm projected Wilde into a premature dotage. 'I have seen old Oscar several times lately, here and there,' he wrote to Ross in 1894, 'wonderfully hale for his great age.' It was at this time that he composed 'A Peep into the Past', a satire upon that same 'old gentleman' which, although it reveals a continuing fascination with Wilde, cruelly converts the genuine admiration of the early *Anglo-American Times* article into an acidulous commentary upon Wilde's faults and failings.

Under the parodic cloak of a supposed journalistic inquiry into the distant past of the 'early Victoria era', Beerbohm wielded his silver dagger. The narrator of the piece, a thoroughly obtuse reporter, tracks the long-forgotten Wilde to his familial home in Tite Street, and sets about damning him with over-enthusiastic praise. Like Beardsley, Beerbohm attacked Wilde's claims to both indolence and originality: Northern 'grit', it transpired, was the secret of Wilde's achievement. He describes Wilde, in the small hours of the morning, disturbing his wife's rest as he paces 'up and down the bedroom in parturition of that same joke of which he sketched for her the outline as they were returning to rest'. Even the effectiveness of these hard-won jokes is called into question, although it is admitted that they very much amuse their creator; 'At the last dinner party [Wilde] ever attended,' Beerbohm's reporter states, 'it was decided he had the rare faculty of keeping a whole table perfectly serious, whilst he himself was convulsed with laughter.'

The journalist then inadvertently reduces the rich variety of Wilde's *oeuvre* (praised in the earlier article as protean) to a mere assemblage of influences – Wilde's poems are parodies of Rossetti, his fairy-tales 'in the manner of Hans Andersen', his novel 'in the style of Poe'; 'Mr Pater is often obliged blushingly to repudiate' the authorship of his volume of essays; *Salome* is described as 'written in collaboration with Mr Louÿs' (who did, in fact, look over the grammar for Wilde); even the English comedies are described as collaborations with Mr G. R. Sims. But, the narrator adds, the impressive thing to realize is how much time and 'unremitting labour' was needed to complete this small 'body of work'. In the drastic foreshortening of time that Beerbohm effects, *Lady Windermere's Fan* (written when Wilde was thirty-seven) becomes a prodigy of 'senile enterprise', and the author's infamous appearance at the curtain with a cigarette in his hand is sympathetically excused as the disorientated forgetfulness of an old gentleman.

Beerbohm also spiced the piece with knowing allusions to Wilde's homosexuality. The reporter catches 'the quickly receding *frou-frou* of tweed trousers' as he enters Wilde's study, and finds his host 'a little dishevelled' upon the sofa, readjusting his wig. There is a quip, too, about 'the constant succession of page-boys' calling at the house, which interestingly was also used by Beardsley in a letter to Ross at the end of 1893. Complaining of the furore over the three unusable *Salome* drawings, Beardsley wrote, 'I can tell you I had a warm time of it between Lane and Oscar and Co. for one week the number if telegraph and messenger boys who came to the door was simply scandalous.' The supposedly 'scandalous' nature of 'messenger boys' had been established back in July 1889 when a homosexual brothel was uncovered at 19 Cleveland Street. It was revealed that young post-office messenger boys were procured there for the pleasure of such aristocratic clients as Lord Arthur Somerset, Lord Euston and Queen Victoria's grandson, Prince Albert Victor. Although, in that less democratic age, the royal implications of the scandal were enough to ensure its prompt suppression, 'messenger boys' acquired thenceforth a *double entendre* among the informed. They were clearly part of the shared armoury employed by Beardsley and Beerbohm against Wilde's authority.

Amazingly, given the real hurtfulness and indiscretion of the satire, Beerbohm considered publishing 'A Peep into the Past'. The title page of the manuscript bears the inscription 'For the first No. of the "Yellow Book"'. Although, in the event, it was not used, the inception (at the very end of 1893) of the said *Yellow Book* offered both him and Beardsley a new means of distancing themselves from Wilde.

The idea for the periodical seems to have originated with Beardsley and an expatriate American author called Henry Harland. Harland was a personable young (or, at thirty-three, perhaps – to Beardsley – old) New Yorker who had come to England in 1889 and rapidly transformed himself from a chronicler of working-class Jewish life into a cultured exquisite. He affected a dressing-gown, a pointed beard, a French vocabulary and an improbable provenance which, amongst its highlights, included the suggestion that he had been born in St Petersburg, the bastard son of the Emperor Franz Joseph, that he had been educated in Rome and that he had gone to university in Paris. *Mademoiselle Miss*, his first slim collection of daintily crafted short stories, had been published in 1893.

Harland shared with Beardsley not only an enthusiasm for art, but also the fatal taint of tuberculosis. Indeed, they had first met in the waiting room of their physician, Dr Symes Thompson. Their friendship had been cemented during the eye-opening excursion to the Paris Salon in May 1893, when Harland and his wife were in the same party as Beardsley and the Pennells.

On New Year's Day 1894 Beardsley lunched with Harland at the latter's home on the Cromwell Road. It was not an afternoon well suited to consumptives as the town was full of what Harland described as 'one of the densest and soupiest and yellowest of all London's infernalest yellow fogs'. But after their repast the pair sat before a glowing fire, almost lost in darkness, complaining happily about the short-sightedness and pusillanimity of London publishers. It was towards the end of this well-rehearsed jeremiad that they had the idea of starting a magazine of their own, over which they could exercise editorial control. They resolved to see John Lane (a short-sighted London publisher) about their idea the very next day.

Beardsley immediately informed Beerbohm of the scheme, and Beerbohm no less promptly passed on the news to Turner, writing excitedly of the project that, 'It is to make all our fortunes'. The news was carried through the cafés, clubs, restaurants and drawing rooms of London. It quickly became the main topic of every literary quidnunc in the capital.

As preparations advanced, there emerged a trivergence of opinion between Beardsley, Harland and Lane as to the exact character of the new periodical. The incandescent imagination of the art editor seized it as – if not quite the flagship of English decadence – a sparkling repository for the work of 'brilliant story painters and picture writers', work which might be 'perhaps a little risqué' for more conventional magazines. The dashing moustache and flowing dressing-robe of the literary editor, however, concealed a surprisingly conventional spirit, and he was inclined to favour a broader spectrum of contemporary taste, a combination of old and new, and a large space specially reserved for his great hero, Henry James. The publisher, for his part, considered it a well-timed commercial exploitation of the up to date, and a convenient show-case for many of the authors on his own list. Nevertheless, these differences were only differences of degree.

From the first it had been understood that the periodical should be modestly daring in content and thoroughly handsome in form. Its very title proclaimed this dual aim. The 'book' element (which apparently received the emphasis in the editorial pronunciation) suggested something more substantial and permanent than the usual magazine; while the adjective 'yellow' conjured up associations with those French novels that were sold in distinctive yellow wrappers. Indeed, Beardsley described the prospective publication to Ross as looking 'like the ordinary French novel'. To most Victorian readers, of course, there was nothing 'ordinary' about the French novel; whether by Flaubert, Zola or Huysmans, it was the epitome of licentious corruption.

By March the two editors and their publisher had issued a prospectus which satisfied their different preoccupations, and titillated still further the curiosity of the public. 'While *The Yellow Book*,' they declared, 'will seek always to preserve a delicate, decorous and reticent mien and conduct, it will at the same time have the courage of its modernness, and not tremble at the frown of Mrs Grundy.' 'Altogether,' they continued with an unrepentant self-assurance which borrowed its note from Wilde's pronouncements before the curtain, 'it is expected that *The Yellow Book* will prove the most interesting, unusual and important publication of its kind that has ever been undertaken.'

The document was fronted by a Beardsley drawing of a predatory female browsing through the boxes outside a curious little bookshop, the shop being recognizable as the Bodley Head building in Vigo Street, and the elderly pierrot standing with a look of disapproval in its doorway bearing the features of John Lane's business partner, Elkin Matthews. On the back there was a list of probable or possible contributors, broad enough to satisfy most tastes. Conspicuous by its absence, however, was the name of Oscar Wilde. There seems to have been a policy decision that Wilde should be excluded from the new quarterly, despite the fact of his being a Bodley Head author. Lane always claimed that it was Beardsley who insisted on Wilde's omission, but although Beardsley probably did suggest the idea, it is interesting that Lane so readily accepted the boycott of his most famous (if not his best-selling) author.

The advent of *The Yellow Book* offered Beardsley and Beerbohm a clear stage for their precocious geniuses, a stage free of Wilde's presence, if not his influence. Indeed, the pull that Wilde exerted over the actions of his erstwhile disciples was readily apparent. Beerbohm's first thought for an article was the recently completed spoof on Wilde. The piece was quite unsuitable, likely to put more than a frown on the face of both Mrs Grundy and Mr Wilde, and in its stead Beerbohm offered an article he had originally begun for the *Pall Mall Gazette*, provisionally entitled 'The Philosophy of Rouge'.

It was a glib reworking of Baudelaire's 'Eulogy on cosmetics' from his long essay, 'The Painter of Modern Life'. Baudelaire's praise of rouge was based on his fundamentally decadent contention that the artificial was necessarily superior to the natural. Beerbohm borrowed this inversion and localized it, setting what he playfully considered to be the welcome return of 'artifice' against both the passing *sancta simplicitas* of the early Victorian era and the boisterous naturalness of those 'new women' who had thrown themselves into every sphere of masculine activity.

The demands of the toilet, Beerbohm suggested, require repose, and repose stimulates thought – while the effects of the toilet, in their turn, conceal the springs of this thought. In a passage that must have summoned up the portrait of Dorian Gray to many of its readers, Beerbohm lamented that for 'too long has the face been degraded from its rank as a thing of beauty to a mere vulgar index of character or emotion', before praising 'artifice' for at last severing this unfortunate connection between 'surface' and 'soul'. While Wilde had contrived to cut this bond through the elaborate device of Dorian's magical portrait, Beerbohm suggested bathetically that it could be achieved with a dab of blusher.

The whole essay, although it conceals its intention with a mixture of sparkling glibness and cod seriousness, is a play upon decadent themes set in a parody of the decadent style. All the expected guests are at the literary feast: the bold neologisms – 'flutterpate', 'ensorcel' – the touches of slang and archaism, the use of technical terms. The required historical perspective is fixed: the late Victorian age is likened not only to Rome 'in the keenest time of her degringolade' but also to those other faded and degenerate epochs, the era of Pompadour and the time of the Regency. The elements, however, are combined with such unfaltering brio, the arguments sustained with such lightness of touch, that it is quite impossible to gauge the level of the author's (un)seriousness.

Beerbohm was, of course, merely playing with decadent ideas and forms. But it was a double game, for he knew that what he treated lightly would shock and confuse sensibilities more sober than his own. Indeed, to the 'respectable', the very idea of make-up was synonymous with the *demi-monde*, if not the underworld. Beerbohm could thus enjoy the fruits of decadence – notoriety and a sheen of modernity – while preserving a degree of distance from any of its more dangerous implications.

Beardsley too was intent on shocking the public. Like Beerbohm, he had to withdraw one of his first submissions because Lane considered it likely to cause too much offence. Although (or because) Beardsley had titled his picture of a rotund woman in a small hat 'A Study in Major Lines', the vigilant Lane recognized it as a caricature of Mrs Whistler, the artist's wife. He was not keen to rouse the ire of

Title page of *The Yellow Book*, Volume

the barbed butterfly and, despite Beardsley's histrionic threats of suicide and insurrection, it was removed.

Some of the other drawings included in the first number of *The Yellow Book* were quite as shocking, but they lacked the hint of personal malice that Lane found unacceptable. The cover itself depicted two masked revellers whose lewd expressions – hers of fatuous sensuality, his of lascivious intent – found a complement in a phallic candle with its wraith of art nouveau smoke. And the title-page was no less alarming. It revealed, in a narrow panel, the back view of a woman standing at a piano in the middle of an open field. The piano – its legs decently covered, of course – was the very symbol of Victorian 'respectability', the focus around which every middle-class household revolved. George Moore lamented its terrible prevalence in the pages of his *Confessions*. Here it was transported, like the easel of some French impressionist, *en plein air* and placed before the strangely elongated form of the 'Beardsley woman'.

Even more extruded than the figure of the pianist was Beardsley's portrait of Mrs Patrick Campbell; and yet more calculated to provoke Mrs Grundy's disapprobation was a quaint scene called '*L'Education sentimentale*'. Beerbohm, on seeing this 'marvellous picture' in proof, had described it breathlessly to Turner: 'A fat elderly whore in a dressing-gown and huge hat of many feathers is reading from a book to the sweetest imaginable little young girl, who looks before her with hands clasped behind her back, roguishly winking . . . you must see it. It haunts me.'

It certainly spooked the critics when the first issue appeared on 15 April 1894. Beerbohm and Beardsley achieved their *épat.* The fiercest fire was directed at their contributions – and that of Arthur Symons. Beerbohm's essay was attacked as 'nonsense', either pure or pernicious. *Punch* cranked out a laborious ditty, ARS COSMETICA, which began, 'How does the little busy bore/Improve on nature's dower/And praise a painted Lais more/Than maidens in their flower.' While the humorist Barry Pain completely lost his sense of proportion and declared the piece, 'the rankest and most nauseating thing in all literature . . . a bomb thrown by a cowardly decadent'.

Beardsley fared even worse (or better). *The Times* could only consider his cover intended to attract by its very repulsiveness and insolence; Frederick Wedmore, writing in the *Academy*, thought his drawings 'meaningless and unhealthy'; while W. E. Henley's *National Observer* produced a sustained bombardment: Beardsley's women, the reviewer found, were not only of ambiguous sex but of doubtful race, if not uncertain humanity – 'They resemble nothing on this earth . . . with their bodies of lath-like flatness, their impossibly pointed toes and fingers, and their small eyes which have the form and comeliness of an unshelled snail.' The *Pall Mall Budget* (edited, ironically, by C. Lewis Hind, who had first promoted Beardsley in *The Studio*) denigrated the image on the title-page as an 'impardonable affectation'. The elongated form of 'Mrs Patrick Campbell' inspired *Punch* to re-dub the picture, 'Played out; or the 252nd Mrs Tanqueray – trained down very fine after a long run'. And the *Westminster Review* despaired completely, declaring that 'nothing would meet the case except a short Act of Parliament to make this kind of thing illegal'.

It was all very gratifying, not only to Lane, who had to reprint the first issue twice to keep up with demand, but also to Beardsley and Beerbohm, who revelled in their *succès de scandale*, watching their fame grow palpably with the rising pile of irate press notices that was gathered at the Bodley Head. They fanned the fire with vigour. Following Wilde's example, both of them entered into public and point-scoring correspondence with their detractors.

On the letters page of the *Pall Mall Budget* Beardsley defended his 'unpardonably affected' al fresco pianist by quoting an account (very probably invented) of how Gluck, 'in order to warm his imagination and to transport himself to Aullis or Sparta, was accustomed to place himself in the middle of a field'; and how in 'this situation with the piano before him, and a bottle of champagne on each side, he wrote in the open air his two 'Iphigenias', his 'Orpheus', and some other works'. What, Beardsley concluded, would the critics have said had he 'introduced those bottles of champagne. And yet we do not call Gluck a decadent.'

Not all his defences were so successful. The reviewer for the *Chronicle* had complained that the picture of Mrs Patrick Campbell was missing from his copy of *The Yellow Book*, and Beardsley had promptly dashed off a note of apology. This was duly published, with a mortifying footnote: 'Our own copy, it is true, contained a female figure in the space thus described, but we rated Mrs Patrick Campbell's appearance and Mr Beardsley's talent far too high to suppose they were united on this occasion.'

Beerbohm replied to his critics in the second volume of *The Yellow*

Book (July 1894), explaining that he had only just become aware of the furore, having previously been up at Oxford – where 'undergraduates see a newspaper nearly as seldom as the Venetians see a horse'. His defence was paradoxical or, rather, contradictory. First he assured the 'affronted mob' that it was the victim of a hoax – a hoax, indeed, which had never been intended to deceive. The essay, he declared, was merely a burlesque upon the 'precious' school of writers. He labelled this 'school' more clearly, and indicated its leader, by remarking that 'if I had only signed myself D. Cadent or Parrar Docks, or appended a note to say that the manuscript had been picked up not a hundred miles from Tite Street', the satire would have been instantly recognized.

Then, however, he changed tack and decried the critics for their lack of sympathy with novelty in literature. Every 'new school', he complained, has been 'rudely persecuted'. Through ignorance and fear they had lambasted 'the dullness of Ibsen, the obscurity of Meredith, the horrors of Zola', and now that there were signs of a fresh 'new school' – of 'literature falling into the hands of the decadents' – they were getting ready to 'pelt' it.

Beerbohm admitted that he had travestied all the qualities of this new school in his own essay – 'paradox and marivaudage, lassitude, a love of horror and all unusual things, a love of argot and archaism and the mysteries of style' – but strangely he did not seem to regard this travesty as akin to 'pelting'. For him, imbued with the self-parodying yet admiring tone of *Intentions*, the distinction was very true. He urged the critics to welcome the 'new queen' (perhaps another sly reference to Wilde?), to 'hang their houses with colours, and strew the road with flowers'. The letter was quite as sprightly and confusing as the original essay.

All this drama, all this publicity, all these sales, Wilde had to endure from the wings. Beardsley seems to have taken a malicious pleasure in pointing up his former mentor's exclusion. The caricature of Mrs Whistler, had it been included, would have proved Beardsley's power to hurt a mutual enemy whom Wilde had famously failed to wound. And the picture of Mrs Patrick Campbell can only have reminded Wilde that it was he who had introduced the subject to the artist. That February he had taken Beardsley to see the actress in Pinero's

The Second Mrs Tanqueray at the St James's Theatre. Beardsley had been captivated by her and Wilde had sent round a fulsome note, explaining that:

> Mr Aubrey Beardsley, a very brilliant and wonderful young artist, and like all artists a great admirer of the wonder and charm of your art, says that he must have the honour of being presented to you, if you will allow it. So, with your gracious sanction, I will come round after Act III with him, and you would gratify and honour him much if you would let him bow his compliments to you. He has just illustrated my play of Salome for me, and has a copy of the *édition de luxe* which he wishes to lay at your feet. His drawings are quite wonderful.

Beardsley marked the unmistakable note of lordly condescension ringing in 'He has just illustrated my play of Salome for me', and drowned it out in the clamour of *The Yellow Book*'s triumph. He took every opportunity to confront the powerless Wilde with evidence of the quarterly's progress. One afternoon Beerbohm encountered Wilde in the Café Royal and was informed that Beardsley had just been there, showing his illustration for the cover of the new *Yellow Book*. Beerbohm impishly enquired what the picture was like; 'Oh,' replied Wilde, his irritation exciting his fancy, 'you can imagine the sort of thing. A terrible naked harlot smiling through a mask – and with ELKIN MATHEWS written on one breast and JOHN LANE on the other.'

When the first number appeared Wilde lost few opportunities to complain of it, calling the publication 'horrid', 'loathsome' and 'dull'. 'It is a great failure,' he told Bosie. 'I am so glad.' He even complained that it was 'not yellow at all'. When Charles Ricketts tried to praise the periodical he was sternly advised not to say 'nice false things about *The Yellow Book*', and then treated to an elaborate account of how Wilde had been trying to 'lose' his copy of it all day – only to have it continually returned to him by over-zealous cabbies and railway guards.

Although his exclusion from the venture was painfully clear to Wilde, it was quite unapparent to the general public. They had been introduced to Beardsley as the illustrator of *Salome* and to them Wilde and his illustrator were inextricably linked. The covers of *The Yellow Book* were clearly by Beardsley, so it was blithely assumed that the contents were very probably by Wilde. In the popular imagination they were twin heads of Beerbohm's 'new school', and *The Yellow Book* was their register.

There was very little that Wilde could do to escape the connection. In June 1894 his poem, *The Sphinx*, was brought out by (of course) John Lane, the publisher of the irritating *Yellow Book*. In eighty-seven long-lined couplets, heavy with jewelled polysyllables, Wilde conjured up visions of sexual perversity in settings of oriental opulence beyond even those of *Salome*. The Sphinx herself – 'half woman and half animal' – combined lust and cruelty with a vigour beyond the energies of most other *fin de siècle femmes fatales*. During the short course of the poem she works through a whole bestiary of imaginary creatures and even the Tiger gets a rough ride from her ('. . . toy with him in amorous jests, and when he turns, and snarls and gnaws,/O smite him with your jasper claws and bruise him with your agate breasts'). The author, at first fascinated by this 'lovely languorous' beast, finally turns away in horror to seek a desperate solace in the contemplation of his crucifix.

The book was issued in a limited edition of 303 copies, with a handsome decorative cover by Ricketts (Wilde having abandoned his initial idea of printing only three copies – 'one for myself, one for the British Museum and one for heaven'). A few informed readers might privately have taken the poem as a coded account of Wilde's own fascinated involvement with an illicit and promiscuous sexual world; the majority took it as another striking work of literary decadence. All the qualities travestied by Beerbohm in his defence of *The Yellow Book* made their appearance in earnest. And even though the text was not illustrated by Beardsley, most people would have been able to imagine how the art editor of *The Yellow Book* might depict a hideous yet alluring Sphinx.

Wilde's antipathy to the Bodley Head quarterly was – like almost everyone else's – focused largely upon Beardsley. Beerbohm was so skilled at playing the double game of flattery through satirical imitation that Wilde was soon praising his contributions. Beardsley's presumption, however, was less easily forgiven. In vain Wilde claimed that he had 'invented' the precocious illustrator. And through a curious chain of connection, his disapproval of Beardsley's art came to be broadcast in print.

Chapter Ten

AT THE beginning of 1894, while plans for *The Yellow Book* were fermenting in Vigo Street, Lord Alfred Douglas was in Cairo, staying with Lord Cromer, the Consul-General. He had been sent there, nominally for his own nervous sanity, partly because he was driving Wilde to distraction with his demanding ways, and largely to escape the after-effects of an ill-suppressed scandal involving him, Robbie Ross and the sixteen-year-old son of an army colonel, Philip Danney – the so-called 'schoolboy Helen'. In Egypt Douglas met up with Reggie Turner, whose wealthy half-brother, Frank Lawson, had taken a splendrous gilded Nile-barge for the winter. Douglas, always drawn to luxury, was a frequent visitor aboard, and together with Turner resolved to make a trip up to Luxor to visit the sights. In Luxor they ran into two other young Englishmen: E. F. Benson, who was still glowing with the recent triumph of his novel, *Dodo*, a satirical portrait based on the brilliant young socialite Margot Tennant; and Robert Hichens, then a modestly successful music journalist with literary ambitions.

Together they all travelled up the Nile to Aswan. They visited Philae. They wrote poems and dedicated them to each other. But mostly they talked, and they talked mostly about Oscar Wilde. He was much in Douglas' thoughts; Douglas had been bombarding him with letters but had received no replies. He had, however, received several letters from his own (divorced) parents, urging him to break his association with Wilde, and to these he responded with increasing rudeness. Turner, too, loved talking about Wilde and was well versed in amusing Oscarisms; he had, besides, a gift for mimicry that gave a living colour to his anecdotes of the great man. Hichens, basking in the convivial – even brilliant – atmosphere, conceived the idea of making a satirical portrait of Wilde.

The idea received a further impetus when the party returned to England at the beginning of April and Douglas introduced Hichens to Wilde himself. During that summer Hichens also met Beerbohm and quickly earned his friendship, for, although Hichens was almost hearty in manner, he shared with Beerbohm the great bond of a similar sense of humour. Very soon he was showing his new friend the manuscript of the Wildean satire on which he was working, and Beerbohm was excitedly offering him encouragement and advice. The finished work bore the trace both of Beerbohm's wit and his knowledge of Wilde's weaknesses.

The book appeared anonymously, under the title *The Green Carnation*, in September 1894, and was an immediate success. It broadcast Wilde's decadent persona, and the details of his daily life, to a public beyond his charmed circle. The portraits of the fluent yet fatuous 'Esme Amarinth' and his slavish young disciple, 'Lord Reggie Hastings', were clearly recognizable as Wilde and Douglas; the element of parody was almost obscured beneath the accuracy of the picture's detail and the dangerous impropriety of its homosexual allusions. That mixture of fascination and annoyance felt by Wilde for Beardsley's *Yellow Book* was deftly conveyed in Mr Amarinth's decision to stay at home and read the last number of the '*Yellow Disaster*'; 'I want to see,' he declares, 'Mr Aubrey Beardsley's idea of the Archbishop of Canterbury. He has drawn him sitting in a wheelbarrow in the gardens of Lambeth Palace, with underneath him the motto *J'y suis, j'y reste.* I believe he has on a black mask. Perhaps it is to conceal the likeness.'

Wilde, who was staying at Worthing with Douglas when the book appeared, responded in good part to the squib – perhaps initially because he thought it was by his friend Ada Leverson. But even when he had discovered the author's true identity – as he soon did – he professed delight, sending Hichens a burlesque telegram of congratulation. In a long career of self-publicity he had become skilled at dealing with satirical attacks, appearing to accept them before turning them neatly to his advantage. He was soon writing to the editor of the *Pall Mall Gazette* to deny the improbable canard that he himself had written the book: 'I invented the magnificent flower. But with the middle-class and mediocre book that usurps its strangely beautiful name I have, I need hardly say, nothing whatsoever to do. The flower is a work of art. The book is not.'

Hichens was not the only young man to usurp the 'strangely

beautiful name' of Wilde's artificial flower. Marc-André Raffalovich wrote a sonnet against the curious bloom. Raffalovich was an early apostate from Wilde's cause and became one his most active rivals. He had arrived in England from Paris in 1882 at the age of eighteen. The youngest son of a Russian-Jewish banker and his accomplished wife, he was distinguished by wealth, literary ambition and personal ugliness. He was dark, with a beaky nose and heavy lips partly concealed by a spreading moustache. His accent never lost the clotted tones of a French-educated, Russian-Jewish émigré. It was unkindly said that his departure for England had been hastened by the distate that his elegant and beautiful mother felt for his physical presence.

The rumour probably owed more to envy than truth, for Raffalovich – whatever his disadvantages of person – was not without charm and intelligence. He moved easily in English literary society. He had been brought up by an English nanny, the formidable Miss Florence Gribbell, and in cultural matters had early become an anglophile. Well before his departure from Paris he was writing articles about, and initiating correspondences with, contemporary English authors. On his arrival in London he very quickly secured introductions to such eminences as Pater, Meredith and Browning.

Given his literary preoccupations it was not surprising that he should seek out Wilde, who – ten years his senior – was then achieving notoriety as the apostle of aestheticism. They lunched together and established a friendly acquaintance. The development of a deeper friendship, however, was not helped by Wilde's casually disapproving review of Raffalovich's 1885 volume of poems, *Tuberose and Meadowsweet*. Wilde complained that Raffalovich's use of 'Tuberose' as a trisyllable was incorrect and summoned up the image of a 'potato blossom' rather than an ivory trumpet. Raffalovich displayed his touchiness in a reply citing the etymology of the word and an example of its trisyllabic use from Shelley. Wilde showed his wit by suggesting that philology should concern itself with the roots of words rather than the roots of flowers, and concluded with a disyllabic example of its use – also from Shelley.

Although Wilde had scant respect for Raffalovich's literary work, he was considerably intrigued by his character. Raffalovich had recognized early on in his life that his sexual orientation was exclusively homosexual, and he accepted the fact with a detachment that developed into a scientific curiosity. On coming to England, although accompanied by Miss Gribbell, he explored some of the covert but cultured homosexual strata that lay beneath the surface of London life. He may have been cautious in his practice but his poetry was a steady record of impassioned male friendships. Indeed, his first picayune volume – brought out in 1884 – bore the suggestive title, *Cyril and Lionel.*

Wilde was interested – and increasingly so – by the subject of homosexuality, his own and other people's. He found in Raffalovich an expert with whom he could discuss the forbidden topic. Wilde's enthusiasm, however, was salacious and camp – he was, as he put it, searching for a 'new thrill' – while Raffalovich's interest (at least according to his own testimony) was purely intellectual. Their regular discussions about 'the more dangerous affections' came to an abrupt end when Wilde's wife innocently told Raffalovich that 'Oscar says he likes you so much – that you have such nice improper talks together'. Raffalovich, who was very touchy about propriety, was 'furious' at Wilde's casual indiscretion, and resolved 'never again to speak with him without witnesses'.

Deprived of its once common ground, the 'friendship' rapidly decayed into enmity and then into rivalry. Wilde's condescension became increasingly irksome. His suggestions that Raffalovich had bought his social position were unjust and hurtful. His famous insult – that 'Dear André . . . came to London to found a *salon* and only succeeded in opening a saloon' – rankled, as did the memory of how Wilde had once arrived for lunch at Raffalovich's South Audley Street house with five other invited guests and suavely informed the butler, 'We want a table for six.' The nicknames, 'Sandy' and 'Little André', were calculated to demean; the remarks upon Raffalovich's appearance were calculated to wound.

Little André was moved to retaliate. In 1890 he published his first novel, *A Willing Exile*, which contained an undisguised portrait of Wilde as 'Cyprian Brome'. Brome is an absurd figure, always surrounded by gushing young men, dedicated to dress, affectation and 'beauty'. Wilde, however, rising in fame, chose to ignore so petty a blow.

Raffalovich continued to agitate fitfully against Wilde in the press, but it was not until the end of 1892 that he saw an opportunity for greater revenge. In November of that year he was introduced – by Arthur Symons – to John Gray, then a very junior civil servant whose small reputation was based upon being Wilde's favoured disciple, if not his lover. It was acknowledged that Wilde's influence over the young man was paramount; he had fostered his poetic talent, introduced him into society, sponsored his membership of the Playgoers' Club, and – at the beginning of 1892 – had introduced his lecture there upon 'The Modern Actor'. He had even undertaken to pay for the production of his first book of poems.

By the spring of 1892, however, this history of patronage was taking place against the background of Wilde's deepening infatuation with Alfred Douglas. Whether Gray felt supplanted by this new rival – or was merely alarmed at Wilde's increasingly indiscreet behaviour – is open to conjecture. It is certain, however, that he plunged into an almost suicidal depression. In this low state he offered an inviting opportunity to Raffalovich; his looks already spoke in his favour, but his disaffection with Wilde was even more appealing. And if Gray was in crisis about his own homosexual urges, who better to discuss them with than the scientifically informed Raffalovich.

He would have been comforted, for Raffalovich had come to the considered conclusion that homosexuality was innate and thus free of any moral stigma, while also maintaining that it was best for homosexuals to remain celibate and channel their energies elsewhere. Although Raffalovich certainly felt a strong physical attraction for Gray, he sublimated it from the outset into an intense fraternal friendship. And finding that the demoralized poet offered very little resistance, he rapidly took over his life.

At the beginning of 1893 Raffalovich renegotiated the *Silverpoints* contract with John Lane, cutting Wilde out of the equation and, apparently, agreeing to guarantee the venture himself. Soon after the book's appearance that spring, he persuaded Gray to break completely with Wilde. By October he had removed his protégé from the Temple to a new address in Park Lane, close to his own house in South Audley Street. From a world of dandified poverty (in which he had often gone without food to finance his elegant pose) Gray was swept up into a life of cultured affluence. Raffalovich took him on his yacht; they went to Paris together. Gray was introduced to Miss Gribbell (who had mutated from governess to companion, to housekeeper, to surrogate mother) and found acceptable.

The basis of their friendship was a common disapproval of Wilde and a common dedication to art. Even within their own London circle there were encouraging models for such productive and passionate (though chaste) partnerships. There were Katherine Bradley and

Edith Cooper, the 'Michael Field' partnership, and, of course, there were Gray's first mentors, Shannon and Ricketts, 'the sisters of the Vale'.

Raffalovich and Gray perhaps aspired to a similar ideal. But although they were both primarily poets, it was not in poetry that they sought to collaborate. The time of their growing friendship was that of Wilde's early dramatic triumph; *Lady Windermere's Fan* ran through most of 1892, *A Woman of No Importance* was the success of the following year. And it was in the spirit of emulous rivalry that Raffalovich and Gray set out to produce a play of their own. Gray had already achieved a (very) limited dramatic exposure with the Independent Theatre production of his translation of *Le Baiser* in February 1892, and the following June the same company had performed Raffalovich's would-be witty duologue, *Roses of Shadow*. Cushioned from real criticism by the club status of the Independent Theatre and by the preciousness of their own plays, they had no reason to doubt their powers.

In April 1894 they made their joint début with a private performance of a thoroughly 'too-too' double-bill: *Sour Grapes*, a masque written in rhymed couplets by Gray, and Raffalovich's *Black Sheep*, a pastoral pantomime 'concluding with a dance'. Then, emboldened by the plaudits of their friends, they decided to put on a proper play. They had been collaborating on a five-act melodrama, called (melodramatically) *The Blackmailers*, and they hired the Prince of Wales's Theatre, Tottenham Court Road, and engaged a company to stage the piece.

The first performance was given on 7 June. It was also the last. The play was a disaster. In apportioning blame for the débâcle it is uncertain whether the production was more at fault than the play, or vice versa. Both, however, were dire. The plot, which centred on the blackmailing exploits of a character called Hal Danger, was without either moral or dramatic focus. What it lacked in force it hoped to make up for by repetition: as the *Theatre* critic observed, 'Blackmail is levied right and left; there is nothing but that in the play.' The logic of the action was further hindered by a thoroughly 'slipshod' production, and frequent unscheduled omissions.

The play's title might have suggested the opportunity for an attack on Wilde, whom the authors knew to be open to blackmail. There is even an intriguing reference to Hal Danger's devoted friend as 'dear Hyacinth' – the very endearment Wilde had used in the letter to Douglas which had been stolen and sold back to him by Clibburn and Allen. This inviting avenue of attack was, however, not explored; indeed Hal Danger is, if anything, the hero of the piece.

The chance to outshine Wilde in his own new medium was also lost. The play's attempts at wit fell flat. The feebleness of the drama was clear to all. *The Blackmailers* was not *Lady Windermere's Fan*. Its production was a very thorough and very public failure. In the wake of this humiliation Raffalovich and Gray retreated. Direct rivalry with Wilde had proved impossible; the options that remained open to them were silence, slander, or some new field of endeavour untouched by 'the Master's' hand. They were to try each in turn.

If John Gray was shy of being thought the model for Dorian Gray, Count Eric Stenbock might have been eager to claim the title. He was perhaps the most determined 'decadent' in London. A dedicated drug addict, a flagrant homosexual, a conspicuous dandy, a writer of horrible poems and horror stories, he became a legend in his own brief lifetime. Such indeed was his proverbial decadence that Arthur Symons, on first hearing of the Comte de Montesquieu, referred to the prototype of des Esseintes as 'that extraordinary Stenbock *plus*'. Stenbock and Wilde did not, however, get on.

The Count (and, in an age of pseudonyms and borrowed robes, he really was a count) was rather older than the very young men of the nineties; he was almost a coeval of Wilde's. He was born in 1860, in Cheltenham, the son of an Estonian nobleman and a wealthy English mother. His father died before his first birthday and his childhood was spent largely in England. His mother remarried and, like Baudelaire, the young Eric found himself out of sympathy with his stepfather, a senior Treasury offical. Eric was dispatched to Wiesbaden to finish his schooling and then – at seventeen – to Oxford, where he was a contemporary of Wilde's (although there is no record of their having met). The Balliol of Jowett, however, did not prove a congenial atmosphere for his burgeoning eccentricity, and he stayed only four terms.

Free of the university, he cultivated the friendship of Simeon Solomon, the homosexual Pre-Raphaelite artist, and indulged a passion for the consumptive son of an Oxfordshire vicar. Some of his feelings towards this ailing youth he transmuted into verse, producing two slender collections – *Love, Sleep and Death* (1881) and *Myrtle, Rue and Cypress* (1883). It was not, however, until 1885 that Stenbock was able to give full expression to his affectations. In that year his grandfather died, and Eric came into his Estonian estates. Clutching a volume of his poems, and accompanied by an evil-smelling monkey, he returned to the family seat at Kalk. The local peasantry were mildly startled by the new lord's shoulder-length hair and iridescent silk shirt.

Stenbock arranged his household along lines that suggest he was perhaps familiar with the recently published *A Rebours*. The upper storey he transformed into an artificial paradise, heavy with the perfumes of incense and opium; tortoises trundled across the thick Smyrna carpets; hot-house flowers and caged song-birds proclaimed the subjugation of nature to artifice; the snake that protruded from the cuff of his dressing-gown and the toads that littered his table made their separate claims for the beauties of ugliness; and the presence of a beloved dachshund called Trixie added a note of unmistakable camp.

The peacock-blue bedroom was a shrine to Count Stenbock's new and private religion. In the middle of the great marble chimney-piece, rising from an artful clutter of rosaries, peacock feathers, oriental shawls and temple lamps, stood a green bronze Eros, naked but for a shroud of incense. Above the bed was emblazoned a gigantic pentagram, while beside it stood an opium pipe.

After two years steeped in this atmosphere of desperate anti-naturalism, Count Stenbock felt the need of a wider audience for his fooleries. He returned to London, settling first in Sloane Terrace and then at 21 Gloucester Walk. His exoticism if not his talent secured him a foothold on the literary scene. He completely captivated Ernest Rhys, who considered him to be 'like an Arabian Nights dream', and the enthusiastic Welshman was not slow to introduce his discovery to the young and impressionable members of the Rhymers' Club.

Count Stenbock was rather a hit. His emotive piano recitals were admired, his improper limericks were repeated. His generous allowance seemed – to the impecunious poets of the day – like real wealth. Yeats called him a 'scholar, connoisseur, drunkard, poet, pervert and most charming of men'; Johnson had doubts about the Count's poetic gifts but recognized a fellow lush; and Symons, though he later condemned him as an 'inhuman and abnormal degenerate', found the Count at first a fascinating companion.

Stenbock was also taken up by Wilde's young disciples. Robert Ross knew him, and Ross's great friend, More Adey, began collaborating with the Count on the translation of some Balzac *contes*. His fame even reached Oxford. The June 1893 issue of Douglas' *Spirit Lamp* – the same one that contained Wilde's 'Disciple' and Beerbohm's essay on 'Modern Dress' – carried a short story called 'The Other Side' by 'Count Eric Stembock.

Wilde's reaction to sharing a title-page with Stenbock is unrecorded, but the Count's offering – a tedious tale of homoerotic lycanthropy – was unlikely to have impressed him. There seems to have been an ill-concealed enmity between the two men for which it is difficult to account. Perhaps Wilde was jealous of Stenbock's evil reputation. Or of his title. Perhaps he found him a bore. There is a tale of how Wilde, paying a visit to Stenbock's house, casually lit a cigarette from one of the little sanctuary lamps that adorned the mantelpiece-cum-altar. The Count took this as blasphemy against his private religion and fell foaming to the floor. Wilde remained unmoved; he kicked his prostrate host lightly out of his path and departed.

If the story is true, Wilde's unkindness seems unnecessary. Stenbock was no sort of rival to him, and deserved more pity than contempt. Drink and drugs were rapidly taking their toll upon his mental health. His feeble literary talent was withering fast. Neither of his two nineties' publications – the poems of *The Shadow of Death* (1893) and the stories of *Studies in Death* (1894) – provoked any critical interest. And although he had commissioned a series of four drawings from Beardsley, such consideration was not enough to secure him a place in *The Yellow Book*. His story '*La Mazurka des revenants*' was turned down for the third number.

By the end of 1894 his health had seriously deteriorated. Suffering from disconcerting delusions, he was dispatched abroad, under the care of a private physician. In the decent obscurity of the French Riviera he loitered palely, accompanied not only by Dr Flanagan but also by a life-size male doll, which he referred to as his son and heir.

Wilde's own health during 1894 was not robust either. Moreover, without a play in production, the incoming flow of cash had dried up, while the outward drain continued. By the summer he found himself in the 'purple valleys of despair'. Nor was his equanimity improved by the ever more taxing conduct of Bosie's father. The Marquis of Queensberry, who at twenty-four had codified the rules of boxing, was now directing his pugilistic energies elsewhere. A man of fierce animosities, he had two particular hatreds – the Church and homosexuality. He was determined to break up what he saw as the 'scandalous' friendship between Wilde and his son. To this end he issued a series of threats and staged several unpleasant confrontations. Wilde was alarmed to discover that neither the sanctum of the Domino Room nor the hearth at Tite Street was safe from the brutish incursions of the 'Scarlet Marquess'. Douglas, fired by familial spite, went out of his way to provoke his father. But Wilde was depressed by the feud; he even tried to appease Queensberry, and once won him over for a few brief hours by discussing religion with him in the Café Royal. The respite proved all too brief. Wilde came to feel that he was being 'dogged by a maniac'. He began to consider recourse to the law, no matter what the scandal.

Yet, in the midst of these cares, Wilde took himself off to the seaside at Worthing, and during the two months of August and September wrote his one undisputed masterpiece. The composition of *The Importance of Being Earnest* was interrupted but not disturbed by a brief 'family holiday', pleasant bathing excursions with local youths, visits from Douglas, the appearance of *The Green Carnation*, and a certain amount of business correspondence.

John Lane and Elkin Mathews were in the process of dissolving their partnership and Wilde, for commercial reasons but rather against his personal inclination, found it advisable to keep all his books with Lane, who was to retain the Bodley Head imprint. In writing his new play, however, Wilde found an opportunity to vent his continuing irritation with the publisher of *The Yellow Book*. Lane's name was ingloriously given to Algernon Moncrieff's bibulous butler. The unmilitary Beerbohm too received an ironic tribute, appearing as 'Maxbohm' in a list of generals read out in the last act. Indeed, a thread of playful and personal subversion runs throughout the piece. The very title, with its play upon Earnest/Ernest, concealed a further twist, for 'Earnest' was one of the contemporary code-words for homosexual.

At the beginning of October the productive calm of No. 5, The Esplanade, Worthing, was shattered by the reappearance of Douglas. He wanted to be amused. He insisted on removing to the Hotel Metropole at Brighton, but promptly fell ill with flu upon arrival. Wilde nursed him dutifully, only to contract influuenza himself. Douglas, however, restored to health, was not interested in the chores of the sick-chamber. He had come to Brighton for pleasure and, (ab)using the prostrate Wilde's credit and cash, he set out to find it. A series of demeaning scenes ensued, terminated only by Douglas' abrupt departure.

Wilde would later claim that he had hoped this rupture might prove permanent, but the assertion seems wishful; he and Douglas were too bound up in the destructive toils of their curious *egoism à deux*. Nevertheless, the reconciliation came sooner and more dramatically than Wilde could have foreseen. On 18 October Bosie's eldest brother, Lord Drumlanrig, while on a shooting party in Quantock, Somerset, was found dead in a ditch, his shotgun having apparently misfired. The coroner's verdict was 'accidental death' but rumours of suicide eddied round the tragedy. Drumlanrig, who was on the verge of marriage, was suspected of being involved in a homosexual circle centred on the Foreign Minister, Lord Rosebery. A scandal at such a level could be very effectively kept from the general public, but Lord Queensberry had a suspicion (which he expressed with characteristic intemperance) that Rosebery and the other 'Snob Queers' might in some way be implicated in his son's death.

The loss of one child as the result of an ill-advised association can only have increased Queensberry's determination to break up the friendship between Wilde and Bosie. Drumlanrig's death had brought that pair back together as Douglas sought sympathy and attention in his bereavement. Soon the routine of champagne suppers, theatrical jaunts and rough trade was re-established.

The new year began with a double dose of glory. *An Ideal Husband* opened on 3 January at the Theatre Royal Haymarket, with the Prince of Wales in the royal box and fashionable London thronging the aisles. The play, with a dramatic irony that would not have escaped the little party of Wilde, Douglas, Beerbohm and Beerbohm-Tree who gathered for a post-performance supper at the Albermarle Club, was about a man whose successful public life is threatened by a terrible private secret. Wilde, however, chose not to dwell on this resonance. As the 'gold' began once more to 'rain' down, he departed with Douglas for a brief holiday in Algiers.

He returned (alone) after a happy fortnight, spent smoking hashish and chasing beautiful Arab boys, to oversee the final rehearsals of *The Importance of Being Earnest* which George Alexander was putting on at the St James's Theatre. The new play opened on St Valentine's night, less than six weeks after *An Ideal Husband*.

It is not always that a masterpiece is recognized on first acquaintance, but on this occasion all were in agreement with the author in their estimate of the piece. Even the critics, whom Wilde had sedulously baited in a series of interviews, could not but applaud. The play received a rapturous standing ovation. Beerbohm was there. Beardsley was a guest in the Leversons' box; but the pressures of his *Yellow Book* work were taking a heavy toll on his fragile constitution and Wilde commented that he looked like 'the most monstrous of orchids'.

Douglas was absent, still in North Africa. But his father had determined to interrupt the proceedings. Fortunately, Wilde was warned. The Marquis' ticket was cancelled, and twenty policemen were stationed outside the theatre to deny him admittance. He duly arrived clutching a large bunch of vegetables and accompanied by a prize fighter, but unable to get at his quarry, he prowled about for three hours in the swirling snow, then 'left chattering like a monstrous ape'.

Part IV

Profit & Parody

Chapter Eleven

JOHN LANE of the Bodley Head has long held a place in the nineties pantheon as the man who made decadence pay. The most distinctive decadent productions of the period – that quartet of seductive sibilants, *Silhouettes*, *Salome*, *Silverpoints* and *The Sphinx* – all bore his name and that of the Bodley Head upon their title-pages. It is true that they also bore another name, that of Elkin Mathews, Lane's partner and sometime friend, but it was Lane who courted the glory – and shouldered the responsibility – for these ventures. And it was Lane, the energetic self-publicist with the Van Dyck beard and the Devonian burr, who, ending the decade in sole charge of the Bodley Head, was able to efface the memory of his former associate.

Nevertheless, Elkin Mathews had been the first to invoke the name of the Elizabethan bibliophile, Sir Thomas Bodley, for business purposes. In the mid-1880s Mathews had opened a little bookshop in the Cathedral Yard at Exeter, the birthplace of Bodley, and emblazoned his first catalogue with the arms of the great man. That Mathews faded from the memory of the nineties cannot perhaps be blamed entirely on Lane. He was, by all accounts, a diffident, even retiring, character, out of temper with the brasher elements of the period. Born in 1851 into a large and cultured West Country family, he was almost forty before the nineties began. His childhood passion was for books, both reading and collecting them, and although after his schooling he was sent up to London to study accountancy, he quickly decided that he would try to turn his hobby into his career.

He trained with a bookseller off the Strand, and worked for a while in Bath. He then returned to London for a stint at Sotheran, which then – as now – had its premises just off Piccadilly. By 1884 he felt confident enough to establish his own business. Deserting the metropolis for the cloistral calm of 16 Cathedral Yard, Exeter, he set up as an 'Ancient and Modern Bookseller' with a specialist interest in local history and topography. He even dabbled in publishing, bringing out an *Index* to Dr Oliver's *Lives of the Bishops of Exeter* and a discursive account of a local lady's donkey trek along the Devon coast. Business, however, was slow.

He was bounced out of this gathering torpor by the busy little figure of John Lane. It is not known exactly how or when Lane and Mathews met, but from the late 1860s Lane was working as a clerk in the Railway Clearing House at Euston along with Elkin's elder brother, Thomas, so an introduction could easily have been made, perhaps even when Elkin was working at Sotheran.

John Lane was three years Mathews' junior. The son of a Devon yeoman and a miller's daughter, he lacked the advantages of a formal education. Nevertheless, there appears to have been some literary inclination in the family, on his mother's side. She was, at any rate, familiar enough with the Reverend Stephen Hawker, the parson-poet of Morwenstow, to seek his help in finding a clerical position for her son. Backed by the Rev. Hawker's sponsorship, John went up to the Clearing House at Euston Station in 1869. He was fourteen.

Arriving in London, innocent, agape and marked by a broad Devonian brogue, he very rapidly began to develop his interests and himself. He had a magpie's instincts for collecting, and soon he took to haunting second-hand bookstalls, print shops and bric-à-brac merchants in a ceaseless quest for curiosities. Although his enthusiasms ran to old pewter, painted fans and antique samplers, his greatest appetite was for books. At his lodgings in Southwick Street, Hyde Park, he gathered what one fellow-tenant described as an 'extensive but peculiar library'. Its peculiarity seems to have been a preponderance of works by George Meredith. And as Lane collected books, so he collected bookmen. He held occasional bookish parties in his little room, and by the eighties had even established himself as a member of the bibliophilic dining-club, the Sette of Odd Volumes.

Given his interests, it was not surprising that he should have taken to Elkin Mathews, the scholarly and knowledgeable bookseller of Cathedral Yard, Exeter. Nor, given his ambition, was it curious that he should have suggested a collaboration. Although Mathews may have expressed some misgivings about the business climate of Exeter, the scheme to bring him back to London, and into partnership with John Lane, was almost entirely engineered by the younger man. Through much of 1887 a barrage of letters descended upon 16 Cathedral Yard – urging, cajoling, bullying letters – propelling Elkin Mathews into the new arrangement.

By June Lane was writing excitedly that he had found the ideal premises: 'a little shop and a W.C. only . . . situated in Vigo St a few doors from Regent St adjoining the R[oyal] G[eographic] Soc: close to Burlington House and the London University etc. Indeed it is surrounded by seats of learning.' The shop belonged to a print-seller called Dunthorne who had recently moved to a larger building in the same street. Lane had approached Dunthorne at a private view with a casual enquiry as to whether there were any 'suitable premises for a high-class bookseller' in the area, and had been rather taken aback when Dunthorne replied, 'Yes! My own "little box" two doors from here.' The shop, Lane admitted, was small, but then so was the rental: eighty pounds per annum.

The location, moreover, was excellent, set between Regent Street and Savile Row, just behind Albany and the Royal Academy. It was close to the bookish centres of Sotheran and Hatchards. It was touched, too, with an air of aristocratic seclusion: horse-drawn traffic was barred from the street by a set of wooden posts.

Mathews obediently came up to inspect the site. But, although he approved it, he still continued to waver, and it was not until the autumn that Lane's undimmable enthusiasm finally carried the day. Despite the fact that Lane put up 'not one shilling of cash' and rather less than half the stock, Mathews found himself swept into a 'partnership' agreement. He was nevertheless to oversee the daily running of the shop, while Lane continued in his job at the clearing house.

Mathews had the satisfaction of giving a distinctive Exeter touch to the new Piccadilly venture. It was decided that Thos. Bodley would be the presiding spirit of the business, and he commissioned a terracotta portrait-medallion of the great West Countryman, tastefully gilded and inlaid, to hang up outside the shop. Mathews moved up to town, renting a house in the 'aesthetic' and unmetropolitan garden-suburb of Bedford Park, close to the Yeats family, to John Todhunter, Florence Farr and Professor York Powell. Meanwhile, 6B Vigo Street was swiftly fitted out with floor-to-ceiling bookshelves. Display cases were made for setting outside on the pavement. And all was ready for 10 October 1887.

The dominant flavour of the shop was antiquarian. It was,

contemporaries recalled, 'a little box of a place' crammed with old books, rarities and fine bindings. Lane's eye for the commercial benefits of controversy could already be glimpsed in the stocklist; he was particularly pleased to have got hold of a copy of *Fanny Hill*. Nevertheless, it was Mathews' interests that were most apparent.

The earliest ventures into publishing by the new firm were both Mathews-inspired projects left over from his Exeter days – indices to volumes of West Country history. The publishing sideline having been established, however, Lane very quickly began to assert his influence upon it. Early in 1888 he 'discovered' a new poet in the pages of the *Academy*. There was a generous review of the poet's first privately printed collection, there were examples of his work, there were references to his great love of books and to his living in Birkenhead. Lane was intrigued. He was intrigued too by the young poet's name: it was Richard Le Gallienne. Lane dispatched a letter addressed simply to 'Richard Le Gallienne, Esq. Poet. Birkenhead'. Le Gallienne's fame, however, had at that time not quite penetrated to the heart of the Liverpool district postal service and the letter was returned. Lane tried again through the offices of the *Academy*, with more success.

Le Gallienne was a provincial aesthete. He had been taken, at the impressionable age of seventeen, to Birkenhead Town Hall to hear Oscar Wilde give some 'Personal Impressions of America and her People'. He had been directly and completely converted to Wilde's creed of beauty and taste for knee-breeches.

He sent off fan letters to Tite Street. He grew his hair. He bought a velvet smoking-jacket and started reading Keats and Rossetti and Pater. He also started writing verse (in the manner of Keats and Rossetti) and prose (in the manner of Pater). It was a striking departure, but Liverpool, even then, afforded some comfort to aesthetic spirits: part of the industrial wealth of the early Victorian period had been ploughed into Pre-Raphaelite art by the new tycoons; there was a thriving local press, and a tenuous network of cultured initiates. Le Gallienne spent many of his free moments haunting the antiquarian bookshops of the area, discussing the cavalier poets with other like-minded romancers and slowly building up a choice little library. And he did all this while studying for his accountancy exams.

A career in double-entry book-keeping was not, however, his ambition. In 1887 he spent his meagre savings on a limited edition collection of his own verse, entitled *My Ladies Sonnets*. The long hours in the second-hand bookshops had given him a well-developed taste for archaic typography and old bindings, and his literary connections had introduced him to a local printer with the ability and the patience to indulge such enthusiasms. As a result Le Gallienne's début volume was decked out in all the trappings of bygone elegance. The blue-grey end-boards were hinged upon a spine of imitation vellum; the poems were printed on fine white hand-made paper, and each was graced with a rubricated initial.

This was the book which had been so favourably noticed in the *Academy* as 'a little volume, the sight and handling of which brings a quick thrill of pleasure to the breast of the book lover'. It was the book of which Lane requested a copy in his letter to the Poet of Birkenhead. And it was the book which was to influence greatly the production values of the new Bodley Head imprint.

What brought a pleasing thrill to John Lane when he received his copy of *My Ladies Sonnets* was that the book looked like an antiquarian volume. Old books were his and his partner's business. They were in their modest way a hot commodity. The tide of cheap, ugly, under-designed and over-produced books churning from the mechanical presses of Victorian England had provoked an inevitable reaction among a discerning minority in favour of well-crafted and elegantly produced work. The book auction records of the late 1880s attest to the growth and strength of such bibliophily – to the desirability of what Pater called those 'pretty volumes of the Bibliothèque Elzevirienne', to the cachet of the simple 'Aldine Poets' series produced barely fifty years before.

As demand grew, so the market expanded. The historical perspective grew shorter and shorter, until people began buying up contemporary works which they thought would become out-of-print rarities. Modern first editions acquired an unprecedented commercial glamour; and Lane was quick to appreciate the glow. He moved promptly to buy up copies of the Mermaid edition of Marlowe's plays (edited by Havelook Ellis) when he learnt that it was going to be withdrawn on account of its blasphemous appendix. He also recognized the potential of Andrew Lang's Pater-inspired edition of 'The Marriage of Cupid and Psyche' published by David Nutt in 1887. And from the time his collaboration with Elkin Mathews was first mooted he urged his partner to gather enough desirable first editions so that they could produce a special catalogue of them.

The 'sight and handling' of *My Ladies Sonnets* convinced Lane that it would be quite possible for him and Mathews to produce something in the same line. They could in effect manufacture their own supply of handsome limited-edition *volumes de virtue*, producing and selling them cheaply enough to widen still further the base of interest in beautiful books.

Lane very sensibly decided to include Le Gallienne in this new vision, and not merely because he needed someone to supply the sonnets; he wanted to borrow the poet's obvious enthusiasm for book production. The Poet of Birkenhead received an invitation to call and, on his next trip to London, Le Gallienne looked in at the little shop in Vigo Street. He met Lane and was introduced to Mathews. He was flattered, encouraged and made much of. The visit was eminently satisfactory for all. Soon plans were afoot to bring out Le Gallienne's next collection under the sign of Bodley Head. It was to be the first venture into verse publishing by the new partnership.

Exactly the same attention to the physical details of paper, print, binding and design that had distinguished *My Ladies Sonnets* was now applied to *Volumes in Folio*. As a further flourish it was decided that the print run should include fifty copies in a large format, each signed and numbered by the author, as well as three de-luxe copies on Japanese hand-made paper. Although the book was to be produced in London by the Chiswick Press, rather than by Mr Robb in Liverpool, Le Gallienne involved himself busily in the minutiae of its construction. He, after all, was the experienced party. Lane was still engaged during the day at Euston, and Mathews, as Le Gallienne rather brutally complained, knew 'as much about the *modus operandi* of book production as a suckling pig'. Le Gallienne's management of the project became even more complete at the beginning of 1889 when he deserted Liverpool and his accountancy studies to take up a short-term post as secretary to the famous actor-manager Wilson Barrett. Up in London he was able to oversee closely the final stages of the book's gestation.

Imaginative and innovatory though Lane's scheme was, it was not unique. Several other small publishing houses, such as David Nutt, Ward Lock and Osgood, McIlvaine & Co, were already producing small but handsome volumes redolent of past times. Indeed the production of *Volumes in Folio* took place against a background of – and was made possible by – a more general revival in the art of printing. Just as the unsightly offspring of the Victorian mechanized presses had stimulated a reactionary interest in old books amongst the public, so they had encouraged an interest in old printing techniques, old type-faces, traditional bindings and classical formats amongst professional printers.

The Chiswick Press, where *Volumes in Folio* was to be printed, had been in the van of this renaissance. As early as the 1840s it had reintroduced the beautiful Caslon old-face type, and the head of the firm in the 1880s and 1890s, Charles T. Jacobi, maintained the high standards set by his predecessors. The field was one that appealed greatly to aesthetes of a practical temper. 'The Revival of Printing' provided the subject for the influential lecture given by Emery Walker to the Art and Crafts Society in 1888, which is said to have inspired William Morris to found the Kelmscott Press.

If the technical expertise was in place for Lane's project, so too were the economic conditions. The prohibitive costs of type-setting had been recently and drastically reduced by the invention of the 'composing machine'. It had also become possible to make stereotype moulds of the set-up pages for use on reprints. Setting costs were kept still lower by Lane's decision to publish poetry, for which fewer and larger characters were required. Furthermore, the simple yet elegant binding – quarter (fake) vellum, three-quarters board – favoured by Lane and Le Gallienne not only looked better but was also cheaper than the vulgar gilt and cloth confections of high-Victorian style. The total printer's bill for *Volumes in Folio* was £24 5s. 2d., which included the cost of the paper.

The risk of the whole enterprise could, moreover, be minimized. Using the same technique that Elkin Mathews had employed in Exeter for subscribing his learned publications on local history, the Bodley Head partners issued a prospectus announcing the imminent appearance of *Volumes in Folio*: giving details of its author, format and price (five shillings), and including a detachable order form. A favourable response encouraged them to print a basic first edition of two hundred and fifty copies (plus the extra fifty-three large-paper versions). And such confidence was not misplaced.

By the time the book was issued in mid-March 1889 many of the ordinary and all of the large-paper copies had been sold. The book was praised in the *Academy* and the *Saturday Review*. Scribners of New York bought fifty copies, and the printing was very soon exhausted.

The experiment had proved a success and, with variations, it provided the basic format and procedure for almost all the books produced under the sign of the Bodley Head during the next five years: limited print-runs and special formats, to titilate the interest of book collectors; distinctive old-world designs; prospecti to gauge the market; and – also – the exploitation of America as a valuable export market. Although poetry would remain the staple of the list, Lane and Mathews soon extended their range to include *belles lettres*, short stories, literary criticism, plays and – in time – even novels.

It was decided that Le Gallienne's next project for the firm should be a critical study of George Meredith, for which Lane would provide a bibliography. Their close collaboration, however, received a setback when Wilson Barrett and his company departed for a tour of the United States towards the end of 1889. Although Le Gallienne, because of his severe asthma, was deemed unfit to travel, without his job he could not remain in London. Disconsolate, he returned north to work on his book and plot a speedy reprieve.

In his absence Lane and Mathews pursued the search for new talent on their own. Lane's gregarious nature, the congenial 'smokers' he held in his Bayswater room, his membership of the Odd Volumes, his 'passion' (as Le Gallienne termed it) for 'everything new under the sun', all equipped him particularly well for the task. The little literary circle centred on the *Academy* magazine provided him with one source of new writers: Gleeson White was persuaded to produce a series of *Letters to Living Artists*, while another young contributor, Cosmo Monkhouse, offered a collection of his own poems under the title *Corn and Poppies*. Lane also wrote excitedly to Le Gallienne about his discovery of William Strang, a young man who, in the tradition of Blake and Rossetti, was both painter and poet. Le Gallienne wrote back, no less excitedly, praising Lane as 'an unexceptionable guide to all manner of *New*dities'.

Mathews had less taste for '*New*dity' (or for excruciating puns). Though also less sociable than Lane, he nevertheless contributed to the partnership's early stock of authors. His residence out at Bedford Park brought him into ready contact with the suburb's aesthetic coteries. Indeed John Todhunter's play, *A Sicilian Idyll* (a work suggested by Yeats and performed at Bedford Park in May 1890 with Florence Farr in the lead role), was one of the dozen publications brought out by the Bodley Head during 1890.

Of the other eleven volumes – four collections of poetry and seven critical studies (including works on Dante, Tennyson and

Browning) – it is difficult, with the exception of the Monkhouse and Le Gallienne books, to ascribe exclusive responsibility to one or other partner. Lane, however, despite his quotidien commitments at the Clearing House (and despite the fact that his name did not appear on the title-page beside Elkin Mathews'), clearly emerged as the more energetic of the pair. His power within the firm increased further during the summer of 1891 when he exerted his influence to secure Le Gallienne the post of literary critic of the *Star*, a popular London evening paper. The appointment allowed Le Gallienne to return to London, and it placed him in a prime position to promote the forthcoming productions from his friends in Vigo Street under his chosen soubriqet of 'Logroller'.

This encouraging new set-up and the steady success of the 1891 publications convinced Lane that the firm could now support his additional weight. At the beginning of the new year (1892) he left his job at Euston and entered into full and open partnership. As the *Publishers' Circular* announced, the new style of the firm was to be 'Elkin Mathews and John Lane'.

Even before he made this step Lane had come into contact with some of the writers who were experimenting with decadent themes and styles. It was not surprising, considering his passion for novelty, that he should have been drawn to such deliberate advocates of what was both modern and strange. He had made the acquaintance of Oscar Wilde and was familiar with many of the young poets who were even then forming the Rhymers' Club. On both these fronts his progress was eased by the solicitous presence of Le Gallienne.

Since his blinding conversion to the aesthetic creed in 1883, Le Gallienne had cultivated a passionate friendship with Wilde. He wrote him fulsome letters, sent him specially bound manuscripts and presentation copies, visited him in London, and flattered him with poetic tributes. One memorable couplet, commemorating a joint picnic excursion in the summer of 1888, ran, 'With Oscar Wilde, a summer-day/Passed like a yearning kiss away . . .' The apparent homoeroticism of these lines seems to have been quite innocent (on Le Gallienne's part at least). Indeed, when Le Gallienne moved up to London and saw rather more of Wilde, he very quickly came to disapprove of him. He disliked Wilde's train of effeminate young men, and he disliked, too, his desertion of the 'English Renaissance' for the corrupt strains of 'French' decadence. But although their friendship dwindled, it dwindled slowly, and Lane – who had met Wilde very occasionally at the Odd Volumes – had time to impose an aquaintanceship.

While the Bedford Park connection gave Mathews access to one section of the Rhymers' Club, Le Gallienne provided Lane with an entrée to the younger members of the group. Indeed, both publishers were occasional guests at club meetings. Lane's interest in young poets was matched by their interest in his publishing business. It might be expected that those of a decadent turn would appreciate the publisher for his commitment to the creation of beautiful books – volumes in which form dared to assert itself at the expense of content. In fact their enthusiasm, though it acknowledged the Bodley Head's commitment to fine production, was pitched at a more mundane level. As Arthur Symons put it, here was a house which 'actually makes poetry pay'.

Symons' youthful enthusiasm rather overstated the case, for – with an average cover-price of five shillings, print-runs often as low as two hundred and a royalty of ten per cent – the poet's remuneration was likely to be slight. Indeed, of the first twenty works produced by the firm (between 1889 and the end of 1891) it was the prose rather than the poetry that achieved the greatest success. Wicksteed's *Six Sermons* on Dante went through three editions, Le Gallienne's study of Meredith and Nettleship's essay on Browning, two apiece. Nevertheless, the perception of the Bodley Head as a successful publisher of poetry was established early and continued long.

Lane recognized the value of a reputation as well as the need for publicity in establishing one. Without the resources to pay for wide advertisement, he became adept at stirring up press – and public – interest through controversy. With Le Gallienne strategically placed at the *Star*, he had a ready conduit for his schemes. Scarcely a single Bodley Head production was left unmentioned in Le Gallienne's weekly column. Johnson's book on Hardy, Symons' *Silhouettes*, William Watson's book of criticism, Norman Gale's milkmaid verses: they were all there. To judge from the pages of the *Star* one might think that the Bodley Head was responsible for the lion's share of British book production during the early 1890s. Le Gallienne, moreover, was not above (or below) mentioning his own books. Meredith received a puff, and when the first *Book of the Rhymers' Club* appeared, he airily confessed to being 'a humble participator', but added that the volume was 'an important event' and could not be ignored.

In his Bodley Head reviews he gave particular prominence to the firm's high production standards. There was praise for 'the wonderful "golden singing coat" in which Messers Elkin Mathews and John Lane have just republished Mr Wilde's poems'; and, a week later, a note that 'Michael Field's' *Sight and Song* had been 'published in delicius buff and sage-green boards by Messers Elkin Mathews and John Lane'. By the time Lord de Tablay's poems came out in the spring of 1893 he was able to describe the volume as 'in every way worthy of the high standards of the Bodley Head'.

Inevitably such publicity, so brash, so unashamed, and so new to the gentle world of book publishing, 'sometimes', as one Bodley Head author recalled, 'offended taste in those more fastidious days'. She even suggested in her memoirs that the term 'log-rolling' was 'first applied in this country' to John Lane. Le Gallienne, moreover, was not the firm's only literary lumberjack. With many Bodley Head authors combining journalism with their more 'serious' work, the network of influence extended far. James Ashcroft Noble, Cosmo Monkhouse, Gleeson White, Frederick Wedmore and John Davidson provided a concentration of influence at the *Academy*. Symons was music-hall correspondent for the *Star*, while Katherine Tynan (whose *Cuckoo Song* was published early in 1894) was a regular contributor to the *Irish Daily Independent*.

When Francis Thompson's *Poems* were issued in November 1893, Alice and Wilfred Meynell (his friends and patrons) launched – together with Lane – a concerted publicity campaign, which included a flattering piece in *Merry England* by Alice (the dedicatee of the volume and herself a Bodley Head author), a glowing review in the *Daily Chronicle* from Le Gallienne, and no fewer than three generous puffs in different magazines by Vernon Blackburn, a close friend of the Meynells. Such tactics, although they brought results (over two thousand copies of the book were sold in the first six months), also engendered resentment and surly mutterings about a 'mutual admiration society'.

Nor was press hyping considered Lane's only offence against the taste of those 'more fastidious days'. Despite widespread praise for Vigo Street's 'artistic' approach to book production, there were some commentators who disapproved of what they thought to be Lane's creation and manipulation of a false market in first editions. By giving second-rate poems first-class clothes and tiny print-runs the Bodley Head, it was argued, was making books desirable for the wrong reasons. The *Fortnightly Review* and the *Pall Mall Gazette* were both censorious. The former lamented that while first editions of Thackeray and Dickens were ignored, 'every ephemeral and often rubbishy tract by living authors' is snapped up by eager speculators. Lane himself, having created the market, was happy to speculate in it. He bought up the remainders of recherché poetry books from the 1880s – works such as Wilde's *Poems* and Théophile Marzials' *Gallery of Pigeons* – and added the stock to the Bodley Head list.

Such actions, and the charges they provoked, created a climate of hostility. As one critic noted, Bodley Head books were often 'attacked . . . through simple dislike of the egregious firm that published [them]'. But attacks, for Lane, were yet more grist to the publicity mill. And it was also as publicity corn that decadence seems to have made its primary appeal.

Lane's 'passion for novelty' was, in fact, quite superficial. Although he was open to what Wilde called 'curious works of art', his personal preferences lay with poetry of a more traditional and insular stamp. William Watson's sub-Wordsworthian sonnets were capable of reducing him to tears (and his tastes were echoed – even more loudly – by both Mathews and Le Gallienne). Nevertheless, as a publisher, Lane recognized the value of supporting both – or all – sides in an argument; he was content to promote representatives from all the modern schools: realists, ruralists, classicists, New Women, Ibsenites, decadents, moralists, Celts. In publishing decadent verse alongside traditionalist work, Lane saw an opportunity to stir up a debate and raise the whole profile of modern poetry.

In direct commercial terms the more conventional poetry easily outsold the self-consciously decadent offerings. But volumes such as *Silhouettes* and *Silverpoints* produced a gratifying amount of outraged press attention, and lent to the traditionalist school an aspect of crusading zeal.

Le Gallienne in his *Star* reviews quickly established himself as a stern critic of decadent verse. He always took care, however, to give such work (especially when published by Lane) generous coverage. He would also temper his strictures with a few sentences of qualified praise, which Lane was able to use for future quotation (out of context) in Bodley Head advertisements. He damned Symons' work for its soulless 'Impressionism' ('the Sadduceism of art') but he also admitted a limited 'Watteau-like, Japanese' charm. Gray's *Silverpoints* was a 'new sensation in format' but the poems 'in theme and treatment are as décadent as can be'; nevertheless, beneath the 'mystic eroticism', Le Gallienne was pleased to note a 'remarkable pictorial gift' and an unexpected interest in 'everyday themes'.

In his enthusiastic review of the original French version of Wilde's *Salomé* ('his *chef d'oeuvre* . . . monstrous . . . evil . . . accursed . . . [but] most cunningly wrought and intensely dramatic'), Le Gallienne so far forgot himself as to attempt to put an apology for decadence into the author's mouth: 'to those who talk of the immorality of the theme,' he suggested, 'Mr Wilde might well ask: Is it not a virtuous act to transform evil things to beauty? Doesn't one thus, so to say, *redeem* them?' By the time the translation was issued, with Beardsley's illustrations, Le Gallienne had, however, revised his position: 'something of the ancient simplicity of soul surviving within us' told him that Beardsley's art, 'though "devilishly" clever', was, 'in the words of Mr Pater, ". . . what I may not see"'. Then, reversing his views on the redemptive potential of beauty, he added: 'From the days of the serpent in Paradise – evil things have taken beautiful forms, and perhaps beauty and evil are more frequently found in company than beauty and good.'

The effect of such reviews was not only to encourage other papers to cover decadent literature but also to forge in the public mind a particular association between the Bodley Head and decadence. This, of course, was to set the equation back to front; for it was decadence that was associated with the Bodley Head. Four of the most distinctively decadent books of the decade were produced under the aegis of John Lane and Elkin Mathews between the autumn of 1892 and summer of 1894, but they were a small part of the firm's output and contributed little to its profits. None of them went into a second edition.

Silhouettes appeared at the beginning of October 1892 in a run of two hundred and fifty copies (with twenty-five in large-paper format). Its cover was grey and its price was five shillings. It seems to have been produced almost as a direct foil to Richard Le Gallienne's stridently anti-decadent, anti-French, third collection of verse, *English Poems*, which was issued the week before in an edition three times the size (even before two subsequent reprintings). In several places they were reviewed together, usually to the detriment of *Silhouettes*.

Lane's decision to issue the French version of Wilde's *Salomé* at the beginning of the next year also smacked of opportunism. After the première of the play had been banned by the Lord Chamberlain the previous June, a French publisher, Paul Schmidt, had agreed to bring out an edition of the text. With copies of the play thus readily and cheaply available, Lane agreed to take three hundred and fifty. He even struck the deal in time for the Bodley Head name to appear together with M. Schmidt's on the title-page (although he delayed paying until after the book was printed). To Wilde's horror, Lane then advertised the book under the sensationalist slogan, 'The play the Lord Chamberlain refused to licence'.

To create a further splash, and to take advantage of the growing public awareness of decadence (as a catchword, if nothing else), Lane planned to bring out Gray's *Silverpoints* on the same day as *Salomé*, a notion which Gray thought 'warrants as little wisdom as it does satisfaction'. In the event Lane's own cautious attitude towards Gray's decadent verses scotched the scheme. There was a delay in publication when Lane insisted that Gray excise the poem 'Song of the Stars' from the collection 'on the grounds of indecency', and the book did not finally make its appearance until two weeks after *Salomé*.

The English version of *Salome* with the Beardsley illustrations followed a year later, in February 1894. The gathering notoriety of Wilde and the sudden emergence of Beardsley gave Lane a commanding platform. There were to be 755 copies of the ordinary cloth-bound edition (505 for England, 250 for America) and an impressive 125 copies of the special, de luxe, thirty-shilling edition, printed on Japanese hand-made paper and bound in green silk. The book achieved an instant and expected infamy. The *Studio* reviewer considered it, '. . . the very essence of the decadent *fin de siècle* . . . the typical volume of the period'.

Such a startling splash could not be easily repeated. When Wilde's *Sphinx* was published in June of the same year, rather than trying to expand the market further, Lane cleverly opted for extreme exclusivity. The poem was brought out in a small but exquisite edition of 303 copies, with the princely cover-price of two guineas.

The book was decorated not by Beardsley but by Wilde's friend

Ricketts. The impact of the illustrated *Salome* had, however, already forged in the public consciousness an irrefragable link between Wilde, Beardsley and decadence. The strength of the connection was revealed very clearly in the spring of 1894 with the launching of *The Yellow Book*.

Although, as has been suggested, the initial inspiration for *The Yellow Book* came from Beardsley and Harland's fog-bound lunch party of New Year's Day 1894, it was Lane who carried their ideas into practice. From the start he involved himself closely and completely with the project, presiding over excited editorial discussions at the Hogarth Club (his informal conference facility in Dover Street), tempering the wilder enthusiasms of his editors and contributing his detailed knowledge of book production. The format of the periodical, its hard cloth-bound covers, its good paper, its Caslon old-face type, all bore the recognized Bodley Head stamp that Lane had worked so hard to create. And, as the publisher, Lane had the final say in all matters.

There can be no doubt that Lane, the arch-publicist, intended to create a stir – even a *succès de scandale* – with his new venture. And he well knew that the mask of decadence was likely to prove the most alarming to both press and public. By sanctioning Beardsley as art editor, and indeed by agreeing to the periodical's very title, he ensured that *The Yellow Book* would have an initial impact that was both arresting and alarming. After all, it is only shallow people who do not judge a book by its cover. The yellow tint was calculated to suggest French literature, and Beardsley's cover illustration could be relied upon to suggest considerably more. His flowing sinuous line, his extraordinary representations of the female form, his very name, had – even in the brief morning of his fame – become the defining symbols of decadence.

It was not, however, that Lane wished to establish a decadent periodical. Far from it. He wanted *The Yellow Book* to reflect the full range of the Bodley Head's interests, to act as an advertisement for his current authors and a sounding-board for future ones. In his editor, Harland, moreover, he had a man who was no particular friend to decadent literature. The first numbers show an impressive variety of 'literature in all its phases': realist short stories, tales of New Women, the more robust forms of verse, the sentimental aestheticism of Le Gallienne and the rural-pagan frolics of Kenneth Grahame, as well as the offerings of Beerbohm and Symons.

Lane seems indeed to have taken deliberate steps to redress any imbalance caused by the magazine's decadent elements. In an attempt to provide 'gravitas', several established names were approached. Harland secured a short story from his hero, Henry James. George Saintsbury promised an article. Frederick Leighton, the President of the Royal Academy, contributed a drawing. And, as a final safety-valve, the first number included an essay by Arthur Waugh on 'Reticence in Literature'. The piece amounted to a condemnation of the 'present tendency to literary frankness' in both its decadent and its realist guises. The former school Waugh castigated for its 'effeminate . . . want of restraint which starts from enervated sensations' and 'plays with the subtle emotions of sensual pleasure'; the latter he condemned for its 'chirurgical' manner and 'brutal vitality, which proceeds from coarse familiarity with indulgence'. In neither could he find that 'unity', that sense of due proportion, which for him (as for Le Gallienne) marked the true work of art.

Despite such elaborate checks and precautions, when the 'Book' appeared it exploded on the public, as planned, with a distinctly decadent boom. Its very look caused a gratifying amount of panic. For publication day the window of the shop in Vigo Street was dressed entirely with *Yellow Books*. The effect of this 'mighty glow of yellow' was, according to J. Lewis May, the office boy at the time, as though 'the sun had risen in the West'. Some, however, were blinded by the brilliance. 'Michael Field' was appalled by the 'incurable jaundice' of so much yellowness. Both aunt and niece considered it to be 'the glare of Hell' no less, and closer knowledge of the book did nothing to alleviate their shock. They quickly recalled the poem that they had submitted for consideration.

While 'Michael Field' retreated, the press attacked. And they attacked their quarry principally on account of its decadent demeanour. Beardsley's drawings were vilified as 'bizarre', 'eccentric' and 'unhealthy'; Symons' poem received a fusillade of abuse; and Beerbohm's squib upon 'Artifice' was considered a 'bomb thrown by a cowardly decadent'. John Lane was able to fill a book with the press cuttings. Although there were a few dissenting voices (and Le Gallienne in the *Star* characterized the volume as 'a refreshing reminder of the diversity of life'), *The Yellow Book* was widely proclaimed as the very clarion of decadence.

This, of course, was a gross distortion, but it was a persuasive one. Even several Bodley Head authors – besides 'Michael Field' – were taken in by it. John Oliver Hobbes announced, on receiving a copy of the book, that he had 'never seen such a vulgar production', and was left to rue his inclusion in it. Alice Meynell and Lord de Tablay declined to contribute. The sober heavyweights took fright too. Frederick Leighton rushed around to Vigo Street to tell Lane that all his friends had reprimanded him for embarrassing the name of serious art, and to excuse himself from any further involvement. Henry James fretted to his brother over 'the horrid aspect and company of the whole production', but lacked the private income to support his qualms; 'for gold and to oblige the worshipful Harland' he would contribute three more stories.

The public, however, recently primed by the press coverage of the Beardsley-Wilde *Salome*, were intrigued as much as alarmed by the furore. There is always a market for scandal. The first volume required two reprints within a week, and sold a healthy seven thousand copies at five shillings each. The price was the same as that for a volume of verse, yet the circulation was some twenty times greater. With *The Yellow Book* Lane projected decadent art beyond the initiated coteries and on to a wider public.

He had borrowed from the aesthetic magazine tradition of the *Germ*, the *Dial* and the *Hobby Horse*, but had added to it the distinctive elements of the Bodley Head house-style, and then marketed the result with all his considerable genius. For most readers *The Yellow Book* must have appeared as something exciting, attractive and daring. It offered access to a previously closed world that was both 'new' and 'shocking'. And nothing, at the time, seemed newer or more shocking than decadence.

Harland suggested to Lane that 'Aubrey must modify himself in Volume II', but there was little sign of any retreat. The publisher was evidently still confident of his shock tactics. Although the second volume, like the first, contained much that was not decadent (including a review of the first number by an independent critic which, amidst the general praise, lamented that Symons should employ 'poetic art to celebrate common fornication'), the decadent elements – provided principally by Beardsley – were still there too.

And to keep the debate simmering nicely there was even a lengthy reply to Arthur Waugh by Hubert Crackanthorpe (a young writer of decidedly 'chirurgical' short stories). Crackanthorpe, who by Waugh's terms was a realist rather than a decadent, was concerned to defend what he considered the 'general return of the literary artist towards nature'. In passing, however, he lamented that the movement's detrators – whether conventional bourgeois Philistines or reactionary 'artistic objectors' – were wont to decry everything new and unconventional as 'decadence'. 'Everything,' he suggested, is called 'decadent nowadays: Ibsen, Degas, and the New English Art Club, Zola, Oscar Wilde, and the Second Mrs Tanqueray.'

He did not, however, attempt to make any finer distinction, and – in his haste to set the individual sensibility above the claims of any artistic creed – he left the reader uncertain as to whether decadence and realism were the same thing, rather than opposite sides of the same coin as Waugh had more helpfully suggested. The Philistines, of course, did not concern themselves with any such confusion of nomenclature. They merely added *The Yellow Book* and Aubrey Beardsley to Wilde, Zola, Ibsen and the more advanced works of Arthur Wing Pinero on that list of things which they considered decadent.

This widespread confusion over the term was not helped by Lane's decision to use Beardsley to design the covers for a series of cheaply produced one-volume Bodley Head fictions. George Egerton's *Keynotes*, which provided both the impetus and the name for the series, had come out in December 1893 and was reprinted twice over the next six months. The book was a collection of realist short stories proclaiming the arrival of the New Woman in the old battle of the sexes. But the cover was by Beardsley, the embodiment of decadence. In the popular consciousness Egerton's New Woman became merged with the Beardsley Woman. Indeed a similar osmosis began to affect the whole list. For many, the Bodley Head and Vigo Street became virtual synonyms for decadence.

Wilde, too, was a victim of such casual classification. Certainly his exclusion from *The Yellow Book* went quite unremarked. An American paper, the *Critic*, even dubbed *The Yellow Book* as 'The Oscar Wilde of periodicals'. Wilde was not amused, and his business relationship with Lane, which had always been fraught, deteriorated still further from this point. Wilde enjoyed being exacting; and he delighted in pointing up the contrasts between his lofty artistic aims and his publisher's narrow commercialism. He would always insist that in book contracts he was referred to not as 'the author' but as 'the poet'. And with *The Sphinx* going to press at the time of *The Yellow Book*'s unwelcome advent Wilde lost no opportunity to be awkward and demanding. He even refused to let Lane put any advertisement pages in the book, for – as he remarked to Ricketts – 'silly things about Le Gallienne are out of place in a work of art'.

Lane's other 'decadent' authors were less troublesome. Although they recognized that his support of their work was based more on commercial canniness than artistic admiration – and although they teased him on this account – they maintained a tone of good-natured exasperation. And they were happy to see him socially. Beerbohm might call him 'that poor fly in the amber of modernity', complain of his dress sense, and pretend that his enthusiasm for Beardsley was based on the fact that '*he never goes over the edges*!' but he readily accepted invitations to the convivial parties that Lane held in his rooms or at the Hogarth Club.

Beardsley seems to have enjoyed rather than resented his frequent battles with Lane. It was a sense of schoolboy naughtiness that led him to hide obscene details and libellous caricatures in his pictures; he wanted them to be discovered. And when Lane duly discovered them, Beardsley was always happy enough to take them out. In most of his dealings with the publisher Beardsley adopted a tone of facetious exaggeration which allowed him to make his points, or vent his resentment, in jest.

If Lane's published authors recognized, and forgave, the trace of opportunism that lay behind his promotion of their 'decadent' work, there were unpublished writers who recognized it too and, with an opportunism of their own, sought to take advantage of the situation. Amongst the bales of unsolicited literature that Lane received during 1894 were two particular manuscripts – one a collection of detective stories, the other a matched pair of paranormal romances – which were deliberately dressed in the fashionable and scented robes of contemporary decadence. He decided to publish them both in his successful Keynotes series.

M. P. Shiel's *Prince Zaleski* is one of the neglected semi-precious stones of 1890s decadence. Matthew Shiel, like Symons, was a child of non-conformism. Unlike Symons, though, he was the youngest of ten children and had been born in the West Indies, where his father was a Methodist preacher on the island of Montserrat. To this exotic background he added, as a defining detail, the vivid childhood memory of a local fiesta at which he had been crowned 'king' of a small, guano-encrusted rock called Rodundo (or Redonda). The uncontested sovereignty of this shit-bespattered outcrop provided the young Shiel with an enduring sense of his own specialness. It sustained him through his university career at King's College, London, through his brief stint as a maths teacher in Derbyshire, and through the first stages of a medical training at St Bartholomew's Hospital. In 1894, however, at the age of twenty-nine, he renounced medicine, after being overcome by nausea while watching an eye operation. To support himself after this break he decided to try literature. And for his début he resolved to create a decadent hero. He had always loved the classics (particularly Greek) but his adolescence had been much affected by the twin discoveries of Edgar Allan Poe and tobacco, heady intoxicants that had combined to 'transport [him] to Nephelococcugia'. It was to that distant region that he returned to gather news of Prince Zaleski.

Zaleski is a detective – or, rather, a solver of problems. Readers of the 1890s were familiar with the type, and were familiar too with the hint of decadence that accompanied it. Sherlock Holmes was in many ways a proto decadent figure: bored by life, tormented by an overkeen intellect, seeking release in drugs and art (or, at least, the violin). (It is perhaps suggestive that *The Sign of Four* – in which Holmes makes his second appearance – was commissioned at exactly the same time as Wilde's *Picture of Dorian Gray*.)

The subtlety of Conan Doyle's characterization is, however, largely absent from Shiel's work. Shiel's hero is a splendid caricature of *fin de siècle* quirks. He is the last of an aristocratic line, and he lives alone (in a decayed mansion) with only a silent manservant, a vast Negro called, revealingly, Ham. We first meet him (having pushed open a door covered in python skin) reclining in the gloom of his curio-filled chamber, a cloud of cannabis smoke about his head, a 'gemmed chiborgue' in one hand and 'an old vellum reprint of Anacereon' in the other.

Apart from the usual knowledge of arcane literature, gemology and Persian word-endings, Prince Zaleski has a very nineties-ish enthusiasm for paradoxical *bons mots*: 'a novel in which there is nowhere any pretence of novelty'; 'Britain, in reality, is a small continent. Near her – a little to the south-east – is situated the large island of Europe.' And so forth. As a further refinement Sheil extended that victory of imaginative vision over active experience manifest in des Esseintes' 'trip' to England, or, indeed, in Swinburne's sex life, to cover the fresh ground of forensic detection; Zaleski is able to solve most mysteries without ever quitting his room. A few mind-clearing bars of Delibes played upon the organ in the corner of his chamber are usually all that he requires to unravel a problem that has long baffled the combined might of Scotland Yard and the British press. Even the subjects of his investigations – the hereditary strain of insanity in Lord Pharanx's family, the mysterious properties of Sir Jocelin Saul's turquoise, an inexplicable epidemic of suicide – bear a decidedly decadent stamp.

The other manuscript that Lane accepted at this time was by Arthur Machen (whose real name was Arthur Llewellyn Jones). Machen was yet another child of the church: his father was a Welsh clergyman. But it was his parents' Welshness rather than their religion which exercised the greater influence over his development. Young Arthur became a passionate explorer of the byways of Celtic lore and mysticism. On coming to London in 1880 at the age of seventeen, he worked as a cataloguer of diabolistic books and as a translator. After dabbling with various arcane sects he was eventually initiated, like Yeats, into the Order of the Golden Dawn.

Machen's interest in an unseen spiritual dimension would later lead him towards an idiosyncratic symbolism, but in 1894 he used his occult knowledge more for decoration. His bizarre Keynotes volume, *The Great God Pan* (containing the title story and another piece, 'The Inmost Light'), was replete with decadent tropes. There was the diabolical *femme fatale* of the first *conte* and the diabolical opal of the second. Both tales have a vivid, contemporary London setting, fixed on the narrow alleys of Soho and the larger streets off Piccadilly (although just how often the characters pass before the little shop in Vigo Street is left to the reader's imagination). As in Shiel's book there is a curious spate of *felos de se* to titillate contemporary anxieties upon the subject. (Some quarters of the press and public had claimed, despite a marked absence of evidence, that the degeneracy of the age had produced a sharp increase in suicide, as more and more 'neurotic' spirits felt unable to sustain either the tedium or the terror of life.) The whole is seasoned with the spice of corruption, a savour which Machen himself characterized as 'the quintessence of yellow bookery'.

Though neither Shiel nor Machen was young – at least by the precocious standards of the nineties – they were, in 1894, both starting out on their literary careers, and both of them, it seems, deliberately slanted their debutant works to catch the yellow rays of the decadent sun, aware that this would give it an appealing tint to John Lane and his public.

The response of John Davidson to the decadent vogue was more complex. Although he acknowledged something of the charm of the artificial by wearing a wig to cover his baldness, as a penurious middle-aged Scot in London he felt it his duty to castigate the glib and fashionable theories of metropolitan youth. The effete strainings of the Rhymers' Club irritated him profoundly. He complained that the society lacked 'blood and guts', and although he regularly attended their meetings, he refused to contribute to their books.

While some of his confrères were seeking tremulously to lose themselves in 'sensation', Davidson was hammering out exuberant ballads, unactable verse dramas and wordy book reviews for the *Academy*. His first taste of success came in 1893 when the Bodley Head brought out his *Fleet Street Eclogues*, a cycle of dramatic poems recounting the seasonal travails and arcadian hankerings of a group of ink-stained newspaper hacks. It quickly ran through two editions, and garnered a bouquet of appreciative reviews, notably from the *Star* and the *Academy*.

His greatest triumph, however, arrived the following year when his 'Ballad of A Nun' was published in the third volume of *The Yellow Book*. Although in both his manner and his work Davidson set himself against the affectations of decadence, this poetic adaptation of a medieval legend in which a nun deserts the cloister to worship 'sinful man' appeared to a public expecting to be shocked by *The Yellow Book* as the latest manifestation of the movement. Davidson found himself swept up in a brief hurricane of publicity; interviewed, caricatured and profiled in the press. Lane, with typical dispatch, rushed out an edition of his *Ballads & Songs*, which netted the author three hundred pounds and the publisher rather more.

Lane left to Ward & Downey Ltd the pleasure of bringing out Davidson's satirical novel, *The Wonderful Mission of Earl Lavender*, a supposedly humorous tale of 'fang-de-seeaycle' attitudes in which the hero discovers (amongst other things) a secret society of flagellants in a subterranean palace beneath Piccadilly Circus. Despite a verse preface (reprinted in *The Yellow Book*) which asserts, 'Though our thoughts turn ever Doomwards,/Though our sun is well-nigh set,/ Though our Century totters tombwards,/We may laugh a little yet', the tone of the book trundles uneasily between the tedious and the prurient. The publishers further confused the author's intention by commissioning a frontispiece from Beardsley. They received a piece of elegant erotica: a commanding woman *en déshabillé* plying the back of a kneeling suppliant with a three-line whip. Even Symons, who knew Davidson well, was unsure what to make of it all. He wrote to Edmund Gosse describing the book as 'an astonishing novel . . . all about flagellation', and remarking, 'Is the man serious or joking, I wonder?'

Although Lane was obliged to pass up Davidson's satire, it was not from any compunction about poking fun at decadence. Indeed, one of the more audacious features of Lane's policy was a willingness to publish satiric parodies of works and authors already on his books. The whole Bodley Head list was honeycombed with self-referential conceits. When, in 1895, Lane brought out Grant Allen's sensational novel of feminist independence, *The Woman Who Did*, he coupled it with a volume by Victoria Cross (Vivian Cory) brazenly entitled *The Woman Who Didn't*. And later in the same year another Grant Allen book, *The British Barbarians, A Hill-Top Novel*, was given the doubtful support of A. D. Traill's parody, *The Barbarian Britishers: A Tip-Top Novel*, in which Allen's hero Bertram has metamorphosed into 'Bunkham'. Beardsley, who had provided the cover illustration for Allen's book (it was in the Keynotes series), even burlesqued his own design for the cover of Traill's version.

There was a trace of self-regard, too, about the publication of G. S. Street's *The Autobiography of A Boy* (1894). Le Gallienne in his reader's report explained – rather laboriously – 'The title is a misnomer. It is evidently meant ironically, but the irony might be made a little more perceptible. The "boy" is actually a "superior" aesthetic young man of the Oscar Wilde type who takes amusingly paradoxical views of his parents and other matters, including, of course, as a starting point, his own importance.' Both the irony and its target seem, however, thoroughly perceptible in the opening description of the 'superior' Tubby's Oxford career: 'In his first year he was a severe ritualist, in his second an anarchist and an atheist, in his third wearily indifferent to all things . . . His humour of being carried in a sedan chair swathed in blankets and reading a Latin poet, from his rooms to the Turkish bath, is still remembered in his college.' As a comedy of unwitting absurdity and egotism it is well done. Street, like Beerbohm a product of Charterhouse and Merton, was himself something of a 'superior' dandy. But it was the hint of Wilde that Le Gallienne had caught in Tubby's portrait that Lane chose to emphasize. He brought the book out on the same day as Wilde's *Sphinx*.

To enhance the moment yet more, Lane issued on the following day a comic novel by Florence Farr called *The Dancing Faun*, which boasted (along with a Beardsley caricature of Whistler on the cover) another sub-Wildean hero: Mr Travers is regarded by polite society as 'a very, very bad man', prone to paradox, 'charming languor' and 'violent' friendships with handsome young men. So, within the space of forty-eight hours, Lane was able to set before the public the work of a self-proclaimed decadent, a deliberate parody of a self-proclaimed decadent and a lightly humorous account of a self-proclaimed decadent.

Despite such stunts the volume of decadent, and decadent-inspired, work produced by the Bodley Head remained quite small in relation to the overall output of the firm. In the Keynotes series the contributions of Machen and Shiel, and indeed of Florence Farr, were easily outweighed by books of a different kind.

The question of female emancipation was a subject just as likely as decadence to provoke controversy – and one more likely to provoke sales. It was the exploration of this theme that fired not only George Egerton's signature volume but also much of the whole Keynotes series. And it was the motive force behind Grant Allen's racily titled *The Woman Who Did*, a work which outsold everything in the catalogue, requiring twenty reprintings within a matter of months.

In his reader's report on the novel, Le Gallienne, while recognizing that 'the book will, of course, create a considerable sensation, and come in for fierce criticism', had thought that 'the worst that can be said of it will be that it is mistaken. No one can say that it is evil.' He had suggested, moreover, that it might be 'like a breath of purity amid the many *décadent* publications of the Bodley Head (!!)'. This last comment – written in November 1893 – gives a revealing glimpse of how some anti-decadents regarded the list even before the advent of Beardsley. To the palate of the disapproving, the small seasoning of decadent work (at that date there was only *Silhouettes*, *Salome* and *Silverpoints*) had, like garlic, imparted its savour to the whole dish.

Lane seems to have become increasingly aware of this fact, and of the danger that it represented. Even towards the end of 1894, when decadence appeared to be riding high on the wave of fashion, Lane was loosening his connections with the movement. He turned down Symons' *London Nights*, and also Theodore Wratislaw's collection, *Caprices*. And although he invited his *Yellow Book* stars, Beardsley and Beerbohm, to spend some of the festive season with him at Windermere, the other member of the party was, significantly, the ultra-traditional William Watson.

If the launch of *The Yellow Book* marked the apogee of Lane's flirtation with decadence, it also marked a decisive rift in his relations with Elkin Mathews. The ungenerous exclusion of Mathews from *The Yellow Book* dinner at the Hotel d'Italia was the clearest, though not the first, sign that all was not well with the Vigo Street partnership. Lane, with his restless energy and thrusting nature, chafed at Mathews' sedate approach to business. They were moving at different paces as much as in different directions. One observer likened the diffident Mathews to an 'ineffective football player vainly endeavouring to push his way into the scrum'. Lane, however, was always in the thick of the game, sweeping into the shop at the head of a pack of 'new geniuses' and sweeping out again on his way to the Hogarth Club.

He had, moreover, managed to gather his own men about him in the business. The chief assistant, Frederick Chapman, was a Lane appointment, the offical reader was, of course, his friend Le Gallienne; the very stock-boys, J. Lewis May and (Wilde's fancy) Edward Shelley, owed their positions to him rather than to Mathews. Increasingly he came to think of the firm as his own, and of Mathews' influence as a negative force. It was inevitable that Mathews should learn of *The Yellow Book* dinner, and after that it was no less inevitable that the partnership would founder and break.

In the negotiations that followed the decision to 'divorce', each partner displayed his characteristics to the full: Mathews in his wish to be scrupulously fair, Lane in his desire to be briskly successful. With regard to the premises it was decided that Mathews would keep the Vigo Street shop but that, in compensation, Lane should receive the terracotta sign of the Bodley Head. This was a rashly made deal, for Mathews did not know that Lane had already negotiated a lease with the Albany authorities for a shop-space exactly opposite number 6B. Lane was thus able to preserve the old business' distinctive name and the familiar Vigo Street location. Mathews was shocked but unable to recall his offer.

Further shocks were in store for him. His suggestion that all the firm's authors should be notified of the split by letter and allowed to choose which of the two partners they would continue with was superficially accepted by Lane – who then promptly set about canvassing for support behind Mathews' back. Many of the authors had, of course, been brought in on Lane's initiative and were thus loyal to him. But Mathews, despite concentrating on the antiquarian side of the business, had been responsible for signing up several important writers. It was his Bedford Park connection that had secured the talents of Todhunter and Yeats. Ernest Radford too was a close friend, and 'Michael Field'. Faced even with this limited competition Lane tried to edge his former partner off the field. At the beginning of September 1894, in an attempt to force the hands of those – like Yeats – who had yet to decide which man to follow, Lane leaked news of the split to the *Publishers' Circular*, providing also a misleading account of the list's division. Mathews was confined to a mere nine unfashionable (or dead) authors, including Todhunter, Wicksteed and Mrs De Gruchy; while Lane was credited with a selection twice as large and many times more glamorous – Grant Allen, Lord de Tabley, Francis Thompson, Norman Gale, the Keynotes series and *The Yellow Book* amongst them. Perhaps his tactics were too brash; Yeats stayed loyal to Mathews.

The decadent authors and their works went, unsurprisingly, to Lane, although Wilde, 'in a desire to be fair and courteous to both', offered Mathews a chance to publish 'The Portrait of Mr W. H.' Such a tale of artistic forgery and homosexual love was, however, quite abhorrent to the fastidious Mr Mathews, who declined to publish it 'at any price'. Lane thus received the rights to all Wilde's recent work – an attractive package in the late summer of 1894, but one with an ominous tick.

Chapter Twelve

AT THE beginning of February 1895 *Punch* published a parody of one of Max Beerbohm's *Yellow Book* essays. Looking back to the distant days of 1894, the supposed author, 'Max Meerboom', considered the 'sect' that had flourished about then, a sect 'that was to win for itself the Title of the "*Decadents*"'. 'What exactly this Title signified,' he admitted, 'I suppose no two etymologists will agree. But,' he went on, 'we may learn from the caricatures of the day what the *Decadents* were in outward semblance; from the lampoons what was their mode of life.'

Certainly there were lampoons upon the decadents; indeed the parody of Beerbohm was one of them. And underneath it there was, indeed, a caricature of another decadent, Aubrey Beardsley. Each, in its way, tells us something about the habits and customs of that supposed 'sect'; but both tell us very much more about how that 'sect' was viewed by the common generality of Victorians.

As a guide to middle-class prejudice throughout the second half of the nineteenth century there is no surer index than *Punch*. Founded in 1841, the magazine had hardened into a national institution by the 1880s. Its half-century was celebrated with commemorative brochures, and *The Times* Publishing Company announced a scheme to reprint and annotate all the past issues in volume form. The magazine's early radicalism had been softened by success to a mild glow of pro-Liberal sentiment.

The man who oversaw much of this development was Francis Burnand, editor for an imposing twenty-six years between 1880 and 1906. He was (according to the historian of *Punch*) 'a vigorous kindly man' who 'believed in fun and in kindly humour'. He had a particular fondness for puns, and an exacting eye for detail. The longevity of his rule, however, perhaps inevitably prompted complaint. Throughout the nineties there was a persistent note in some quarters of the press that *Punch* was in decline – that it had, indeed, its own part in a more general decadence. Nevertheless, despite such carping, *Punch*'s appearance, on a Wednesday morning, remained the hebdomadal highlight of many Victorian households.

Satirical humour relies for its success upon an arsenal of shared assumptions. *Punch*, although it did on occasion draw directly from life, seems throughout the nineties to have taken much of its ammunition from the pages of other periodicals. There were spoofs of essays, poems inspired by articles, reviews of books, plays and exhibitions, mock interviews, and mocking profiles. The novel and distinctive ploys of the contemporary press – the so-called New Journalism – were all used or parodied in *Punch*: interviews, sensationalism, banner headlines and gossip. The intellectual debates of the established *Reviews* provided further fodder for fun. *Punch*, as a result, served as a digest for the whole range of contemporary journalistic concerns.

Although Mr Punch had founded his reputation upon political satire, he increasingly turned the barbs of his wit to the excesses of fashionable culture and society. Throughout the early 1880s the pretentions of the aesthetes had been subjected to regular ridicule in the drawings and skits of George du Maurier. A cast of extravagant characters – including the Pre-Raphaelite beauty Mrs Cimabue Brown, the intensely poetic Mr Jellaby Postlethwaite (who behaved like Oscar Wilde) and Mr Maudle, the languorous painter (who looked like Oscar Wilde) – struck mannered poses, contemplated lilies, if not sunflowers, and resolved to be worthy of their blue-and-white china tea-sets.

By the beginning of the 1890s, however, although long-locked 'aesthetes' still appeared in occasional cartoons, the fashionable force of the aesthetic movement was spent. There were new watchwords and new targets. Indeed, almost everything was 'new' unless it was '*fin de siècle*'. Or rather to be '*fin de siècle*' was to be 'new'. Neither term required or enjoyed an exact definition; both were chronologically presumptuous. As Beerbohm remarked, the 'new humour' was new only in the sense that the New Forest was new; while the *Punch* theatre critic rather pettily complained of a farce called *Paris Fin de Siècle*, which appeared in June 1890, on the grounds that, 'If it is the Paris of today that is pictured, it certainly cannot be the Paris of five years hence, and the century has yet ten years to run.' He did

Oscar Wilde and Lord Alfred Douglas, about 1893

Max Beerbohm and William Rothenstein, 1893

Robbie Ross and Reggie Turner

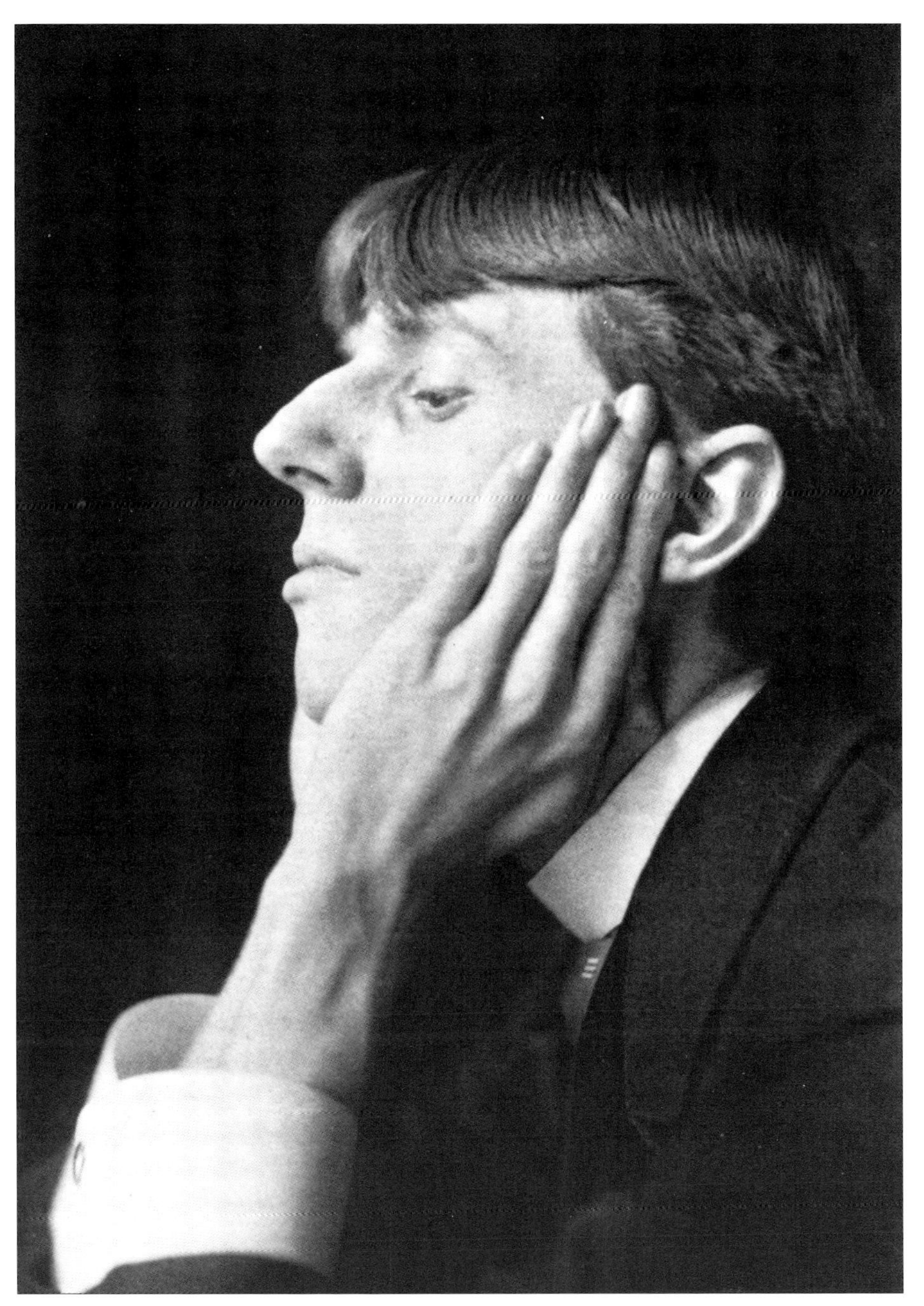

Aubrey Beardsley by Frederick Evans

Marc Andre Raffalovich
from a painting by
A. Dampier, May 1886

John Lane

Ada Leverson

Owen Seaman

POST-PRANDIAL PESSIMISTS.

SCENE—*The Smoking-room at the Decadents.*

First Decadent (M.A. Oxon). "AFTER ALL, SMYTHE, WHAT WOULD LIFE BE WITHOUT COFFEE?"
Second Decadent (B.A. Camb.). "TRUE, JEOHNES, TRUE! AND YET, AFTER ALL, WHAT IS LIFE *WITH* COFFEE?"

Above: An early 'decadent' cartoon, by George du Maurier, 15 October 1892

A Beardsley parody by E.T. Reed, *Punch*, 26 November 1894

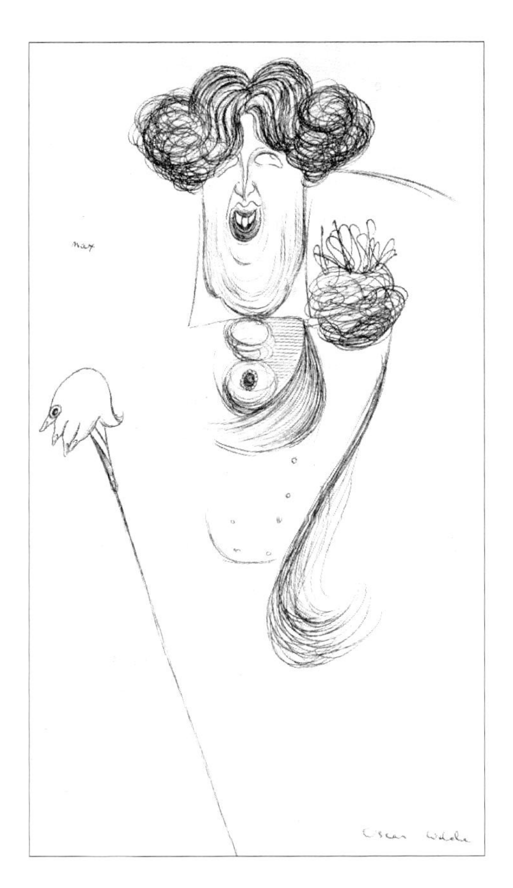

Oscar Wilde by Max Beerbohm

The Marquess of Queensberry by Phil May

Queen Victoria by William Nicholson

nevertheless attempt his own definition of the epithet, based on the knowledge gained from watching the said farce. '*Fin de siècle*,' he considered, 'seems to involve being engaged but forgetting to get married, and playing Baccarat instead of attending to business.'

Moral latitude certainly emerged as one of the distinguishing features of the term. Others included female emancipation, fashion-consciousness and spiritualism. A skit called 'Cinderella Fin de Siècle', in *Punch*'s Christmas number for 1890, had Cinders refusing to go to the ball on the grounds that it would bore her. She was, besides, busy – studying for the Senior Wranglership – and would, as a final impediment, only tolerate dresses bought in Paris. Eschewing the offer of a pumpkin coach from her fairy-godmother, she wants instead to be taught the secrets of hypnotism. Soon '*fin de siècle*' was being applied to any and every manifestation of novelty, even to industrial action and the revival of church-going. Such was its vogue that by August 1891 Mr Punch was advertising for a 'word slayer' to deliver the public from the 'pest term'.

The course of the 'new' was entirely similar. The epithet was attached with significant emphasis to morality, women, art, humour and a host of other phenomena before *Punch* finally lost patience and lumped everything together as 'the new newness', complaining that the whole thing had become a 'new-sance' and that henceforth the proverb should be amended to, 'There's nothing old under the sun.'

The artistic expressions of this *fin de siècle* novelty were several. Decadence was certainly one of them, but its place – in the eyes of Mr Punch – was, at first, small. It had to wait its turn. As the fashionable lure of 'aestheticism' ebbed away during the 1880s the satirists were eager to scout out the next plausible 'fad'. In the early years of the new decade their favoured targets included 'Ibsenism', 'Zola-ism', realism and the 'New Poetry'.

The controversial productions of *A Doll's House* and *Rosmersholm* at the beginning of the nineties, together with the translations of many other of Ibsen's works by William Archer, prompted a barrage of satirical abuse. Throughout 1891 *Punch* ran a series of (over)detailed and (over)long parodies, under the general title 'Mr Punch's Pocket Ibsen'. They printed also an 'ABC of Ibsenity', which begins:

> A is the Archer who booms in the *World*,
> B is the Banner of Ibsen unfurled.

C the Commotion it makes for the minute,
D is the Doll's House, and all there is in it.

The particular qualities of Ibsen's work that seemed to alarm were his frankness ('Ibsenity'), his interest in heredity as a force in human life, and his portrayal of repressed yet independent women. After seeing 'Ibsen's dramas', one *Punch* contributor was moved to compose some 'New (Norwegian) Nonsense Verse' on this last particular theme:

There was a young female from Norway
Who fancied herself in a poor way,
Because she felt that
Her sweet sex was squeezed flat,
As though caught in cold Destiny's doorway.

Zola-ism, too, received the tribute of parody. Number XIV in 'Mr Punch's Prize Novels' series (published at the beginning of 1891) was a two-part story called 'Le Petroleum; ou les Saloperies Parisiennes' by Zorgan-Gola, 'Auteur de "La Fange", "499 Pages d'Amour" etc.'. The tale, written not even in Franglais but in French, lays out the perceived characteristics of Zola's *oeuvre*: working-class squalor and sex. Set in 'Les Slums Parisiens', it concerns the 'degringolade' of the unfortunate family 'Ogwash'. None of them turns out well, but our heroine's fate is wrapped up particularly briskly as 'l'hôpital, trente pages de délire alcoolique, et la fosse commune'.

Zola and Ibsen were conspicuous foreign imports, but there were also home-grown 'fads' and 'booms' to be pilloried. During 1892 *Punch* instituted a prolonged inquiry into the nature of the 'New Poetry' which 'has asserted itself by the mouths of many loud-voiced boomers'. This was just part of the trend of self-examination and appraisal that – with Browning gone and Tennyson on the way out – late Victorian poetry subjected itself to. Given Mr Punch's concern with poetic novelty, it might be supposed that his inquiries would have taken him to the Cheshire Cheese. The decadent experiments of Arthur Symons might even have come under his scrutiny. But, it seems, the fame of the Rhymers' Club did not, in 1892, extend much beyond its membership.

Three distinct types of 'New Poetry' were discussed, but all of them were linked by a common characteristic – boisterousness. There was 'the "blustering hob-nailed" variety, which clatters up and down with immense noise', 'the "coarse but manly" kind which swears by the great god Jingo!' And there was the sort that 'doesn't rhyme or scan properly and is called "impressionism".' Mr Henley was cited as a master of the first and third varieties, and Mr Kipling of the second.

The parodic examples were excellent: there was the clattering fury of 'The Song of the Poker' (borrowed from Henley's 'Song of the Sword'), which begins, 'The Poker/Clanging/I am the Poker, the straight and the strong,/Prone in the fire-grate/Black at the nether end/Nobby and nebulous.'; and the rollicksome brutality of 'K-pl-ng's' 'Knocked Out' ('Oh it's bully when I land 'em with a counter on the jaw,/When the ruby's all a dripping and the conks are red and raw,' etc./While the impressionistic poem on a kitchen – by 'W.E. H-nl-y' – with its mass of sensory detail ('the odours of the meat/The cabbage and sweets all merge as in a pall') and its mixture of low subject-matter with high style ('the black beetle seems/A plumed Black Prince arrayed in gleaming detail'), points up clearly why Symons would later try to claim Henley as an ally and a decadent. To *Punch*, however, the three varieties of 'New Poetry' were all aspects of contemporary vigour, energy and restlessness – not of decadent hypersensitivity.

Nevertheless, despite these assertions of native vitality, there were occasional hints at something more perverse. Oscar Wilde was too large a personality and too good a butt to be ignored for long. And although Burnand was anxious not to give him again the sort of blanket coverage he received in the 1880s at the height of the aesthetic boom, Wilde continued to warrant regular name-checks. In July 1890 his 'Decay of Lying' (which had just appeared in the *Nineteenth Century*) was spoofed as 'A Dialogue Up To Date, with some remarks on the Importance of Talking an Infinite deal of Nothing'. Gilnest and Erbert sit about exchanging paradoxes and cigarettes until Erbert tries (apparently) to seduce Gilnest (he taps him 'lightly on the cheek', then 'pinches his cheek', and finally 'attempts to detain him'). A fight ensues and Gilnest's banjo is broken.

Paradoxical nonsense, homosexual undertones and cultural name-dropping are the basic elements of the parody. Erbert compares his friend's expression, when he makes a *moue*, with 'the divine sullenness that broods upon the pale brow of the Antinous'. His fancy then races on to a scene in which pale HELEN steps out upon the battlement and turns to FLAUBERT her appealing glance, and CELLINI paces with Madame DE SÉVIGNÉ through the eternal shadows of unrevealed realism. And BROWNING, and HOMER, and MEREDITH and OSCAR WILDE are with them, 'the fleet-footed giants of perennial youth', while on 'the vine-clad bank of Ilyssus . . . Mr PATER stands contemplative, like some mad scarlet thing by DVOŘÁK . . .'

The picture contained some of the key decadent figures (Antinous, Oscar Wilde and Pater in his 'mad scarlet' mode), and also showed that Wilde's 'sinister' reputation was even then gaining a general currency, albeit that it was taken merely as another 'pose'. Nevertheless, it displayed too the foreshortened perspective common in popular descriptions of the cultural scene. Everything remotely unconventional or foreign – Flaubert, Meredith, Pater, Dvorak, even Browning – was heaped together, then the whole was labelled with the nearest available 'ism' or tag – in this case 'realism'. And this despite the fact that Wilde's dialogue had specifically condemned 'realism' as an inadequate artistic creed.

The review of Wilde's *Dorian Gray* in the very next issue did not even have recourse to a convenient 'ism'. It dismissed the whole novel as an exercise to show 'what an easy thing it is to frighten the respectable MRS GRUNDY with a bogie'; though the relation between Wilde and the unmentioned tradition of decadence was fleetingly pointed to in a passage comparing the novel's literary style to 'the sensuous and hyperdecorative manner of "Mademoiselle de Maupin".' By and large Wilde was regarded in the early nineties as an exceptional case: a circus performer rather than the representative of any literary movement. His debts to other authors were always gleefully exposed, but the use he made of these borrowings was generally considered personal and distinctive. His each successive work was hailed – and derided – as the 'Wildest and Oscarest' yet. It was only gradually that he was drawn into relation with his artistic contemporaries.

The term 'decadent' did not make its début in the pages of *Punch* until the autumn of 1892, and even then it appeared in a social rather than an artistic context. The issue for 15 October discovered two 'Post Prandial Pessimists' sitting in the 'the Smoking-room at the Decadents'. Beneath the picture of the two young men lounging in evening dress ran the caption:

First Decadent (M. A. Oxon.): 'After all, Smythe, what would life be without coffee?'
Second Decadent (M. A. Camb.): 'True, Jeohnes, true! And yet after all, what is life *with* coffee?'

The cartoon provided a remarkably concise portrait of the decadent type – weary of life, over-educated, intensely alive to sensory gratification (and artificial stimulants), yet resignedly aware that such pleasures were but a fleeting respite from the grand futility of existence. Having proffered this useful and quite exact definition, *Punch* then proceeded to confuse it. Over the next two years 'decadent' cartoons became almost a regular feature. The word could be attached to languorous females who turned down over-boisterous dancing partners, to bespectacled girls who discussed divorce cases, to a young art critic who mistook a child's scribble for an 'Impressionist' sketch, even to a lecherous middle-aged roué who tried to chat up a pert young girl with the line, 'Don't you find existence an awful bore?' (Only to be told, 'Well, some people's existence, most decidedly.') Applied in this cavalier fashion to every threatening aspect of modernity – to the New Woman and the New Art critic, as much as to the New Hedonist and the old libertine – the word was in some danger of becoming a new 'pest term'.

It was only in 1894 with the emergence of Aubrey Beardsley and the publication of *The Yellow Book* that the artistic aspect of this supposed decline came under examination. Beardsley was a gift to an illustrated paper, his style easily recognized, easily parodied and easily printed. Sickert's hazy 'Impressionism', for example, was much less susceptible to mass production, and thus, though his name was often taken in vain, his pictures seldom were. 'Mortarthurio Whiskersley' or 'Danby Wierdsley', however, became frequent contributors of 'Japanese Fan de Siecle' illustrations to *Punch*'s little skits and parodies. E. T. Reed, one of the magazine's leading artists, developed a real enthusiasm – and ability – for burlesquing Beardsley's style.

In April 1894 the excitement generated by Beardsley's poster for the Avenue Theatre production of Todhunter's *A Comedy of Sighs* provoked Mr Punch to his first extended notice of Beardsley. This was the poster at which, according to the show's producer, 'even the cab horses shied': a daring arrangement in blue and green showing a mysterious female looming behind a screen of large dots. It prompted a *Punch* broadside under the heading 'ARS POSTERA OF LET'S AVENUE POSTER'. Beardsley, addressed as 'Mr Aubrey Beer de Beer', was told that his 'Japanee-Rossetti girl/Is not a thing to be desired', while 'A beauty raised on Nature's rules . . ./Is worth a dozen spotted ghouls.'

Beardsley had become elevated to the level of a named celebrity, although it was his work – and particularly his 'women' – rather than himself, that continued to be the main focus for attack. A week later the *Punch* critic (along with everyone else) was lambasting the first number of *The Yellow Book*. After accounting for the cover ('like a poultice made of mustard') and the letterpress ('silly . . . neo-pagan . . . starred with spluttering sparks of paradox'), the poetic reviewer turned to 'the things called "Illustrations!"': 'Ill drawn objectless abominations! Supernatural silliness!. . . Void of beauty, meaning, charm, proportions.' And just in case anyone had failed to recognize this as a critique of Beardsley, the week after that there was a detailed review of his work (then on view at the New English Art Club Exhibition) complete with a spoof version of his portrait of Mrs Patrick Campbell, or 'The 252nd Mrs Tanqueray' by 'our Yellow Book Impressionist'. The review, while admitting that Mr Beardsley was 'perhaps not so black as he paints', condemned the 'wickedness' of his characters' faces and the impossibility of their figures – 'the old lady in No. 17,' readers were told, 'is nothing but a preposterous parallelobiped, while those in No. 19 would shock any right-minded giraffe.'

In late July the magazine even carried a special 'Art Recipe', explaining exactly how to construct one of these giraffe-shocking abominations. It was a complicated matter:

Take a lot of black triangles,
Some amorphous blobs of red;
Just a sprinkling of queer spangles,
An ill-drawn Medusa head
Some red locks in Gorgon tangles,
And a scarlet sunshade spread:
Take a 'partiere' quaint and spotty,
Take a turn-up nose or two;
The loose lips of one 'gone dotty',
A cheese-cutter chin, askew . . .
Take an hour-glass waist, in section,

Shoulders hunched up camel wise;
Give a look of introspection
(Or a squint) to two black eyes . . .

The basic ingredients of anti-naturalism, ugliness and fatal womanhood are recognizably decadent, although *Punch* still preferred to label Beardsley with the parallel term, 'Impressionist'. The two words were indeed almost synonymous in the journalistic mind; it was only two weeks before the appearance of the 'Art Recipe' that 'Our Decadent Art Critic', Mr Flipbutt, suffered his confusion between the child's drawing and the Impressionist's sketch.

Punch generated much of its copy in response to articles in other periodicals, and it was the arrival of the much-discussed, and supposedly decadent, *Yellow Book* which launched the new phase in the magazine's coverage of decadence. Max Beerbohm was attacked (in very poor verse) for the strained artificiality of his piece on cosmetics. Symons too was condemned – though more obliquely – for his morbid fascination with sex. He was surely the principal addresee of Owen Seaman's 'To A Boy-Poet of the Decadence', a poem that asserts:

The erotic affairs that you fiddle aloud
Are as vulgar as coin of the mint;
And you merely distinguish yourself from the crowd
By the fact that you put 'em in print.

The figure – or, rather, the poetry – of Symons also lurked in the works of 'Clarion Blair', the pretentious anti-hero of 'Lyre and Lancet', the regular serial that ran throughout the second half of 1894. The story concerns a young poet who has recently had a minor success with his first slim volume, *Andromeda*, and on the strength of it has been invited to a fashionable house-party at Wyvern Court. By an unfortunate accident a young vet, who has just won first prize at Crufts with a bulldog also called Andromeda, is going down to Wyvern Court on the same train to give his opinion on a sick horse. The two men are duly mistaken for each other with (what are generally called) hilarious results.

In the second instalment of the story the expectant house-guests read out several extracts from Blair's *Andromeda*, including one Symons-esque offering called 'Abasement' about the 'strange delight' that 'lurks in self disgust', which draws the praise, 'Now, do you know I rather like that – it's so very decadent.' John Gray, rather than Symons, seems to have provided the model for Blair's 'Disenchantment'; the lines 'My love hath sickled to a loath/And foul seems all that fair I fancied – /the lily's sheen a leprous growth/The very buttercups are rancid' echo the daisies' leprous stain in Gray's 'Poem'.

Although these poetic parodies show a first-hand – if cursory – knowledge of the subject, the common journalistic assumption that all distinctively 'modern' movements were somehow connected was not avoided. Clarion Blair is depicted as not only an ardent sensualist but also an ardent socialist. One poem, warning the 'Pale patricians, sunk in self-indulgence' to prepare for the dawning of 'Demos', has the story's ultra-conservative host anxious that his poetic guest might arrive at the house with a bomb.

The Bodley Head, meanwhile, endured a similar distortion in the prism of *Punch*'s wit. The firm, as publishers of *The Yellow Book*, became enveloped in a generalized yellow haze; and 'yellow', as *Punch* pointed out, was 'the colour of age, decay and bile, and mustard'. All Bodley Head authors were regarded as equally modern, equally dangerous and equally silly. They were all reduced to items of confectionery at the OBC (the 'O'erated Bosh Company (Ltd), caterers by self-appointment to the *Yellow Book*, the Rhymers' Club, and Nobody Else in Particular'). This poetical version of the Aerated Bread Company offered 'highly spiced productions at unpopular prices' with 'particular attention . . . given to ensure imperfect cleanliness in all details'. Although customers could order 'Sonnets' ('with wide margins, on hand-made paper and quite unintelligible') at two pounds each, they were pointed towards such specialities as 'John Silvergray's Blue Points (3d. a dozen), 'Arthur Sillywit's Symnels' and 'Oscar's Masterpieces (each 2d.)'.

Even those Bodley Head poets opposed to decadence found themselves convicted of licentiousness and obscurantism. Le Gallienne (who had recently given a lecture decrying the institution of marriage) earned the tribute of 'Le Billygoat's Lovers Liquorice', while William Watson was implicated in 'Watrot's Eloping Sally Lunns' and Norman Gale's pastoral jollity was fixed in sugar as 'Norty Gal's Richmond Maids'.

This confusion became even more marked when George Egerton's *Keynotes* was parodied in *Punch* as '*She-notes*' by 'Borgia Smudgiton' (with an illustration by 'Mortarthurio Whiskersley'). The skit, with its mannish young heroine who – over her pipe and whisky (taken neat and served by her husband) – likes to read Oscar Wilde because, as she puts it, 'he shocks the middle classes', presents a general *mélange* of nineties' fads. Egerton's 'New Woman' (independent, sexually emancipated, politically and athletically active) has become casually confounded with the newly arrived 'Beardsley Woman' (morally dubious, sexually ambiguous and improbably thin). This, of course, was a confusion that John Lane inadvertently (or deliberately) encouraged by using Beardsley to decorate Egerton's *Keynotes*, but it was seized upon eagerly by the *Punch* satirists, as was the more general equation that Wilde, Egerton and Beardsley all shared a common publisher and a common creed: the desire to 'shock the middle classes'.

Having forged the association between the Bodley Head, cultural decadence and insubstantial naughtiness, *Punch* increasingly pointed it up through its selective coverage of the literary scene. Wilde's *Sphinx* and the subsequent volumes of *The Yellow Book* all received ample space – pages given over to spoofs and parodies. Significantly, with *The Yellow Book* the items chosen for satirical treatment were always the most 'decadent' and provocative.

From Volume III (October 1894) it was Beerbohm's revisionist essay, 'A Note on George the Fourth', and Beardsley's teasing portrait of himself (as a bedridden pierrot) that drew the fiercest satirical fire. The skits that appeared on these two pieces were, however, very different in kind: the one was an 'inside job', written by an intimate member of the decadent coterie – Ada Leverson; the other was a condescending and hostile squib thrown by a schoolmasterly opponent on all modern 'booms and fads' – Owen Seaman. Together they reflect, in miniature, the twin reasons for *The Yellow Book*'s (and decadence's) vogue: log-rolling and provocation.

Leverson was a fashionable literary hostess with a delight in all that was 'new'. She was adored by Wilde (who called her the 'Sphinx of Pleasure'); she was a childhood friend of Beerbohm's; she was much taken with Beardsley (and was even rumoured to have tried to seduce him). As a diversion for her wit and a supplement to her dress allowance, she wrote occasional articles for various magazines. Her gift for social comedy drew her to *Punch*, and her first piece appeared there in July 1893 (not long after she had been introduced to Wilde). It was an ingenious dialogue between various contemporary dramatic heroines, including Ibsen's Nora (from *A Doll's House*), Charley's Aunt, and the Princess Salome. When her next spoof included a cameo appearance by Dorian Gray, Burnand had to warn her against dragging Wilde too often into her work.

After that she concentrated her talents for a while in a series of 'Letters to a Débutante'. But even in these little skits on the contemporary social scene she could not altogether resist the temptation to introduce her friends into the work. The poised, precocious figure of Beerbohm stands neatly behind her creation of 'Baby Beaumont', so very young, yet 'wonderfully well-preserved, very clever and so cynical that he is quite an optimist'. (Beaumont's interest in cross-dressing cannot be traced to Beerbohm but perhaps owes something to Beardsley's supposed proclivity in that direction.) The 'Débutante' is amused by this diminutive dandy, but her stolid, conventional fiancé dismisses him hotly as being 'gay and decadent'.

With the launch, scandal and success of *The Yellow Book* Leverson felt justified in adopting a more direct mode of address: parody. The work of her decadent friends was in the news and under discussion; it was visible enough to be travestied. Even Burnand had acknowledged this, although with his cusomary reservations. In July 1894 he published Ada Leverson's skit upon Wilde's *Sphinx* – 'The Minx', a mock interview between the poet and his subject (which delighted Wilde). And in October of the same year Ada's parody of Beerbohm appeared (which delighted Beerbohm). Given that Beerbohm's own essays for *The Yellow Book* were so hedged by irony as to be almost self-parodies, the parodist was faced with a difficult task. And certainly Ada Leverson's attempt was not altogether successful. She relied heavily on neologisms (borrowed either from Carroll's 'Jabberwocky' or directly from Beerbohm's own 'Defence of Cosmetics') and words beginning (in the Regency manner) with 'ph' ('Mrs Phox', for instance, drives 'phorth'). The happiest conceit was a Wildean paradox about looking for 'a wisp of hay in a packet of needles'. Burnand, although amused by the piece, was not quite convinced of Beerbohm's – or 'Meerboom's' – celebrity,and insisted upon the explanatory subtitle, 'A Brown Study in a Yellow Book'. The parody, like the skit on Wilde's poem, was more of an advertisement than an attack; certainly both authors were flattered by the tribute.

This miasma of mutual admiration was absent, however, from Owen Seaman's poems on Beardsley. Although the London literary world was small enough for Seaman (who was born in 1861) to have dined with Lionel Johnson and to have met Arthur Symons in the Crown, he had no particular enthusiasm for the young prodigies of the day. He seems to have been particularly irked by the strain of decadence he detected in much modern art; it brought out in him a priggish, disparaging tone (which is absent from his best work). The 'Boy-Poet of the Decadence' he dismissed with the magisterial pronouncement: 'For your dull little vices we don't care a fig,/It is *this* that we deeply deplore;/You were cast for a common or usual pig,/But you play the invincible bore.' Beardsley (first castigated for his 'Comedy of Leers' poster as 'Mr Aubrey Beer de Beers') was, by October 1894, being slated in even coarser terms. Beneath an imitation of Beardsley's picture – recaptioned as 'Portrait of the Artist in Bedlam' – Seaman trotted out a Rossetti-like poem, beginning 'Under a canopy as dark-hued as – well/Consult the Billious Book page 51 – /Lies pallid Whiskersley's presentment done/By Whiskersley's own weird unearthly spell.'

On the same page there was also a short poem called 'Morbidezza' – a title borrowed from Symons. The unknown poet complains that 'morbid fleshliness' is now the mark of 'the modern (sham) Art-lover', an accusation that could be readily substantiated from the pages of October's *Yellow Book*, where Symons' 'Credo' (with its call to a life of 'strenuous sin') lay close by Wratislaw's overheated 'To Salome at St James's', which sought to fuse the image of a *décolleté* chorus girl with the eternal spirit of Salome, over a supper table at the St James's restaurant. 'Morbidezza' ends its brief rant against the tyranny of anti-naturalism and perversion with the shot that 'caught in Sham's sepulchral mesh/Art now raves at *Green* Carnations'.

The artificial bloom (which had first marked out Wilde as the leader of a coterie if not a school) was greatly in the news during the autumn of 1894. Heinemann published *The Green Carnation* on 15 September, and the appearance of Hichens' anonymous, satirical *roman-à-clef* stirred up a maelstrom of discussion and speculation. Almost anyone with wit, literary facility and a knowledge of Wilde was accused of perpetrating the book. Reflecting the mood of the moment, Leverson's 'decadent' man-about-town, 'Baby Beaumont', is heard of, writing to seventeen newspapers to deny that he wrote 'The Mauve Cornelia'.

As the book provoked intrigue, it also prompted imitation. *Punch* attempted a satire upon the satire: 'The Blue Gardenia' ('A Colourable Imitation'). Burnand had been obliged to concede that Wilde was now at the centre of a new cult and that this was an opportunity to poke fun at him. *Punch*'s satire, nevertheless, remained strictly conventional. It was restricted to a string of nonsensical paradoxes ('To be appreciated is to be found out' etc.), and the relationship between Cecil Paragraph (the Wilde figure) and his young friend, Lord Archie ('he was not a Lord really, but Cecil always insisted that a title was a matter of temperament'), was less fraught with homosexual undercurrents than the friendship between Esme Amaranth and Lord Reggie in Hichens' book.

Rather more revealing was a full-page dualogue called 'The Decadent Guys (A Colour Study in Green Carnations)' which appeared three weeks later, on 19 November 1894. Two bonfire-night guys – 'Lord Raggie Tattersall' and 'Fustian Flitters' – clearly recognizable as Alfred Douglas and Wilde, or at least as Lord Reggie and Mr Amaranth – sit in their respective handcarts exchanging the usual epigrammatic banter ('The true impromptu is invariably premeditated' etc.) while awaiting their imminent immolation.

It is difficult to gauge the exact level of irony intended in the numerous references to the pair's impending doom, but the light and generalized tone of homoeroticism detectable in 'A Dialogue Up To Date' (back in July 1890) seems to have hardened into something more knowing and sinister. At least some people at *Punch*, it seems, were now aware that Wilde's proclivities were not merely a pose, and were prepared to poke veiled fun at them for the amusement of the informed. When a policeman approaches the two guys, Lord Raggie muses excitedly, 'Can we be going to become notorious – really notorious – at last?' At another point he says to Fustian, 'Are you going to blow up tonight? You are so brilliant when you blow.' Wilde's explosion was, however, some months in the future – and so was Fustian Flitters'. 'The Decadent Guys' are saved (temporarily) from the bonfire: 'with gentle resignation, as martyrs whose apotheosis is merely postponed, LORD RAGGIE and FUSTIAN FLITTERS allowed themselves to be moved on.'

The year ended, in the pages of *Punch*, on a resounding note of decadence; the Christmas number was graced by an elaborate cartoon of 'Britannia *à la* Beardsley' (by 'Our Yellow Decadent' or, rather, E. T. Reed). Over the year Reed's delight in parodying Beardsley's style seemed to have become tempered by a genuine admiration for the young genius' use of line. The parodic element had been slowly displaced by a desire to imitate. Even Owen Seaman was struck by it. In later years he would remark that 'not even the original artist himself ever did a better or more typical Beardsley than Mr Reed's Britannia'. Britannia had developed all the characteristics of the Beardsley Woman: the 'turn-up nose', the 'loose lips of one "gone dotty"', the 'cheese-cutter chin' and 'hour-glass waist'. Although she was posed in her usual position, upon the cliffs of Dover, there was now the suggestion that, instead of surveying the waves of the channel, she was looking to France for cultural inspiration.

Reed's drawing came at the end of a year of gathering interest and controversy. Beardsley, Beerbohm, Wilde, Douglas, *The Yellow Book*, *The Green Carnation* and the Bodley Head had stepped to the fore as representatives of a new and disturbing art movement. And if 'Britannia *à la* Beardsley' marked the high-water mark of popular decadence, the level did not subside immediately.

Volume IV of *The Yellow Book* received even more comprehensive coverage than its predecessor. A whole page was laid out in the manner of 'The Queer and Yellow Book' and dominated by Reed's spoof version of Beardsley's frontispiece for the poems of Juvenal (which had appeared in the January *Yellow Book* as a special double-page supplement) and which was here refashioned as the 'Preface to Juvenile Poems' by 'Daubaway Weirdsley'. The picture showed Beardsley in drag, pulling a cart-load of whores and rakes. The side of the cart is emblazoned with an advertisement for *The Yellow Book* and its publisher, 'The Bogey Head'. In the background stands an imposing building marked with the sign, 'This fine Doll's House to Let', a detail which reflects the continuing confusion between the different strains of progressive art.

Ada Leverson provided the written matter, and rather exposed her ignorance of the popular prejudices against *The Yellow Book* by providing a satirical narrative to accompany the 'Weirdsley' picture. Burnand, turning it down, had to explain that the whole (comic) point about *The Yellow Book*'s illustrations was that they bore no relation to the text. She was obliged to try again. And perhaps in an effort to break the very narrow and 'decadent' frame of her reference, Burnand supplied her with a detailed synopsis of Victoria Cross's story 'Theodora', which was duly transmuted in 'Tooraloora' by 'Charing Cross' – an absurdly over-coloured account of an argument in a pub between a lout and his doxy; a parody of high style and low matter.

Pride of place on the page, however, was given to '1894' by 'Max

Meerboom', a parody of Beerbohm's cod-historical survey of aestheticsm, '1880'. Coming across a 'sketch of a lady with a Mask on, playing the piano in a Cornfield, in a low dress, with lighted Candles, and signed "Aubrey Weirdsley"', the author feels impelled to discover more of 'the remote period' in which it was drawn. Although much must inevitably remain 'mobled in the Mists of Antiquity', he does know that it was about then that there flourished 'the sect that was to win for itself the Title of the "*Decadents*"'. And, while admitting that an exact definition of the title is impossible, he ventures to suggest various distinguishing traits. 'Nightly' he explains, the *Decadents* 'gathered at any of the Theatres where the plays of Mr WILDE were being given. Nightly the stalls were fulfilled by Row upon Row of neatly curled Fringes, surmounting Buttonholes of monstrous size.'

The plays of 'Mr WILDE' were, of course, much in the press during the first two months of 1895. When *An Ideal Husband* opened in January the *Punch* critic pointed out its debt to Sardou's *Dora*, and then compounded the criticism by having a Wildean mouthpiece demand, 'And why not? A dramatist has only one virtue; he never invents a drama.' The reviewer also condemned the playwright for his deficient moral sense, accusing him of 'confus[ing] black and white'.

The opening of *The Importance of Being Earnest* was presaged with 'The O. W. Vade Mecum' ('Vade Mecum' was a regular *Punch* series, usually focused on types not individuals). 'O. W.', asked whether it was 'easy to become a dramatist', helpfully lists the requirements as 'A West End Theatre, a first rate troupe of artists, a trained audience and a personality'. When pressed as to what he means by 'a personality', the Wildean voice replies, 'More or less – an insouciant manner, and a rather startling button-hole'.

Ever since Wilde's espousal of the green carnation, the buttonhole had occupied a prominent position in all popular descriptions of decadence and of Wilde. A buttonhole (particularly a dyed one) was the very image of nature tamed, shackled and turned to the service of art. Ada Leverson's *Punch* spoof of *The Importance*, entitled 'The Advisability of Not Being Brought Up In a Handbag', has two principal characters, Algy (a Flutterpate) and Dorian (a Buttonhole). 'Dorian' was a thinly disguised caricature of Alfred Douglas. Another cast-member, the 'Duke of Berwick' (a character without equivalent in Wilde's play) would have been no less recognizable to the cognoscenti as the Marquis of Queensberry. And behind the inconsequential chatter of the piece some might have detected the breath of a greater drama. At one point when Dorian is giving his views on life ('To be really modern one should have no soul. To be really medieval one should have no cigarettes. To be really Greek . . .') the 'Duke of Berwick' 'rises in a marked manner and leaves the garden'.

Part V

The Decline of Decadence

Chapter Thirteen

THE Marquis of Queensberry, denied the chance to confront Wilde at the first night of *The Importance of Being Earnest*, switched the angle of his attack. Four days after the play's opening he visited Wilde's club – the Albermarle – and left his card, addressed with a scrawl so illegible that even the porter's curiosity could not decipher it. There the card languished for over a week until Wilde called by on the morning of 28 February. Wilde too was unable to make out exactly the Marquis' fierce and hasty script. Did it read, 'For Oscar Wilde ponce and Somdomite' or 'For Oscar Wilde posing Somdomite'? He was unsure. But though the writing might be appalling and the spelling inaccurate, the message was horribly clear.

Wilde's sense of being besieged, his exasperation at Queensberry's ceaseless irruptions into the very fastnesses of his London life, carried him beyond the bourn of endurance – and wisdom. 'My whole life seems ruined by this man. The tower of ivory is assailed by the foul things,' he wrote in bitter exasperation to Robbie Ross. 'I don't see anything now but a criminal prosecution.' Ross counselled restraint, but Wilde was too vexed to be wise, and also too goaded by the vehement urgings of Alfred Douglas, who saw in a libel suit the opportunity to humiliate that 'funny little man', his father.

The Marquis in leaving his 'hideous note' had hoped for an interview. Instead he received a libel writ. The terrible, and seemingly inevitable, course of Wilde's action has been detailed too often to need repeating here: the weight of evidence Queensberry's private detectives were able to produce to justify (and more) the Marquis' assertion that Wilde was 'posing' as a sodomite; Wilde's defiant wit in the witness box; the rapid collapse of his case; his arrest at the

Cadogan Hotel; his remand at Bow Street; the removal of his name from outside the theatres where his comedies continued to play; the forced sale of his possessions to pay off the damages against Queensberry; his own trial on charges of committing homosexual acts and writing immoral books; the parade of unsavoury evidence (much of it provided by unsavoury witnesses who were being maintained at the Crown's expense); Wilde's impassioned speech in defence of 'the Love that dare not speak its name'; the inability of the first jury to reach a verdict; the need for a retrial; Wilde's brief respite of bail when, after being hounded across London by Queensberry's hired thugs, he found refuge first at his mother's house in Oakley Street, and then with the Leversons in South Kensington; his steadfast refusal to flee, despite the pleas of his wife, and Frank Harris' dramatic assertion that he had a yacht waiting in the Thames with its steam up; the second trial; the swift conviction; the heavy sentence – two years' hard labour – the maximum the law would allow.

The spring of 1895 (Queensberry's trial began on 3 April, Wilde's finally ended on 25 May) marked the climacteric of the decadent nineties. The identification of Wilde with decadence was, in the popular mind, complete. And the ruin of one demanded the ruin of the other. The press (with few exceptions), having been scrupulous in reporting every last salacious detail of the case, was noisy in its condemnation of both Wilde and his artistic creed. Indeed, even before Wilde's first appearance in the dock W. E. Henley's *National Observer* (6 April) saluted the Marquis of Queensberry for 'destroying the High Priest of the Decadents', while – on the same day – the *Daily Telegraph* lamented Wilde's contamination of English art and life with a 'French and Pagan plague'.

Punch picked up the mood and grew pompous and patriotic in its displeasure. What, it versified at some length, has 'Art' to do with 'pseud-Hellenic decadence, effete, /Unvirile,' or with 'debased Petronian ways'? 'Is this your "culture",' it asked, 'to asphyxiate with upas perfume sons of English race?' And what, it wondered, could be said of the supposed 'devotees of "Beauty"' who of late 'displayed the symbol of the vitriol-tinted flower'? The list of further offences by which these 'aesthete heirophants fair Art betray' ran to 'unsexed "Poetry"', 'scarlet sins', 'garbage epigrams' and 'poisonous hints', before, in a final outburst of revulsion, the *Punch* poet was moved to cry:

> If such be 'Artists', then may Philistines
> Arise, plain sturdy Britons as of yore,
> And sweep them off and purge the signs
> That England e'er such noxious offspring bore.

Public sentiment was both reflected and inflamed by such impassioned calls. Queensberry's acquittal, and Wilde's eventual conviction, were cheered from the public gallery. In a scene which neatly encapsulated the late-Victorian faith in hypocrisy and market forces, prostitutes are said to have danced on the pavement outside the Old Bailey to celebrate the downfall of 'unnatural vice'. Messages of congratulation rained in upon the Marquis of Queensberry; indeed, after years of ill-tempered conflict with various sections of society, he was quite dazed to receive so much warm approval: letters from the aristocracy, telegrams from the clubs. One message ran succinctly, 'Every man in the city is with you. Kill the bugger!'

Although Wilde's supposed witticism, 'The working classes are behind me to a boy', appears to be apocryphal, the reaction of the working classes to his plight (with the exception of the prostitutes' competitive spite) seems to have been markedly uncondemnatory. They turned the drama into a fiesta. Street ballads were hastily run off to capitalize on the scandal, and perhaps the public bars really did ring to rousing choruses of:

> Oh Oscar, you're a Daisy, you're a Sunflower and a Rose,
> You're a thick old Dandylion, from your pimple to your toes,
> You're the sweetest lump of Boy's Love that's been picked for
> many a day
> Oh! Oscar Wilde, we never thought that you was built that way.

A handful of newspapers – *Reynold's Weekly*, the *Daily Chronicle*, the *Star* and the *Illustrated Police Budget* – carried sympathetic notices of Wilde's demise, suggesting that he was 'the object of a most cruel persecution at the hands of Lord Queensberry', or (after the verdict) that 'No matter how one might deplore the criminal actions for which he was justly found guilty, it was impossible to keep down a certain amount of pity.'

Meanwhile, 'Cultivated London', as Yeats recalled, which 'before the action against Lord Queensberry had mocked [Wilde's] pose and his affected style and refused to acknowledge his wit was now full of his advocates.' Yeats, as he did so often, was overstating the case. He was in Ireland when the crisis broke, and he instantly set about gathering letters of support for Wilde from amongst Ireland's literary circles. He was remarkably successful; only Professor Edward Dowden refused to voice support. Yeats then brought this cache of letters over to London while Wilde was out on bail before his second trial. Nevertheless, although these Irish supporters were not alone in admiring Wilde for making 'of infamy a new Thermopolye', there were many supposedly 'cultivated' people in England who were all too ready to forget their classical educations.

Although the claims of the judiciary to 'cultivation' might not perhaps have been admitted by Yeats, it was noticeable throughout the case that the lawyers and judges acted with an almost punitive zeal. At the end of Queensberry's trial Mr Justice Collins made no attempt to curtail the applause from the gallery, but, gathering up his papers, retired to his room to dash off a brief note of congratulation to the Marquis' counsel, Edward Carson. And Wilde, after his arrest, was persistently and unnecessarily refused bail by a succession of magistrates, all ready to pronounce with irresponsible haste on what they considered to be the heinous nature of Wilde's (supposed) crime. Mr Justice Wills, who presided over Wilde's second trial, declared it 'the worst case I have ever tried' even before the verdict; and after it, he said considerably more.

It has been suggested that there was a political motive behind this remorseless campaign, a determination to be seen to be against homosexuality in an effort to scotch 'the abominable rumours' (as Sir Frank Lockwood, the Solicitor-General, called them) circulating about the beleaguered Liberal Prime Minister, Lord Rosebery. Rosebery's name had been mentioned in court at the Grand Jury hearing which preceded Queensberry's trial, quoted in a ranting letter from the Marquis to his father-in-law, Alfred Montgomery. Although we know of Queensberry's suspicions concerning the role of 'Rosebery and the other snob-queers' in the tragic death of his son, Drumlanrig, the reference on this occasion was concerned with a political slight, and was scarcely germane to the proceedings. It was, nevertheless, enough to link Rosebery's name with the case, and to alarm his advisers. With an election approaching in June, any thought of alleviating Wilde's predicament, such as Rosebery apparently entertained, had to be abandoned. Nothing less than the full and awful rigour of the law would serve.

Although a skein of political intrigue might have lain behind the Solicitor-General's tenacious refusal to let the case drop, either before or after Wilde's first trial, it seems inadequate to explain the general tenor of revulsion that rang loudly through the court proceedings. All the legal actors were public-school men, brought up in an educational tradition which promoted Greek culture and accepted – if it did not approve – homosexual acts between boys. Although the *National Observer* tried to suggest that Wilde had imported his vices from Dublin, many must have recognized the falseness of this charge. Indeed the *Star*'s terse comment on Wilde's conviction (it ceded priority on the front page to an account of W.W. Reed's Testimonial Match at the Oval) was that 'the lesson of the trial ought not to be lost upon the headmasters of our public schools. It rests with them, more probably than with anyone else, to exorcise this pestilence.' And behind the virulent homophobia of the lawyers there was, perhaps, a trace of both guilt and hypocrisy.

There is no doubt that the Victorian middle-class obsession with 'appearances' added a keenness to the general condemnation of one who had been exposed. The desire for 'respectability' is a great encouragement to hypocrisy, and many were happy to distract attention from their own failings by pointing out Wilde's. As Gleeson White sagely remarked at the time of the trial, 'Wilde will never lift his head again, for he has against him all men of infamous life.'

To these strains of human weakness was added a note of 'intellectual' justification, for, with that sense of dramatic timing which he enjoyed in every sphere of his life and art, Wilde's self-precipitated downfall coincided with the publication in England of Max Nordau's international best-seller, *Degeneration*, a highly charged account of contemporary cultural decadence. In his survey of the whole European scene Nordau professed to have discovered numerous signs of a general decline into unhealthy – even insane – egomania. This 'ego-mania' he considered to be the principal fault in all modern art, from the Parnassians to Ibsen, from Wagner to Nietzsche. He catalogued its advance amongst the decadents of France, tracing it through Baudelaire and Gautier to Huysmans and Verlaine. And he followed its course across the channel. In England, he considered, the 'ego-mania of decadentism, its love of the artificial, its aversion to nature, and to all forms of activity and movement, its megalomaniacal contempt for men and its exaggeration of the importance of art, have found their English representatives among the 'Aesthetes', the chief of whom is Oscar Wilde.'

The polemical force of Nordau's book, and its almost hysterical tone of condemnation, won for it many admirers, especially amongst those who were predisposed to admire it. Amongst those who were not, it provoked a nauseated contempt. The combination of responses fuelled a lively debate in the press. The book was widely reviewed and its conclusions provided plentiful fuel for the correspondence columns. As a result the image of the artist as an insane ego-manic degenerate was much before the reading public in the spring of 1895, and it was not an image that was useful to Wilde as he stood in the dock at the Old Bailey having his indiscretions paraded before him.

In this essentially hostile climate it is not surprising that even the literary and artistic enclaves of 'cultivated London' presented a less united front than Yeats imagined. Henry Harland's estimate that 'six hundred gentlemen crossed from Dover to Calais' on the night of Wilde's arrest was clearly a facetious exaggeration. But several young men did feel the wisdom, if not the necessity, of flight. Others took the lesser precautions of getting their hair cut or joining a cricket club.

Wilde's close friends did not desert him. The departure for Calais of Ross and Turner (who had both been with Wilde at the time of his arrest) was at the insistence of their families and their friends, and was also for Wilde's good. (Ross's family offered to contribute five hundred pounds to Wilde's defence if the errant Robbie would leave the country.) Alfred Douglas and Maurice Schwarbe, who joined them at the Hotel Terminus, were also urged to decamp for Wilde's benefit: it was feared that otherwise they might be called to give evidence. But Douglas, who was only too keen to attack his father in court, sailed under protest, and not before he had received a note from Wilde commanding him to go.

They left behind them a busy cell of friends working on Wilde's behalf: More Adey and the Leversons; the Reverend Stewart Headlam and Bosie's brother Percy (who together put up Wilde's two and a half thousand pounds bail). Frank Harris was full of implausible schemes; Robert Sherard reversed the flow of exodus by coming over from Paris to help. And there are glimpses too of other benefactors: Edmund Backhouse (Beerbohm's wealthy undergraduate friend) was raising money for the defence fund; Adela Schuster, a banking heiress, contributed one thousand pounds to the cause. Rothenstein went about 'the minor clubs' insulting anyone who was not for Oscar's part. And a 'New Woman' (unspecified) wrote a pamphlet (unknown) – in the Leversons' drawing room – defending Wilde's position 'from first principles'.

Beyond this immediate group of intimates, however, spread the broader circles of English art and letters. Many of these conventional Victorian spirits had disliked Wilde in his fooleries and his triumphs, and were quite content to dislike him even more in his disgrace. Wilde, for them, presented a far greater threat to the probity of art than did the 'philistine' British public. Robert Bridges confessed to a feeling of 'satisfaction in the collapse of the traducer of idealism'. Mrs Humphrey Ward gave vent to a righteous indignation. Henley crowed at the 'pleasing sight' of 'Oscar at bay'.

A few bold individualists, such as Shaw, Robert Buchanan and John Davidson, while having little or no sympathy for Wilde's predilections or philosophy, nevertheless asserted his right to a fair trial, or cast doubt upon the moral certainties of the mob. (As Davidson remarked to Lane, 'What the law has to do with it [sodomy] so long as there is no rape I fail to see.') But the vast majority of established figures preferred to contemplate the scene from a position of fascinated detachment. Henry James, writing to Gosse, told of how he found the whole case 'hideously, atrociously dramatic and really interesting' in a way that Wilde in his pomp had never been interesting.

Detachment, however, was not possible for those young writers and artists who, through their own associations with decadence (or indeed any other manifestation of cultural modernity), found themselves inextricably linked with Wilde and his fortunes. However little they might have known – or cared for – Wilde personally, they soon recognized that they could not insulate themselves from the reverberations of his fall. The scandal could not be ignored.

If the extraordinary scenes which occurred in Paris – where Catulle Mendès insisted on fighting a duel with Jules Huret (and Jean Lorrain demanded the rather less dramatic 'satisfaction' of a printed apology) after the journalist had referred to them both as intimate friends of Oscar Wilde – were not repeated in London, it was not from want of concern. Arthur Symons wrote to Verlaine on 9 April, 'We can think of nothing here but the Oscar Wilde case.'

Symons himself had nothing to fear directly. Sleeping with chorus girls and then writing explicit verse upon the subject was not, to the irritation of some, a criminal offence. Nevertheless, as the storm clouds of an enraged puritanism gathered, Symons' way of life and art laid him open to attack. So, at least, Herbert Horne considered. The bisexual editor of the *Hobby Horse* wrote from the safety of Paris, urging circumspection. Symons replied with a bantering friskiness which reveals a real sense of excitement:

> I have carried out your wishes in living a quiet and virtuous life. I have been nowhere, seen nothing; in fact I have stayed in so much that I have broken one of the castors of my sofa and two of the springs. If M[uriel Broadbent] tells you that we discussed s-d-my at the Empire, don't believe her. If Rothenstein tells you he saw me in earnest conversation with a small, but comely, person in a remote neighbourhood at a late hour, and that, with his usual fine sense of fitness, he yelled out 'Arthur Symons!' don't believe him . . . I have corrected a few proofs, had dinner every few days, and said my prayers when I didn't forget them.

John Gray was more anxious than excited. With *The Picture of Dorian Gray* cited specifically in Queensberry's 'plea of justification' as an 'immoral work', he was worried lest the connection between himself and that novel's hero should be brought up in court. He took the precaution – doubtless at Raffalovich's prompting and expense – of retaining a barrister to hold a watching brief for him during the three trials. In the event, his name was not mentioned.

The awful fascination of the events unfolding at the Central Criminal Court was too much for Raffalovich. Despite – or perhaps because of – his rift with Wilde he felt unable to keep away. His attempt to gain admittance to the public gallery was, however, unsuccessful. The duty officer turned him away with the gnomic admonishment, 'It is no place for you, sir; don't go in.' Whether this trip to the Old Bailey was fired by a scientific curiosity about the origins of sexual inversion (a subject upon which Raffalovich was writing a thesis), or by a malicious desire to see Wilde humbled, is uncertain. Deprived, however, of the chance to stare, Raffalovich directed his energies elsewhere.

Both he and Gray asserted their own continuing creativity in the face of Wilde's collapsing career by bringing out two short dramas, *A*

Northern Aspect and *The Ambush of Young Days*, on the very eve of Wilde's first trial. Then, before the final verdict was delivered, they removed themselves to Berlin, arranging to be wired the news of Wilde's fate by their (and Wilde's) hairdresser.

Gray's reaction to Wilde's fall has gone unrecorded, but Raffalovich's was hot with bitterness – the bitterness of literary rivalry, of disapprobation for Wilde's lack of self-restraint, of resentment at the misery which Wilde had caused Gray. Many years later he tried to explain his position, saying, 'If you had lived through that time and seen at least one tortured victim as I did, and sinister shadows cast on tracts of human relationships, you would have understood my feelings.' His immediate response was to write a long and hostile article on '*L'Affaire Oscar Wilde*' for a French journal of criminal anthropology. The piece was hurried into print with opportunistic swiftness, appearing just five weeks after the verdict had been delivered.

Lionel Johnson's attitude to Wilde was ambivalent. Whether through guilt or jealousy he had come to resent Wilde's friendship with Alfred Douglas, a friendship which he himself had initiated. He damned Wilde in his poem, 'To the Destroyer of a Soul', and on the eve of the first trial wrote to Yeats denouncing his erstwhile friend for the 'sense of triumph and power' he got 'at every dinner table he dominated, from the knowledge that he was guilty of that sin which, more than any other possible to man, would turn those people against him if they but knew.'

Yet in the face of Wilde's savaging by the philistine press, the fastidious Johnson altered his position completely. When Yeats replied to his letter, in what he took to be a conciliatory tone, regretting Wilde's 'downfall, but not that of his imitators', Johnson wrote back sharply, 'Why do you not regret the fall of Wilde's imitators? They were worthless but should have been left to criticism.' Even Yeats' opinion that Wilde was a martyr who might yet draw a new and deeper note from his sufferings was brushed aside. Johnson refused to grant Wilde's enemies even that much merit. He considered that the playwright 'would produce, when it was all over, some comedy exactly like the others, writing from an art where events could leave no trace.'

The kind-hearted Dowson, though his acquaintance with Wilde was quite slight, gave rather more concrete support. He called at Oakley Street during Wilde's brief period of bail between the two trials; and he attended the Old Bailey – with Robert Sherard – on the final morning to hear the verdict and sentence pronounced. It is said, too, that he suffered for his unembarrassed sympathy. One evening a prostitute, overhearing his views on Wilde, called after him, ''Ere's another of the dirty buggers.' But Dowson, though he might have been wary of newts, was unafraid of names.

Robert Hichens called on his publisher, William Heinemann, during the trials, and together they decided to withdraw *The Green Carnation* from circulation. It was a courageous move, for the book was selling hotly, but the story's nudging indiscretions suddenly seemed in 'doubtful taste'. The firm of Ward Lock & Bowden showed rather less scruple, rushing out a second edition of *The Picture of Dorian Gray* in May 1895, to take advantage of the court room publicity. Most publishers, however, shied nervously – even blindly – in the other direction. Grant Allen, who had achieved notoriety earlier in the year with his sensational novel, *The Woman Who Did*, found himself 'lumped' together with the decadents, and his next work turned down by two timid publishing houses. The whole topic of homosexuality – which had been opening up to broader and more informed discussion – became, overnight, taboo once more. The reputable academic firm of Williams & Norgate hastily returned the manuscript of Havelock Ellis' scientific study of sexual inversion. And T. Fisher Unwin insisted that Edward Carpenter come and remove the remaining stock of *Towards Democracy*, his Whitmanesque poem of a socialistic and homosexual ideal.

But it was at the Bodley Head that the shock waves of Wilde's downfall were most keenly felt. The tremor was even carried – telegraphically – across the Atlantic. Lane, on the very eve of the débâcle, had departed for America on a business tour to New York and Boston, with the aim of perhaps establishing a branch of the Bodley Head in the States. He was accompanied by Richard Le Gallienne, who planned to give a series of lectures on English poetry. And although Beardsley, who had hoped to be of the party, had been obliged to stay behind due to his chronic ill-health, another key *Yellow Book* contributor, Max Beerbohm, was already in America, accompanying his half-brother on a theatrical tour, in the unlikely capacity of 'private secretary'.

As Lane and Le Gallienne disembarked in New York they were greeted with the news of Wilde's arrest. Worse even than this, the press report stated baldly that Wilde had been led away from the

Cadogan Hotel with a copy of '*The Yellow Book* under his arm'. At a distance of almost four thousand miles Lane could not be aware of the painful irony behind the headline, for the yellow-bound volume in Wilde's clasp had not in fact been the (in)famous Bodley Head quarterly, but a French novel, *Aphrodite*, by Wilde's young friend Pierre Louÿs. Beardsley's excited description of *The Yellow Book*'s design as, 'in general get-up . . . like the ordinary French novel' had proved only too accurate. The deliberate effort to exclude Wilde from the periodical was brought to nothing. Coincidence, and the British journalist's knack for factual inaccuracy, conspired to link the two in a blaze of lurid publicity.

The British public had always assumed the connection, and they were quite content to accept the erroneous assertions of the press. An angry mob gathered in Vigo Street and hurled stones through the elegant bow-window of the Bodley Head shop. In the first flush of alarm – before he even knew of this fenestral outrage – Lane had cabled to his assistant, Frederick Chapman, advising him to withdraw all Wilde's books from sale. The situation, however, was not to be so easily calmed. Six prominent Bodley Head authors sent a cable to Lane demanding the removal of all Beardsley's work from the next number of *The Yellow Book*. The publisher demurred, but left matters at the discretion of Chapman.

Chapman looked for advice to the senior authors Wildfrid Meynell and William Watson; they both demanded the removal of Beardsley's drawings from *The Yellow Book*. The curious nexus that – despite the best efforts of all the concerned parties – bound Beardsley to Wilde and both to *The Yellow Book*, was, it seemed, unbroken, even in the eyes of such 'cultivated' Londoners as Watson and the Meynells. And Mrs Humphrey Ward regarded it as her duty, in view of her 'position before the British public', to support their call for Beardsley's dismissal. She was unmoved by Gosse's plea that although 'the British public considered Beardsley's art immoral, [it] was not sufficient reason for an act that would connect him [Beardsley] in the public mind with a form of vice with which he had no connection whatsoever'. In the minds of many the connection had already been made; and their principal concern now was not to be connected with Beardsley.

That was certainly William Watson's desire. Watson was a modestly popular and thoroughly conventional poet – 'an unswerving upholder of the classical tradition' in the phrase of a contemporary.

Gladstone admired his work. Although his books sold by the thousand (singular) – which was very much more than could be said for Gray's or Symons' – he was certainly not the financial prop of the firm. Lane, nevertheless, held him and his verse in extremely high regard. From the beginning of the 1880s, however, when his first volume of poems was slated by the critics and ignored by the public, Watson had been subject to bouts of paranoid insanity. In December 1892 he stopped the carriage of Prince Alfred, the Duke of Edinburgh, in the park at Windsor, apparently in the hope of bringing the Prince to a fuller appreciation of his verse. The attempt failed. The Prince drove on, and Watson was shut up for a spell in an asylum.

Watson had never cared for either Wilde or decadence. In the summer of 1892, when the Lord Chamerlain's refusal to licence a production of *Salomé* had prompted Wilde to threaten to emigrate, Watson had written a rather feeble ditty of celebration in the *Spectator*. (Wilde had remarked at the time that there was 'not enough fire in William Watson's poetry to boil a tea-kettle'.) By 1895, however, Watson's hostility had hardened into something altogether more cranky. Perhaps he believed that he had a chance of gaining the still vacant laureateship, and had become hypersensitive about any connection with a scandal that might damage his hopes. Or perhaps the periodic mental instability to which he was subject had confused further his views upon the Wilde-Beardsley-*Yellow Book* question. Yeats favoured the latter explanation, and offered it as a partial excuse for the strident cable which Watson dispatched across the Atlantic: 'WITHDRAW ALL BEARDSLEY'S DESIGNS OR I WITHDRAW MY BOOKS.'

Lane was still not inclined to take so drastic a step. It would be, he cabled Chapman, 'a great injustice to Beardsley'. There had obviously been much debate upon the subject amongst the British party in America, for in his resolve he claimed to be supported not only by Le Gallienne, but also by Beerbohm Tree and Rudyard Kipling (who happened to be touring the States). He gave instructions that 'If Beardsley is attacked' – either at the trial or in the press – it should be argued that 'he has been a modern Hogarth in pointing out and, as it were, lampooning the period and its customs'.

In fact Beardsley was not mentioned in court. It was another Vigo Street employee who dragged the name of the Bodley Head into the Old Bailey proceedings. Edward Shelley, the firm's erstwhile junior clerk, was one of the young men to give evidence against Wilde, and

Lane rapidly diverted his concern and energy to scotching any suggestion that he had introduced the pair or encouraged their intimacy. He sent numerous cables to Chapman, urging him to place a denial in the press, and begging for more detailed news of proceedings than could be found in the New York papers. (In Lane's absence Elkin Mathews even appeared at the second trial to confirm that Shelley had been asked to leave the firm when it was discovered that Wilde was writing him fulsome letters.)

Meanwhile, Beardsley's position was weakening. He was only too aware of his inescapable connection with Wilde. He is said to have received the news of Wilde's arrest with the morbid jest that he himself would have to go into exile. During the course of the trials, he called on Symons at Fountain Court and, staring into the mirror above the fireplace, conceded dolefully, 'Yes, I do look like a sodomite.' But while Beardsley mocked his own predicament, others exploited it.

Wilfrid Meynell cabled to Lane urging him to act decisively against the young illustrator, and he put pressure, too, upon the hapless Chapman. Harland, who might have shielded his co-editor, was away in France with his wife, recovering from a bout of tuberculosis and the strains of bringing Volume V of *The Yellow Book* to the press. His assistant, Ella D'Arcy, though she had no natural enthusiasm for decadent art, tried gallantly to defend Beardsley. But she was alone and ineffectual. As she later contended, 'If Harland had only been at the Bodley Head everything would have been different. He would have made Chapman wait until Lane got back. But Chapman was a little man and he didn't like Beardsley. He took this opportunity to be important.'

Lane, stuck in America with only inadequate cables and the strident headlines to the New York papers to guide him, oscillated between impotent exasperation and outright panic. Finally, in desperation, on the eve of boarding a ship to recross the Atlantic, he cabled Chapman authorizing him to do whatever was necessary to save the firm. Chapman took this opportunity. He recalled Volume V from the press and set about excising all evidence of Beardsley's presence. Five illustrations were removed, and the cover design – of a girl and faun – was replaced with a picture by Patten Wilson. Chapman, in his haste, forgot, however, to alter the spine and back-cover, which were also by Beardsley.

Nevertheless, when the emasculated volume finally appeared on

30 April 1895 it created a splendid absence of outrage. The wags remarked that *The Yellow Book* had 'turned grey' overnight, while the newspapers considered that Beardsley's removal raised the moral tone of the whole publication. *The Times* applauded a new 'striving towards healthiness'; while the *Bookman* (an American periodical) pronounced the new issue altogether 'far more wholesome' than its predecessors. The Philistines cheered, and in the *World* (8 May) Mostyn Piggott, under his name 'Testudo', commemorated the victory with a poem in the manner of Lewis Carroll:

> Twas rollog, and the minim potes
> Did mime and mimble in the cafe;
> All footly were the Philerotes,
> And the Daycadongs outstrafe.
>
> Beward the Yallerbock, my son!
> The aims that rile, the art that racks,
> Beward the Aub-Aub Bird and shun
> The stumious Beerbomax.
>
> . . .
>
> Then, as veep Vigo's marge he trod,
> The Yallerbock, with tonge of blue,
> Came piffling through the Headley Bod,
> And flippered as it flew. . .

In the immediate wake of the débâcle Beardsley went over to Paris to see Harland, and to tell him of the long knives that were being wielded in Vigo Street. Harland condemned Chapman's interference as 'deplorable', and even seems to have entertained a hope that the situation could be redeemed. Writing to Gosse at the beginning of May he blithely asserted that 'He [Beardsley]'ll be in the July number, I hope, larger than ever.' Beardsley, however, seems to have known that his job was forfeit.

The loss precipitated a crisis for him. It deprived him of his only regular income and it seemed to confirm his unwanted and dangerous association with Wilde. Beardsley's own reaction to Wilde during the course of the trials was non-committal: it had begun with a facetious note to Ada Leverson, 'look[ing] forward eagerly to the first act of Oscar's Tragedy' (while suggesting that 'the title *Douglas* [had] been used before'), but as the case progressed it had swiftly modified itself into a distant – though not unkindly – concern. When Wilde was on remand at Holloway between his trials, Beardsley announced his intention to write to the 'poor dear old thing'. (The letter, if it was written, has, however, been lost.) Nevertheless, the camp banter that he kept up on the subject with Ada Leverson perhaps masked a deeper perturbation.

Beardsley returned to London during the first week of May apparently in a state of some distress. He had a 'difficulty' (as he termed it) and, on discussing it with his sister Mabel, she suggested that he consult Andre Raffalovich. Although Mabel had encountered Raffalovich socially upon a couple of occasions, Aubrey had only been introduced to him for the first time 'not many weks' beforehand, when Raffalovich (at Mabel's invitation) had attended a small drawing-room lecture given by Beardsley. Raffalovich had been unimpressed by the lecturer, the lecture (and, indeed, the sister) and – as he later recalled – 'left without any wish to encounter the Beardsleys again'.

Happily, Aubrey was unaware of these sentiments, and following Mabel's suggestion, he presented himself at South Audley Street on the very morning of his return from Paris. Raffalovich was out, but Beardsley said he would wait. When the wealthy émigré returned home soon afterwards he found his 'strange visitor in the drawing room near Gustave Moreau's *Sappho*'.

Beardsley (according to Raffalovich's account) came straight to the point: 'He was in a fix . . . Could I advise help?' The nature of Beardsley's 'fix' and Raffalovich's 'advice' or 'help' is left unstated. There is an understandable temptation to regard the incident as merely financial: Beardsley had just lost his job; Raffalovich was a wealthy and generous art lover. Was Beardsley, the impecunious artist, seeking to stave off starvation? In his first letter to Raffalovich, written directly after their morning interview, Beardsley did indeed thank his new friend for the gift of some chocolate, and for an invitation to lunch. And his almost bi-diurnal letters over the next few weeks were littered with expressions of gratitude for presents, invites and opera trips. There were references also to possible commissions: a full-length portrait in pastel on brown paper (not done), and a frontispiece for Raffalovich's latest verse collection, *The Thread and the Path* (done, but turned down by the nervous publisher, David Nutt, on the grounds that the central figure was, 'whatever you may say . . . hermaphrodite'). Certainly Beardsley's friends were quick to assume an economic motive behind the burgeoning friendship. As early as 23 May Aymer Vallance wrote to Ross, remarking that Raffalovich was 'financing Beardsley to any amount'.

Nevertheless, even by the lush standards of nineties' letter-writing, a curiously intimate – and most un-business-like – note is detectable throughout the correspondence. Beardsley, for example, addressed his new friend as 'Mentor' and signed himself 'Telemarque' – allusions to the young son of Odysseus and his trusted guide (an old man who, in true classical style, turned out to be the goddess Athene in disguise). Although with an ironist of Beardsley's stamp it is unwise to leap to sober conclusions, the names would seem to suggest some element of moral guidance, beyond the mere provision of expensive chocolates and elegant walking-sticks. Raffalovich, it should be remembered, besides being a rich man and a poor poet, was an 'expert' on the subject of homosexuality. He had recently completed a study of *L'Uranisme. Inversion sexuelle congenitale*, and he was even then working on his '*L'Affaire Oscar Wilde*' for the *Archives de l'anthropologie criminelle*. He showed – or perhaps read – both of these works to Beardsley during the first days of their friendship. Beardsley pronounced the 'study of inversion' to be 'quite brilliant', while he considered the passing reference to his own *Salome* illustrations in the Wilde pamphlet to be harmless.

Raffalovich was as vain as most authors. He was always angling for praise; and he was rather awed by Beardsley's fame. So it is possible that he forced these writings upon his young supplicant in the same spirit that he presented him with his *The Thread and the Path* and another unnamed sonnet. Nevertheless, there remains an alluring suspicion that Beardsley might have consulted Raffalovich at a particular crisis in his own sexual development, a crisis brought into sharper and more painful focus by the revelations of the Wilde trial. Although from the subsequent (and prior) course of Beardsley's brief life it would seem very doubtful that he was a congenital invert, perhaps the shifting tide of his oceanic curiosity and the fierce squalls blowing from the Old Bailey had brought him to confront at least the possibility of his own homosexuality. And perhaps, understandably, he was alarmed.

In the face of this alarm he could try to escape through Wildean exaggeration (claiming to 'look like a sodomite' when, as Yeats remarked, 'he certainly did not'); through diversionary tactics (he was accompanied on his visit to Symons' rooms by a conspicuous 'young woman' called 'tuppence coloured' – or, perhaps, 'penny plain'). Or he could confront his problem directly and intellectually by asking for the advice of a noted student of the condition.

If this was the reason Beardsley called at South Audley Street in such a state on that morning in early May 1895, Raffalovich's comforting theories (accepting inversion as a congenital condition free of moral taint, while urging chastity and the redirection of sexual energy into art) might either have convinced him that he was not an invert, or at least given him the necessary ballast to ride out the difficult moment.

Whatever Beardsley's exact motives, he emerged from his immediate 'fix' with a new friend and 'Mentor'. By the time of Wilde's conviction (25 May) he could write breezily to Raffalovich – away in Berlin – thanking him for his kindnesses, his advice, his flowers, and his photograph, before adding, 'I suppose the result of the Oscar trial is in the German papers – two years' hard. I imagine it will kill him.'

Beerbohm, who, if he lacked Beardsley's public association with Wilde, owed a far greater and more real debt to the Irishman, was also much affected by the great débâcle. He was in Chicago when the news of Wilde's action against Queensberry broke, and, like Lane, he felt the desperate frustration of relying on inadequate and second-hand news. Although he never allowed his dandefied mask to fall completely, his first words on the subject had almost the ring of sincere emotion sincerely expressed: 'Poor, poor Oscar!' he wrote to Turner on 3 March. 'How very sad it is.' He could not 'bear to think of all that must have happened' to bring Wilde to such a pass. But he begged Turner for '*real long* details & *full accounts*' of all the proceedings.

Nevertheless, by 9 April he was able to write from New York to Ada Leverson, lamenting the arrest of 'poor Oscar', but tempering his own sorrow at the situation with an idle note of concern for 'poor Mrs Robinson', the society fortune-teller who had prophesied a brilliant life for Wilde.

Beerbohm (also like Lane) cut short his American sojourn, and returned to London in time for the opening of Wilde's first trial (26 April). On arrival in England he immediately threw himself into the plans and schemes for Wilde's assistance. The waning of his admiration for Wilde was completely forgotten, and with a commendable lack of concern for his own reputation Beerbohm attended the court hearings. In this act of friendship he was perhaps lent a new confidence by an attachment he had forged on his American tour with a young actress in his half-brother's company – Grace (Kilseen) Conover – 'a dark Irish girl of twenty, very blunt and rude'. He had even begun proposing to her (as he was to do, off and on, for the next six years). With his own heterosexuality clearly defined – at least to himself and his family – he perhaps felt more able to support the cause of his homosexual friend.

Beerbohm's account (written to Turner) of Wilde's speech on 'the Love that dares not tell his name', is touching in its simplicity and enthusiasm. Max said that the peroration 'affected the Gallery'; it certainly affected him. Although he could not resist a jest about 'Ned Clarke' (Sir Edward Clarke, QC, Wilde's counsel) being 'implected with Hoscar' and considering 'shaving his whiskers', the tone of the whole letter rings with real feeling at the horror of Wilde's plight.

Beerbohm's courage and lack of self-consciousness even prompted him to join a deputation to Scotland Yard to petition for an improvement in Wilde's prison conditions while on remand. There, on the walls of the police inspector's room, he was horrified to see one of his own caricatures of Oscar – gross, fleshy and proud – stuck up 'as though it were evidence against the inspector's latest malefactor'. He felt the pang of an unwitting Judas. And in an effort to distance himself from the awful deed he looked at his hand and wondered how it could have done such a thing. It gave him, as he remarked many years later, 'quite a turn'.

Down at Brighton, Count Stenbock was oblivious to events. He was oblivious to everything. Chronic cirrhosis of the liver and dropsy of the abdomen had recently combined with his periodic bouts of insanity. At the beginning of the year he had been brought down to his mother's house to die. He lingered on until 26 April (the day of Wilde's first appearance in the dock). But then, after falling into the fireplace of his bedroom while attempting to assault one of his relatives with the poker, he lapsed into unconsciousness and died. His heart was extracted and sent to Estonia; his body was interred in the extra-mural section of Brighton's Catholic cemetery. His personal jewellery was bequeathed to Wilde's – and his – friends, More Adey and Robert Ross.

Chapter Fourteen

In the wake of Wilde's conviction there was a general reaction against all that was modern and outré in art, and against decadence most particularly. The results of too much artistic licence had, it seemed, been made only too clear. There was a feeling that the decadent emperor had been exposed in his nakedness, and the public was quick to suggest that it had never really been taken in by his extravagant 'new clothes'. The charade was over.

Punch's verse-maker heaved a hugh sigh of relief:

> At last! I see signs of a turn in the tide
> And O, I perceive it with infinite gratitude.
> No more need I go with a crick in my side
> In attempts to preserve a non-natural attitude.

He was delighted that he was free from the chore of pretending to love 'horror' and 'muck', or believe that 'egomania' was 'the last word of latter day wisdom'. He rejoiced that he no longer had to 'worship the maudlin', and 'aim at the mad', and could once more enjoy his Dickens without appearing 'insane'. He did admit that the exact details of this great respite were slightly blurred; he was unable to 'quite understand/How they've suddenly found all our fads are degenerate;/Why MAETERLINK, IBSEN, VERLAINE, SARAH GRAND/ TOLSTOI, GRANT ALLEN are "lumped" but', as he concluded cheerily, 'at any rate,

> I Know I'm relieved from one terrible bore, –
> *I need not admire what I hate any more.*'

The shout was speedily taken up by others, and by the end of the summer Beerbohm was writing regretfully to the *Daily Chronicle*, suggesting that Wilde's ruin had 'given the public its cue. "Art," it cries, "is all wickedness." It dives into the pages of the genial Nordau. "Art," it cries, "is all madness. We were right after all . . ." Now this, it seems to me, is the extent of the revolution – that the public need pretend no longer.'

Other contributors to the paper's correspondence columns made greater claims for the supposed 'revolution'. It was, they countered, a burst of vital energy following on the years of morbid 'degeneration'. Nordau, as one letter-writer put it, had 'opened the eyes of many people to the real character of extravagance and levity and the Nemesis that awaits them'. New and healthier philosophies were required and, happily, they were to hand.

The General Election of June 1895 had brought down Rosebery's Liberal government and returned Lord Salisbury to office. A new mood of unabashed imperialism was already making itself felt. And then there was the widely-remarked enthusiasm for sport – for football, for cricket, for cycling – an indication, it seemed, of 'a more healthy and manly spirit'. It was even hoped that this new and salutary aura would soon make itself known in a literature at once 'more restrained, healthier and brighter'. The language was that of the sanatorium, but the tone was one of bracing optimism.

The letter-writer's overview was certainly perspicacious, although his optimism would prove misplaced. The second half of the 1890s did indeed usher in a period of energetic, even frenetic, imperial activity. Joseph Chamberlain crossed over from the Liberal benches to take up a position as Colonial Secretary armed with the firm belief that Britain's social and economic ills could best be cured though a course of overseas expansion, in search of 'new markets . . . new countries which will be free to take our goods'. The pulse of this expansion was quickened by fear. The rapid industrialization and obvious ambition of both France and Germany seemed to threaten the Rule Britannia. It was a climate conducive to chauvinism. The imperial ideal had always rested in part on a belief in Britain's 'divine mission' as 'a great civilizing people' (as Rider Haggard termed it), and this belief was now easily extended to condemn Britain's imperial rivals.

The empire became increasingly a focus for national pride, an arena of blood and proxy excitement that could distract the mob – and also the middle classes. Kipling, Haggard, Stevenson and the forgotten story-tellers of the Anglo-African Writers Club created the tales and songs of what was inevitably called the New Imperialism, while the popular press broadcast the message in its basest form. This was the era of 'jingoism'.

It was an era that ended in the Boer War (1899–1902), when half a million British and imperial troops struggled under incompetent generalship to subdue fifty thousand disaffected Dutch farmers. By then even sport, far from being seen as 'healthy and manly', was regarded (by Kipling at least) as a dangerous distraction, the pastime of 'flannelled fools' and 'muddied oafs'. In the years immediately after 1895, however, a spirit of rather self-conscious healthfulness and vigour did for a while assert itself, and in the face of this bracing new spirit the purveyors of 'horror' and 'muck' were thrown back. Their options were limited: capitulation, defiance, retreat, realignment, or perhaps even oblivion.

In fact, despite a contemporary alarm that *felo de se* was epidemic, very few took the option of suicide. Hubert Crackanthorpe was the one writer of note to end his own life (in the Seine, in 1896). But, although one newspaper considered that his mode of death confirmed him as the 'most pronounced type of decadent', he was more of a 'chirurgical' realist; and he was brought to his end not by any existential angst but by the vexed state of his marriage.

Some decadents fired off a final defiant salvo and then hoisted the white flag. Theodore Wratislaw presented his monstrous *Orchids* to an ungrateful world and then entered the Estate Duty Office at Somerset House. Others who had but recently picked up the 'decadent' mask, quietly set it down again. M. P. Shiel's second book, *The Rajah's Sapphire* (1896), was a piece of Haggard-escapism. (Over forty years later Shiel added a personal note to this tergiversation by choosing – in a literary questionnaire – as the 'deceased man of letters whose character you most dislike', Oscar Wilde.)

Arthur Symons, however, had invested too much in the movement to consider such an easy escape. The most doctrinaire of the decadents was, moreover, the first to feel the blast of the 'more healthy and manly spirit' then abroad. His third collection of verse, *London Nights*, was published by Leonard Smithers towards the end of June 1895. It was issued in an edition of five hundred copies (with an addition fifty in a large format) and was received – as the author later recalled – with 'a singular unanimity of abuse'. Verlaine (the dedicatee) was nice about it in the *Revue encyclopédique*, and Yeats strove to be positive in his review for the *Bookman*, but they were the rare exceptions. The depiction of so many 'light loves', the description of so much joyless copulation (although offset by a brace of nature poems), were not well calculated to appeal to a self-righteous press.

The *Saturday Review* tried gamely to excuse Symons' 'lack of reticence' on the grounds that he was 'merely posing . . . anxious to appear a much more abandoned sensualist than he is'. But the ploy was wholly unconvincing – and perhaps was even a deliberate slur on Symons, who prided himself on his bad reputation. The *Glasgow Herald* was less circumspect; it asked rhetorically whether it was 'wise . . . to print such things', before answering, 'Distinctly, we think not.' The *National Observer* thought it 'a most disagreeable volume', with a style that 'recalls the cold-blooded catalogues of a semi-educated house agent'. While the *Pall Mall Gazette* excelled itself with a page of fulsome spite under the heading 'Pah'. 'Mr Symons', the reviewer sermonized, 'is a dirty little man, and his mind is reflected in the puddle of his bad verses'.

Smithers, Symons' publisher, seems to have been quite unperturbed by such attacks. He appeared, on the contrary, to relish his first exposure as the new champion of decadent art, successor to the mantle so hastily discarded by John Lane. Symons himself was less sanguine. He instructed a solicitor to ask for an apology from the *Pall Mall Gazette* but was forced to back down when the journal refused it.

At the same time that Symons' decadent verse was bringing him brickbats, his decadent lifestyle was also causing him grief – or rather, the impossibility of maintaining a truly decadent detachment was causing the grief. For all his experience of sampling exquisite sensations (or uneducated chorus girls) Symons had slipped and fallen. He had become infatuated with Lydia, the dark-eyed dancer from the Empire. His agonized fascination over what he saw as her strange mixture of saintliness and perversity was complicated further by the fact that she was promised to another – a wealthy, older businessman. This commitment placed an additional strain upon their already fraught relationship. Love was slowly turning into hate, as Symons' rather hectic poems of the time record. Yet he continued to feel an oppressive 'hunger' for her flesh. 'The Sphinx' had her claws in his breast. There were frequent rows. In early August, after one 'final scene' at Fountain Court, Symons tore himself free, and fled to Dieppe.

He packed only a few things in his small suitcase, but his head was full of plans. Earlier in the summer (indeed just before the publication of *London Nights*) Smithers had called by at Fountain Court with an exciting proposal. He suggested that together they should launch a new advanced periodical as a rival to *The Yellow Book*, which was in a state of very public turmoil. Smithers saw the value of a flagship periodical to draw new authors to his list and advertise the existing ones. And with his natural bent for the risqué encouraged by Symons' advanced artistic theories, it was to the decadent authors that he hoped to make his appeal.

While the rest of the literary establishment was drawing back from the movement, Smithers advanced boldly. He had signed up Symons and taken on Wratislaw. He reiterated his boast that he would 'publish anything the others are afraid of'. And, indeed, for a man who had dealt extensively in under-the-counter pornography, the over-heated effusions of a few young versifiers must have seemed quite tame.

Although Yeats credits Symons with proposing Beardsley as art editor of the new venture, it would seem just as likely that the whole impetus behind Smithers' initial idea was sparked by Beardsley's sudden availability following his dismissal from Lane's publication. Beardsley's bizarrerie and eagerness to shock would certainly have appealed to Smithers (who had once famously offered, in a catalogue of rare books, two volumes bound in human skin). And by mid-1895 Beardsley had already discovered Smithers' little shop of curiosities in Arundel Street, off the Strand, lured inside by a display of Fragonards in the window.

Whether it was Smithers or Symons who first suggested the appointment, they both agreed on it. Smithers proposed that a generous retainer (often quoted as twenty pounds a week, but in reality closer to twelve pounds) should be offered to Beardsley not merely for work on the new periodical but for exclusive services to the new publishing house. Symons hurried round to Cambridge Street to sound out the artist. He was shocked on arrival. He found Beardsley stretched out on the sofa, 'horribly white'. For a moment Symons wondered if he had come too late. But mention of the new magazine, and the hint of a regular income, worked a quasi-miraculous cure. Beardsley was soon firing off ideas for drawings, stories, contributors and titles. It was he who suggested the *Savoy* as a name.

It was a typical piece of Beardsley wit, with its obvious topographical, historical and theatrical associations concealing both a private reference to Smithers (whose shop and publishing office were situated in that area of London once known as the Savoy), and a nudging allusion to the magnificent new hotel (opened in 1889) which had figured so prominently in the Wilde trials. This sly allusion did not go unnoticed, and there was considerable resistance to the title. Thomas Hardy (when asked whether he would allow his name to go on to the prospectus) expressed his distaste for the title; and both Symons and Smithers were hesitant. But, after 'endless changes and uncertainties', it was adopted.

Meanwhile, the gathering of materials commenced. Symons spent his days in Dieppe, sitting in the writing-room of the casino dashing off letters to potential contributors on the notepaper provided. Towards the end of the summer he was joined by Beardsley, who was only just well enough to travel (under the supervision of his mother), but was eager to plot out a strategy for the magazine. Also party to their discussions were the other members of the seaside town's artistic colony: Charles Conder, the painter of 'fine shades', who was seeking oblivion in drink after the failure of his love affair with an American girl called Louise Kinsella; Jacques-Emile Blanche, the French portraitist, who came to paint both Symons and Beardsley; and Fritz Thaulow, a vast Norwegian painter with a trawlerman's physique and a red beard. Smithers himself made several trips across the channel to give his views, and so too did Ernest Dowson and William Rothenstein.

Symons wrote a mauve-tinted impression of those months (and published it in the first number of the *Savoy*). For him the summer beside the sea passed in sunlight amidst friends, ideas and work. The old-fashioned little town with its faded lawns, its line of white hotels, its peppermint-coloured casino, its medieval church, its tawdry fun-fair, its large-pebbled beach, held an indefinable charm. The *petits chevaux* and the matinée concerts provided entertainment, and the Café des Tribunaux offered a forum for debate. Beardsley amazed him with his iron will and cool detachment; while to be with Conder was, he felt, 'an education in Fine Shades'. Even the painter's passion for *menthe verte* was, Symons considered, a matter of aesthetics.

Conder for his part reported on the 'excitement' surrounding the *Savoy* discussions with rather more directness: 'Beardsley,' he told Rothenstein, 'is being very pompous about it all'; while Symons, he considered, was 'too awful for words', although 'very good-hearted'. His worst fault seems to have been his dress-sense: he decked 'himself out in a whole suit of French summer clothing from the Belle Jardinière' which, 'although it suits his particular style very well', did not make Conder 'exactly proud of his companionship'. The painter, however, managed to set aside his pride and he passed many hours in debate over the new quarterly with both Symons and Beardsley.

Beardsley, although he spent some time soliciting pictures from possible contributors (including Conder, Blanche and Rothenstein) and was engaged on some drawings of his own, devoted most of his energy to writing. He went everywhere with a large, gilt-hinged, antique morocco-bound portfolio under his arm, ready, when inspiration struck, to jot down some fleeting thought, choice phrase or snatch of dialogue. His literary imagination was certainly aflame. He would amuse – and startle – his friends with ideas for stories 'so daring', as Blanche recalled, 'that it would have been better had he told them in Greek'. He spent two days in writing, with 'strenuous application', his short poem, 'The Three Musicians'. But his principal concern was to work on his story of Venus and Tannhäuser, a wickedly recast telling of the Wagnerian legend. The story had already been advertised by Lane in his list of forthcoming titles, but Beardsley was determined to transfer it to Smithers and the *Savoy*, perhaps even under an assumed name. He suggested 'The Queen in Exile' as a possible new title.

The editorial discussions held around the tables of the Café des Tribunaux (and at Fountain Court, after Symons and Beardsley returned to England in the autumn) cast the new periodical in an unapologetically 'advanced' mould. The writers and artists approached for contributions represented the more challenging end of the broad spectrum of taste and style that had been gathered for the launching of *The Yellow Book*: George Moore, Crackanthorpe, Dowson, Beerbohm, Johnson, Rothenstein and Sickert. The whimsicality of Le Gallienne and Harland was excluded, its place taken by the intellectual playfulness of Shaw and the intellectual earnestness of Havelock Ellis.

Nevertheless, although Symons might privately tell Ada Leverson that the *Savoy* was 'going to be much more artistic and interesting that *The Yellow Book*', or Dowson might refer to it as a 'very advanced Review', publicly the same disingenuous disclaimers were issued as to the periodical's artistic programme. Arthur Waugh duly reported to the readers of his 'London Letter' that the *Savoy* would contain 'nothing decadent, nothing revolutionary'. And Symons' opening editorial was largely taken up with pre-emptive denials. 'We have no formulas,' he wrote, 'and we desire no false unity of form or matter. We have not invented a new point of view. We are not Realists, or Romanticists, or Decadents. For us, all art is good which is good art.'

Setting aside the fact that Symons' very apologies were underpinned by such decadent assumptions as the autonomy of art and the part's superiority to the whole, the line-up that he had gathered together for the *Savoy*'s first number was deliberately diverse, impossible of too easy characterization. The lead-off piece – a breezily ironic article by Bernard Shaw – suggested that far too much modern art, literature and journalism was the product of 'the teapot, the bottle and the hyperdermic syringe', and that such stimulants were 'especially dangerous' to 'creative artists' since 'they produce that terrible dream glamour in which the ugly, the grotesque, the wicked, the morbid, begin to fascinate and obsess, instead of disgusting'. Shaw proposed 'going to church' as a less deleterious (and non-toxic) alternative for those wishing to lose their sense of self and increase their artistic efficiency.

Many of the other *Savoy* contributions might well have been inspired by ecclesiastical attendance rather than by strong liquor or hard drugs. Havelock Ellis' cautious estimate of 'Zola: The Man and His Work'and Joseph Pennell's overview of book illustrators from the 1860s were eminently sensible. The four muted vignettes of contemporary realism (although they treated, as convention demanded, with a music-hall performer, an ill-assorted couple, a casual pick-up and a drunken tailor) were so reticent as to be almost unintelligible. A poem by Mathilde Blind told of the strange noises made by the sea. Symons himself contributed an account of his summer holidays at Dieppe and a poem on the joys of a wandering gipsy life. Blanche provided a portrait of Thaulow with his family. Even Beerbohm's offering, though playful, was too slight to shock: a camp little squib on 'A Good Prince' whose name is untouched by 'one breath of scandal'. (The 'Prince', however, is then revealed as Edward of York – the future Edward VIII – who was then only two years old, and quite unknown to Mrs Simpson.)

There were touches of strangeness. Yeats contributed a symbolical story called 'The Binding of the Hair', the tale of a Dark Age bard in love with an Irish queen, together with two symbolical love poems. Dowson in his poem, 'Impedimenta Ultima', sought shelter in his beloved's hair, although the effect is more conventional than the peculiarly fetishistic symbolism in Yeats' contributions. Nevertheless, Yeats and Dowson were clearly writing about love – and love, as Shaw remarked in his 'Church-Going' essay, although quite as disturbing as drink, is much more readily excused.

Indeed, the whole of the first issue of the *Savoy* could have been very readily excused as a worthy, disciplined, intelligent, cultural exercise – but for the all-pervading presence of Beardsley. He was simply irrepressible. The schoolboy naughtiness that had alarmed Lane and irritated Wilde was unchastened. The bizarre imagination was undimmed. His state of 'distress', which had led him to seek Raffalovich's advice earlier in 1895, had passed.

In a curious but suggestive move he had, on his return from Dieppe, taken rooms at 10 and 11 St James's Place, SW1. The location was conveniently equidistant from Smithers' offices in Arundel Street and Raffalovich's house in Mayfair, but the place was also heavy with particular resonance. Wilde had rented the same rooms in 1893-94, and had written most of *An Ideal Husband* there, and, like the Savoy (Hotel), St James's Place had been cited specifically in the charges against Wilde as a setting for 'acts of gross indecency'. Beardsley, after his initial flurry of fright, seems to have been courting association with Wilde, seeking, in true dandiacal fashion, to escape an emotion through exaggerating it.

Nor was 'emotion' the only thing that Beardsley was exaggerating at the time. George Moore on receiving a prospectus for the forthcoming *Savoy* (with his name included in the list of future contributors) was shocked to note that the figure of John Bull on the pink-tinted cover was enhanced by what appeared to be a tumescent bulge. It is hard to believe that Moore himself can have been seriously upset by the discovery of a bump in John Bull's breeches, but with the 'Oscar-Beardsley-*Yellow Book*' débâcle still fresh in everyone's mind, he was aware of the danger it represented. He summoned Shaw, Image and Edgar Jepson (Herbert Horne's roommate in the Temple) and they went as a deputation to Arundel Street.

Smithers was at first nonplussed. As a successful dealer in erotica his experience was all of the public's appetite for such lewd details. When, however, the little embassy had impressed upon him the seriousness of the situation, he looked suitably serious and promised to look into the matter. Any immediate looking was academic as many of the eighty thousand prospecti had already been distributed. But Smithers was put on his guard, and when Beardsley presented his proposed cover-design for the first issue, the publisher queried the presence of a little cherub who appeared to be on the verge of urinating over a copy of *The Yellow Book* which happened to be lying in the grass at his feet. Perhaps he thought it shocking; perhaps he was anxious about libel; perhaps he was just reluctant to afford the rival periodical even this doubtful flash of publicity. Whatever, the cover – when it appeared – was minus *The Yellow Book*. And, indeed, the cherub was minus his genitalia.

Nevertheless, the very fact that the cover was by Beardsley (and the *Savoy*'s large format gave the image – of a statuesque woman with a riding whip in a neo-classical garden – a ready prominence) ensured the periodical's association with the shocking tradition of the early *Yellow Book*. And inside the cover, although John Bull made a second appearance, minus the offending bulge, Beardsley's literary contributions confirmed the suspicion. His limpid little poem, 'The Three Musicians', offered a playful portrait of English probity confronted with continental licence; but the decisive blow was dealt by the first three chapters of his 'Romantic Novel' – now titled *Under The Hill*.

Although the more flagrantly erotic passages of Beardsley's original manuscript were expurgated, and the names of Venus and Tannháuser were altered to Helen and Abbé Fanfreluche, the story – and its illustrations – still constituted a fanfare of unrepentant, if ironic, decadence. The three chapters were preceded by an elaborate piece of cod-seriousness, an 'epistle dedicatory' addressed to an entirely imaginary Cardinal of the Holy Roman Church, excusing the 'mere venery' of the subject-matter on the grounds that the story 'treats of the great personal contrition of its chiefest character'.

The style of writing, the tone of affectation, the proliferation of details, the choiceness of setting, the absence of plot, all marked the

Design for the cover of *The Savoy*

book out as a determinedly decadent work. In Chapter I the Abbé arrives at the gateway to 'the mysterious Hill' and decides to enter; in Chapter II Helen is dressed by her attendants; in Chapter III Helen and Fanfreluche sit next to each other at a banquet. There is no more to the story than that, and yet the details make it superb.

The Abbé, an exquisite, androgynous dandy, whose 'gold hair' is like 'a finely curled peruke', has achieved such a level of artificial niceness that, when set beside a rose, his delicate accoutrements are quite offended by the flower's 'hardy petals'. On every page nature cedes her position to art. The toilet of Helen is one long progress of artificialities; her garden too is carefully marshalled – even the trees wear sashes. The moths that guard the portal of her court owe their richly decorated wings to a diet of 'tapestries and royal stuffs'.

And over everything hangs that 'terrible dream glamour', that fascination for 'the ugly, the grotesque, the wicked, the morbid', which Bernard Shaw considered to be a function of drinking too much tea, but Beardsley makes at once somehow personal, 'natural' and playful. Around Helen's dressing-table scamper 'dwarfs and doubtful creatures', while Helen herself is attended by a vast lesbian 'manicurist and fardeuse' whose nicknames include 'Dear Toad', 'Naughty-Naughty' and 'Mrs Manly'. At dinner the guests leer from behind masks and fans and make-up; some of the women (in a touch that combines sexual ambiguousness, strange beauty and anti-natural presumption) sport 'delightful little moustaches dyed in purples and bright greens, twisted and waxed with absolute skill'; their 'spotted veils' seem to 'stain the skin', creating the illusion of disease, or perhaps the symbol of corruption.

The studied perversity is, however, undercut. The lavish eleven-course meal, with its *ragoût aux langues de carpes* and *glaces aux rayons d'or*, rapidly degenerates into comical tipsiness. By the close the 'tragedian', Tala, is swaying on his feet, endlessly repeating the first line of a favourite speech. Natural appetite, together with natural weakness, has pulled the rug from beneath cold artifice.

Beardsley accomplishes all this in a prose which is quite extraordinary: strung with neologies and archaisms, with words borrowed, unitalicized, from the French ('chevelure', 'pantoufles', 'cochonnieres'). It is enlivened with unexpected and felicitous juxtapositions; Fanfreluche's cravat is in a state of 'mutiny'; Helen's coiffeur makes 'delicious intelligent curls'; her breasts are 'malicious', while the Hill under which she holds her court is 'wan'. Yet the writing is quite devoid of the portentous 'poetical' avoirdupois that weighs down, say, Wilde's attempts at high style. Beardsley notes everything in his imaginary world with an unimpassioned precision. As in the three drawings that accompanied the three chapters, the details are piled and piled, but the line always remains strong, fluid and cool. The fantastical galaxy of disparate details (and the fantastical galaxy of disparate sentences) are bound together by sheer force of style.

Beneath, or above, it all lies Beardsley's wit. The cod introduction, although it might perhaps have taken in a (very) few people, served more to unsettle the reader over the seriousness of the whole piece. The heroic tale – and the visit of a beautiful Christian noble to the court of Helen in exile is the stuff of epic – is consistently guyed with bathos. The erotic carvings on the pillars at Helen's gateway not only 'surpassed all that Japan has ever pictured from her maison vertes, all that was ever painted in the cool bathrooms of Cardinal la Motte [but] even outdid the astonishing illustrations to Jones's "Nursery Numbers". Fanfreluche readies himself for his entry into Helen's kingdom not with any martial preparations but by 'undoing a tangle in the tassel of his stick'. And Helen's divine proportions are mapped out with prosaic exactitude: 'From the hip to the knee, twenty two inches; from the knee to the heel, twenty-two inches.

There were in-jokes too, to amuse (or annoy) his friends. The story's very title was borrowed from the family home of More Adey – Under-the-Hill, at Wooton-Under-Edge, Gloucestershire. The mass of painted fans, although a detail entirely in keeping with the pervasive *dix-huitemèrie* of the piece, would have reminded some that Conder had made a reputation with such work. And by the same token 'the stories of Scaramouche' found on some of the said fans would have conjured up thoughts of Davidson, whose 'Plays', including *Scaramouch in Naxos*, had been memorably decorated by Beardsley two years before. There was a distinct glimpse of Wilde at his worst in the merciless description (and illustration) of Mrs Marsuple, with her 'short respiration . . . corrupt skin . . . great flaccid cheeks . . . chin after chin' and voice 'full of salacious unction'. And perhaps Wilde's famous description of his *dîners intimes* with London rent-boys as 'Feasting with Panthers' inspired those of Helen's dinner-guests who dressed in 'tunics of panthers' skins . . . over pink tights'.

The effect of Beardsley's prominent contributions – both pictorial and literary – was to ensure the *Savoy* a lively reception. Indeed his very name (and, to a lesser extent, Symons') had been enough to alert the critics. Despite Symons' own efforts and Arthur Waugh's helpful notice, most of the snippets of pre-publicity (which began appearing in the press from November 1895) were quick to characterize the quarterly as a refuge for (as the *Globe* put it) those 'young decadents who once rioted . . . in *The Yellow Book*' but had been cast into 'obscurity by the metamorphosis of that periodical and the consequent exclusion of themselves'. Owen Seaman contributed a ditty to the *National Observer* on 'The New Quarterly Blue Book' ('Our heads are light, our tales are blue'), suggesting that although *The Yellow Book* lost all its 'spice' when 'Aubrey went', the new Beardsley-Symons magazine would be even more highly seasoned than its rival ever was:

> A racier journal stamps its pages
> With Beardsleys braver far;
> A bolder editor engages
> To shame the morning star,
> On *London Nights*, not near so chilly,
> Sampling a shadier Piccadilly.

Although delays occasioned by the need to amend Beardsley's cover-design meant that the first number did not appear until January 1896, the memory of Wilde's fall and Beardsley's (unwitting) association in it was still current. A few reviews were generous. The *Sunday Times* pronounced it 'a "Yellow Book" redeemed of puerilities', and, while acknowledging Beardsley's 'audacious decadence', praised particularly the 'splendid decorative effects' of his designs. But then Beardsley had got Smithers to send them a review copy specially, by hand, because – as he put it – 'They are so very friendly to me.' And certainly there were a select few amicable to Beardsley and his art: the *Academy* and the *Scotsman* always recognized his gifts.

The majority, however, were less well-disposed. The *Star* (with its intimate ties to John Lane and *The Yellow Book*) predictably enough found the rival periodical 'dull – at once eccentric and insipid', and – much to Beardsley's delight – singled out 'Under the Hill' as particularly offensive. *Punch* wondered whether to notice it at all. When Ada Leverson, ever ready to promote her friends, suggested a skit upon the *Savoy* to Burnand, he queried whether anyone would really be interested. Mrs Leverson, however, persuaded him.

Her mock review of the *Saveloy* as 'Book of the Week' duly

presented parodies of exactly those three contributors who had given the first number of *The Yellow Book* its sere and decadent hue – Symons (Simple Symons), Beerbohm (Max Meerboom) and Beardsley (Daubaway Weirdsley). Although Mrs Leverson's skit was written to amuse and advance her friends, the effect was to present the *Savoy* as an exclusively decadent production. This would have unfortunate repercussions, but the immediate impact was happy enough. Indeed, the tone of mock approbation employed in the 'review' was left blatantly open to misappropriation; and Symons duly quoted much of the piece out of context as an advertisement in the *Savoy*'s second number. 'Weirdsley's' story, 'Under Ludgate Hill', was praised for its terse, vigorous style, its 'absolute truthfulness to nature, and . . . its high moral tone', while the overall verdict was, 'There is not an article in this volume that one can put down without feeling the better and purer for it.'

The small celebratory dinner that Smithers held at the New Lyric Club on 22 January for some of the *Savoy*'s contributors was enlivened when Symons produced two letters addressed to Yeats condemning him for writing in the new periodical. One was from the Irish Rhymer, Rolleston, the other from George Russell (or A.E., as he signed himself), another nationalistic Celtic poet. Russell went so far as to describe the *Savoy* as the 'organ of the Incubi and Succubi', much to the indignation of Smithers, who lunged at Symons shouting, 'Give me the letter, give me the letter, I will prosecute that man.' There was an unintended irony in Russell's charge, for even as his attempt to rescue Yeats from the forces of darkness (as represented by the *Savoy*) was being read out, Yeats himself was sitting, just down the table, discoursing 'in deep vibrant tones' upon 'Dyahbolism', to Beardsley, who – for all his devilish reputation – was quite uninterested and replied only with such camp asseverations as 'Oh really? How perfectly entrancing!' and 'Oh really? How perfectly sweet!'

Although the names of both Symons and Smithers contributed their bit to the decadent miasma that quickly gathered around the *Savoy*, it was Beardsley's presence – and his provocative performance – that ensured the connection. It was a connection, moreover, that came increasingly to irritate Symons. Relations between him and Beardsley deteriorated rapidly in the months leading up to the appearance of the second number. Beardsley was obliged to spend most of that time in Paris and Brussels on account of his ill-health, and communication with Symons was largely via Smithers. The specific cause of their falling out was Beardsley's poem, 'The Ballad of the Barber', which Symons (who seems rather to have resented Beardsley's encroachment of the literary domain) considered 'poor'. Beardsley was incensed. He had planned to include the poem in the second instalment of 'Under the Hill', but he now suggested that it should be published separately, under a pseudonym. He proposed 'Symons' as his *nom de plume.* Thereafter Symons' name never appeared in his letters without some arch jibe or several exclamation marks.

Nevertheless, despite the reservations about the ballad (which eventually appeared, separately, but under Beardsley's own name, in the third issue), Symons did not attempt to modify the influence of his art editor over the periodical's illustrations. These, if anything, became even more eccentric and extreme. For Volume II Beardsley gathered several curiosities, including Philipe Caresme's licentious 'Bacchantes' and three very weird 'Visions' by a young artist called William T. Horton (one of them, 'illustrating' a text from the Book of Timothy – 'Giving heed to seducing spirits' – was a close-up of a disgruntled man with a squid on his head). Beardsley's own illustration for 'The Bacchanales of Sporion' in 'Under the Hill' was missing due to illness (as a publisher's note explained), but the art editor was represented by two other 'Under the Hill' pictures and by his magisterial title-illustration for Pope's *The Rape of the Lock*.

And in a self-referential flourish worthy of John Lane, there was also Beerbohm's caricature of Beardsley, together with Beardsley's own bat-eared self-portrait, in which he depicted himself as a devilish imp with a giant pen under his arm, tethered to a slender herm. Perhaps the image was supposed to suggest an artist tethered to the world and to worldly subjects. (Having completed his magnificent illustrations for Pope's poem, Beardsley was embarking on his next major Smithers' commission – eight obscene drawings for a privately published edition of Aristophanes' *Lysistrata;* and the play was indeed much taken up with herms and their phallic properties.) Nevertheless, if Beardsley did feel tied, the bonds – in the picture at least – looked suspiciously light, and the captive suspicously easy.

Beardsley's travels during the first four months of 1896, although coloured by a series of bad haemorrhages, and structured by much serious work (including most of the *Savoy* illustrations and all the magnificently detailed baroque drawings for 'The Rape of the Lock'), had also been an occasion for pleasure. Perhaps too much so. In Paris he saw Dowson (who was also in France struggling with the effects of consumption), and the French writers Henry Davray and Gabriel de Lautrec ('le Prince des humoristes'). Smithers too came over to visit. There were trips to the theatre. In February he went with Dowson to the enthusiastically received première of Wilde's *Salome* at the Theatre de l'Oeuvre. On another occasion he was persuaded to take some hashish by Dowson and Smithers. The drug had no noticeable effect until several hours later when, with the trio sitting down to dinner at a restaurant, it 'began to work very powerfully'. As Dowson wrote to Davray, 'Luckily we were in a *cabinet* or I think we would have been turned out – for Beardsley's laughter was so tumultuous that it infected the rest of us – who had *not* taken hashish & we all behaved like imbeciles.'

Beardsley's health survived that escapade but was dealt a more damaging blow in the middle of March when he went to see Smithers off at the Gard du Nord and (according to Dowson at least) decided on a whim, at the station, to accompany the publisher to Brussels. While Smithers was obliged to return from there to London, Beardsley settled at the Hotel de Saxe, and although he continued to work fitfully on 'Under the Hill', his physical condition deteriorated steeply. He suffered another tubercular haemorrhage, and was confined to his room. Friends and relatives hurried round. His sister came over to nurse him. Smithers, on request, sent a lightweight suit. Vincent O'Sullivan, yet another young consumptive with literary ambitions, visited Brussels and found him in a 'half-invalid state', unable to walk without the aid of a stick, scarcely capable of climbing the short flight of stairs to his room. Raffalovich took him out to lunch; while the doctors, for their part, aggravated his condition by putting on blisters that did nothing but give him a 'dreadful pain in the spine'.

Nevertheless, even in the face of such troubles, Beardsley strove to make light of his illness. At the beginning of May, just before his mother arrived to escort him back to England, he sent Smithers the first two lines of an autobiographical limerick:

> There once was a young invalid
> Whose lung would do nothing but bleed –

suggesting that Symons, '*if* he is a good boy', should be allowed to finish it.

Beardsley, although very much engaged upon projects for Smithers, continued an occasional association with the Bodley Head. Lane still used him to design covers for the popular Keynotes series. But the awkwardness of *The Yellow Book* business stood between them, even if it remained unvoiced. Of the decadent coterie it was only Beerbohm – the least threatening – who stayed on close terms with Lane.

Lane's abandonment of decadence had begun before Wilde's fall and it continued during and after it. It had received a spur in March 1895 (on the eve of Wilde's action) when Owen Seaman had published his parody of Davidson's 'Ballad of a Nun' in the *World*. Seaman's 'Ballad of a Bun', told of a young woman writer who, struggling unsuccessfully to make a name for herself with 'songs and tales of pleasant cheer', decided to discover the 'knack of Belletterie'. She set off for the 'neighbourhood of Regent Street' where she encountered a 'decadent . . . dribbling by'. He offered her a 'sample of the Bodley Bun' ('It is fulfilled with precious spice,/ Whereof I give the recipe, – /Take common dripping, stew in vice,/ And serve with vertu; taste and see!'). She tasted the bun 'and went away and wrote a book'. Her new volume was hailed by the critics amidst the 'thunder of the rolling logs'. But then the 'seasons went and came again', and 'the languid public' grew tired. 'We want a little change of air,' they cried. 'We cannot any longer bear/The seedy sex-impressionist.' 'It is,' they said, 'a sorry sort of Lane/That hardly ever turns aside.' The publishers duly started 'going in' for 'songs and tales of pleasant cheer'. But our heroine, having eaten of the Bodley Bun, is unable to change her ways.

The poem 'delighted London' and it stirred Lane. He realized, especially after his hasty return from America, that he must make it very clear that he was 'turning aside' from the 'seedy sex-impressionist' school. In June 1895 he sought out Seaman and offered to publish *his* verses. Even by Lane's own standards of self-referential publishing this was a bold move. Seaman was amazed but impressed; he accepted the offer.

Despite such drastic measures the 'languid public' was infuriatingly slow to recognize any break between decadence and the Bodley Head. At the very beginning of 1897 *Punch* published 'From the Log of a Log-Roller', a flippant satire upon a decadent poet who had, in

1890, turned his back on 'the Good, the Beautiful and the True' in order to write verse for the Bodley Head. His collection, '*Sodom and Gamorrah*', had achieved a modest success. But soon after 1895 he had suffered a setback when 'decadence' became 'a recognized form of lunacy'. He was carried from his 'sumptuous' flat and incarcerated in 'a padded room in Hanwell'.

Ada Leverson was appalled at what she considered an unworthy attack on the imprisoned Wilde, and she wrote to Burnand to complain. But decadence in 1896-97 was obviously still too good a target to be ignored. The desire to discredit it was still widespread. Lionel Johnson, who had poked fun at the decadent pose back in 1891, was still at it in 1896-97. The *Pageant* for that Christmas contained his story 'Incurable', complete with three parodies of 'sex-impressionist' verse, including 'A Decadent's Lyric' with its memorable last verse:

> Her body music is: and ah
> The accords of lute and viola
> When she and I
> Play on live limbs love's opera.

It was not, however, only decadent poetry that was under attack at this time. The election of Alfred Austin to the long-vacant laureateship in the New Year's Honours of 1896 had released a torrent of ridicule. The diminutive poet's first stab at official verse appeared less than two weeks after his accession; it was a celebration of Dr Jameson's ill-judged and ill-fated 'raid' into the Transvaal to aid the European Uitlanders who were being oppressed by Dr Kruger's Boer regime. Austin's melodramatic opening, 'Wrong! Is it wrong? Well, maybe./But I'm going, boys, all the same', was soon being echoed in a dozen parodies: 'Say, is it song? Well – blow it!/ But I'll sing it boys, all the same'; 'Wrong? are they wrong? Of course they are,' and so on.

The poem and its author came in for rather more censure than did Dr Jameson and his raid. There was a new philistinism abroad. Its god may have been 'jingo', but its weapon was laughter. Yeats lamented how, during the years immediately after Wilde's fall, he 'was in despair at the new breath of comedy that had begun to wither the beauty that I loved just when that beauty seemed to have united itself to mystery'.

Yeats was determined not to let the 'beauty' die, and he sought an ally in his struggle. In October 1895 he moved to Fountain Court, into Havelock Ellis' rooms, adjacent to and connected with Symons' set. Although Yeats had not been drawn to Symons during the early days of the Rhymers' Club, a friendship had gradually grown up between them. The Rhymers' Club itself was breaking up: the dissolution of the Bodley Head partnership (and the emergence of Smithers) made any further group-publishing projects all but impossible. Meetings had become infrequent (the last recorded one was in 1896. Moreover, during the first half of the decade, Lionel Johnson, who had been Yeats' closest friend in the group, was descending deeper into the alcoholism that would eventually kill him in 1902. But while Johnson was becoming less approachable and coherent, Symons seemed to offer a fresh perspective. He and Yeats had always been the theorists of the group, and they perhaps recognized in each other a useful sounding-board – or, at least, someone who would listen to their ideas.

For Yeats, Fountain Court also represented a taste of independence. He was, till the age of thirty, still living at home in Bedford Park. A garret in the Temple gave him freedom from immediate parental constraints and, more specifically, the chance to explore the possibilities of a relationship with Olivia Shakespear, a married novelist (and a cousin of Lionel Johnson's) who had, rather flatteringly, fallen in love with him.

Yeats, embarking tentatively on an affair, deferred to Symons' greater experience in such matters; indeed, unlike some, he seems to have been quite impressed by Symons' amatory reputation. He was particularly delighted by his observation one evening, 'Oh Yeats, I was never in love with a serpent charmer before.' But it was Symons' less dilettante-ish 'passion' for Lydia that most engaged him. For Yeats considered 'passion . . . as the greatest god in life', and he had, moreover, his own unfulfilled love for Maud Gonne to hold up for comparison.

Symons and Yeats were an earnest and self-absorbed pair. On one occasion they punctuated their excited discussions of Catullus and Blake and Verlaine to experiment with the potential of excess; they solemnly drank two whiskies every night for a fortnight to see whether this would make them crave a third. Their natural continence prevailed. They did not become alcoholics, and after the two-week trial period they returned to their habitual tumblers of hot water, remarking ruefully that 'if we had felt a tendency to excess, we would have been better poets'.

They would have to achieve the liberation of excess by other means. The pair had, however, very different artistic outlooks. Yeats with his creed of 'passion', and particularly 'religious passion', was unconvinced by Symons' unimpassioned and decadent impressionism. As Yeats recalled in his biographies, 'I was quite unlike others of my generation in one thing only. I am very religious.' Yeats' 'religious' interest, however, was not remotely orthodox. It comprehended all manifestations of the supersensual world. Having lost the 'simple-minded religion of [his] childhood' he was trying to fashion a new and personal system of belief. His spiritual vision included belief in the Faery Kingdom of his native Ireland; it led him to study mystical philosophies and the occult; it prompted him to found the Dublin Hermetic Society (1885), to join Madame Blavatsky's Theosophists (1887), and to become an initiate of the Hermetic Students of the Golden Dawn (1890). He manipulated arcane symbols, he saw visions, he heard prophesies, he performed rites, he wore ridiculous clothes.

To some tempers this very direct belief in occult powers and rituals might seem rather absurd, even embarrassing, but in the late nineteenth century it was (in a minor way) fashionable. It marked an extreme reaction to the claims and presumptions of 'modern' science – claims that had swept away the security of 'child-like' faith, that had fostered a barren materialism, that had reduced man from a romantic hero to a ruthless ape, that had made every fixed point shifting and relative. Yeats' desire to reach beyond the limited exigencies of this disparate material world to an unseen spiritual domain was one shared by many young men – and women – of 'religious' temper and fractured faith. And 'magic', whether Druidical, Egyptian, Kaballistic, Rosicrucian, Masonic, Theosophical, or an admixture, seemed a perfectly sensible way of getting in touch with this other realm.

Yeats certainly believed seriously in his occult experiments, despite the scorn of his father. And the occult, together with Irish nationalism, provided much of the force behind his poetry during the 1890s. He began to experiment with a poetic symbolism derived not only from Irish myths but also from his knowledge of magic. The dominating image of the rose, used as a symbol of transcendent love and mystic truth, which occurs throughout his 1892 volume, *The*

Countess Kathleen, was, for example, taken from the arcana of The Golden Dawn.

Such experiments encouraged Yeats in his belief that art too could provide a revelation of the unseen reality – an art not of description and argument but of evocation and imagination; an art not of sense impressions, but of symbols. The three-volume edition of William Blake's works that Yeats produced, together with the painter and Rhymer Edwin Ellis between 1889 and 1893, contained a lengthy examination of the poet's elaborate symbology. And Blake's ideas seemed gloriously to confirm those Yeats was drinking in with the Hermetic Students of the Golden Dawn. In his excitement Yeats even went so far as to suggest that Blake might too have been a member of some unknown prototype of the Order.

The notion of the artist as a mage was particularly prominent in Paris in the early nineties. The city was a centre for occultism, its very air (so Huysmans claimed) polluted by the forces of Black Magic. The Kabbalistic Order of the Rosy Cross, founded there in 1888 by two pre-eminent magicians, Stanislas de Guaita and the Sar Péladan, had split two years later when Péladan deserted to establish his Order of the Catholic Rosy Cross of the Temple and of the Grail, with the bold aim of reconciling Rosicrucianism and the Catholic Church. But around these two poles a host of smaller cults proliferated and warred. And in 1892, when the Abbé Boullan claimed that Guaita and Péladan were attempting to poison him through magical agencies, he was taken seriously. When he died suddenly and mysteriously the following year, many considered him the victim of a supernatural assassination.

Both Guaita and Péladan were quick to equate the worlds of art and magic. Guaita made experiments with writers, getting them to compose under his magical influence, and at least one young decadent poet considered that his best work was done in this fashion. Péladan, for his part, wrote a vast series of novels (*La Vice suprême*) and a handful of plays. From 1892 onwards he arranged an annual Salon of the Rose+Croix at the Durand-Ruel gallery, for painters who were inspired by his mystical vision. Satie composed a fanfare for the first opening, while Péladan himself presided in the garb of a medieval knight.

Despite such dressing-up box absurdities, many young writers and artists were attracted by the grand claims Péladan made for their caste. 'Artist,' he declared resoundingly, 'you are a priest . . . artist you are a king . . . artist, you are a mage.' Even Mallarmé was respectful, for the fact was that these florid 'magical' pronouncements were very close to the theories which he had been adumbrating tentatively, allusively, in the little drawing-cum-dining room in the Rue de Rome. The notion that there was a higher, truer, reality, unseen beyond the world of appearances, yet related to it – a world that could be glimpsed by the artist in strange '*correspondances*', flashed upon the mind by esoteric symbols (and evoked by unexpected tricks of language), was one familiar to those who attended his *mardis*. It was the very root of his theory of symbolism.

It was a theory that he and his circle had been able to trace back through the poems of Baudelaire and the prose works of Villiers de l'Isle Adam. It could be found, too, in the posthumously published verse of Rimbaud, and the critical writings of Poe. The theory, so daring and so un-Anglo-Saxon, was, however, remarkably little understood in London at the time. 'Symbolism' was discreetly subsumed into 'decadence' by Symons in his 1893 *Harper's* article. George Moore dismissed it with a cheap crack, and admitted that he only used the word as a 'pistol in his pocket' to frighten newspaper editors. Dowson considered that it meant no more than 'musical', euphonious verse, largely devoid of sense.

Yeats, however, with his grounding in the occult, and his own tentative and independent experiments with poetic symbols, was intrigued by what he heard of such ideas. And some information did make it across the channel. At the beginning of 1893 Mallarmé contributed an article on '*Magie*' to Henley's *National Observer*, in which he not only discussed Boullan's mysterious death but also drew an elaborate analogy between the writer and the magician, calling the former an 'enchanter of letters'.

Yeats wanted to know more. Symons could help. He was, after all, the acknowledged expert on the avant-garde of contemporary French literature, while Yeats had only an imperfect grasp of the French language. Symons had met Mallarmé, had attended a *mardi*, had read Villiers de l'Isle Adam. Perhaps inevitably the evening discussion at Fountain Court came to focus less on the poetic possibilities of whisky-drinking and more on the theory and practice of French symbolism.

The topic was a challenge to Symons, forcing him to reappraise the writings of his favourite authors and to reconsider the position of his 1893 *Harper's* article, in which symbolism was characterized as a subsection of decadence. Perhaps he had mistaken the proper order. Perhaps 'decadence' was not the final answer. Perhaps the senses did lead on to some form of higher reality. And perhaps symbolism could effect this leap.

Certainly Symons was beginning to feel the strain of his rootless, relativistic decadent existence. His succession of 'light loves', his round of dilettantish hedonism, had become a progress of inevitable disillusionment. Even his love for Lydia had brought him only agony and rejection. His mother, of whom he was fond, died in the spring of 1896. A mood of bitterness began to pervade his verse. There was a fitful hankering, too, for the release of oblivion. To one in such a state, Yeats' passionate belief in the possibility of spiritual unity must have seemed very attractive. And, moreover, Yeats' ideas of how to achieve this spiritual unity seemed to follow on from – rather than negate – Symons' own theories of life and art.

The intensely felt and finely fixed impression (which Symons had come to regard as the key feature of his own decadent art) might offer, Yeats suggested, a point of contact with that other, supersensual, world. The art of the senses could yet become a means of transcendence. This, of course, was the imaginative progression that had turned many Parisian '*décadents*' into Parisian '*symbolistes*' during the late 1880s and early 1890s. But in the mighty confusion of terms and voices that raged up and down the Boul' Mich' its proper significance had never been made clear. And it was only now, in 1896, that Symons, prompted by Yeats, set off to explore this avenue.

Symons' conversion to symbolism was gradual. He slowly relinquished his decadent affiliations. In the preface that he prepared for the second edition of *Silhouettes* (published by Smithers in April 1896), he replied with Gautier-esque *élan* to the critics who detected a faint and 'unwholesome' whiff of 'Patchouli' about his verses. His pleas were for artistic freedom – and freedom particularly to treat of 'artificial' rather than 'natural' subjects. 'After all,' he pointed out, 'All art . . . is a form of artifice.'

Although the argument was based squarely upon the French decadent tradition of Gautier and Baudelaire, Symons shrank from making Baudelaire's claim that artifice was *superior* to nature. He merely asserted that 'both exist and both . . . are charming in their way'. Even this apparent assumption of equality was undermined by an admittance that his 'little pieces' were perhaps 'somewhat deliberately frivolous'; and, a few paragraphs later, by the fuller capitulation:

'Nor do I affect to doubt that the creation of the supreme emotion is a higher form of art than the reflection of the most exquisite sensation, the evocation of the most magical impression.'

Symons was already beginning to reduce the claims of his 'decadent' art, and – indeed – to weaken his own association with it. 'I do not wish to assert,' he wrote of his poetry in *Silhouettes*, 'that the kind of verse which happened to reflect certain moods of mine at a certain period of my life is the best kind of verse, or is likely to seem to me, in other years, when other moods have made me their own, the best kind of verse for my expression of myself.'

Symons' use of the word 'moods' was suggestive. It was a favourite of Yeats', indeed Yeats had published an essay with that very title only the year before. To Yeats, 'moods' were earthly manifestations of the supersensual world, and it was the artist's peculiar gift to discover such 'immortal moods in mortal desires', to discover 'an undecaying hope in our trivial ambitions, a divine love in sexual passion'. In the second number of the *Savoy*, which appeared in the same month as Symons' reissue of *Silhouettes*, Yeats had a story, 'Rosa Alchema', the hero of which talks of a 'mood' 'first discovered by Poe, Baudelaire and Pre-Raphaelites which was even now abroad, enlarging its power as it goes, awaiting the time when it shall be, perhaps, alone or with other moods, master of a great new religion'.

Nevertheless, despite the draw of this new symbolist 'mood', Symons continued to find space for decadent themes in the *Savoy*. Besides three pieces in honour of Verlaine, who had died at the beginning of the year, the second number boasted an apologetic essay by Vincent O'Sullivan 'On the kind of Fiction called Morbid', and the unapologetic evidence of the fourth chapter of Beardsley's 'Under the Hill' (which included a description of Fanfreluche's morning bath and lengthy footnotes upon Saint Rose of Lima and the 'Bacchanals of Sporion', an imaginary ballad by Phillippe Savarat and Titunel de Schentefleur.

Other, rather different artistic strains were, of course, represented too. There was the usual gathering of muted realist tales; Ellis wrote of Nietzsche; and John Gray announced his renunciation of decadent themes with a resounding poem about a blacksmith's forge. Nevertheless, it was still only too possible for casual observers to regard the whole periodical as a dangerous and decadent production.

Sales were modest. The print-run was set at three thousand but the costs were high. In an effort to reduce these Smithers announced that after the third issue the two-hundred-page quarterly would become a one-hundred-page monthly. The move, although bold, was ill-timed.

When the third volume appeared in July 1896, the guardians of morality at the offices of W.H. Smith were shocked. They announced that they were no longer prepared to handle the title. Then (as now) Smith's influence on the publishing trade was great. They controlled all the railway bookstalls and magazine stands, and without their support, and with the fresh burden of monthly production, the *Savoy*'s survival was imperilled. Symons hastened round to the company's offices in an effort to get them to reconsider their verdict. It was difficult to guess what had caused the offence. The most obvious culprit, Beardsley's 'Under the Hill', was absent – discontinued, as an editorial note announced, due to the author's 'severe and continued illness'. True, Beardsley had contributed his 'poor' poem 'The Barber', which was a distillation of decadent attitudes towards art, artifice and desire, but the whole was set in such decorous lines as to seem remote rather than threatening.

The W.H. Smith manager, however, felt threatened by something – or perhaps it was by everything. He was unmoved by Symons' pleas. And to emphasize his point he opened the magazine at what he considered to be a particularly disgusting illustration. Ironically, this drawing was not by Beardsley but by William Blake. It was one of four pictures accompanying an article by Yeats on Blake as the illustrator of Dante, and it showed the giant Anteus (regrettably unclothed) 'setting Virgil and Dante upon the verge of Cocytus'. When Symons pointed out that Blake was considered 'a very spiritual artist', he was told, 'O, Mr Symons, you must remember that we have an audience of young ladies as well as an audience of agnostics'. As a final insult, the manager (who by his intransigence had virtually ensured the future demise of the magazine) sent Symons on his way with a parting shot: 'If contrary to our expectations the *Savoy* should have a large sale, we should be very glad to see you again.'

There was no second meeting. The print-run had to be cut to two thousand four hundred (for the fourth issue) and then to one and a half thousand (for the last four). The *Savoy* came to rest at the end of the year, with the editorial complaint that it had received 'the too meagre support of our friends', and the more general observation that 'art cannot appeal to the multitude. It is wise when it does not attempt to.'

There was little doubt within the periodical's circle that the failure was occasioned by the presence of Beardsley. He was too conspicuous, too obviously decadent, too thoroughly disliked by large sections of the press and public. Yeats (who always maintained that the W.H. Smith manager had been looking for a Beardsley picture when he turned up the Blake) wrote later that 'but for our association with Beardsley . . . the *Savoy* might have survived'. As early as October 1896 Hubert Crackanthorpe was writing to the young publisher Grant Richards urging him to take over the periodical (and install Crackanthorpe as editor), convinced that if the magazine could but make 'a fresh start' and 'break away from the Beardsley Tradition' then it would have a 'very fair chance of success'. In the event Richards decided against the plan, and Crackanthorpe committed suicide the following month. Nevertheless, the letter reveals a lack of support, even amongst young, progressive artists, for the 'Beardsley Tradition'. By 1896 Beardsley's strain of decadence already appeared outmoded and inconvenient.

Chapter Fifteen

THE failure of the *Savoy* certainly hastened Symons' own move away from decadent art. He had drawn from the débâcle the conclusion that art should not attempt to appeal to the multitude and, although popular applause had never been his aim, this latest rebuff from the public seemed to sanction the unashamedly esoteric vision put forward by his friend Yeats.

Although Yeats had moved out of Fountain Court in March 1896, to take up rooms in Woburn Buildings, just off the Euston Road, his close association with Symons continued. They spent the late summer of that year together in Ireland. And Symons, introduced to the mysterious twilight of Yeats' Celtic world, had veered even more towards his friend's spiritual perspective. At Rosses Point, on the West Coast, he had composed a preface for the second edition of *London Nights* which Smithers was planning to bring out.

Again, Symons was concerned to assert the artist's right to freedom of choice in the subject-matter, but the angle of his defence had shifted. 'The whole visible world,' Symons wrote, 'is but a symbol made visible that we may apprehend ourselves.' Thus, if we can but read the symbols, everything in the visible world can lead back to the transcendent, invisible world, and it is quite 'laughable' that 'we should busy ourselves, with serious faces, in commending or condemning . . . this subject for the "moment's monument" of a poem'. Symons had moved his ground again: rather than reducing the importance of his 'frivolous' decadent verse, he was claiming that all subjects had the potential to lead on to transcendence.

Although in the case of *London Nights* the argument was no more than post-facto justification, the effect of such ideas was already making itself felt in Symons' new verse. In the August number of the *Savoy*, for instance, his poem, 'Stella Maligna', attempted to evoke spiritual transcendence through sexual passion, although the notion was dressed up rather awkwardly in the borrowed robes of Yeats' particular symbolist imagery. The poet hopes that his lover's 'passions shall release/The secret light that in the lily glows,/The miracle of the Secret rose'. The dancers in Symons' poems developed increasingly from alluring images of self-absorbed sensuality into the suggestive embodiments of 'shadowy and immutable forces'.

Nevertheless, despite these new leanings, the critic who had defined 'Decadence' (at least for the readers of *Harper's* magazine) was reluctant to relinquish the term completely. The last number of the *Savoy* contained a publisher's advertisement for a forthcoming book by Mr Arthur Symons, entitled 'The Decadent Movement in Literature'. It was to be a study of Verlaine, the Goncourts, Huysmans, Villiers de l'Isle Adam and Maeterlinck. Throughout 1897, however, the usefulness of the term became eroded still further. Yeats tried deliberately to break Symons' association with the word. In his review of Symons' fourth verse collection, *Amoris Victima* (published in January), he described his friend as 'in no accurate sense of the word a 'decadent', but a writer who has carried further than most of his contemporaries that revolt against the manifold, the impersonal, the luxuriant, and the external, which is perhaps the great movement of our time'.

Symons himself, when attempting to give an 'accurate sense of the word', in a *Fortnightly Review* article on Meredith that November, reduced its scope to a stylistic quirk. 'What decadence, in literature, really means,' he wrote, 'is that learned corruption of language by which style ceases to be organic, and becomes . . . deliberately abnormal.' He considered that this 'abnormality' could be found more readily in the works of Meredith and Carlyle than in those of any 'particular school of very recent writers'.

It was not surprising, then, that the title of Symons' collection of essays on that 'school of very recent writers' should change from 'The Decadent Movement in Literature' to something else. Yeats had no doubt that Symons' writers were part of his 'great movement of our time'. The movement only wanted a name. They chose 'symbolist' as their adjective. Symons' book duly reappeared in the publisher's advertisements as *The Symbolist Movement in Literature*. Publication, however, was delayed. Smithers' bankruptcy (in 1899) and Heinemann's protracted attempt to secure an American co-publisher meant that the book did not appear until March 1900. It was, though, largely made up of work written – and published separately – over the previous five years. At every point it revealed the new direction of Symons' artistic thought. The original line-up had been altered to exclude the Goncourts and include Mallarmé, Nerval and Laforgue. The book was dedicated to Yeats ('the chief representative of the movement in our country') with thanks for the many happy hours of discussion, argument and elucidation.

In his introduction Symons reversed the order that he had suggested in his 1893 *Harper's* article, and instead of symbolism being a sub-section of decadence, symbolism is the new movement and 'decadence' is dismissed as a mere 'mock interlude' that 'diverted the attention of the critics while something more serious was in preparation'. The concern of decadence, such as it was, was merely stylistic – an 'ingenious deformation of the language', comparable to the 'Greek and Latin of the Decadence' – while the aim of symbolism was now nothing less than to 'attempt to spiritualize literature', to make art 'a kind of religion, with all the duties and responsibilities of the sacred ritual'.

Although, as a result of its piecemeal composition, Yeats found the book disappointingly 'vague in its philosophy', all the writers discussed were fitted by Symons into the same broad pattern of mystical revelation. They were all depicted as having renounced the comforts of life for the religious mystery of art. They all glimpsed, in their different ways, the unseen unity that lies behind the fragments of outward experience, and tried to evoke it in magical, musical, allusive language. And they all subscribed to the elitist, anti-bourgeois notion that beauty is an hieratic mystery that can never (and should never) be comprehended by the crowd.

The book achieved a modest vogue, and although it did not produce a movement it was certainly an important and continuing evangel of French symbolist practice in England, Ireland and America. Joyce, Eliot and Pound, as well as Yeats, owed a debt to Symons' work; and it is as a precursor of early twentieth-century modernism that Symons' reputation chiefly endures.

For Symons himself the future was less happy. The quest for transcendence through symbolism proved unrewarding. On a trip to Italy in 1908 he suffered a complete and devastating nervous breakdown. He was confined to an institution for over a year, and although he recovered some degree of equilibrium, his spiritual perspective returned irrevocably to the Methodist vision of his early childhood.

He became tiresomely obsessed with sin, damnation and girls' underwear. He eked out his long decline in a small cottage at Wittersham in Kent, struggling to regain his critical wits and rewriting the history of his amorous conquests with lubricious enthusiasm.

For Beardsley the collapse of the *Savoy* was a severe blow; it coincided with, and perhaps hastened, a further sharp decline in his health. Throughout 1896 he had been struggling against the debilitating effects of his consumption, but although Symons had been obliged to announce in the July *Savoy* a premature end to the serialization of 'Under the Hill' on account of the author's 'severe and continued illness', Beardsley had still managed to produce much very fine work during the year. He executed his illustrations for *The Rape of the Lock*, *Lysistrata,* and Dowson's insubstantial verse playlet, *The Pierrot of the Minute,* besides starting half a dozen lesser projects, writing two excellent poems and commencing a narrative version of *Das Rheingold.*

In style his drawing moved constantly in search of new modes of expression. For the *Lysistrata* pictures he experimented with bold outlines against white backgrounds, to produce a sense of unabashed frankness. For *The Rape of the Lock* he looked to Watteau and the French illustrators of the eighteenth century for inspiration, and to embroidery for technical effect, forging a richly decorative whole out of the myriad lines and dots.

The choice of subjects was made in conjunction with Smithers, but certainly it revealed no desire to abandon the banner of provocative decadence. *Lysistrata* offered the chance for blatant obscenity; Dowson's play was the diversion of a *fête galante*; while *The Rape of the Lock*, although suggested as a project by Gosse, gave Beardsley an opportunity to obliterate Wilde's rebuke about his appreciation of Pope.

The public perception of Beardsley as a – if not *the* – decadent continued unchecked. In November 1896 the *Magazine of Art* carried an article entitled 'Aubrey Beardsley and the Decadents'. And the following month a journalist from the determinedly middle-brow *Idler* went down to Boscombe to interview Beardsley in some dread of a discussion on 'decadent art'.

Beardsley was only too happy to connive in this portrait. Despite his invalid condition he presented himself as an unflappable dandy, immaculately attired in what the interviewer described as 'fine raiment'. He confessed to being 'equally fond of good books, good furniture and good claret', and he lightly recommended that the journalist should 'lay down' some Château Latour 1865 – a fanciful notion which achieved its aim of shocking the journalist's views on extravagance, but which also revealed a dying man's desire to project himself boldly into an uncertain future. With perverse eclecticism he claimed an interest in the literary works of 'the French Catholic Divines', but supposed that his 'favourite authors' were 'Balzac, Voltaire, and Beardsley'.

He voiced his disdain for bourgeois motives and bourgeois tastes, saying, 'I have always done my sketches, as people would say, for the fun of the thing,' and 'of course, I have [but] one aim – the grotesque. If I am not grotesque I am nothing.' His views on the superiority of the artificial to the natural (including the claim that he could not work by daylight) were rather undercut (when the piece was published in March 1897) by the interviewer's innocent observation that Beardsley had 'a young man's natural preference for life in London or Paris'. Beardsley's ideological enthusiasm for the artificial delights (and lights) of 'big cities' was thus inadvertently transformed into a 'natural preference'. The paradox, however, went unremarked.

In a last, and horribly touching, pronouncement on his future schemes, Beardsley said that he planned to go on working despite his illness. 'How can a man die better', he asked, 'than by doing just what he wants to do most . . . To be a slave to one's lungs . . . seems to me utter foolishness.'

Nevertheless, a 'slave' he increasingly became. The year 1897 marked the beginning of the end. He became less and less able to do just what he wanted to do most. The haemorrhages, the suffocating fits of coughing, the outbreak of other symptoms over his weakened frame, the crushing waves of exhaustion, all came more frequently. Work became almost impossible. The effort of lifting a pen was often too much. Nursed always by his mother, he continued the halting peregrination that had already taken him from Crowborough to Epsom, from Epsom to Boscombe.

Changes of scene seemed to have a stimulating effect upon his spirit, and a firm pattern of collapse, relocation, brief revival of health, eager return to work, inevitable relapse, asserted itself during 1897–98, as the Beardsleys moved from Boscombe to Bournemouth, to Paris, to Germain-en-Laye, to Dieppe, back to Paris, and (finally) down to Menton.

If Beardsley could rarely draw during his last year and a half, he did write numerous, almost daily, letters, many of which have survived to give a vivid portrait of his decline. In the face of great pain and horrible frustration he maintained a cheerfulness which bordered on the heroic. His principal correspondents were Smithers and Raffalovich. Both were sources of patronage, and the spectre of necessity lurked behind some of Beardsley's letters. His financial position continued to be precarious; more than once the bailiffs appeared at the sick-bed.

Smithers and Raffalovich were, however, very different from each other: one a cynical libertine and erstwhile pornographer, the other a serious, sensitive, responsible Maecenas. Beardsley recognized these differences, and played up to them generously in his letters. This can leave a disturbing impression when reading his collected correspondence; often, in letters written on the same day, Beardsley describes the same event in very different terms to his very different friends. Christmas 1896, for example, was praised to Raffalovich as 'the most beautiful of all feasts', while to Smithers Beardsley wrote with irreverent exasperation, 'Ye gods what a feast is Christmas.'

The letters to Smithers (especially in the last months of 1896) were filled with puerile obscenities – with 'lace pantaloons' and 'cockstands'; one letter is signed 'John Thomas', another contains a limerick about a lady from Lima who 'played dirty tricks/With a large crucifix/Till the spunk trickled right down her femur'. There is a sketch of one of Beardsley's teeth (which had been extracted) with the caption, 'even my teeth are a little phallic'; but then, as he added unkindly and unamusingly, '*everything* is phallic . . . except Symons' prick'. Against all this there is the more measured tone of his letters to Raffalovich. These are usually thank-you letters, for gifts of chocolates, flowers, and particularly books. There are plentiful medical details but no flashes of either wit or indecency.

In February 1896 Raffalovich had become a Roman Catholic. The conversion had been a sudden one; his friend, John Gray, later described it as a '*coup de foudre*'; but when one considers that Gray himself was a Catholic and that Miss Gribbell (Raffalovich's other intimate companion) had also just gone over to Rome, his decision seems quite unsurprising. He adopted his new faith and its observances with a punctilious zeal, and it was inevitable that he should attempt to interest his brilliant invalid protégé in the consolations of religion.

His effort on this front has earned him a dubious position in the Beardsley myth. He is conventionally portrayed as a pious bore, bullying and bribing the impecunious Beardsley into the arms of the Jesuit Fathers against the artist's will and better judgement. None would dispute that Raffalovich was pious and could be boring, but Beardsley's susceptibility to his message should not be lightly dismissed.

Beardsley had long been attracted to the trappings of the Catholic faith. His usual place of worship in London was the very High Anglican church of St Barnabas in Pimlico, but he had also developed the habit of going to the Brompton Oratory ('such a lovable church') for Christmas mass. As early as April 1895 he was inviting Father Williamson (an Oratory priest) to tea, and giving him a ticket for the New English Art Club show. There is no doubt that the appeal of the Roman Church was partly aesthetic, but throughout the first half of the 1890s Beardsley felt quite happy to enjoy and employ Catholic motifs without the necessity of a formal conversion. 'Under the Hill' is suffused with Catholic camp from its cod dedication to its elaborate footnote on the girlhood of St Rose of Lima.

By 1896, however, he was perhaps more inclined to consider seriously both religion and conversion. He was increasingly conscious of the fact that his disease could not be cured, and that even the retardation of its progress was uncertain. He had come (as John Gray later put it) 'face to face with the old riddle of life and death' and, unable to escape into either concerted work or social distraction, he turned with interest to religion and to Catholicism in particular.

For further encouragement there were several examples of conversion, besides that of Raffalovich, already close to him. His beloved sister had been received into the Catholic Church at the beginning of March 1896. Amongst the *Savoy* contributors, Dowson, Johnson, Verlaine and Gray were all converts; and Beardsley had a particular affection for the 'really admirable' *Spiritual Poems* that Gray had brought out that year. Wilde had flirted with the idea but not gone through with it (he was said to have sent to the Oratory a bouquet, instead of himself, on the day fixed for his confirmation), while in the more distant past, Watteau, Beardsley's 'Master' of the moment, had also submitted to Rome.

Despite these useful supports, Beardsley's spiritual progress was not untroubled. Raffalovich's attempts to bring him into the fold do not appear to have begun until the autumn of 1896. He had by then already proved his friendship with many gifts and solicitous kindnesses. And although some have chosen to see these presents as the long-term strategy of an accomplished emotional blackmailer, it would seem more likely that Raffalovich regarded Roman Catholicism as but another – and yet more valuable – gift and kindness that he might bestow upon his unfortunate friend. He began to dispatch books of pious instruction. He arranged for priests, and particularly Jesuit priests, to call on Beardsley. His letters contained church gossip and advice on how to combat the arguments of Anglicans who were anxious about Beardsley's interest in Rome.

To all this Beardsley responded with gratitude and diligence. He read the 'pi books', he received the visits of the kind Fathers of the Sacred Heart, he asked eager questions about sermons, and even expressed a desire to assist at services. There were touches of his familiar ironic camp; he exclaimed at one moment, 'What a lovable creature [St Aloysius] must have been.' But there was a steadier note of unaffected piety muffled by genuine doubt.

Beardsley was particularly concerned with the problem of reconciling his (famously amoral) art and his (famously moral) religion. At the beginning of February 1897 he wrote to John Gray about two Dominican painters, wondering at the 'stumbling block such pious men must find in the practice of their art.' The following week, in a letter to Raffalovich, he expressed his envy for Raffalovich's Swiss butler, 'whose conduct of life puts no barriers in his way to the practical acceptance of what he believes in'. Beardsley obviously considered that his own conduct of life (or, at least, art) would pose a very awkward barrier to the practice of religion. He cited Pascal as 'the great example to all artists and thinkers', because he 'understood that, to become a Christian, the man of letters must sacrifice his gifts, just as Magdalen must sacrifice her beauty'.

In the event Beardsley decided to ignore the barrier and avoid the sacrifice. His solution was typical. He chose to adopt both courses. He would alternate between the familiar 'Mask of the Artist' and the new 'Mask of the Convert'. This was really no more than an amplication of his existing practice in writing to Smithers and Raffalovich in different tones. It is, of course, tempting to regard one of these poses as somehow truer and more sincere than the other, but both were deliberate and dramatic, and both, one suspects, were sincerely believed in during the moment of their expression.

Any practical difficulties in maintaining this double position were almost completely removed by Beardsley's invalid status. He did not go out. He was away from London. And, although both Smithers and Raffalovich did visit him occasionally, it was easy to keep them apart. Most of Beardsley's contact with the outside world was through letters, and in them he could exercise complete control.

Beardsley converted on 31 March 1897. He wrote to Raffalovich from Broadstairs telling him: 'This morning I was received by dear Father Bearne into the Church, making my first confession, with which he helped me so kindly. My first communion will be made next Friday. I was not well enough to go up to the Church, and on Friday the blessed Sacrament will be brought me here. This is a very dry account of what has been the most important step in my life, but you will understand fully what those simple statements mean.' To Gray he wrote of his relief at being 'folded after all my wandering'.

The sentiments seem sincere, and it is too jejune to place a cynical interpretation on the fact that Raffalovich began paying Beardsley a regular allowance of one hundred pounds a quarter only a few weeks before he made his decisive step. Certainly for the final year of his life Beardsley was always scrupulous in his religious observances. On arriving at each new stop-over on his invalid odyssey he would immediately visit the local church and search out a sympathetic priest. He seems to have derived a real comfort from his conversion; it was not the idle act of a naughty boy hoping to please a patron and gain an income.

Nevertheless, his new religion had no noticeable effect upon his artistic work. He did mention the fact of his conversion to Smithers, but obliquely, as an afterthought concealed in a foreign language: '*Je suis catholique*,' he added as the last line in a letter to his publisher, probably written on the very day of the 'important step'. But the new artistic projects which Beardsley took up, in the face of a steady cycle of 'bed and blood', were all thoroughly – even deliberately – irreligious. He was interested in Casanova's *Memoires*, he did several pen-and-wash illustrations for *Mademoiselle de Maupin* (that famous hymn to art's moral irresponsibility); in May 1897 he enquired whether Smithers wanted 'any erotic drawings'; and at the same time he did a series of risqué pictures for a wealthy young patron called Jerome Pollitt, including a 'scrumptious' one of Bathylle – the Greek dancing-boy, mentioned in Juvenal, who had inspired the infamous tribute of Jean Lorrain's salacious poem fifteen years before.

If his art was not affected by his conversion, some people supposed that his manner was. Rothenstein recalled meeting him in

Paris during the autumn of 1897 when 'All artifice had gone'. Beardsley had become 'gentle and affectionate' and, according to Rothenstein, 'spoke with great regret . . . of many drawings he had done and his anxiety to efface the traces of a self that was now no more'. Perhaps the 'Mask of Religion' was already beginning to impress its contour on to the face beneath, or perhaps Rothenstein (who was writing some time later) overstated the case.

Beardsley's friends were notoriously eager to find excuses for what they considered to be the unneccessary indecency of his work. Lane had claimed that Beardsley was a satirist of the unpleasant in the manner of Hogarth. Yeats tried out a number of plausible explanations: he blamed Beardsley's illness which, he thought, 'parade[d] erotic images before his eyes'. He asserted (rather as Lane had done) that all the drawings were 'inspired by rage against iniquity'. (When he told Beardsley of this, he received the deliciously evasive reply, 'If it were so inspired the work would be in no way different.') Finally he developed an elaborate (and typically Yeatsian) theory of 'victimage', suggesting that Beardsley (like some medieval saint deliberately contracting a disease so that others might be cured of it) had 'take[n] upon himself . . . the knowledge of sin' so that the corrupt age in which he lived might 'recover innocence'. For Symons, in his symbolist phase, Beardsley was a 'profoundly spiritual artist' who expressed 'evil with an intensity which lifted it into a region almost of asceticism'. In his art 'sin' was 'transfigured by beauty'.

Beardsley, for his part, studiedly avoided making such claims. Even with his last major project – a set of pencil illustrations and decorative initials for *Volpone* – his principal concern was that the pictures should be 'scrumptious and amusing' (and promptly paid for).

Although Beardsley occasionally mentioned Raffalovich (usually as 'Raff' or 'the Russian Prince') in his letters to Smithers, and though he sometimes made facetious references to his new faith in his letters to Pollitt (the discharge of blood that he suffered on the train journey from Paris down to Menton was dismissed lightly as 'a punishment . . . for taking Gibbon with me to read. In future,' he added, 'I won't travel without the *Imitation* or St Therese at least') he was careful to protect Raffalovich from anything that might upset him.

In July 1897, when Beardsley was quartered at Dieppe, Oscar

Wilde, recently released from prison, arrived in the town. Beardsley alluded to his advent in a letter to Raffalovich ('Some rather unpleasant people come here'), but he did not think it necessary to mention that he actually met and dined with Wilde, and that Wilde had persuaded him to 'buy a hat more silver than silver'. This rapprochement with Wilde was short-lived, but it was not broken on account of any jealousy felt by Raffalovich. For, keen though Raffalovich's animosity to Wilde was, Beardsley had his own good reasons for being wary of the man. He did not forget that he owed his dismissal from *The Yellow Book* to the unfortunate association that existed between them. So, although he briefly considered providing a frontispiece for Wilde's *Ballad of Reading Gaol*, he soon reverted to his more accustomed position. When Smithers put forward a plan at the end of 1897 for a new artistic periodical, to be called the *Peacock*, Beardsley consented to provide a cover on the condition that it 'is quite agreed that Oscar Wilde contributes nothing to the magazine anonymously, pseudonymously or otherwise'.

The *Peacock* was never hatched. And early the following year Beardsley died. He had been moved down to Menton in the south of France at the end of November 1897, in search of a kinder climate, but that winter was exceptionally damp and his lungs soon became congested. From 26 January 1898 he was unable to leave his room at the little Hotel Cosmopolitan. He suffered a major haemorrhage on 6 March; the disease had touched on a major artery. Breathing became an agony. The tension between the artistic and religious sides of his life, which had become painfully stretched, could be ignored no longer. On 7 March he picked up his pen for the last time and scrawled his famous note to Leonard Smithers:

> Jesus is our Lord and Judge
>
> Dear Friend
> I implore you to destroy *all* copies of *Lysistrata* and bad drawings. Show this to Pollitt and conjure him to do same. By all that is holy *all* obscene drawings.
>
> Aubrey Beardsley
> In my death agony.

Even *in extremis* he had a sense of dramatic style; for his final pose he had slipped on the mask of the death-bed penitent. One wonders whether he really expected Smithers and Pollitt to comply with his request; it was probably enough for him that he had expressed the sentiment.

His 'death agony' rattled on for nine more days. He clutched a crucifix and rosary, and was soothed by frequent doses of morphia. His body finally capitulated on the morning of the 16th. Mabel, who had travelled down to Menton to help nurse him, considered that the boy-genius of the decadence 'died as a saint'. He was buried the next day after a solemn Requiem Mass in the Cathedral.

Smithers cheerfully ignored Beardsley's death-bed plea. He continued to distribute the *Lysistrata* drawings, even after his bankruptcy, when all his rights in Beardsley's work were bought up by Lane. And towards the end of his life (he died in 1907) he would even raise money by selling off forgeries of the 'last letter' itself.

Beardsley's association with decadence had been so complete and so close that his death inevitably broke, if it did not destroy, the movement. To some the repentant manner of his end was especially significant. John Gray, on receiving the news from Menton, was said to have wandered around Piccadilly for hours, murmuring over and over, 'I must change my life.' He was already devoting himself to writing religious verse but he clearly felt that even this renunciation of his former ways was not enough. By the autumn of 1898 he announced that he would never write again; and in October he entered the Scots College in Rome to prepare for the priesthood. The tedium of his studies was relieved by regular food parcels of caviar and asparagus, sent by his ministering angels, Raffalovich and Miss Gribbell.

Others followed a less drastic path. While Gray disappeared into the bosom of the Church, Beerbohm made good his escape from the decadent legacy with a series of graceful arabesques. He had begun his discreet withdrawal almost at the moment of his first appearance, and he had completed most of the major steps of his retreat even before Beardsley's final illness. In 1895 he had announced, with mock solemnity, at the age of twenty-three, his retirement.

At the end of that year a new, elegantly produced, literary annual appeared, published by Messrs Henry & Co. It was edited by Gleeson White and Charles Shannon and called the *Pageant*. Although largely taken up with the rather lush Pre-Raphaelitism of the Vale circle it did contain a short essay by Beerbohm entitled 'Be It Cosiness'. The piece was a droll study in disappointment, charting – or purporting to – Max's disillusionment with the creed of aesthetic decadence. Being a Beerbohm article, however, the line between praise, parody and critique was thoroughly obscured by shafts of irony.

Max recounted his awed arrival at Oxford, his excited plan to attend Walter Pater's lectures, his shock on first seeing Pater in Rymans. The Philosopher of Beauty was, it transpired, 'a small, thick, rock-faced man' with a bristling 'moustachio' and gloves of bright dog-skin. From that moment Beerbohm recognized that the man might be fallible.

Beerbohm, however, claimed – in an inescapable parody of Pater's literary style – never to have cared for Pater's literary style ('that sedulous ritual wherewith he laid out every sentence as in a shroud – hanging, like a widower, long over its marmoreal beauty or ever he could lay it at length in his book, its sepulchre'). The attraction was always Pater's philosophy. This Beerbohm misrepresents as a concentration upon the 'more exquisite intervals' of 'our physical life'.

'Physical life', however, proved either disappointing or impossible for Beerbohm. Oxford, which he had hoped to find 'comely', he found full of trams, electric lights, newspaper-sellers and vulgarity, its medieval loveliness and distinction all but obliterated. In London he discovered the whirl of life even more hectic. He pretended to consider the Prince of Wales (the coarse and worldly Edward) as the true disciple of Pater's philosophy. He was, Max insisted, a man from whom no 'experience has been withheld', who was 'present always at the focus where the greatest number of forces unite in their purest energy'. Max, however, felt himself unfitted constitutionally and financially for such a course of life.

He decided that his only hope lay in retreat from 'those external experiences' so dear to the heart of Pater. He would 'unswitch' himself from his surroundings and guard his soul from 'contact with the unlovely things that compassed it about'. He resolved to dedicate his life to 'the pleasure of intellect . . . the pleasures of imagination'. He would 'shield' his body from the 'world' that his mind might range over it, unfettered and unhurt.

This apparent renunciation of decadent sensation-seeking he likened to the happy existence of those monks who, living in the cloister, retain their sense of wonder about the world. But he then subverted this picture with a second analogy: 'I thought, *pardie*, of the lurid verses written by young men who, in real life, knew no haunt more lurid than a literary public house.' The effect is funny and deliberately confusing. Were Arthur Symons, the Rhymers, indeed the whole decadent school, no different from wide-eyed monks? Or was, perhaps, the escape into the intellect a yet further refinement of the decadent spirit? Max's notion of a retreat from the world was, after all, curiously reminiscent of des Esseintes' scheme in *A Rebours*.

The details of Max's plan, however, were rather different. He proposed a move to some 'pleasant little villa' in the suburb of '–ham'. There he expected to sit in placid idleness, free from all 'sensations' and 'pulsations' (other than intellectual ones), reading his newspaper and his books, and thinking his thoughts. As for writing, he would renounce that too. He found it too stressful. He was not interested in that 'Art with a capital H' which alone brought worldly consolations. 'I shall write no more,' he explained 'I feel myself to be a trifle outmoded. I belong to the Beardsley period. Younger men, with months of activity before them . . . have pressed forward since then. *Cedo junioribus*.' He was, moreover, quite happy to stand aside, for – as he remarked – 'to be outmoded is to be a classic, if one has written well'. The closing note was one of farewell. The party was over.

Beerbohm's readers could not be quite sure that he was not serious. The gods having given Beerbohm the 'gift of eternal old age', he was determined to use it to his advantage. He would try to leap directly from *enfant terrible* to *vieux maître*. The pose of outmodedness and retreat in the face of change, mapped out in 'Be It Cosiness', was made complete in the early summer of 1896 when his collected essays (all seven of them) were brought out by John Lane under the title, *The Works of Max Beerbohm*.

Beerbohm, although he contributed to the *Savoy*, and was planning to bring his caricatures out with Smithers, always maintained his friendship with Lane. Unlike Symons and Beardsley he even continued to write for *The Yellow Book* (before it expired in April 1897). Lane, for his part, delighted in Beerbohm's work, and to add a yet further gloss of classic sheen to Max's début collection, he appended a full bibliography of Beerbohm's slender output, accompanied by a cod-antiquarian preface in which he described Max with the hushed reverence usually reserved for the great and not-quite-dead. Beerbohm was characterized as one who, 'though resigned, yet yearns for the happier past'.

Beerbohm's own immediate past was, at the same time, unashamedly revised in the epigraph that introduced the work: a single elaborate sentence, set out in the form of an inverted triangle, claiming that the author's attitude was that of a scholar and that his one aim was 'that [he] will not offend'. This from a man who, barely a year before, had provoked outrage with his views on cosmetics; who was a known associate of both Wilde and Beardsley; who had been denounced as a 'cowardly decadent'. It was yet another veil with which to confuse the reader. Was Beerbohm being serious? Was Beerbohm ever serious? Was he really an admirer of maquillage, and the manners of the Prince Regent, or was he an inoffensive scholar hoping to retire to a suburban villa, after the shock of his *Yellow Book* '*succès de fiasco*'? Was he neither? Or even both? The whole production of the *The Works of Max Beerbohm* was calculated to confuse perceptions and make criticism impossible. The image of the 'cowardly decadent' was dissolving in the mists of irony and pastiche.

In his personal life, too, Beerbohm marked a new phase of development. Although he remained quite public in his support of Wilde both during and after the trials, and continued to see much of Reggie Turner and Robbie Ross, his association with Kilseen provided a heterosexual counterbalance to these friendships. Certainly Max's family regarded Kilseen as a godsend. They might disapprove of her voice and manner (and her habit of dining so very often *chez eux)* but she was, nevertheless, 'a boon at what was a critical time'; she had 'diverted' Max away from 'his dangerous friends' and even (Max's sister, Constance, noted) 'had the courage to tell him that the *rumour* of his being friendly and intimate with them was misunderstood by outsiders, and harming him'.

Beerbohm was too self-aware not to recognize the danger that some of his friends posed to his own reputation. Although he was too good a friend to let them see it, he was always careful to guard his good name. When Ada Leverson marked the appearance of 'Be It Cosiness' with a little poem in *Punch*, Beerbohm obliged her to remove a stanza which, he feared, 'would rather suggest to people at large that I use rouge'. His regular appearances with Miss Conover – the theatre trips, the restaurant suppers, the gallery openings – must have done much to reassure 'people at large' on this score. They remained engaged for six years before they agreed to break it off.

Despite the claims of 'Be It Cosiness' (or 'Diminuendo', as it was retitled in *Works*), Beerbohm did, of course, continue to write, and he also continued to sport with 'decadent' ideas and poses. To the eleventh number of *The Yellow Book* he contributed a short 'fairy story' called 'The Happy Hypocrite', which conflated the doctrine of the mask with *The Picture of Dorian Gray*, and the series of 'Commentaries' he wrote for Alfred Harmsworth's recently established, halfpenny paper, the *Daily Mail*, included such a Baudelairian *jeu d'esprit* as an essay on the aesthetics of house fires (and the philistinism of the fire brigade). It was, however, impossible now to take Beerbohm or his views at face value. He had claimed – and won – a jester's licence, or perhaps it was an OAP's concession. He had admitted proudly that he belonged to the 'Beardsley period', but he had set that era in the distant past of 1894. This freed him not only from the attacks of all but the most purblind critics but also from the responsibility of continuing the decadent tradition. He was able, instead, to bask in the warm glow of an (ironic) nostalgia. It was a glow that suffused nearly all his subsequent writings.

The retirement from the world that Beerbohm had so lovingly – if playfully – mapped out in 'Be It Cosiness', he actually achieved in 1910 when he married Florence Kahn and moved with her to a quiet little villa, not in the suburb of '–ham' but at Rapallo on the Ligurian coast of Italy.

Wilde's prison sentence, despite frequent pleas for its reduction from both the prisoner and his friends, was served to the day. Two years of incarceration, of malnutrition, insomnia and illness, had broken the great man's constitution and fractured his spirit. That he survived at all was impressive, if not incredible. A Parisian chiromancer whom he consulted soon after his release was puzzled by his hand, for – as she said – 'By your line of life you died two years ago.' And certainly something of him had died in Reading prison.

While in gaol Wilde had been unable to write. He had tried to stir himself to creative work; he considered taking up again his unfinished 'Florentine Comedy' but, as he told More Adey, his brain had become 'fettered to monotony of suffering' and he was unable to invent. Even news of his past work failed to stimulate him. On hearing of the French production of *Salomé*, he recorded his conventional thanks to the producers but regretted that he could not feel more pleasure in the event. He was 'dead to all emotions except those of anguish and despair'.

Out of these, he did fashion one substantial literary work, the long letter of extravagant self-recrimination and magnanimous self-forgiveness addressed to Alfred Douglas, which was later published as *De Profundis*. The letter was not sent at the time of its composition and Wilde carried it with him when he was released from prison on 19 May 1897.

His friends, particularly Ross and Adey, had been active on his behalf. They had raised a sum of eight hundred pounds to launch him back into life. Many people had sent presents. Reggie Turner provided a full set of luggage embossed with the initials S.M. (for Wilde had decided to travel abroad under the pseudonym Sebastian Melmoth). Wilde's wife, Constance, had agreed to provide him with an income of one hundred and fifty pounds a year on the conditions that he did not try to communicate with her against her will, or associate with Alfred Douglas.

In the first hours of his liberty Wilde hatched an impulsive scheme to retire for six months to a Catholic retreat, but his application was turned down; so, instead, he left with Adey on the night-boat from Newhaven to Dieppe. They were met on the French quayside at four the following morning by Turner and Ross. All were in high spirits, and Wilde – luxuriating in the novelty of freedom – immediately began to romanticize his experiences: Reading gaol 'became for him a sort of enchanted castle', Ross recalled. 'The hideous machinalated turrets were already turned into minarets, the very warders into benevolent Marmelukes and we ourselves into Paladins welcoming Coeur de Lion after his captivity.'

Dieppe with its sea air and holiday savour must have made a very happy and very striking contrast even to the 'enchanted castle' of Reading gaol. The town was, however, a popular English resort, almost a satellite of London. This had its attractions but also its drawbacks. Wilde was too well known not to be recognized. His alias – which combined the name of his favourite saint and the title of a novel by his great-uncle – was almost more of an advertisement than a disguise. And although some people were happy to greet him, others felt that they could not publicly acknowledge so celebrated a gaol-bird. There were painful snubs, as well as happy reunions.

Wilde chose to remove himself from the hub of the town. He took a ride along the coast and discovered in the nearby fishing village of Berneval-sur-Mer a refuge of welcome quietude and dullness. He took rooms in the small hotel, but soon decided upon renting a chalet. Throughout the summer a steady stream of friends continued to visit him, and often he would go into Dieppe to write letters at a table outside the Café Suisse. He saw Beardsley during the artist's invalid sojourn at the Hotel Sandwich. The Norwegian painter, Fritz Thaulow, hosted a reception in his honour, and a deputation of young French poets decamped from Montmartre to pay their respects. Rothenstein called on him too. But one of the happiest encounters of the summer was with Ernest Dowson, who called at Berneval with Conder and a young composer named Dalhousie Young at the beginning of June.

Dowson, although never an intimate, had always been an admirer of Wilde's. He had lionized him at an early Rhymer's Club gathering, seen him occasionally, and even called on him during the horrible days between the two trials. His own circumstances during the middle years of the decade had, however, been only slightly better than Wilde's. The death of both his parents within six months of each other (his mother by her own hand) had left him an orphan early 1895. The family dry-dock business was by then in terminal decline and the inheritance due to him from his parents' estates was thoroughly entangled with it. As a result, although he lived in constant expectation of a settlement, he had almost no income. His health suffered badly. He gave up any practical interest in the dry-dock and spent most of his time adrift in France. Much of 1896 he passed on the Brittany coast at Pont Avern, a little village which had the virtues of being cheap and quiet, although its damp climate was not calculated to benefit his consumptive lungs.

He had followed Symons and Beardsley away from John Lane's Bodley Head, to the new circle of writers and artists gathering around Smithers. The association was an important one. Smithers provided him with a regular trickle of translation work, and in the summer of 1896 brought out his *Verses* with an elegant cover by Beardsley. The *Savoy*, which published both poems and prose by Dowson, included in its August issue a *causerie* upon him by Arthur Symons. Dowson was unnamed in the article but the 'dilapidated' habitué of the cabmen's shelters, enduring a self-imposed exile upon some 'remote foreign sea-coast', would have been clearly recognizable to many.

Symons presented Dowson as a 'decadent' seeker after sensations, a lover of the sordid and the curious. Dowson, however, although he acquiesced in the general tenor of Symons' portrait, specifically denied that particular trait. He claimed that he had 'long since outgrown [his] old "curious love of the sordid" and [was] grown the most pastoral of men'. Certainly the colours and scents of the Brittany coastline had begun to inform the stories and few poems that he wrote at this time.

His old life was breaking up. Missie, the young girl to whom *Verses* was dedicated, had not only grown up beyond the alluring state of girlhood, but was now also officially engaged to a young 'cylindrical' German who worked in her parents' restaurant. It was in a sorry condition – sad, ill, lonely and desperately short of funds – that Dowson met Wilde at Berneval in June 1897. Wilde, however, seems to have taken to his visitor. He was happy to have 'a poet' to talk to and to be reminded that he himself had 'the soul of a poet'.

Wilde made a few characteristic attempts to give the friendship a gloss of romance. Dowson (despite his unkempt appearance) was praised for his dark Hyacinth locks as well as for being 'persistently and perversely wonderful'. Why Wilde should consider Dowson 'perverse' is unclear. It was Dowson, after all, who persuaded Wilde to try heterosexual sex again. Their trip to a Dieppe brothel was not an unqualified success. Wilde described his carnal encounter as 'like chewing cold mutton'. But he did also urge Dowson to 'tell it in England where it will entirely restore my reputation'. And generally it was Wilde's naturalness, rather than his artificiality, that appealed to Dowson. He described excitedly how he had found Wilde in 'splendid health and spirits . . . but unlike he was of old in the extreme joy he takes in the country and in simple things'.

Dowson also enjoyed his new friend's prodigality. Wilde was happily making inroads into his eight hundred pounds. He celebrated Queen Victoria's Diamond Jubilee (22 June 1897) with a lavish tea party for the children of Berneval, complete with music, toasts, going-home presents and a large pink cake. Dowson was always amused by the 'unconscious contrast' that existed between Wilde's profession of rigid economy and his practice of extreme extravagance:

'He does not realize in the least that nobody except himself *could* manage to spend the money he does in a petit *trou de compagne.*'

There was no doubt that the money brought moments of mirth and happiness, but these were short-lived. The presence – all in one place – of Wilde, Dowson, Conder, Beardsley, Rothenstein and Smithers (who came over to France during the course of the summer and was introduced by Dowson to Wilde) might have been the occasion not only for social jollity but also for artistic excitement. Instead it served painfully to point up the discrepancy between that summer and the one of two years before, when the cafés of Dieppe had been full of talk and plans for the *Savoy*. Since then the *Savoy* had folded, Beardsley had become a chronic invalid, and Dowson scarcely more than one. Conder was subject increasingly to fits of delirium tremens, Wilde had passed two years stitching mail-sacks.

Wilde's 'splendid health and spirits' were both subject to wild fluctuation. After the first flush of freedon he became acutely and increasingly aware of the constraints that a life of penurious exile imposed upon him. His memories, moreover, of the savage injustice of the British penal system were too present to be easily escaped. Barely a week after his release he felt compelled to write a lengthy letter to the *Daily Chronicle* about the treatment of children in prison and the cruelty inseparable from a 'stupid system' of punishment. This was an Oscar Wilde that the public had not seen before. It was an Oscar Wilde that Oscar Wilde had not seen before.

He had convinced himself that his own fall had been occasioned not by any sin or crime but by a betrayal of the artistic creed. As he told Major Nelson, the benign governor of Reading prison, 'I am terribly ashamed of the materialism of life that brought me [to prison]. It was quite unworthy of an artist.' Yet here he was apparently offending against the creed again, though in a different fashion. The crusading urge, which he had always ridiculed in other artists, was upon him. And although he emerged from prison determined to reassert himself as a poet, to prove that he had survived philistia's torments unbroken, he was equally determined that his art should point up the iniquities of modern justice.

Having dispatched his letter to the *Daily Chronicle*, he set about composing the poem with which he planned to announce his artistic return. He fretted to Laurence Housman that it was 'terribly realistic' and 'drawn from actual experience', indeed 'a sort of denial of my own philosophy of art in many ways'. In style (although it owed something to 'A Shropshire Lad' by Housman's brother) Wilde described it as an attempt to 'out-Kipling Henley'. Every night he heard the cock crow, but, as he told Vincent O'Sullivan, 'catastrophes in life bring about catastrophes in art'. It was something he *had* to do.

The Ballad of Reading Gaol was brought out in February 1898 by Smithers. The first edition, bearing only Wilde's prison number, C33 on the title-page, was 'exhausted on the day of issue'. Other editions followed. It was translated into French. Everyone talked of it. Smithers took out advertisements to broadcast the book's success. The reviews were generally 'sweet'. Despite the 'decadent' tone of its paradoxical moral – 'each man kills the thing he loves' – most people took the poem as a piece of polemical realism. Indeed, Wilde was left complaining peevishly that the papers did not seem to understand that it was 'not *altogether* a pamphlet on prison reform'.

After he had achieved this success, however, Wilde's artistic energies collapsed completely. He felt that he had discharged his duty, both artistic and social. Thenceforth he was quite unable to settle to any work. In one letter to Smithers he suggested a decidedly decadent project – a novel based upon the life of Heliogabulus, the dissolute Roman Emperor (with that severe beauty sometimes discoverable in 'young Oxonian[s] of a very charming kind'). Nothing, however, came of the idea. A proposed essay on the virtues of drunkenness and a plan to adapt Scribe's period comedy, *Le Verre d'eau*, were similarly still-born. He considered his own abandoned plays, *La Sainte Courtisane*, *Pharaoh* and *The Florentine Tragedy*, but he did not write them. His friends tried to encourage him with eager enquiries, confident prophecies of success, even with commissions, but – as Wilde confided to a young visitor – he had 'lost the joy of writing'.

He had lost much of his joy in living too. Existence in Berneval, although enlivened by occasional, even frequent, visits from friends, was dull. By the end of August 1897 the terrible attraction of Alfred Douglas had already begun to exert itself once more over his imagination. Despite the vituperation of the *De Profundis* letter, despite the warnings of his friends and his solicitor, despite the rumour that the Marquis of Queensberry was resolved to shoot him if he ever met with Bosie again, Wilde wrote to Douglas. After everything he was still prepared to believe that his best hope of happiness lay with his young friend. They met in Rouen and travelled to Naples.

It was a mad and pathetic reunion. It endangered Wilde's income from Constance and it brought him nothing but the set round of extravagance, ingratitude, recrimination and desertion. Wilde tried gamely to justify his actions to the disapproving tribunal of Adey, Ross and Turner. He even claimed that the reunion would do wonders for his work, as Bosie was 'the first of all the young poets of England'. The claim deceived no one. Wilde's income was stopped and Bosie promptly abandoned him. After that Wilde limped back to Paris, full of contrition, and there – with occasional trips to the Riviera, to Switzerland and to Rome – he eked out a tenuous existence in a succession of cheap hotels.

He was given the comfort of some literary work by Smithers' decision to bring out editions of both *The Importance of Being Earnest* and *An Ideal Husband*. But even the pleasant chores of proof-reading, choosing dedicatees and complaining about cover-designs failed to provide a lasting solace. He was struck instead by the awful gap that had opened up between his past success and his present condition. 'It was extraordinary reading [*The Importance*] over,' he told Turner. 'How I used to toy with that tiger life!' The tiger had now got him in her jaws.

Even in Paris he was 'much alone', unhappy and unwell. The 'pilgrimages to the sinner' continued, of course, but so did the hurtful snubs, the hushed asides, the disapproving glances. He was, moreover, agonized by financial worry; 'without money and with that detestable preoccupation with money that poverty entails – a mood of mind fatal to all fine things'. Every detail of life, his hotel bill, his cigarettes, his bus fare, now assaulted his calm.

Death too confronted him. He heard first that Beardsley, his one-time collaborator, had died 'at the age of a flower'. Then barely a month later Constance was dead, struck down by a disease of the spine. She was only forty. They had not met since his release. Dowson, that 'poor, wounded, wonderful fellow', wheezed and coughed for another year before expiring in February 1900. Smithers, whose irresponsible example was supposed by some to have hastened the end of both Beardsley and Dowson, was not dead, but his firm had collapsed into bankrupt extinction.

In Piccadilly Circus the grotesquely won victories of the Boer War might provoke outbreaks of hysterical revel amongst the great

British public, but in Paris Wilde was overcome by exhaustion and despair. He was ill, too, covered in a red splotchy rash and assailed by a painful ear infection. The doctor called often and Wilde was forced to borrow money for an operation.

His last improbable scheme to restore his financial position hinged upon the outline for a drawing-room drama which he sold – separately – to five different parties. Frank Harris, one of the purchasers, turned it into a play, *Mr and Mrs Daventry*, and with no less dispatch got it produced at the Royalty Theatre by October 1900. In clearing a path for his production he was obliged to buy off the other parties who thought that they had secured rights to the play, and – not unnaturally – Harris deducted this hidden expense from the 175 pounds he had promised to pay Wilde.

Wilde was furious, frantic and full of self-pity. He desperately needed the money to pay his doctor's bills. It was not forthcoming. Ross and Turner came over to Paris to nurse him, but his condition deteriorated. On 30 November 1900, a few days after being received into the Catholic Church, he died – as he had lived – beyond his means.

Epilogue

WILDE'S DEATH at the end of 1900 served to confirm the nineties as a decade apart, and to fix Wilde's place at the centre of it. In *De Profundis* he had claimed with characteristic extravagance, 'I was a man who stood in symbolic relations to the art and culture of my age.' With his death the pattern seemed complete: eighties aesthete to nineties decadent, to victim of the outraged forces of middle-class philistinism, to lonely outcast dying in the arms of the Catholic Church. With his gift for self-dramatization Wilde had managed to give the course of his life the form of grand tragedy, and others were able to see an echo of their own fates in the lines of his drama.

Although decadence in England during the 1890s never quite managed to refine itself into a movement, it did create a pungent and distinctive flavour. Despite the best efforts of Arthur Symons, no definition of the word was ever really accepted either by those inside or those outside artistic circles. London lacked that ready familiarity with literary movements and fashionable 'isms' that has provided decadence with a firm location in Paris.

Nevertheless, even in England, amongst the informed, various literary values and artistic positions did become loosely associated with the term; distrust of Victorian confidence in society's common aims and standards – both artistic and moral; belief in the essential loneliness of the individual consciousness and the consolation of aesthetic impressions; belief too in art's superiority to nature – and to life.

The art produced by those sympathetic to such ideas, for all its diversity, did share some common traits. It was intense and personal – or strove to be. Where previous generations had sought to entertain or educate their audience, the decadents sought to shock and confuse. That this should, for a while, prove a successful marketing ploy was an irony both the artists and their publishers were happy to enjoy.

The press, which at first had been happy to use decadence as an all-purpose term of abuse, became willing collaborators in the decadents' campaign to shock. The decadent desire to turn art into life presented the media with the notion that morbid poems and pictures must be produced by morbid poets and painters. Newspapers and their readers are, of course, happier with people than ideas, and decadence very rapidly became reduced to a cult of personalities.

Symons, for all his critical knowledge of the 'decadent movement' and his self-advertised indiscretions with the Empire chorus girls, lacked the necessary profile to become a popular personality. Wilde and Beardsley, though, were ideal; unnatural, ironical, dandified, morbid and incomprehensible. From 1893 to 1895 they represented the twin peaks of decadence for the British public.

Their bourgeois-baiting had, however, a limit. The public, intrigued at first, became vexed and angry. In the spring of 1895 the sense of mounting irritation found a spectacular outlet in the trials and conviction of Wilde. His fall marked the symbolic revenge of the middle-class public upon the presumptious artist.

The brief moment when decadence had been fashionable was over. In literary and artistic circles decadence – in the Symons-ish sense of amoral aesthetic impressionism – would probably have died away of its own accord, as it did in Paris, where it evolved gradually into the broader school of symbolism. But, faced with the widespread distrust of all artistic experimentation in the years following the Wilde trials, the end was artificially abrupt. The venture of the *Savoy* foundered for want of support, and the symbolist experiments of Symons and Yeats took place against a background of hostility and indifference. Henry James characterized the second half of the decade as a 'desert of Boetian betise'.

It was not until the new century that some of the essential ideas behind nineties decadence – the cultural relativism, the intense personal vision, the contempt for the general audience – re-emerged in the first works of modernism. The modernists, however, were not keen to acknowledge the debt; their concern was to reject the past. Given the existence of the Wilde-Beardsley-*Yellow Book* tradition, it was not difficult for Yeats and others to dismiss the nineties as a closed period of extraordinary and doomed personalities. The nineties became – and have to a large extent remained – the victim of their own successful mythologizing.

Select Bibliography

EVERY STUDENT of the nineties must acknowledge a debt to Linda Dowling's *Aestheticism and Decadence: A Selective Annotated Bibliography* (1977) not only for its wealth of bibliographic information but also for its lucid and amusing 'Introduction'.

I have not listed primary works below because, generally, they appear in the text with their full title and date of publication. It should, however, be mentioned that many of the novels, stories, essays, poems, plays and periodicals of the nineties are long out of print and difficult to discover outside of major libraries or expensive second-hand bookshops. The works of Wilde are, of course, an exception, but for the rest one is grateful to several excellent anthologies for providing a readier access to much interesting prose and verse. *An Anthology of 'Nineties' Verse* (1928), compiled by A. J. A. Symons, was an early and influential attempt to revive interest in the period; broader in scope is *The Eighteen-Nineties: a Period Anthology in Prose and Verse* (1948), edited by Martin Secker, with an amiable introduction by John Betjeman. Derek Stanford's *Poets of the 90's* (1965) and *Stories of the 90's* (1968) both contain amusing biographical vignettes. Karl Beckson's *Aesthetes and Decadents of the 1890's* (1966) has an excellent introduction. The Penguin *Poetry of the 'Nineties* (1970), edited by R. K. R. Thornton, provides a useful selection. *British Poetry and Prose 1870–1906* (1987), compiled by Ian Fletcher, sets the work of the nineties in a wider context. Recent years have seen the first two *Dedalus Books of Decadence – Moral Ruins* (1990) and *The Black Feast* (1992) – edited by Brian Stableford, which combine choice examples from both England and France.

Of the general surveys of the period *The Eighteen Nineties* (1913) by Holbrook Jackson is the first and fullest; although it remains essential, it is now usefully supplemented by Karl Beckson's *London in the 1890s* (1992).

The decadent aspects of the period are traced in several general works and essay collections: *The Beardsley Period* (1925) by Osbert Burdett is eccentric but interesting, while *The Men of the Nineties* (1920) by Bernard Muddiman is disappointingly slight. *Edwardians and Late Victorians* (1960), edited by Richard Ellmann, contains several important essays. Anything in which Ian Fletcher had a hand is worth reading: *Romantic Mythologies* (1967) and *Decadence and the 1890s* (1979), both of which he edited, are full of excellent material. *Dark Passages* (1965) by Barbara Charlesworth and *The Decadent Dilemma* (1983) by R. K. R. Thornton deal interestingly with the major decadent figures. In *Language and Decadence in the Victorian Fin de Siècle* (1986) Linda Dowling examines the subject from the linguistic angle. *Ripe Was The Drowsy Hour* (1977) by J. E. Chamberlain takes a thematic approach. John Stokes' entertaining *In the Nineties* (1989) selects several areas of contemporary fascination for detailed study. As general background to the subject Mario Praz's classic, *The Romantic Agony* (1933, new edition 1951), is wonderfully good.

Although the English 1890s cannot boast a Pepys or, indeed, a pair of Goncourts, 'Michael Field's' journal, edited as *Works and Days* (1933) by T. and D. C. Sturge Moore, provides a fascinating contemporary account of nineties artistic life. Other figures of the period wrote their memoirs at a distance of time. Nevertheless, despite the occasional outbreaks of exaggeration, mythologizing, score-settling and mis-remembering, there is much information – and even more colour – to be gleaned from the pages of *Autobiographies* (1922) by W. B. Yeats, *My Life* (1939) by Havelock Ellis, *Memories of a Victorian* (1933) by Edgar Jepson, *The Romantic 90's* (1925) by Richard Le Gallienne, *Everyman Remembers* (1931) by Ernest Rhys, *Opinions* (1959) by Vincent O'Sullivan, *As We Were* (1930) by E. F. Benson, *Contemporary Portraits* by Frank Harris (1920), *Time Was* (1931) by W. Graham Robertson, *Men and Memories* (1931) by William Rothenstein, *The Puppet Show of Memory* (1932) by Maurice Baring and *Author Hunting* (1934) by Grant Richards.

Contemporary newspapers and periodicals are rich sources: I particularly enjoyed trawling through the pages of the *Daily Chronicle*, the *Star*, the *National Observer*, the *Idler* and *Punch*.

Part I

For the French background *The Idea of Decadence in French Literature* 1830–1900 (1959) by A. E. Carter is as useful as its title suggests. *Paul Verlaine and the Decadence 1882–1890* (1974) by Philip Stephan provides a commanding study of Verlaine's role in the decadent movement, while Erich Auerbach's *Mimesis* (1953) has a very good chapter on the Goncourts' aesthetic sensibility. *Artists and Writers in Paris* (1964) by Malcolm Easton and *Dreamers of Decadence* (first English trans. 1971) by Philippe Jullian provide much biographical information. There are many works on the individual authors but I found particularly useful *Baudelaire* (1987) by Claude Pichois and Jean Ziegler, *Théophile Gautier* (1975) by Philip Tennant and *Verlaine* (1973) by C. Chadwick.

The English roots of decadence can be traced at first hand in *The Aesthetes, a Sourcebook* (1979), edited by Ian Small, or in the rollicking pages of *The Aesthetic Adventure* (1945) by William Gaunt. The philosophical concerns of the period are lucidly laid out in *The Last Romantics* (1949) by Graham Hough. There is an interesting essay on the subject in *Fin de Siècle and its legacy* (1990), edited by Teich and Porter. Amongst individual studies *Swinburne* (1973) by Ian Fletcher, *Walter Pater* (1959) by the same author and *George Moore: A Reconsideration* (1955) by Malcolm Brown stand out.

Part II

Arthur Symons, after a slow start, is now receiving much critical attention: *Arthur Symons: A Critical Biography* (1963) by Roger Lhombreaud was followed by John M. Munro's *Arthur Symons* (1969); since then there have been *The Memoirs of Arthur Symons: Life and Art in the 1890s* (1977), edited by Karl Beckson, *Arthur Symons: Selected Letters, 1880–1935* (1989), edited by Karl Beckson and John M. Munro, and *Arthur Symons, A Life* (1987), also by Beckson. Symons' role in interpreting French decadent ideas for the English has been examined in *The Romantic Image* (1957) by Frank Kermode and in *The Critic's Alchemy* (1953) by Ruth Z. Temple.

The world of the Rhymers' Club is brilliantly examined in *The Rhymers Club: A Social and Intellectual History* (1988) by Bruce Gardiner, and there are biographical studies of several significant Rhymers and their guests.

For Dowson, see *Ernest Dowson 1888–1897: Reminiscences, Unpublished Letters and Marginalia* (1914) by Victor Plarr, *The Poetical Works of Ernest Dowson* (1934) edited by Desmond Flower, *Ernest Dowson* (1944) by Mark Longaker and *The Letters of Ernest Dowson* (1967) edited by Desmond Flower and Henry Maas. There is very little on Johnson besides Ian Fletcher's 'Introduction' to *The Complete Poems of Lionel Johnson* (1953). Fletcher also contributed an 'Introduction' to his edition of *The Collected Poems of Victor Plarr* (1974) and a biographical monograph on *Herbert Horne: the Earlier Phase* (1970).

For John Gray, see *The Poems of John Gray* (1988) edited by Ian Fletcher, *In Dorian Mode: A Life of John Gray, 1866–1934* by Brocard Sewell, and Jerusha McCormack's excellent new biography, *John Gray: Poet, Dandy, and Priest* (1991). For Yeats, see *Yeats: The Man And The Masks* (new edition, 1979) by Richard Ellmann.

Part III

Few nineteenth-century figures have received quite so much biographical attention as Oscar Wilde: Hesketh Pearson's *Oscar Wilde* (1946) and H. Montgomery Hyde's *Oscar Wilde* (1976) are both good, but dominating the field is Richard Ellmann's magisterial *Oscar Wilde* (1987). Ellmann only just managed to complete the book before his death, and the pressure of time upon him caused a few minor errors to creep into the text. Pedantic critics have been swift to point these out, and most of the slips have been gathered together in *Additions and Corrections to Richard Ellmann's 'Oscar Wilde'* (1989) by Horst Schroeder. *The Letters of Oscar Wilde* (1962) and *More Letters of Oscar Wilde* (1985), both brilliantly edited by Rupert Hart-Davis, are an extraordinary record of wit and perspicacity. For a discussion of Wilde's works *Oscar Wilde: The Critical Heritage* (1970) edited by Karl Beckson provides an historical perspective, while Norbert Kohl's *Oscar Wilde, The Works of a Conformist Rebel* (1989) is full of valuable insights.

For Wilde's circle of friends and rivals, see *Oscar Wilde's Devoted Friend, a life of Robert Ross* (1990) by Maureen Borland, *Reggie, A Portrait of Reginald Turner* (1965) by Stanley Weintraub, and *Bosie* by Rupert Croft Cooke (1963), *Yeats, Stenbock and the Nineties* (1969) by John Adlard, *The Sphinx and her Circle: A Biographical Sketch of Ada Leverson, 1862 to 1933* (1963) by Violet Wyndham. *Love in Earnest* (1970) by Timothy d'Arch Smith explores the homosexual milieu of the 'Uranian' poets. *Feasting With Panthers* (1967) by Rupert Croft-Cooke provides a hugely entertaining account of the seamier side of the period.

For Beerbohm, see *Max, a biography* (1964) by David Cecil and *Conversation with Max* (1960) by S. N. Behrman. There are three collections of his letters: *Letters to Reggie Turner* (1964) edited by Rupert Hart-Davis, and *Max and Will: Max Beerbohm and William Rothenstein their friendship and letters, 1893 to 1945* (1975) edited by Mary M. Lago and Karl Beckson, and *The Letters of Max Beerbohm, 1892–1956* (1988) edited by Rupert Hart-Davis. *The Dandy: Brummell to Beerbohm* (1960) by Ellen Moers has an interesting section on Beerbohm, while Lawrence Danson's *Max Beerbohm & the Act of Writing* (1989) provides an excellent critical account.

For Beardsley, see *The Letters of Aubrey Beardsley* (1970) edited by Henry Maas, J. L. Duncan and W. G. Good, *Aubrey Beardsley, Imp of the Perverse* (1976) by Stanley Weintraub, *Beardsley* (1967) by Brian Reade, *Black and White: A Portrait of Aubrey Beardsley* (1968) by Brigid Brophy, *Aubrey and the Dying Lady: A Beardsley Riddle* (1972) by Malcolm Easton, and *Aubrey Beardsley: An Account of His Life* (1981) by Miriam J. Benkovitz. *Fin de Siècle: The Illustrators of the Nineties* (1992) by Simon Houfe and *High Art and Low Life: The Studio and the fin de siècle* (1993), the special centenary number of *Studio International* magazine, set Beardsley in a wider context. Philip Healey's essay, 'Monitor and Telemaque: A Beardsley Friendship', in the *Journal of the Eighteen Nineties Society* (1992) gives an interesting account of Beardsley's relationship with Raffalovich.

Part IV

For John Lane and the Bodley Head, see *John Lane and the Nineties* (1936) by J. Lewis May and *The Early Nineties: A View from the Bodley Head* (1971) by James G. Nelson. *England in the 1890s* (1990), a bibliographic exhibition catalogue edited by M. D. Stetz and M. S. Lasner, contains some interesting sidelights. For Richard Le Gallienne, see *The Quest of the Golden Boy: The Life and Letters of Richard Le Gallienne* (1960) by Richard Whittington-Egan and Geoffrey Smerdon. For Henry Harland, see *Henry Harland: His Life and Work* (1978) by Karl Beckson. For *The Yellow Book*, see *A Study in Yellow: The Yellow Book and its Contributors* (1960) by Katherine L. Mix and, also, Fraser Harrison's introduction to *The Yellow Book: an anthology* (1914).

For *Punch* and its contributors, see *A History of Punch* (1957) by R. G. G. Price, *Owen Seaman, His Life and Work* (1977) by John Adlard, *Ada Leverson* (1973) by Charles Burkhart and *Wonderful Sphinx, the Biography of Ada Leverson* (1993) by Julie Speedie.

Part V

The Wilde trials and their effects upon the other figures of the period are, generally, dealt with in the books listed above. For the trials themselves, however, see *The Trials of Oscar Wilde* (revised edition, 1962) edited by H. Montgomery Hyde. For the *Savoy*, Stanley Weintraub provides a brief 'Introduction' to his anthology *The Savoy: Nineties Experiment* (1966). For *The Symbolist Movement in Literature* see Richard Ellmann's 'Introduction' to the 1958 edition.

Index